Praise for *Capernaum*

The fascinating story of ancient Capernaum has attracted the attention of scholars for over 150 years, as it involves an early Roman Jewish village that came to be known as "the town of Jesus" and in late antiquity developed into a prominent Christian pilgrimage destination. Relying on a sound historiographical methodology, this sophisticated and well-argued book leads the reader through main topics regarding the village and its social and religious makeup, analyzing and synthesizing abundant archaeological data and textual evidence.

—Uzi Leibner, professor of classical archaeology,
The Hebrew University of Jerusalem

This book is a treasure. Few scholars can effectively weave historical and archaeological evidence together as Cirafesi has done in his study of Capernaum. This wide-ranging study is not only a fantastic overview of the ancient village of Capernaum, but also a major contribution to the study of early Judaism, early Christianity, and Jewish-Christian relations.

—Jordan J. Ryan, associate professor of New Testament,
Wheaton College, Illinois

This volume is of utmost importance for anyone interested in the relationships between Jews, Jewish Christ-followers, and non-Jewish Christians in antiquity. Wally Cirafesi presents a stimulating historical construction of the dynamic socio-religious fabric in Capernaum from the first century to the seventh century CE. He critically examines texts, archaeological evidence, socioeconomic networks, local and non-local elements, and the impact of buildings on their social and spatial setting. He even imagines the interreligious relations in everyday life and brings new insights to Judeo-Christian interactions in the Galilee.

—Rina Talgam, professor of art history,
The Hebrew University of Jerusalem

This is an extraordinary book. At a time when studies of ancient Jews and Christians—and all those in between—have increased dramatically, often concentrating on either texts or archaeology, pinpointing a single moment in time or making sweeping descriptions lacking geographical and chronological anchors, Wally Cirafesi breaks new ground in this fascinating study. By focussing attention on one specific site and analysing all available sources, and then following historical developments closely over several centuries, Cirafesi substantially increases our knowledge of ancient Jewish-Christian relations, all the way from the first century into the early Islamic period. This is exactly what the field needs at this moment. Highly recommended!

—Anders Runesson, professor of New Testament,
University of Oslo

CAPERNAUM

CAPERNAUM

JEWS AND CHRISTIANS IN THE ANCIENT VILLAGE FROM THE TIME OF JESUS TO THE EMERGENCE OF ISLAM

WALLY V. CIRAFESI

FORTRESS PRESS
Minneapolis

CAPERNAUM
Jews and Christians in the Ancient Village from the Time of Jesus to the Emergence of Islam

Copyright © 2024 Fortress Press, an imprint of 1517 Media. All rights reserved. Except for brief quotations in critical articles or reviews, no part of this book may be reproduced in any manner without prior written permission from the publisher. Email copyright@1517.media or write to Permissions, Fortress Press, PO Box 1209, Minneapolis, MN 55440-1209.

Library of Congress Cataloging-in-Publication Data

Names: Cirafesi, Wally V., author.
Title: Capernaum : Jews and Christians in the ancient village from the time of Jesus to the emergence of Islam / Wally V. Cirafesi.
Description: Minneapolis : Fortress Press, [2024] | Includes bibliographical references and index.
Identifiers: LCCN 2024003144 (print) | LCCN 2024003145 (ebook) | ISBN 9781506474564 (hardback) | ISBN 9781506474571 (ebook)
Subjects: LCSH: Judaism--Relations--Christianity--History. | Christianity and other religions--Judaism--History. | Jews--Israel--Capernaum (Extinct city)--History. | Christians--Israel--Capernaum (Extinct city)--History. | Capernaum (Extinct city)--History. | Church history--Primitive and early church, ca. 30-600.
Classification: LCC BM535 .C5798 2024 (print) | LCC BM535 (ebook) | DDC 275.694/5--dc23/eng/20240409
LC record available at https://lccn.loc.gov/2024003144
LC ebook record available at https://lccn.loc.gov/2024003145

Cover design: Laurie Ingram Art + Design.com
Cover image: Capharnaum the Town of Jesus/richardernestyap/Shutterstock

Print ISBN: 978-1-5064-7456-4
eBook ISBN: 978-1-5064-7457-1

For
Anders, Anna, Rebecca, Rachel, and Noah
and
Karin, Magnus, Sofia, and Eric
with
Gratitude

CONTENTS

	List of Images	ix
	Preface	xi
	Introduction	1
1.	Capernaum in the Time of Jesus and the Socioeconomic Context of the Earliest Christ-Followers	15
2.	Was There a Public Synagogue in Capernaum during the Time of Jesus? *History between Texts and Archaeology*	43
3.	Jewish Christ-Followers in Capernaum before the Fourth Century *Reconsidering the Texts, Archaeology, and Institutional Context of Jewish–Christian Relations in Capernaum before Constantine*	79
4.	Architecturalizing Jesus in the Fourth Century *Jewish–Christian Relations and the Capernaum Christaeum*	117
5.	Architecturalizing Power and Resistance *Capernaum's Octagonal Church and Limestone Synagogue*	153
6.	Beyond Monumental Architecture *Jewish–Christian Relations and Everyday Life in Capernaum in Late Antiquity*	201
7.	Capernaum and the Byzantine–Islamic Transition	225
	Epilogue *In Lieu of a Conclusion*	249
	Bibliography	255
	Ancient Sources Index	277
	Subject Index	285

LIST OF IMAGES

Image I.1	One of the entrance signs to the modern archaeological park of Capernaum.	1
Image I.2	Satellite view of the Lake of Galilee (also known as Lake Kinneret or Lake of Tiberias).	2
Image I.3	General plan of the Franciscan side of the Capernaum site.	3
Image I.4	Greek Orthodox side of the Capernaum site.	4
Image 2.1	Gamla synagogue.	56
Image 2.2	Magdala synagogue.	57
Image 2.3	Plan of the fifth-to-sixth-century limestone synagogue. Earlier structures are beneath it in the areas of the side aisles (trenches 814, 821, 819, and 817).	61
Image 2.4	The black basalt wall running underneath the western wall of the white limestone synagogue.	68
Image 3.1	Ariel view of Capernaum, with the octagonal church and limestone synagogue in center view. Picture taken August 16, 1972.	101
Image 3.2	Ariel view (looking northeast) of *insula* 1 (*insula sacra*), with the location of Room 1 (*sala venerata*) marked at the center of the octagon.	102
Image 3.3	Detail of the town plan, focusing on *insula* 1.	104
Image 3.4	Some fragments of the wall graffiti from Room 1.	107
Image 4.1	Reconstruction of *Insula* 1 in the early Roman period (first to second century CE).	119
Image 4.2	Reconstruction of *Insula* 1, after renovations in the mid- to late fourth century CE.	120
Image 4.3	Late Roman Fine Wares stamped with crosses found in Capernaum, mostly dated to the fifth and sixth centuries.	135

List of Images

Image 5.1	Aerial view (looking south) of the octagonal church and limestone synagogue.	164
Image 5.2	Looking southeast. Central octagon set on the walls of *sala venerata*.	165
Image 5.3	Plan of a mid-fifth-century octagonal church.	166
Image 5.4	Hypothetical reconstruction of the mid-fifth-century octagonal church.	167
Image 5.5	Photo looking southeast of the damaged mosaic pavement containing the image of a peacock. This was the floor of the octagonal church, which, when first laid, sealed the earlier phases of Room 1 from view.	172
Image 5.6	Photo (looking north) of the apsidal baptistry added sometime in the sixth century.	176
Image 5.7	Plan of the limestone synagogue.	183
Image 5.8	Details of finely decorated friezes and capitals from the limestone synagogue.	185
Image 6.1	Segmentation of Capernaum's Byzantine houses and shops with commentary by Sharon Mattila as published in "Capernaum, Village of Naḥum," 224.	209
Image 6.2	Photo looking north of Areas 3 and 4, comprised of houses and workshops, and flanked to the left (west) by the main north–south street (L39).	210
Image 6.3	Photo looking southeast of the houses in Area 2.	211
Image 6.4	The photo on the left is of an area looking north of Area 3. This is Mattila's House 8 and 8a, which included an olive press complex attached to the house, labeled in the photo L270. The photo on the right is of the same area looking east.	213
Image 7.1	The photo on the left is of an area looking southwest from Street L514, where two decorated stones are in reuse, into room L512. The photo on the right is of a detail of a stone with light scratching of a menorah.	234
Image 7.2	The lintel above the main entrance, southern façade, of the Capernaum synagogue, with effaced relief.	240
Image E.1	Aerial view of Capernaum's modern memorial erected over the remains of the octagonal church. Picture taken in 1999.	250

PREFACE

The idea for this book emerged in the Fall of 2017, when I was still a PhD candidate at the University of Oslo. Anders Runesson, my supervisor at the time, had invited me to cowrite a large essay on the art and architecture of the Christ-oriented buildings at Kefar ʿOthnay, Capernaum, and Dura Europos for volume 3 of the now award-winning book *The Reception of Jesus in the First Three Centuries*, edited by Chris Keith, Helen Bond, and Jens Schröter. I was tasked with writing the sections on Kefar ʿOthnay and Capernaum, and, in the process, became deeply enthralled with the archaeology of Capernaum and the complicated historical questions to which it gives rise.

I am not an archaeologist by training, although I took doctoral coursework in archaeology and have experience excavating in the field. I am not particularly interested in Capernaum or other sites in the Galilee for personal religious reasons, although I can appreciate those who are, and I do think that Capernaum has contemporary significance on a humanistic level. The reasons for my fascination with Capernaum, I think, have to do more with it being a sort of "laboratory" in which several of my intellectual interests could be brought together with some coherence: the practice of "microhistory"—that is, the kind of history that aims to ask "large questions in small places"[1]—material culture, the early history of Jewish–Christian relations, and the *longue durée*. Writing about Jews and Christians in Capernaum from multiple disciplinary, theoretical, and methodological perspectives has, I hope, allowed me to grow into a creative, yet not fanciful, historian of Judaism and Christianity within the broader settings of the ancient and late ancient Mediterranean world.

In light of my approach to Capernaum as a kind of intellectual laboratory, I wish to highlight for readers that there is a way *to* read and a way *not* to read

---

1. C. W. Joyner, *Shared Traditions: Southern History and Folk Culture* (Urbana: University of Illinois Press, 1999), 1.

this book. The book is neither an archaeological report nor a general profile or survey of the site. Neither is it intended as a comprehensive history or a grand narrative about Capernaum. Rather, it is a study of what I think are seven key historical questions that any historian who wants to understand Jewish–Christian relations in the ancient village needs to address. Undoubtedly, there are other important archaeological and historical questions that could have been featured. Therefore, I have been quite selective of the issues covered in the book. The selection process was determined usually because of my own interests and curiosities, but also, at times, because of limitations of my subject competencies, and often because of space constraints. As such, not all parts of the history and archaeology of Capernaum are given equal attention. For example, while the Greek Orthodox side of Capernaum is fascinating in its own right, the remains are relatively small, un- or under-published, and mostly, though not exclusively, date to the late Byzantine and early Islamic periods. Thus, I do not spend much time, until chapter 7, discussing the significance of the Greek Orthodox side. Readers are referred to Sharon Mattila's excellent survey of it in her essay "Capernaum, Village of Naḥum, from Hellenistic to Byzantine Times,"[2] and, of course, the single archaeological report that was published, *Excavations at Capernaum*.[3] While I hope a broad range of readers will find the present book engaging, I have written it mainly for advanced graduate students and scholars in the fields of ancient Judaism and Christianity, including the fields of Second Temple Judaism and the New Testament, the archaeology of ancient Palestine, rabbinic Judaism, and late Roman/early Byzantine (i.e., fourth to seventh century) history.

* * *

While the idea of this book originated in 2017 at the University of Oslo, it primarily took shape within three other institutional contexts. The project officially launched in January of 2019 with the start of a postdoctoral research fellowship at the MF Norwegian School of Theology, Religion, and Society

---

2. Sharon Mattila, "Capernaum, Village of Naḥum, from Hellenistic to Byzantine Times," in *Galilee in the Late Second Temple and Mishnaic Periods*, vol. 2, *The Archaeological Record from Cities, Towns, and Villages*, ed. D. A. Fiensy and J. R. Strange (Minneapolis: Fortress Press, 2015), 226–237.

3. V. Tzaferis, ed., *Excavations at Capernaum*, vol 1, *1978–1982* (Winona Lake, IN: Eisenbrauns, 1989).

Preface   xiii

in Oslo. I am thankful to MF and to my former colleagues for creating such a friendly and stimulating environment within which my ideas could take off and develop. In particular, thanks are due to Karl Olav Sandnes, Ole Jakob Filtvedt, Liv Ingeborg Lied, Matthew Monger, Brent Nongbri, and Mary Jane Cuyler, each of whom warmly supported the initial stages of my research in various ways.

The COVID-19 pandemic was a tragic interruption for the world, and it was no different for me and my family. As such, progress on the project was extremely slow, even non-existent at times, from the spring of 2020 to the spring of 2022. However, in July of 2022, I was fortunate to start a new position in Sweden as a Fellow in the Pro Futura Scientia XVI, a research program facilitated by the Swedish Collegium for Advanced Study (SCAS) and my nominating institution, the Centre for Theology and Religious Studies (CTR) at Lund University, and generously funded by Riksbankens Jubileumsfond. More than half of the book's writing was done in the first year and a half of this position. During the 2022/23 academic year, I had the privilege of being in-residence at SCAS, which provided a broad and immersive intellectual experience that was catalyzed by the idyllic setting of the sights, sounds, and smells of Uppsala University's botanical garden. I wish to thank my SCAS colleagues, many of whom quickly became good friends, for the many engaging conversations we had over daily lunches that were brilliantly designed and executed by SCAS's in-house chef, Ulrika Andersson. Thanks are especially due to Jeffrey Paller, Mathieu Grenet, Katharina Ó Cathaoir, Lisa Hellman, Janina Neufeld, Eliel Camargo-Molina, Valentyna Savchyn, Skylab Sahu, Gonda Van Steen, Sofia Näsström, Valbona Muzaka, Claudia Merli, Fredrik Logevall, Elizabeth Lambourn, Eric Cullhed, Gísli Pálsson, and Carol Upadhya. Many thanks also to the wonderful SCAS administrative staff: Mattias Bolkéus Blom; Bjarne Graff; Pia Hultgren; Maria Odengrund; Sandra Maria Rekanovic; Ellen Werner; and, of course, Christina Garsten, principal of SCAS.

The book finally found completion upon my coming to the CTR at Lund University, now my home department. I am extremely grateful for the new colleagues I have gained and for having the opportunity to be part of such a vibrant community of researchers and teachers. In particular, I wish to thank my colleagues in the New Testament seminar, the Jewish studies seminar, and in the Department of Archaeology and Ancient History, all of whom provided valuable feedback on aspects of the book in a joint gathering during the winter of 2023. Furthermore, the CTR has supported me not only professionally but also personally, as my family and I have made the transition to what we hope will be a long life ahead in Sweden. In particular, I wish to thank Alexander Maurits, who has been instrumental in facilitating this process.

Beyond these institutions, many smaller groups and individuals need to be thanked for their support and contributions to this project. Many thanks to Marianne Bjelland Kartzow for inviting me to join her seminar in October of 2018 on the topic of the "Ambiguous Neighbor," in which I was able to pilot some initial ideas that eventually formed the basis of chapter 6. In the Spring of 2019, I was invited to present some of the first fruits of my research at two international conferences, one at the University of Lausanne devoted to the topic of early Galilean synagogues ("Les prèmiers synagogues en Galilée") organized by David Hamidovic, and another at Lund University on ancient Jewish and Christian identity formation ("Negotiating Identities") organized by Karin Hedner Zetterholm, Cecilia Wassén, Anders Runesson, and Magnus Zetterholm. The research presented in these settings eventually formed the bases for chapters 2 and 3 of the book. I offer my thanks to all the colleagues involved in these two conferences for their precious feedback, but especially to Danny Sion, Rina Talgam, Benjamin Arubas, and Uzi Leibner in Lausanne; and Paula Fredriksen, Christine Hayes, and, again, Rina Talgam in Lund. Rina and I had a third occasion to interact, at a symposium organized by Karin Zetterholm in Lund in the late winter of 2020 just before the pandemic, and I am very grateful to her for the time she spared.

Thanks are due to Marcela Zapata Meza (Universidad Anáhuac) for the invitation to present research related to what is now chapter 1 at the Seminario Vida Cotidiana en la Antigüedad. Since excavating with her at Magdala in 2016, she, as well as her colleagues Rosaura Sanz Rincón and Andrea Garza, have been constant sources of archaeological information, inspiration, and, most importantly, friendship. Similarly, I wish to thank Zeev Weiss, one of the first people I spoke to about this project. Since our first meeting in his office in Jerusalem almost eight years ago, he has offered nothing but encouragement, enthusiasm, and a wealth of professional wisdom. Zeev has, to me, become a trusted friend, and I am thankful that we now have the opportunity to work together on an upcoming project, *The Oxford Handbook of Ancient Synagogues*.

During the Spring of 2023, I had the opportunity to present work related to the project in three research groups at or connected to Uppsala University. Thanks to James Kelhoffer, Cecilia Wassén, and the Biblical Studies research seminar for reading and commenting on an initial draft of chapter 1; to Patrik Klingborg and the seminar in Classical Archaeology for providing excellent critical feedback on parts of chapter 5; and to members of the Jewish Studies Forum who attended a keynote lecture I gave in Stockholm on ancient synagogue architecture at Paideia–The European Institute for Jewish Studies in Sweden. While the book, therefore, has the fingerprints of many people all over it, I alone, of course, am responsible for any remaining errors or inconsistencies.

Many thanks are due to two staff members of the Terra Sancta Museum in Jerusalem. Fra Eugenio Alliata, OFM, director of the museum, graciously provided access and spent time with me during two visits I made to work hands-on with some of the artefacts from Capernaum, particularly the ceramics, being held in the archaeological storerooms. Fra Alliata was a close colleague of Virgilio Corbo and Stanislao Loffreda, having excavated with them at Capernaum, and his almost encyclopedic knowledge of the site and the Capernaum excavation reports is, in my view, unparalleled. He was, therefore, an extremely valuable resource for me, and I am very thankful for the kindness he showed in hosting me during those two short visits. I also thank Dr. Daniela Massara, curator of the museum and a scholar of Byzantine archaeology, for several stimulating conversations and for providing access to the electronic versions of the Capernaum reports.

Thanks to Roberto Orlandi and the Terra Santa Edizioni for permission to reproduce many images from the Capernaum archaeological reports, but especially from Stanislao Loffreda's *Cafarnao V: Documentazione fotografica degli scavi (1968–2003)*, which collects a large amount of the photographs taken of the site over the course of its excavation history. Thanks also to Brepols, Fortress Academic/Lexington Books, and Routledge, for permission to reproduce content here in edited form: Chapter 2 represents an edited version of an article published as "A First-Century Synagogue in Capernaum? Issues of Historical Method in the Interpretation of the Archaeological and Literary Data," *Judaïsme ancient—Ancient Judaism* 9 (2021): 7–48; Chapter 3 represents an edited version of a chapter published as "Jewish Christ-Followers in Capernaum before the Fourth Century? Reconsidering the Texts and Archaeology," in *Negotiating Identities: Conflict, Conversion, and Consolidation in Early Judaism and Christainity (200 BCE–600 CE)*, ed. Karin Hedner Zetterholm, Anders Runesson, Cecilia Wassén, and Magnus Zetterholm (Lanham: Fortress Academic/Lexington Books, 2022), 293–327; and Chapter 6 represents an edited version of a chapter published as "Imagining the Everday Life of Jewish and Christian 'Neighbors' in Late Antique Capernaum: Beyond Church and Synagogue—and Back Again," in *The Ambiguous Figure of the Neighbor in Jewish, Christian, and Islamic Texts and Receptions*, ed. Marianne Bjelland Kartzow (London: Routledge, 2022), 189–212.

My editor at Fortress Press, Carey Newman, deserves many thanks as well. Carey believed in this project at a very early stage and has been a strong advocate and gracious guide ever since our first interactions in 2019.

The Harald and Louise Ekmans Research Foundation provided a one-week fellowship at Sigtunastiftelsen, where I was able to put the finishing touches on the manuscript. A hearty thanks to the Foundation and to the staff at Sigtunastiftelsen for their expert hospitality, top-notch food, and for making those six days some of the most productive I have ever had.

Lastly, a few others deserve special thanks. Jordan and Joy Ryan, with whom I have shared not a few adventures wandering around Israel during excavation seasons, were hugely encouraging during the two professionally unhappy years I spent in the Chicago area during the pandemic. Jordan has been a constant dialogue partner in all things dealing with early Jewish archaeology, ancient synagogues, and ancient churches, and I continue to learn a great deal from him. Greg Fewster, whom I have now thanked in every book I have written, continues to be a source of great personal and professional support. He has also recently entered uncle status for my two young kids, who with humor and affection, know him as Dr. Uncle Greg.

Huge thanks to Jessie, my spouse and friend, for all the support she has offered during this project. My kids, Levi and Camille, have had to live with the project for almost longer than they have been alive. I am deeply thankful to both of them for letting their dad drag them around the world to pursue his academic dreams. For better or worse, they have been part of it all. Thanks, kiddos.

As thankful as I am to my own family for their support, I want, finally, to thank two other families for the impact they have had, and continue to have, on me and mine. The Runessons—Anders, Anna, Rebecca, Rachel, and

Noah—have been with us, in various ways, as we have journeyed back and forth between three countries (Canada, Norway, Sweden) in the last decade. Anders, of course, has been a fundamental influence in my professional life since 2014, and his own work on Capernaum is a major reason why I wanted to take it up in a large-scale project like this one. But he, Anna, and their kids have played big roles in helping me cope with a number of challenges that have characterized my life over the last ten years, from the difficulties of (several) international transitions to the uncertainties of a volatile job market. I thank them all for the support they have given, much of which they might not even be aware of.

The Zetterholm family—Magnus, Karin, Sofia, and Eric—have quickly come into the same relational sphere for me. Karin was my Rabbinics teacher during my days as a PhD student, and she continues to be the strongest influence on my thinking about Judaism in late antiquity. But she has become an even stronger friend. Likewise with Magnus, whose work on Jewish–gentile relations and the New Testament shapes much of my thinking today. But even more than the intellectual influences they both have had on me, I want to thank them, as well as Sofia and Eric, for how they have welcomed me and my family to Sweden, loved on my kids, and opened their home.

This book, despite its imperfections, is dedicated to these two families.

Wally V. Cirafesi
Sigtuna
Lucia 2023

Introduction

1. Capernaum, the "Town of Jesus"?

THE IMAGE ON the cover of this book alludes to a sign that all visitors to Capernaum today see when they enter the modern-day archaeological park, which sits immediately off the northwestern shore of the Lake of Galilee. The sign is dressed in the garb of an ancient mosaic, with the image of a five-fold cross (also known as the Jerusalem cross or cross-and-crosslets type) at the top and the words "Capharnaum[,] the Town of Jesus" presented below in the form of black tesserae.

Image I.1. One of the entrance signs to the modern archaeological park of Capernaum.

Image accessed on Wiki Commons. Used here under Creative Commons Attribution-Share Alike 4.0 International license.

Image I.2. Satellite view of the Lake of Galilee (also known as Lake Kinneret or Lake of Tiberias).

From Loffreda, *Cafarnao V*, 38 (DF 2). Used here with permission.

The sign is artistically creative and, I would think, pleasing to the eyes of many who walk through Capernaum's gates. But it is also ideologically loaded, and it would be remiss of me not to spend at least some time at the outset of this book unpacking its complicated cargo, even if ever so briefly. After all, neither the construction of archaeological parks nor the writing of history is done in a social, cultural, or political vacuum. The ways we think about and represent the human past are always shaped by our modern contexts, always entangled with matters of power and epistemology, with patterns of production and consumption, with decisions about what we value and what we do

Introduction 3

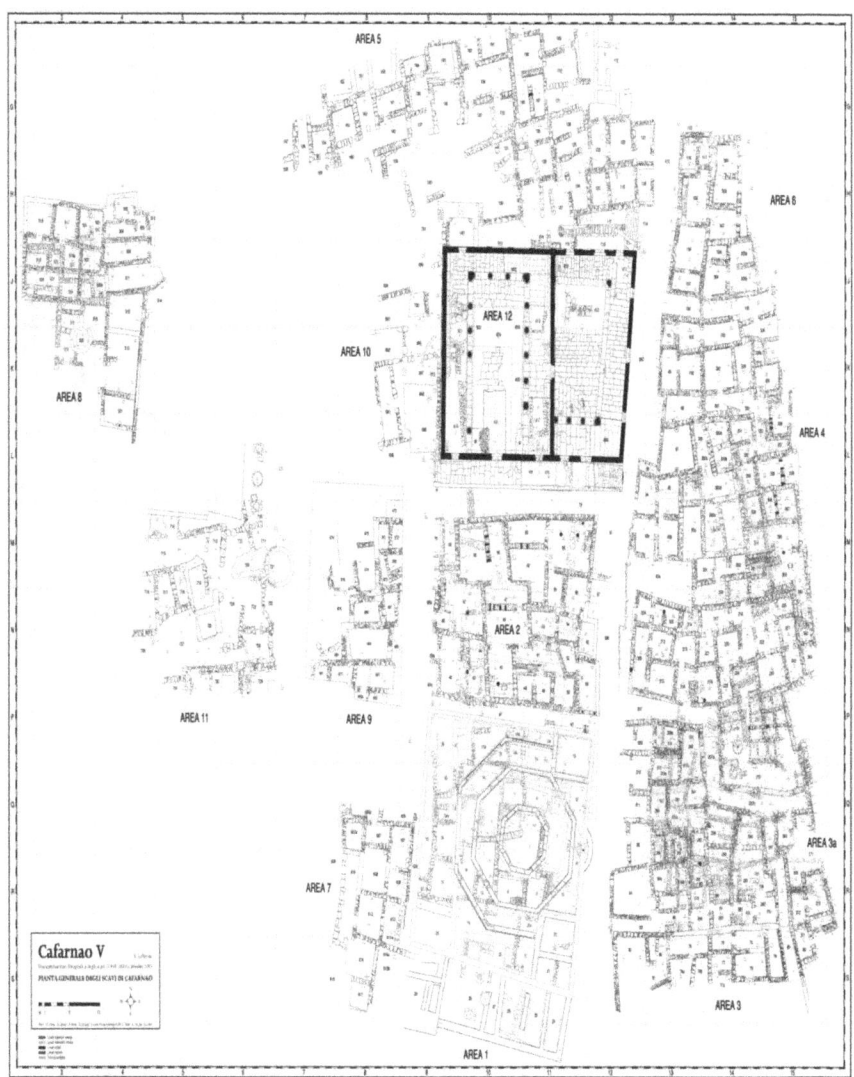

Image I.3. General plan of the Franciscan side of the Capernaum site.

From Loffreda, *Cafarnao V*, 247. Used with permission.

not.[1] The more we recognize these entanglements, the more we can critically engage both the past and our present.

---

1. See Michel-Rolph Trouillot, *Silencing the Past: Power and the Production of History* (Boston: Beacon Press, 1995).

Image I.4. Greek Orthodox side of the Capernaum site.

From V. Tzaferis, ed., *Excavations at Capernaum: 1978–1982* (Winona Lake, IN: Eisenbrauns, 1989).

The description of Capernaum as "the Town of Jesus" immediately conveys the significance that this site has for many Christians. Today, the archaeological park operates as a major tourist attraction along the so-called "Jesus Trail," a sixty-five-kilometer hiking trail that leads from Nazareth and passes by important pilgrimage sites in the Lower Galilee.[2] Interested devotees can choose from two hiking packages operated by Abraham Tours: for NIS 4,000, or just over USD 1,000, one can purchase the six-day package;

---

2. Jesus Trail, accessed January 24, 2024, https://jesustrail.com/.

Introduction

for NIS 1,100, or almost USD 300, one gets the three-day package. Both, however, promise Capernaum as the *telos* of the journey, "the city that was the center of Jesus's ministry." Similarly, contemporary Christian music artists, such as Joshua Aaron, have capitalized on Capernaum (and other sites), even performing concerts, shooting videos, and providing virtual tours in the setting of Capernaum's limestone synagogue.[3] In such contexts, the words "the Town of Jesus" do not function merely as a historical designation. Rather, they constitute the language of an economy of religious devotion, as they offer the pilgrim, at a cost of course, an opportunity to step into not just any past but the sacred past of a particular place, whose history begins and ends with Jesus.

And herein lies the potential problem. It is not that the words "the Town of Jesus" are, necessarily, untrue. On a historical level, the archaeological remains located at the modern site of Tell Ḥum have now been firmly identified as ancient Capernaum.[4] This means that, if the New Testament Gospels are reliable in their assertion that Jesus and his disciples, particularly the apostle Peter, made their homes in Capernaum (e.g., Matt 4:13, Mark 2:1, John 2:12), then its description as "the Town of Jesus" is arguably apropos and relevant for modern scholars. As Eve-Marie Becker has observed, since its "rediscovery" by American explorers in the nineteenth century, "Capernaum has formed an integral part of scholarly work, even among New Testament exegetes."[5] The problem, rather, is that the historical Jesus, the historical Peter, and thus the data of the New Testament are, together, just one sliver of a much larger historical pie. Some of the earliest archaeological remains found in Capernaum go as far back as the early Bronze Age (ca. 2000–1500 BCE) and some of the latest

---

3. Joshua Aaron, "Joshua Aaron & Friends Live at the Garden Tomb 'Resurrection Premiere' (Gather the Nations)," April 7, 2023, YouTube video, 1:00:49, https://www.youtube.com/watch?v=m6D_Iv4Ma8A. Aaron also does a "Worship in Israel Tour," which costs anywhere between USD 3,955 and USD 5,309. A visit to Capernaum is on Day 3 of the itinerary. See https://www.premierisrael.com/joshua-aaron-2024.

4. In my view, the best analysis of the location and identification of ancient Capernaum is by J. C. H. Laughlin, "The Identification of the Site," in *Excavations at Capernaum*. ed. V. Tzaferis, vol. 1, *1978–1982*, (Winona Lake, IN: Eisenbrauns, 1989), 191–199. As Laughlin notes, the evidence in favor of identifying the modern archaeological site with ancient Capernaum is overwhelming.

5. E.-M. Becker, "Jesus and Capernaum in the Apostolic Age: Balancing Sources and Their Evidence," in *The Mission of Jesus: Second Nordic Symposium on the Historical Jesus, Lund, 7–10 October 2012*, ed. S. Byrskog and T. Hägerland, WUNT 2.391 (Tübingen: Morh Siebeck, 2015), 118.

extend all the way to the early Crusader period (eleventh to twelfth century CE).[6] Thus, Capernaum was "the Town of Jesus" for only a small fraction of a past that spans almost three thousand years. The label has the potential to obscure this point and the fact that, although their names might be lost to us, many other humans populated this space who were not Jesus, who were neither Jewish nor Christian, or who were *both* Jewish *and* Christian. One of the basic aims of this book—which itself covers only a few pieces of Capernaum's historical pie—is to convince its readers that Capernaum was more than just "the Town of Jesus." Long before any sign was hung that claimed Capernaum for Christianity, the village was a place in which Jews, Christians, and, eventually, Muslims all rubbed shoulders and made do in everyday life on the one hand, and, on the other, interpreted their traditions and constructed their identities in constant interaction with each other. Some of these identities, I will argue, were compatible with each other; others were not.

The image of the five-fold cross on the entrance sign—a type of cross that appears on the coat of arms of the Franciscan Custodia Terrae Sanctae—is also not neutral. While its precise origins are unclear, the early history of the design is bound up with the development of medieval European heraldry and the colonial formation of the Crusader Kingdom of Jerusalem.[7] Some traditions even associate the design directly with Godfrey de Bouillon (1060–1100), the French leader of the First Crusade and first ruler of the Jerusalem Crusader state. To be clear, I am in no way intending to associate today's Custodia with the violent imperial ideology of the medieval crusaders. But what I *am* suggesting is that the image on its coat of arms—and which appears at the gates of Capernaum and on the cover of this book—has a long and complicated past that is wrapped in the ideology of Christian ownership and control of land, in particular the "Holy Land." Indeed, the story of Capernaum's acquisition by the Custodia in September of 1894, as told by the Custodia itself, is a winding and dramatic, if not altogether romanticized, account that revolves around a heroic leader's relentless pursuit of property (Fra Giuseppe Baldi), his struggle against a morally suspect antagonist (the Samakieh Bedouin tribe), his battles with competing buyers ("the Jews") and an opposing colonial power (the

---

6. S. Loffreda, *Recovering Capharnaum,* Studium Biblicum Franciscanum Guides 1 (Jerusalem: Franciscan, 1993), 27.

7. See the dated but still relevant discussion in W. W. Seymour, *The Cross in Tradition, History, and Art* (London: G. P. Putnam's Sons, 1898), 364–365.

Ottoman government), and an ending in which the Custodia, against all hope, comes out victoriously in command of the land.[8] The five-fold cross—whether on a sign, a flag, or a book—is conceptually connected to stories like this, which are fundamentally about Christian assertions of the power to possess.

Admittedly, this book is not, or at least not primarily, about modern religious politics or the history of Christian colonial ideology. Nevertheless, the modern story of the competitive struggle between Jews and Christians over the right to "own" Capernaum is, I suggest, a helpful way to think about the village in its ancient iterations. It challenges us to keep at the forefront of our minds that Capernaum was home to multiple religious traditions and multiple pasts, no matter how those pasts are constructed by historians. And it reminds us that Capernaum continued to be a site of Jewish–Christian interaction well *after* the seventh century, the period with which this book ends its analysis. While Christians, namely the Roman Catholic Church, seem to have won the day, the story generates an interesting exercise in counter-factual history: How would the site be represented differently today if "the Jews" mentioned in the Custodia's account had won the bid for Capernaum's ownership over 125 years ago? One guesses that it would not be marketed as "the Town of Jesus" or have the five-fold cross as its logo.

2. The Aims, Approaches, and Interventions of This Book

This book is about certain aspects of the early history of Jews and Christians in Capernaum—certain questions about their interactions, their institutions, and their identities—from around the time of Jesus up to the Byzantine–Islamic transition in Palestine. As a whole, it aims to investigate the development of these social dynamics diachronically and contextually by considering the available literary and archaeological sources, which will be introduced along the way. The book is, among other things, a historiographic exploration of

---

8. See the account given on the Custodia's website: https://www.custodia.org/en/sanctuaries/capernaum (click on the "Archaeology" tab to the left). Left out of this story, for whatever reason, is the broader nineteenth- and early twentieth-century context of European involvement in the antiquities trade and colonial practices of purchasing, owning, collecting, and extracting artifacts from Ottoman Palestine (and other areas). In some ways, the story of Fra Baldi could be seen through the lens of other Christian collectors during this period. In this context, see O. Shay, "Collectors and Collections in Palestine at the Conclusion of the Ottoman Era," *Le Muséon* 122, no. 3 (2009): 449–471.

how a predominately Jewish and generally prosperous village in first-century Galilee gradually transformed in later centuries into an important site of non-Jewish—perhaps even *anti-*Jewish—Christian memory and imagination. It seeks to place this Christianization process within the context of Byzantine imperialism to understand how the colonization of Palestine—first by Christians and then by early Muslims—impacted Jewish–Christian interactions at the local level.

To accomplish these aims, I take several different, though not mutually exclusive, methodological approaches, depending on the nature of the question being asked. Because so many existing scholarly opinions on Capernaum's Jewish and Christian pasts boil down, in my view, to issues of method, my choice of approach is often equivalent to the intervention in research I am attempting to make. Specifically, there are three method-centric issues to which the book variously speaks. I sketch them briefly here not only as a means to clarify what I hope are the book's main contributions to scholarship but also as a way to summarize its contents for the hurried reader.

Capernaum and the Task of History

One of the general yet central contributions this book makes to Capernaum scholarship is critical reflection on historical method. While Capernaum has received no shortage of attention from archaeologists and historians of the New Testament, as well as of Jewish and Christian antiquity more broadly, there has been a striking lack of attention to the idea of history itself and what it means to practice it in relation to the historical questions that Capernaum presents us with.[9] How one answers questions about, for example, the existence of a first-century synagogue in the village (chapter 2) or the presence of Jewish Christ-followers there in the time after Jesus but before Constantine (chapter 3), are deeply indebted to what one thinks "history" is and what it means to make a historical argument. My own answers to these questions, and others, represent a reaction to what I perceive as a gross empiricism underlying

---

9. My use of the phrase "the idea of history" of course alludes to the title of Robin Collingwood's famous treatment of the topic in *The Idea of History*, rev. ed., ed. J. van der Dussen (Oxford: Oxford University Press, 1994 [orig. 1946]). Collingwood's ideas about history and historical construction provide the central methodological platform for chapters 2 and 3 in this book.

some Capernaum scholarship that reduces the total task of history to the simple description of observable phenomena. This empirical orientation often leads to the demand—whether made explicitly or not—for "definitive" or "irrefutable proof" (usually thought of as an archaeological datum) in order for a historical judgment to be considered valid. However, as I argue in not so many words in chapters 2 and 3, if the jobs of ancient historians depended on the procurement of "irrefutable proof" for their views, then most would be unemployed. Rather, as most historians in most fields of study today recognize, and have for a long time, the study of the past is not an empirical science; we cannot observe it as onlookers in a laboratory. As such, we avoid the language (and thus the mythical standard) of "definitive" or "irrefutable" proof, especially when we study places and people whose pasts are so far removed from our modern contexts.

Instead, we think of history as a construction project not altogether different than an archaeological park like Capernaum itself. History is not equivalent to the past. We study the past through the medium of "evidence," in all its forms, but history is the portrait of that past we paint in our minds as we critically interpret that evidence. We, therefore, cannot "*re*construct" history any more than we can "recover" or "uncover" the past as an unmediated static object that exists "out there" just waiting to be revealed by the historian's pen. Rather, we "construct" history—we build it—which necessarily involves creativity, imagination, and invention, but not necessarily novel fancy.

Synagogue Studies and Greco-Roman Associations

Every chapter in this book has been variously informed by recent developments in the study of ancient synagogues and/as Greco-Roman associations. Chapter 1, in large part, draws from new research on trade associations throughout the Roman East to intervene in scholarship that has characterized Capernaum in the early Roman period as a village of mainly "subsistence level" farmers and fishermen. Chapter 2 engages with advancements in the social history and archaeology of synagogues from the Second Temple period to reconsider the question of whether one stood in Capernaum during the time of Jesus. Chapters 3 and 4 use the model of Greco-Roman cult associations to re-examine the architecture and institutional settings of the pre-fifth-century phases of the so-called House of Peter, that is, Room 1 (the *sala venerata*) of the *insula sacra* (*insula* 1). Chapter 4, in particular, uses these comparanda to criticize the use of the term *domus ecclesia* to describe Room 1 in its late fourth-century phase; it then proposes an altogether new term to use in its place.

Chapter 5, which moves the book more squarely into the period of late antiquity, incorporates recently discovered synagogues from Palestine during that period, such as at Huqoq, Hurvat Kur, and Wadi Hamam, in its new interpretation of the monumental architecture of Capernaum's limestone synagogue. The chapter argues, among other points, that the synagogue's architecture needs to be interpreted as a strategy of Jewish identity formation that took shape *in response to* the architecture of the contemporaneous Byzantine octagonal church that was erected just twenty-five meters to the south. I suggest that the two monuments projected toward one another certain ideas about "Jewishness" and "Christianness" and thus participated, through their built form, in broader cultural discourses of Christian power and Jewish resistance. Chapter 6 takes its point of departure from the interpretation of monumental architecture presented in chapter 5 and then shifts analytical gears down to the social realia of Jewish–Christian relations in the fifth and sixth centuries. Scholars have often mapped the contrasting architecture of Capernaum's synagogue and church directly onto their understanding of the nature of Jewish–Christian relations "on the ground" in the village. The result has been that conflict and separation are often the social paradigms through which these relations are interpreted. But monumental architecture, just like the rhetorically charged heresiological literature and laws of late antiquity, needs to be "read" critically and against the grain. In Capernaum, when synagogue and church are re-interpreted within (1) the intensely relational space of the village's domestic landscape, and (2) the literary sources that document the phenomenon of Christian attraction to synagogues, the categories of conflict and separation to describe Jewish–Christian relations become woefully inadequate. On the other hand, insights from social theorists on the concepts of "neighbors," "neighborhoods," and "everyday life," suggest that descriptions such as the "friendly hypothesis" and "coexistence" also tend to fall flat, lacking contour and neglecting attention to the practical realities of social life. In the end, I suggest Michel de Certeau's notion of "making do" is a better way forward. Indeed, this type of approach shapes my argument in chapter 7, where I integrate new research on art and iconoclasm in Palestinian synagogues during the early Islamic period to challenge the long-held view—often derived from scholars' taking the seventh century Jewish and Christian apocalyptic literature at historical face value—that the emergence of Islam necessarily meant the end of the Jewish and Christian communities in Capernaum.

The "Parting of the Ways" and the Formation of Judaism and Christianity

While this book is not about the so-called "parting of the ways" between Judaism and Christianity per se, it does draw upon some recent research on the topic to underpin several of its claims. Two general points are worth mentioning here.

First, many scholars have highlighted the artificiality of a Judaism/Christianity divide in the early centuries CE and, relatedly, have understood that adherence to Jesus remained a valid option within Judaism during this period.[10] But a few have gone further, rightly in my view, in arguing that the Judaism and Christianity we know today simply did not exist in these early centuries but rather trace their beginnings to the intense heresiological identity-building projects of rabbinic Judaism and Roman Christianity in late antiquity.[11] To be sure, the terms "Judaism" and "Christianity" do appear as early as the second century CE, particularly in the boundary-obsessed theological writings of

---

10. E.g., J. Lieu, *Neither Jew nor Greek? Constructing Early Christianity*, 2nd ed. (London: T&T Clark, 2016), 31–49; D. Boyarin, *Borderlines: The Partition of Judaeo-Christianity* (Philadelphia: University of Pennsylvania Press, 2004); A. H. Becker and A. Y. Reed, eds., *The Ways That Never Parted: Jews and Christians in Late Antiquity and the Early Middle Ages* (Minneapolis: Fortress Press, 2007); and K. H. Zetterholm, "Alternate Visions of Judaism and Their Impact on the Formation of Rabbinic Judaism," *Journal of the Jesus Movement in its Jewish Setting* no. 1 (2014): 127–153.

11. See A. Runesson, "What Never Belonged Together Cannot Part: Rethinking the So-Called Parting of the Ways Between Judaism and Christianity," in *Jews and Christians: Parting Ways in the First Two Centuries C.E.? Reflections on the Gains and Losses of a Model*, ed. J. Schröter, B. A. Edsall, and J. Verheyden (Berlin: De Gruyter, 2021), 33–56; K. H. Zetterholm, A. Runesson, C. Wassén, and M. Zetterholm, eds., *Negotiating Identities: Conflict, Conversion, and Consolidation in Early Judaism and Christianity (200 BCE–600 CE)* (Lanham/Minneapolis: Lexington Books/Fortress Academic, 2022); and K. H. Zetterholm and A. Runesson, eds., *Within Judaism? Interpretive Trajectories in Judaism, Christianity, and Islam from the First to the Twenty-First Century* (Lanham/Minneapolis: Lexington Books/Fortress Academic, 2023).

the Christian literary elite, but, as I argue variously throughout chapters 3 to 6, what these sources often betray, when read between the lines, is a *lack* of boundaries between "Jewishness" and "Christianness" at the grassroots level. While most scholars would agree that the late first and second centuries, and perhaps also the third century, were marked by unpoliced borders among non-Jesus–oriented Jews, Jesus-oriented Jews, and non-Jewish Christ-followers, I suggest that such socioreligious entanglements are also discernible, if not characteristic, of the fourth, fifth, and sixth centuries as well. As chapter 6 highlights, we have solid evidence that some non-Jewish Christ-followers continued to attend Jewish gatherings in synagogues in these centuries, apparently seeing no contradiction between their "Christian" identity and a simultaneous attachment to Jews and Judaism.[12] In chapter 4, I propose that we view the increase of non-Jewish Christian pilgrimage to Capernaum through the lens of this type of positive, not necessarily supersessionist, interest in Jewishness on the part of non-Jews.

Second, some of the same scholarship noted above, especially in the 2023 volume edited by Karin Hedner Zetterholm and Anders Runesson titled *Within Judaism? Interpretive Trajectories in Judaism, Christianity, and Islam from the First to the Twenty-First Century*, has argued that historians need also, in some way, to take account of the emergence of Islam as they investigate the formation of Judaism and Christianity. Methodologically speaking, although Islam is a seventh-century development, later historical phenomena can provide insight into the dynamics of earlier periods. For example, understanding developments in Judaism and Christianity in late antiquity can and do help us understand with more clarity and greater contrast what is or is not transpiring in earlier documents like the New Testament and the Mishnah. Indeed, there is a reason why it is often said "hindsight is always twenty-twenty." While this

---

12. P. Fredriksen, "'If It Looks like a Duck, and It Quacks like a Duck...': On *Not* Giving Up the Godfearers," in *A Most Reliable Witness: Essays in Honor of Ross Shepard Kraemer*, ed. S. A. Harvey et al., BJS 358 (Providence, RI: Brown University Press, 2015), 25–33, where on p. 30 n.17 she says: "Non-Jews continued to frequent Jewish community gatherings even after they became Christian: Origen (ca. 230, Caesarea) tells his Christians not to discuss in church questions they heard raised the day before in synagogue, and not to eat meals in both places (*Hom. Lev.* 5.8; *Sel. Exod.* 12.46); John Chrysostom, notoriously before the high holidays in 387 in Antioch, said: "Christians fast, keep Sabbath, go to synagogue, take oaths in front of Torah scrolls, co-celebrate Passover and Sukkot [...]. Church canons forbid such co-celebration on through the Visigothic and Byzantine period in the seventh century [...]."

book could have ended with, say, the time of Justinian I (527–565 CE)—*From Jesus to Justinian* would have, perhaps, made for a catchier subtitle—there is, in my view, analytical value in extending its temporal framework well into the seventh century and considering, even if briefly and restrictedly, the impact of early Islam on Jews and Christians in Capernaum. The main idea that I advance in chapter 7, then, is that the arrival of Islam did not signal the *ultimi giorni*, that is, the last days, of Capernaum;[13] it just meant that Christians were no longer in control. Importantly, it also meant that Jews and Christians in the village were equipped with socioreligious resources that allowed them to engage constructively with an ethnoreligion that had as many things in common with them as it had differences.

* * *

What holds the individual parts of this book together is not a grand narrative about the hopes and hurts, the conflicts and comradery, of Jews, Christians, and Muslims in a village of pilgrimage fame and religious liberalism. Rather, it is the conviction that the case of Capernaum, in fact, complicates and resists such narratives. Capernaum, thankfully, forces the historian out of the comfort zone of telling tidy teleological tales about, for example, the inevitability of orthodox Christianity's triumph and Judaism's struggle for survival, or about how "the synagogue" was nothing but an irreconcilable rival to "the church." On the one hand, to be sure, our stories need to account for sources that indicate Jewish communities were sometimes targets of rhetorical and physical violence by both pagans and, later, imperial Christians. But, on the other hand, when we look at Capernaum from a broader diachronic and comparative perspective, we might begin to see that sympathetic entanglements, porous identity boundaries, and a healthy dose of pragmatism were more often the driving social forces in the village, forces that are generally eschewed in Jewish and Christian heresiologies. Thus, offering this broader perspective is the central impetus of this book.

---

13. This was the view of Fra Virgilio Corbo ("Gli ultimi giorni di Cafarnao," *Liber Annuus* 33 [1983]: 373–390), who was one of the main excavators of the Capernaum site in the 1960s, 70s, and 80s, and whose ideas we will have many occasions to engage with throughout this book.

CHAPTER ONE

Capernaum in the Time of Jesus and the Socioeconomic Context of the Earliest Christ-Followers

1. Introduction
The Galilee of Jesus between Rich and Poor

SINCE THE LATE Seán Freyne published his seminal work in 1980, the study of ancient Galilee has been a hot spot for scholars working in a wide range of disciplines. Whether it is the history and politics of the Roman East, Jewish life in the Second Temple and rabbinic periods, or Jewish–Christian relations in Palestine in late antiquity, the Galilee has intensely occupied the pens of modern exegetes, historians, and archaeologists alike.[1] One of the subfields of Galilean studies that has, perhaps, absorbed the greatest amount of ink from those pens is the study of the historical Jesus. Whatever other advancements the "quests" for the historical Jesus have made to our understanding of Jesus and his aims, two stand out as foundational and are now essentially taken for granted. The first is that Jesus must be understood not simply "against the background" of his first-century Jewish environment but as, and in every way, *within* and *a part of* the fluid and flexible nature of Jewish identity in

---

1. S. Freyne, *Galilee from Alexander the Great to Hadrian: A Study of Second Temple Judaism* (Wilmington, DE: Glazier, 1980). The bibliography on Galilee research is too large to list here. For surveys, see S. Freyne, "Galilean Studies: Old Issues and New Questions," in *Religion, Ethnicity, and Identity in Ancient Galilee: A Region in Transition*, ed. J. Zangenberg et al., WUNT 210 (Tübingen: Mohr Siebeck, 2007), 13–29; R. Deines, "Galiläa und Jesus: Anfragen zur Funktion der Herkunftsbezeichnung ‚Galiläa' in der neueren Jesusforschung," in *Jesus und die Archäologie Galiläas*, ed. C. Claußen and J. Frey, BThSt 87 (Neukirchen-Vluyn: Neukirchener Verlag, 2008), 271–320; and D. A. Fiensey and J. R. Strange, eds., *Galilee in the Late Second Temple and Mishnaic Periods*, 2 vols. (Minneapolis: Fortress Press, 2014, 2015).

Greco-Roman antiquity. Jesus, in other words, self-identified as a Jewish man from Nazareth, who lived under Roman cultural and political domination like every other Jewish person in the first century, and never did or said anything that suggested he rejected his Jewishness, Jewish law, or Jewish institutions. The second advancement, now acknowledged by most scholars, is that the Galilee of Jesus was predominately inhabited by Jews and was characterized by the everyday practice of what Andrea Berlin has called "household Judaism," that is, "the practice, beginning in the early first century BCE, whereby people living in the regions of Judea, the Lower Galilee, and southern Gaulanitis adopted identical new household goods that distinguished their homes, and therefore their daily lives, from those of people living in adjacent regions."[2] Thus, *Jewish* Galilee—as embedded as it was within the larger Hellenistic Roman world—functioned as the geopolitical matrix of Jesus's activity.[3]

While the importance of the historical Galilee for the study of Jesus has been widely recognized, there continues to be debate about the nature of the region's socioeconomic landscape.[4] Some scholars envision the Galilee as a region marked by widescale poverty, subsistence-level fishing and farming, and strong antagonism between its rural village "peasants" on the one hand and its wealthy urban elite on the other. Also, part of this picture is the view that the region was cut off economically from, and even hostile toward, the "mainstream" culture and politics of Judea. But as archaeological finds from all around the Galilee continue to multiply—a trend that has intensified even within the last ten years or so—the notion that the region was a socioreligious

---

2. A. Berlin, "Household Judaism," in *Galilee in the Late Second Temple and Mishnaic Periods*, vol. 1: Life, Culture, and Society, ed. D. A. Fiensy and J. R. Strange (Minneapolis: Fortress Press, 2014), 208–215.

3. See especially M. A. Chancey, *The Myth of a Gentile Galilee*, SNTSMS 118 (Cambridge: Cambridge University Press, 2002).

4. For a helpful presentation of the debate, see the cowritten essay by D. E. Oakman and J. A. Overman, "Debate: Was the Galilean Economy Oppressive or Prosperous?" in Fiensy and Strange, 1:346–65. Oakman favors the former view, while Overman favors the latter view. See also the discussion by D. A. Fiensy, "Introduction," in *The Galilean Economy in the Time of Jesus*, ed. D. A. Fiensy and R. K. Hawkins, ECL 11 (Atlanta: SBL, 2013), 1–4. For a larger discussion of issues surrounding the socioeconomic context of the early Jesus movement, see A. Keddie, *Class and Power in Roman Palestine: The Socioeconomic Setting of Judaism and Christian Origins* (Cambridge: Cambridge University Press, 2019).

and socioeconomic backwater has been called into question. Recent excavations at Magdala alone—including its richly decorated synagogue, marketplace, ritual areas, and domestic complex—have suggested to some that late Hellenistic and early Roman Galilean towns had considerable access to both local and nonlocal resources, an interest in art, the ability to engage in trade, and a high level of connectivity to Judean culture.[5] This, as well as other data gleaned from recent and not-so-recent excavations around the region, have led some scholars to paint an opposing picture of the Galilee as a place of general economic prosperity, healthy and constructive relations between rural areas and urban centers, and reverence for Judean culture and the Jerusalem temple cult.

While my aim in this chapter is not to solve this debate, I do wish to integrate into the study of the social history of early Roman Capernaum, specifically, recent research that has drawn attention to the role of trade associations, in particular those related to the fishing industry, within the social and economic landscape of the Roman East. Of course, this research has implications for the "poverty versus prosperity" debate, and, throughout this chapter, my view on this debate, especially as it relates to Capernaum, will become clear. However, here, I am less concerned with arguing that Capernaum was simply rich or poor. Rather, I am concerned with showing how Capernaum was a village of *connections*, a village shaped socially by trade networks and associations, which provided an important institutional framework for the recruitment of Christ-followers and the development of the early Jesus movement in the Galilee. My argument is that while Capernaum was not marked by widespread elite wealth as seen in some of the major cities of the Roman East, the village's economy in the early Roman period was largely supported by the work of trade associations that were able to maximize local production from natural resources and contribute to a dynamic marketplace; and, as such, these associations possessed a relative amount of social and political influence. I will suggest that it was within this context of socioeconomic connectivity that the Jesus movement in Capernaum emerged and competed for influence with other Jewish associations within the village more broadly.

---

5. See, e.g., the essays collected in R. Bauckham, ed., *Magdala of Galilee: A Jewish City in the Hellenistic and Roman Period* (Waco, TX: Baylor University Press, 2018).

2. Socioeconomic Networks and Access to Wealth in Early Roman Capernaum
Patronage, Pottery, and a Connected Economy

Capernaum, in many ways, represents a microcosm of the larger debate about the social and economic fabric of Jewish life in the Galilee during the time of Jesus.[6] This is despite the fact that the sources for early Roman Capernaum are relatively slim. There are no literary references to Capernaum in the periods before Jesus. The Gospels and Josephus are the first. Josephus, for his part, does not say much. As Jonathan Reed notes,[7] in one place Josephus simply refers to Capernaum as a village to which he was taken after he was injured, having fallen off his horse during a battle against the Roman General Sylla.[8] In another place, as part of his larger description of the lake and the lush land of the Gennesar Plain,[9] Josephus says that the high agricultural quality of the area was due to the "good temperature of the air" and "a productive spring" that the locals call "Capharnaum."[10] The precise relationship between this named spring and the actual village of Capernaum is uncertain; there is really

---

6. For a thorough discussion of the debate as it relates to Capernaum specifically, see S. L. Mattila, "Revisiting Jesus' Capernaum: A Village of Only Subsistence-Level Fishers and Farmers?" in Fiensy and Hawkins, 75–138.

7. J. Reed, *Archaeology and the Galilean Jesus: A Re-examination of the Evidence* (Harrisburg, PA: Trinity Press International, 2000), 140.

8. Josephus, *Life* 403.

9. Josephus, *J.W.* 3:506–521. The Gennesar Plain, Josephus says, renders a diverse vegetation profile. All sorts of trees, which usually require different types of environmental conditions, can grow upon the land, although walnuts, figs, and olives are specially singled out. While the land gives forth fine produce, it also preserves its fruit longer than other places; grapes and figs are supplied ten months out of the year, and other ripe fruits grow year-round. Josephus's description does not seem far afield from modern descriptions of the region's fertility. Commentary on the Gennesar Plain/region: see M. Aviam, "People, Land, Economy, and Belief in First-Century Galilee and Its Origins: A Comprehensive Archaeological Synthesis," in Fiensy and Hawkins, 14; U. Leibner, *Settlement and History in Hellenistic, Roman, and Byzantine Galilee*, TSAJ 127 (Tübingen: Mohr Siebeck, 2009), 180–191; and U. Leibner, "Identifying Gennesar on the Sea of Galilee," *JRA* 19 (2006): 229–245.

10. Κεφαρνόκος in the manuscripts. There has been some discussion about the various spellings of "Capernaum" in Josephus and thus his intended referents. On the variant spellings in the manuscripts, see F.-M. Abel, "Le nom de Capharnaum," *JPOS* 8 (1928): 24–34; E. Bishop, "Jesus and Capernaum," *CBQ* 14 (1953): 427–437.

no way of knowing whether Josephus understood the spring to correlate with the village at all. But, if he did, then Josephus's reference might somehow associate the village with an important natural resource that, as he saw it, stood at the center of the entire region's agricultural prosperity.

The Gospels give us some more data to work with, since Capernaum is frequently mentioned as a place of Jesus's activity, especially in the Gospel of Mark.[11] It is presented as a predominately Jewish village (Matt 11:23 // Luke 10:13–15; Luke 7:1–5), and the presence of crowds going after Jesus (Mark 2:1) might suggest that the village was understood to have a sizable population, at least compared to other Galilean villages, or that it was easily accessible from other locations around the lake, whether by boat or road.[12] While, in past scholarship, population estimates of the village were as high as twenty-five thousand inhabitants, more recent archaeological studies have shown that those estimates were grossly exaggerated, and that first-century Capernaum had a modest population in comparison to the major Galilean cities, with no more than fifteen hundred inhabitants and probably closer to one thousand.[13] The Gospels indicate that fishermen lived in Capernaum (Matt 4:12–22 // Mark 1:16–21; Luke 4:31; 5:1–11; John 6:22–59) and that there was a *telōnion* in the village, often interpreted as a "tollbooth" or "tollhouse" (Mark 2:14 // Matt 9:9 // Luke 5:27).[14] While a significant amount of scholarly attention has been given to the role of the fishing industry within the early Roman Galilean economy, very little has been given to the Gospels' reference to a

---

11. Until recently, it was largely taken for granted that the historical Jesus used Capernaum as a major "hub" for his Galilean activity. Christopher Zeichmann has argued, however, that the prominence of Capernaum in the Gospels stems from the narrower interests of the Markan evangelist rather than the historical Jesus himself. See C. Zeichmann, "Capernaum: A 'Hub' for the Historical Jesus or the Markan Evangelist?" *Journal for the Study of the Historical Jesus* 15 (2017): 147–165.

12. Reed, *Archaeology*, 140.

13. Mattila, "Revisiting Jesus' Capernaum," 85, agreeing with Reed, *Archaeology*, 152. For a larger discussion of Capernaum's population levels over the centuries, see S. Mattila, "Capernaum, Village of Naḥum, from Hellenistic to Byzantine Times," in Fiensy and Strange, 2: 242–254.

14. Reed, *Archaeology*, 140. Reed, however, devotes no attention to the socioeconomic significance of the Capernaum *telōnion*. Judging from what he writes elsewhere in his chapter on Jesus and Capernaum, it would seem he understands it as having functioned to collect imperial duty on goods in transit on the regional and interregional trade-routes that ran nearby the village.

telōnion in Capernaum. Both will be discussed later in this chapter, where I will suggest that there was an important relationship between the two—fishing and the *telōnion*—and that this relationship tells us something about the socioeconomics of Capernaum. Lastly, Mark, Luke, and John all mention the presence of a synagogue (συναγωγή) in Capernaum (Mark 1:21; Luke 7:5; John 6:59). Luke alone, however, mentions that this "synagogue" was a physical building, which had been gifted to the Jews of the village by a "centurion" who loved the Jewish people.[15] Since many scholars have doubted the reliability of Luke's account of a synagogue building in Capernaum during Jesus's lifetime, I have chosen to treat this issue separately in the next chapter.[16] What I want to discuss now is the possible socioeconomic significance of Luke's reference not only to the presence of a centurion in Capernaum but, more specifically, to his role as a patron to the local Jewish population.

Roman legions in Palestine were quite rare before the Jewish War, especially in small villages. The Galilee did not have a long-term Roman garrison until 120 CE, when *legio VI Ferrata* came to Kefar ʿOthnay/Legio.[17] This has led a number of scholars to conclude, rightly in my view, that the centurion in Capernaum mentioned in the Gospels was probably not a commander of a formal Roman detachment of legionnaires but rather an official in the

---

15. Matt 8:5 also mentions the presence of a "centurion" (ἑκατόνταρχος) in Capernaum but does not say anything about a synagogue. Conversely, while John mentions a synagogue in Capernaum, it lacks reference to a centurion. Some scholars have interpreted John's story of Jesus's healing of the royal official's son in Capernaum (John 4:46–54) as a Johannine reworking of the tradition and, thus, as evidence that the centurion was probably not a commander of legionaries in a Roman detachment but an official in Herod Antipas's administrative and military apparatus (Reed, *Archaeology*, 162; M. A. Chancey, *Greco-Roman Culture and the Galilee of Jesus*, SNTSMS 134 [Cambridge: Cambridge University Press, 2005], 52–53). While this interpretation is possible, it is also possible that the two traditions are entirely unrelated and represent two separate stories. After all, the differences between the stories are stark: one involves a non-Jewish centurion, his patronage and affection for the Jewish people, and his "respected" (ἔντιμος) slave, while the other involves an administrative official and his son. In my view, the latter interpretation is more likely.

16. E.g., H. C. Kee, "Early Christianity in the Galilee: Reassessing the Evidence from the Gospels," in *The Galilee in Late Antiquity*, ed. L. I. Levine (New York: JTS Press, 1992), 9–10; Reed, *Archaeology*, 155. Mattila, "Revisiting Jesus' Capernaum," also expresses skepticism about the existence of such a synagogue in Capernaum.

17. Chancey, *Greco-Roman Culture*, 55.

royal forces of the client kingdom of Herod Antipas.[18] As Christopher Zeichmann has shown, there is indeed some evidence for centurions in the royal client armies of Palestine.[19] Zeichmann makes the important observation that centurions, including those in smaller detachments, could function in a range of non-combat roles, from administrative positions to service in public works.[20] For example, according to some Egyptian papyri, centurions could oversee the security of tax collection, in some cases intervening on behalf of civilians who experienced abuse from tax collectors and, in other cases, providing aid and protection for collectors who were themselves being harassed by local would-be tax payers.[21] One of the best examples of the direct involvement of centurions in the mechanics of tax collection comes from the mid-first-century text known as the *Periplus of the Erythraean Sea*, a text composed of short entries describing the navigation and trading activities of ports from Roman Egypt to the Indian Ocean.[22] One entry (no. 19) mentions a harbor with a fort at a place called Leukē Kōmē ("White Village"), from which there was a road leading to the flourishing Nabataean city of Petra. The harbor of Leukē Kōmē served the function of a port for small vessels loaded with cargo coming from Arabia. For security purposes, a customs officer (παραλήπτης τῆς τετάρτης) was dispatched there to oversee the collection of a fourth of all incoming goods; also dispatched was "a centurion with a detachment of soldiers" (ἑκατοντάρχης μετὰ στρατεύματος). As Zeichmann notes, because Capernaum was positioned at the nexus of interregional roads, was a port village with a tax office (on which see section 3 below), and was on an international border, it would have been an ideal

---

18. Reed, *Archaeology*, 162; Chancey, *Greco-Roman Culture*, 43–44; and, more recently, C. B. Zeichmann, *The Roman Army and the New Testament* (Lanham: Lexington/Fortress Academic, 2018), 68.

19. Zeichmann, *Roman Army*, 67. See especially the inscription he cites, §38 from the Database of Military Inscriptions and Papyri of Early Roman Palestine (www.ArmyOfRomanPalestine.com), which also has the inventory numbers *AE* 1966.493; *IGLS* 16.1475.

20. Zeichmann, *Roman Army*, 23–41 (esp. 31).

21. Zeichmann, *Roman Army*, 31.

22. Noted by Zeichmann, *Roman Army*, 31. The edition of the *Periplus* that I have consulted is Lionel Casson's *The Periplus Maris Erythraei: Text with Introduction, Translation, and Commentary* (Princeton, NJ: Princeton University Press, 1989).

place for a regional centurion to be stationed.²³ Even though direct evidence for a Roman military presence in Capernaum does not appear until the second century—a Roman milestone from the time of Hadrian was found during site excavations²⁴—it is historically plausible that a centurion was stationed there along with a small contingent of soldiers both to safeguard civilian interests and, as in the case of Leuké Kōmē, to "ensure the protection of those exacting tolls and taxes from merchants on regional trade routes, or perhaps those exacting a fish tax."²⁵

One way centurions seem to have been able to accomplish this dual security aim was by pouring money back into local populations through various patronage activities and, thus, engendering a level of goodwill with the public. Rebecca Runesson has recently argued that Luke's description of the centurion's patronage to the local Jewish community in Capernaum "is consistent with what we know about Roman military relationships with civilians."²⁶ Runesson notes the broad range of economic relationships Roman military personnel could have with local civilian populations, from the arrangement of personal loans to formal patron-client relations. As she shows, centurions were especially active in patronage relationships among civilians, including Jews, channelling both wealth and goodwill through local social and material infrastructure.²⁷ Accordingly, some were honored as patrons and benefactors of cities, some were hailed for their extensive local benefactions, some were thanked for their patronage to local trade associations, and some, including one mentioned in an inscription from war-time Judea, could be praised for their general goodwill toward the people.²⁸

---

23. Zeichmann, *Roman Army*, 67–68.

24. On which, see Loffreda, *Recovering Capharnaum*, 18–20.

25. Zeichmann, *Roman Army*, 31.

26. R. Runesson, "Centurions in the Jesus Movement? Rethinking Luke 7:1–5 in Light of the Gaianus Inscription at Kefar 'Othnay," *JBL* 142, no. 1 (2023): 131, where she also engages thoroughly with the range of source-critical issues involved. Showing how Luke presents the centurion as doing the things that centurions were known to do, Runesson's study also indirectly addresses the debate over whether a first-century synagogue existed in Capernaum. This debate is the main topic of chapter 2.

27. Runesson, "Centurions in the Jesus Movement?" 147.

28. For primary sources and discussion, see Runesson, "Centurions in the Jesus Movement?" 148.

In so far as centurions acted as patrons to local Jewish communities, they were quite similar to other types of non-Jewish elites who established economic ties with Jews through their donation to synagogue buildings. For example, an inscription from Ptolemaic Egypt (second or first century BCE) mentions a synagogue (here called a προσευχή) that was dedicated to "the god most high" by "Ptolemaios son of Epikydes, the superintendent of police, and the Jews of Athribis."[29] The fact that this inscription singles out a certain Ptolemaios, who apparently sat high within the civic administration of the entire tenth Lower Egyptian nome, is almost certainly due to his role as one of, if not *the*, main patron of the building. Similarly, and perhaps most famously, is the case of Julia Severa, a Roman high priestess and "director of contests of the whole household of the Augustan gods" who also built a synagogue (called an οἶκος) for a Jewish community in Akmoneia in western Anatolia.[30] Thus, although we do not have a great deal of other evidence from early Roman Palestine, Luke's presentation of the centurion sits comfortably alongside other sources from throughout the eastern Mediterranean that document, specifically, the patronage of high-status non-Jews toward Jewish communities and their "synagogues."

---

29. See *ASSB* no. 151. While there has been debate about this Ptolemaios's ethnic identity, John Kloppenborg (*Greco-Roman Associations*, vol. III, 36–38) provides persuasive evidence that Ptolemaios was likely not an *Ioudaios*: (1) the overwhelming majority of the 3,700 occurrences of the name Ptolemaios in Egyptian papyri are not Judean/Jewish; (2) there are very few examples of Egyptian Jews in this period engaged in local administration; and (3) the fact that Ptolemaios is mentioned with the Jews of Athribis does not immediately identify him as an *Ioudaios*. As Kloppenborg notes, he is not identified in relation to a role in the προσευχή, as are the Jewish men Theodoros and Achillion (described as προστάται [presidents] of the προσευχή in Xenephyris in *Jewish Inscriptions of Greco-Roman Egypt* 24 [=*Greco-Roman Associations*, vol. III, 156]), but rather in relation to his quite prominent civic role as superintendent of police (ὁ ἐπιστάτης τῶν φυλακιτῶν) for the entire nome.

30. See *Monumenta Asiae Minoris Antiqua* VI 263, ca. 100 CE; *Monumenta Asiae Minoris Antiqua* VI 264; *IJO* II 168 = *Greco-Roman Associations*, vol. II, 113; late first to early second century CE. The notion that this οἶκος was a synagogue, built by Julia Severa and donated for use by the Jews of Akmoneia, is firmly established in the scholarly literature. There is also no real doubt about Julia Severa's status as a non-Jew (see discussion in P. Trebilco, *Jewish Communities in Asia Minor*, SNTSMS 69 [Cambridge: Cambridge University Press, 1991], 57–60). She, along with her Italian husband, L. Servenius Captio, were members of a prominent family in the mid- to late first century that was full of high-ranking imperial officials, especially throughout Asia Minor (*ASSB*, 135; P. Harland, *Greco-Roman Associations*, vol. II, 153), and she held an important civic position as high-priestess in the imperial cult.

What then might have the presence of a regional centurion meant for Capernaum socioeconomically? As Zeichmann notes, soldiers in general were deeply involved in the everyday economy of Roman Palestine, since items such as food, clothing, and even weapons had to be bought locally.[31] In short, soldiers, like everyone else, needed the stuff of life to survive.[32] And this meant they brought their paychecks and purchasing power to local markets. In the case of the Capernaum centurion, his purchasing power might have been considerable. While perhaps not himself a formal Roman legionnaire, like a Roman centurion, he is presented in Luke as a patron with his own "circle of power," a term used by Pedro López Barja de Quiroga to describe the network of social relationships patrons often created around themselves with slaves, freedmen, and clients.[33] The power of a patron, de Quiroga notes, "was measured by the number and the quality of the people belonging to it, and by their *status*."[34] According to Luke, the Capernaum centurion not only had soldiers (στρατιώτας) under his authority but also at least one "highly regarded" (ἔντιμος), that is, "quality" slave, who very well could have been responsible for managing the centurion's wealth and property.[35] Also in the centurion's circle were local Jewish elders who were not only his clients, that is, beneficiaries of his donation of the synagogue, but were also connected socially to him as his agents, as he "sends" them to ask Jesus for help for his ailing slave (Luke 7:3). In other words, the centurion, as a patron, is presented as a source of wealth in the village and, therefore, a wielder of significant social capital.

---

31. Zeichmann, *Roman Army*, 35–36.

32. Zeichmann, *Roman Army*, 35 notes, e.g., a legionary pay record found at Masada (*P. Masada* 722; 72–75 CE), which lists some of the things a solider named Gaius Messius, son of Gaius, purchased at the market: barley, a linen tunic, boots, and, generally, food expenses. On the local purchase of weapons, see Josephus, *Ant.* 17.282–283; and Dio Cassius, *Hist. rom.* 69.12.2, although the date of reference is around the time of the Bar Kokhba War.

33. P. de Quiroga, "Patronage and Slavery in the Roman World: The Circle of Power," in *The Oxford Handbook of Greek and Roman Slaveries*, ed. S. Hodkinson, M. Kleijwegt, and K. Vlassopoulos (Oxford: Oxford University Press, 2020), published online: https://doi.org/10.1093/oxfordhb/9780199575251.013.31

34. de Quiroga, "Patronage and Slavery," 1.

35. Household slaves were often mediators of their masters' wealth. On the relationship between slavery and economy in the larger Roman world more broadly, see W. Scheidel, "Slavery," in *The Cambridge Companion to the Roman Economy*, ed. W. Scheidel (Cambridge: Cambridge University Press, 2012), 89–113.

And, although nothing is said explicitly in the sources about it, his potential as a private lender to local civilians—a role we know other centurions played in Roman Palestine[36]—would have only amplified his position within this circle of power.

In addition to his function as a *source* of wealth in Capernaum, the centurion was probably also a *supervisor* of wealth. That is, judging from our earlier discussion about the link between centurions and tax collection, it is quite possible, even likely, that supervising the importing and exporting of goods at the village's harbor—and the orderly exacting of taxes—were at the very heart of his mandate. This might suggest that, instead of interpreting the socioeconomic situation in Capernaum as being characterized by poverty-inducing abusive tax practices, we interpret the situation in the village as tending toward fairness, at least by Roman legal standards. At least according to Luke's account, the Capernaum centurion, like other lower-level officers known from inscriptions in other parts of the Roman East,[37] had engendered goodwill among the local population through building a synagogue for them. Another contributing factor of such goodwill could have been the protection he offered from greedy tax farmers.

Patronage, however, was only one aspect of early Roman Capernaum's economy. Douglas Edwards and, more recently, Sharon Mattila, have noted that there is strong evidence for the development of craft and agricultural specialization in the region already during the Hasmonean period (ca. 140–63 BCE), as well as for local and intraregional market exchange.[38] For example, in this period, the Galilee saw the rise of a thriving chalkstone vessel industry—likely connected to a general increase in ritual purity observance among the population of Jewish Galilee[39]—the emergence of the mass production of olive

---

36. For a discussion of military personnel in Roman Palestine and the transaction of private loans, see Zeichmann, *Roman Army*, 38.

37. Zeichmann, *Roman Army*, 39–40, notes two examples (inscriptions) from Batanaea, in which villagers honor a centurion as "friend and benefactor."

38. Mattila, "Revisiting Jesus' Capernaum." D. R. Edwards, "Identity and Social Location in Roman Galilean Villages," in *Religion, Ethnicity, and Identity in Ancient Galilee: A Region in Transition*, ed. J. Zangenberg, H. W. Attridge, and D. Martin, WUNT 210 (Tübingen: Mohr Siebeck, 2007), 367.

39. On the archaeology—and its interpretation—of ritual purity practices in early Judaism, including the production and use of chalkstone vessels and ritual baths, see Y. Adler, *The Origins of Judaism: An Archaeological-Historical Reappraisal* (New Haven: Yale University

oil, and the establishment of large pottery production centers at sites like Kefar Hananya, Shikhin, and Yodefat.[40] And all of these products *moved*, that is, they were exported and imported throughout Roman Galilee and Judea, and, in the case of olive oil, beyond these borders.[41] Edwards, thus, concludes that rather than constituting an isolated backwater, the villages of the Galilee were "active in the economic buzz of the early Roman period."[42]

Capernaum, too, seems to have been a part of this buzz. The village may have been a site for glass production, and its ceramic record includes common pottery fired at important kilns throughout the region.[43] This, of course, is not necessarily a sign of wealth, but it does signal connectivity to larger pottery production networks in the Galilee. Similarly, 264 chalkstone vessel fragments were found in the village, which not only might attest to a concern for Jewish purity practices there but also shows Capernaum's participation in a larger regional and interregional industry dealing in such vessels. For example, recent excavations at nearby 'Einot Amitai and Reina (both in the vicinity of Nazareth in the Lower Galilee) have uncovered two large-scale chalkstone vessel production sites that likely fed high local demand. According to Yonatan Adler, the activity at production sites like these "strongly supports the understanding that Galilean Judeans shared with their Jerusalemite brethren a similar market demand for this unique product."[44]

The large olive press complexes discovered in Capernaum probably belong to the Byzantine period,[45] so it is difficult to know what the village's precise relationship to the otherwise thriving olive oil industry would have been in

---

Press, 2022), 50–86, as well as his myriad of articles written on the topic. For a different methodological perspective on the material, see S. Miller, *At the Intersection of Texts and Material Finds: Stepped Pools, Stone Vessels, and Ritual Purity among the Jews of Roman Galilee* (Göttingen: Vandenhoeck & Ruprecht, 2015).

40. Mattila, "Revisiting Jesus' Capernaum," 106–107.

41. Mattila, "Revisiting Jesus' Capernaum," 108–109.

42. Edwards, "Identity and Social Location," 367.

43. Especially at Kefar Hananya, Shikhin, and Yodefat. See Mattila, "Capernaum, Village of Naḥum," 244.

44. Adler, *Origins of Judaism*, 71.

45. Mattila, "Capernaum, Village of Naḥum," 229. It was in the Byzantine period that the number of olive-presses in the Galilee peaked among both Jewish and non-Jewish communities, becoming a particularly important part of the Galilean economy in late antiquity.

the early Roman period. But the remains of large basalt Roman millstones, mortars, bowls, and craters certainly indicate the village's engagement in agricultural production. These basalt vessels were apparently produced in Capernaum itself.[46] However, an even more interesting point to note is that in an often overlooked geochemical study published in 1988 by Carolyn Xenophontos, Carolyn Elliott, and John Malpas, the authors determined that several basalt Roman millstones found in Cyprus had likely been originally produced in Capernaum and its environs.[47] They suggested that after their production, the basalt vessels were then carried overland on the Tiberias–Akko (Ptolemaïs) road, with the port of Akko being "the outlet for millstones intended for the Cypriot market."[48] The vessels traveled by sea and were then offloaded at Salamis, a prominent Roman city in eastern Cyprus known as the "emporium of the East."[49] This would seem to indicate that at least part of Capernaum's commercial portfolio included the making, selling, and exporting of basalt products—basalt being an important natural resource in the area[50]—to one of the Roman world's most diverse and vibrant markets. Far from isolated, Capernaum's economy apparently participated in networks that extended not only beyond the Galilee but beyond Palestine as whole.

The idea that early Roman Capernaum had such economic connections should not be too surprising. After all, there is no question that it had such connections in other periods of its history, both earlier and later. For example, seven stamped Rhodian amphorae handles with Greek inscriptions and many fragments of a fine ware known as Eastern Terra Sigillata A (ETSA) imported from the Mediterranean coast populate Capernaum's ceramic record from the late Hellenistic period.[51] These imported fine wares, overlooked in Reed's study, are rightly interpreted by Mattila as indicators of wealth in Capernaum

---

46. Loffreda, *Recovering Capharnaum*, 20, noting the presence of unfinished pieces.

47. C. Xenophontos, C. Elliot, and J. G. Malpas, "Major and Trace-Element Geochemistry Used in Tracing the Provenance of Late Bronze Age and Roman Basalt Artefacts from Cyprus Edwards," *Levant* 20 (1988): 182. The study, however, is mentioned by Edwards, "Identity and Social Location," 366.

48. Xenophontos, Elliot, and Malpas, "Roman Basalt Artefacts," 183.

49. Xenophontos, Elliot, and Malpas, "Roman Basalt Artefacts," 182.

50. Xenophontos, Elliot, and Malpas, "Roman Basalt Artefacts," 182.

51. Loffreda, *Cafarnao VI*, 120–121. For photographs, see DF 825:1–7 in Loffreda, *Cafarnao VIII*, 57. Unfortunately, the Greek inscriptions have not been published yet. For

and, more importantly, a kind of wealth derived from the village's participation in international economic networks.[52] Furthermore, both coins and pottery from periods after 135 CE show that the village continued to have significant socioeconomic connections to a wide range of regions in the Roman and Byzantine East, especially Syria, Cyprus, and Asia Minor, and to a lesser extent Northern Africa.[53]

While there was, apparently, a sharp downturn in imported fine ware to Capernaum in the early Roman period, Mattila asserts that this does not mean the village suddenly sank into subsistence-level living. Mattila argues that the drastic decrease in imported pottery—especially ETSA, which is found so profusely at contemporaneous non-Jewish sites—reflects, rather, an intentional change in trade patterns among Jewish communities in the Galilee toward introversion, that is, a general resistance to trading with non-Jews. For Mattila, this anti-Romanization strategy coupled with the rise of chalkstone vessel production and the concomitant widespread religious concern for Jewish purity regulations. It would not be until after the Bar Kokhba war ca. 135 CE, when chalkstone vessels (and ritual baths) largely fell out of use, that more direct economic relations with non-Jews would resume, as is reflected in the archaeological record and, to a degree, in early rabbinic textual sources such as the mishnaic tractate *Avodah Zerah*.

Economic introversion—whether or not an anti-Romanization strategy—does not entirely explain the decrease in imported vessels to Capernaum in the early Roman period. After all, *some* fragments of ETSA were, indeed, found in the village belonging to this time. But Mattila's general claim is sound, that the absence of imported fine wares in the early Roman period should not be taken as a sign of Capernaum's poverty or economic backwardness. Indeed, it is much more likely to see continuity of economic vitality in Capernaum—from the Hellenistic period, through the Roman period, and on to the Byzantine period—rather than a sudden decrease in the early Roman period and a sudden increase in the Byzantine period.

---

the statistics on these fine wares in the larger context of Capernaum's ceramic record, see Mattila, "Capernaum, Village of Naḥum," 239–240.

52. See Mattila, "Revisiting Jesus' Capernaum," 90–93.

53. Mattila, "Capernaum, Village of Naḥum," 246, 251; Loffreda, *Recovering Capharnaum*, 19.

Excursus
The Early Roman Houses of Capernaum

Capernaum's domestic landscape has often been invoked as evidence that the village was marked by poverty and low-level living conditions.[54] In particular, the remains of the walls of houses—constructed out of unworked dark basalt blocks packed with mud or clay with smaller rocks in the interstices—have been taken as a sign of their poor-quality construction. However, what is sometimes overlooked is that there is a huge methodological hurdle to clear when attempting to say something about Capernaum's early Roman houses. That is because, while lead excavators Virgilio Corbo and Stanislao Loffreda did reach *some* early Roman strata of houses in Areas 1, 3, 7, 9, 10, and 11, there currently exists no fully excavated house from the early Roman period at the stie. The walls of the houses that one sees standing in Capernaum today date almost entirely to the Byzantine period. This means it is very difficult to draw firm conclusions about the size and quality of the construction of houses from the first century. And it is even more difficult to say anything about how they relate to the socioeconomic character of the village overall. In light of this, it is striking that some scholars have felt able to make broad and sweeping claims about the supposed "poor quality" of Capernaum's first-century houses and, therefore, the supposed poverty in which most or all of Capernaum's villagers lived.

This, of course, does not mean that we cannot say anything about Capernaum's houses in the early Roman period. For example, it is probably safe to assume, as the excavators do, that Capernaum's early Roman houses would have followed a similar peristyle courtyard layout that we see in most of the excavated houses from the late Roman and Byzantine periods. But, more specifically, as Mattila has argued, there are two factors about Capernaum's houses as they relate to the village's socioeconomic character that are worth reconsidering. The first concerns their size; the second concerns their quality of construction.[55]

Concerning house size, despite the rather impressionistic claims of some scholars to the contrary, Mattila has shown that for the three houses identified in *insula* 2, the tendency was for houses to get progressively smaller in

---

54. See, e.g., Reed, *Archaeology*, 151–153, 157–160.
55. The following paragraph depends largely on Mattila's essay "Revisiting Jesus' Capernaum."

later periods. While two of these three houses—the so-called Triple Courtyard House and the Northeast House—date from the late Roman to Byzantine periods, the partially excavated Western House seems to have had its beginnings in the early Roman period; and it, too, shows the same tendency of getting progressively smaller over time. In the early Roman period, the Western House was home to what the excavators called "il grande cortile," the large courtyard, which measured around 100 m². Only in later periods was this courtyard subdivided into other rooms and courtyards. This suggests that the Western House was quite large in the early Roman period, significantly larger than the so-called Patrician House (ca. third to fourth century) from the town of Meiron in the Upper Galilee, which scholars have suggested was the home of a wealthy "nuclear family."[56] While, of course, it is impossible to know how many people or families inhabited Capernaum's Western House, Mattila has convincingly argued that it is an *assumption* to claim that it was occupied differently than Meiron's Patrician House, that is, that it was instead home to several different family units who each occupied a single room: "The standing remains and recovered finds scarcely demand such a conclusion."[57] It is just as easy to assume that the Western House in Capernaum was a large home to a family with a moderate level of wealth.

Concerning the quality of construction, many scholars have interpreted the use of undressed local basalt stone as an indication of poor quality and, subsequently, subsistence-level poverty in Capernaum. Mattila notes, however, that this interpretation is also based on an *assumption*. She says, "The distinct possibility needs to be kept in mind that the undressed basalt stone walls and floors of the domestic structures excavated by the Franciscans at Capernaum are but the bare bones or skeletons of the houses that once existed, whether in the Byzantine or in the earlier periods."[58] Mattila goes on to suggest, based on comparative evidence from some houses from Karanis in Roman Egypt, that it is quite possible that the basalt walls of Capernaum's houses had once been smoothed over and even finely decorated with layers of limeless mud plaster, which have not survived the test of time and the climate.[59] To

---

56. Mattila, "Revisiting Jesus' Capernaum," 114–124.
57. Mattila, "Revisiting Jesus' Capernaum," 120.
58. Mattila, "Revisiting Jesus' Capernaum," 124.
59. Mattila, "Revisiting Jesus' Capernaum," 124–129.

Mattila's argument we could add the point that basalt stone, while local to Capernaum and its broader environment around the lake, is not necessarily a building material of poor quality. There are many benefits to using basalt in construction. It is a very hard stone, which makes it excellent for building sturdy foundations, floors, and walls that can support upper levels. Its hardness also explains why most of the basalt blocks used in Capernaum were not finely worked. It is very difficult, even for modern builders, to dress basalt. Basalt also has excellent resistance to weather and moisture, and it has a high level of thermal inertia.[60] This makes basalt, in fact, a rather ideal building material, considering the sweltering and humid summers and wet winters characteristic of the region's climate.

In my view, interpretation of Capernaum's basalt houses as a sign of poor construction and poverty emanates from an assumption that itself stems from two errors involving comparison with the use of white limestone (the material out of which Capernaum's synagogue of late antiquity is constructed) and the houses of elites in major cities throughout the Roman East. While, today, the black basalt of the village landscape might contrast sharply with the grandeur of the white limestone synagogue, and while basalt may not glisten in the sunlight in the same way, modern ideals of domestic decor should not inform our value judgments about ancient basalt houses. Limestone was simply not a readily available commodity for Capernaumites; it had to be brought into the village from at least ten kilometers away from Mount Arbel. Basalt was an important part of Capernaum's local and translocal economy, and it made good sense to construct dwellings out of it. Thus, while it should be obvious that Capernaum's domestic landscape does not resemble the elite and wealthy homes of major Roman cities like Pompeii, Sepphoris, or Jerusalem's Herodian quarter, neither do they necessarily reflect a village struck by abject poverty across the board. My statement here basically reflects Loffreda's comments made in 1993, which very few scholars seem to acknowledge or engage: that Capernaum's houses are "rather unpretentious but by no means poor, at least according to the living standard of an ancient village."[61] What is more, Loffreda goes on to mention that "they also betray no sharp economic differentiations."[62] This suggests, then,

---

60. G. Evola et al., "Thermal Inertia of Heavyweight Traditional Buildings: Experimental Measurements and Simulated Scenarios," *Energy Procedia* 133 (2017): 44.

61. Loffreda, *Recovering Capharnaum*, 20.

62. Loffreda, *Recovering Capharnaum*, 20.

that while there was almost certainly some type of socioeconomic stratification in the village, there was, it seems, a general standard of living that defies characterization as merely subsistence level.

3. The Fishing Industry, Trade Associations, and Capernaum's *Telōnion* in Social-Historical Context

Capernaum rested on the border of Antipas's and Philip's respective tetrarchies and, with the founding of new sites such as Tiberias in 19 CE and Bethsaida/Julias in 30 CE, it experienced an increase in regional and interregional trade traffic on its nearby roads. Travelers on these roads, according to Reed, would have included affluent merchants, Herodian officials, or "ostentatious elites."[63] This traffic enhanced Capernaum's role in the local economy and multiplied its interregional contacts.[64] The *telōnion* in Capernaum is seen by some scholars to have served the purpose of taxing transit between the borders of the tetrarchies; it was, therefore, a roadside "toll station." For Reed, for example, while the people of Capernaum would have had exposure to "visible signs of wealth" via its proximity to the trade routes, this wealth did not actually find a home in the village, and the toll money collected at the *telōnion* would have directly fed imperial coffers.

In his recent book, *Class and Power in Roman Palestine*, Anthony Keddie has suggested another possibility for understanding the Capernaum *telōnion*. He suggests that, rather than serving the purpose of taxing border transit, the *telōnion* might have served as an office for other types of indirect taxes. These taxes were variably exacted on products and exchanges of commercial goods, usually overseen by local elites, and, besides roadside toll stations, primarily collected at harbors and markets.[65] Thus, Capernaum's *telōnion* might have been more directly, and restrictedly, related to tax collection at its harbor, for example, on fishing and lake transport, which were the two primary uses of Capernaum's ancient harbor.

Two points substantiate Keddie's suggestion. First, the Gospel of Mark, after all, specifically locates Capernaum's *telōnion* "along the lake" (παρὰ τὴν

---

63. Reed, *Archaeology*, 165.
64. Reed, *Archaeology*, 148.
65. See Keddie, *Class and Power*, 133, 141 n. 113.

θάλασσαν, 2:13–14).⁶⁶ Second, if tax receipts from Roman Egypt (especially from the Fayyûm) are any indication, roadside toll stations were commonly referred to using the synecdoche *pulē* ("gate") rather than *telōnion*. *Pulai* ("tax-gates") were tax stations through which traveling merchants had to pass and at which they paid duty on their goods as they exited administrative districts. Hence, rather than the formula we see in some Egyptian papyri mentioning a *telōnion*—"so-and-so paid/registered X amount of money in the *telōnion* (ἐπὶ τὸ τελώνιον)" or something similar⁶⁷—in *pulē* receipts we see the formula, literally, "it has been paid through the gate" (τετέλ[εσται] διὰ πύλ[ης]), meaning "it has been paid at the [roadside] toll station."⁶⁸

It is better, then, to see Capernaum's *telōnion* not as a *pulē*, that is, a roadside toll station, but rather as a tax office or customs-house,⁶⁹ and to understand its primary function in relation specifically to activities at the village's harbor. As Keddie notes, Galilean *telōnai*—those who busied themselves in the *telōnia*—"collected indirect taxes on local commerce and transport, and particularly on sales and exchanges at village fairs or the markets at Magdala, Sepphoris, Tiberias, on the fishing industry and use of harbors around the lake."⁷⁰ This would mean that *telōnia*, like the one in Capernaum, were apparently linked to the buying and selling of goods

---

66. A point also noted in Mendel Nun, "Ports of Galilee," *Biblical Archaeology Review* 25, no. 4 (1999): 18–23, 25–31, 64.

67. See, e.g., *Chrest. Wilck.* 223 (tax declaration; ca. 250 BCE, found in Gurob [Egypt], written in Alexandria, destination Arsinoites [Fayyûm]); *PSI* 4.383 (petition against unjust tax; 248–247 BCE, written in Arsinoites, found in Philadelphia); *SB* 1.5729 (contract of sale of land or declaration that normal takes have been paid; 210 BCE, Feb. 12–15, Dios Polis, written and found); *UPZ* 1.112.8 (instructions to financial employees on the collection of taxes; 204 BCE, July 22–September 8, written in Oxyrynchites, found in Memphis); *BGU* 6.1234 (register of taxes; 141 BCE, Egypt); *BGU* 4.1118 (contract of lease of shoal-waters for produce; receipt for the payment of taxes; 22 BCE, March 14, written in Alexandria, found in Bousiris); *SB* 10.10266 (177 CE, June 13, Egypt).

68. See, e.g., *P. Fay.* 67–76 and the introduction to this set of papyri published in B. P. Grenfell, A. S. Hunt, and D. G. Hogarth, *Fayûm Towns and Their Papyri* (London: Offices of the Egypt Exploration Fund, 1900), 195–204. Many thanks to Gregory Fewster for directing my attention to these documents.

69. This rendering coincides with the use of *telōnion* in some epigraphic and papyrological sources. To the papyrological sources already mentioned above, we could add several inscriptions: *ILS* 8858 (second century CE, Halikarnassos); *IEph* 20 (54/59 CE, Ephesos); *IEph* 1503 (138/161 CE, Ephesos).

70. Keddie, *Class and Power*, 142.

and services in market contexts. Thus, it is quite possible that Capernaum's harbor front *telōnion* was *intentionally* located where it was for the economic benefit of local fishermen, since it would have served as a logistically convenient first stop in the commercial process of bringing catches of fresh fish to market.[71] A *telōnion* that was παρὰ τὴν θάλασσαν would have established a highly efficient supply chain that allowed producers easy access to the market and consumers easy access to fresh fish, a food product whose transportation normally required careful management and rapid consumption.[72] While there is extensive evidence for the production and consumption of preserved fish (e.g., processed through salting or pickling) in the Greek and Roman worlds,[73] fresh fish was clearly the more highly valued commodity. This would explain why it was sometimes transported over great distances and, conversely, why some buyers traveled far and wide to the coast for fresh fish.[74] In the case of Capernaum, the speedy movement from fresh catch to docking at harbor to processing at customs to consumption at market would have translated, for fishermen, into drachma signs.

How much would fishermen have had to pay in taxes on their catch? We do not have much evidence from early Roman Palestine on this question, but, as John Kloppenborg notes, comparative data from Ptolemaic and Roman Egypt suggest that there could be great variability in levels of indirect taxation. Kloppenborg mentions that levies on fish could be anywhere between 25 to

---

71. See a few paragraphs below where I compare this historical construction with a similar scenario (albeit one on a larger scale) involving the *telōnion* mentioned in *IEph* 20 / *IK*, 11.1a-Ephesos, 20, an inscription from the harbor of Roman Ephesos.

72. T. Theodoropoulou, "Salting the East: Evidence for Salt Fish and Fish Products from the Aegean Sea in Roman Times," in *Fish & Ships: Production et commerce des salsamenta durant l'Antiquité*, ed. E. Botte and V. Leitch, Bibliothèque d'Archéologie Méditerranéenne et Africaine 17 (Arles Cédex: Édition Errance, 2014), 219–220.

73. Magdala, whose Greek name was apparently Taricheaea (although there has been some debate over this identification), which means "the fish salting house," is sometimes taken as evidence that fish salting was common around the eastern Galilee and, indeed, Magdala's primary economic activity. See S. De Luca and A. Lena, "The Harbor of the City of Magdala/Taricheaea on the Shores of the Sea of Galilee, from the Hellenistic to the Byzantine Times: New Discoveries and Preliminary Results," in *Harbors and Harbor Cities in the Eastern Mediterranean from Antiquity to the Byzantine Period: Recent Discoveries and Current Approaches*, ed. S. Ladstätter, F. Pirson, and T. Schmidts, BYZAS 19 (Istanbul: Yayinlari, 2014), 122.

74. Theodoropoulou, "Salting the East," 219–220.

50 percent of the initial catch during the time of Ptolemaic Egypt, a range he cautiously adopts for early Roman Palestine as well.[75] Scholars have often interpreted these high percentages to mean that fishermen could not have profited from the industry. But, as Kloppenborg shows, it is an assumption to assert that the apparently high taxation rate meant that village fishermen were left with no economic surplus and lived only at a subsistence level.[76] In other words, profitability is not reducible to the percentage of taxation, but also involves how much one puts into production (e.g., labor, materials) as well as the volume and value of what is produced. Fishing, for example, was apparently in high demand in Roman Palestine, as it certainly was in Egypt, so much so "that local fisheries (both in the Kinneret and on the coast) could not keep up with the demand."[77] Archaeological evidence—especially the distribution of saltwater and freshwater fish bones in areas far from both the Mediterranean coast and the Kinneret—suggests that the fishing industry in Roman Palestine represented a highly organized commercial network, involving the importing and exporting of fish across significant distances and tetrachial boundaries. This, coupled with other evidence from around the Kinneret that suggests the importance of fishing to the Galilean economy,[78] leads Kloppenborg to conclude that "the fishing industry around the Kinneret was thriving, and that accordingly, fishermen were also thriving."[79]

---

75. J. Kloppenborg, "Jesus, Fishermen, and Tax Collectors: Papyrology and the Construction of the Ancient Economy of Roman Palestine," *Ephemerides Theologicae Lovanienses* 94, no. 4 (2018): 575–576. See also Keddie, *Class and Power*, 135. Most estimates like these derive from the extensive information given on the Greco-Roman taxation system in Egyptian documentary papyri. Kloppenborg provides careful and insightful justification for using this data to talk about the situation in Roman Palestine.

76. Estimates for agricultural tax rates could be even higher, yet still not necessarily imply subsistence-level living. Kloppenborg says that "a typical crop share lease on a vineyard had the owner taking between half and two-thirds of the harvest, and this still left the lessee with more than a subsistence-level agricultural endeavor" ("Jesus, Fishermen, and Tax Collectors," 575).

77. Kloppenbrog, "Jesus, Fishermen, and Tax Collectors," 596.

78. For which, see R. Hakola, "The Production and Trade of Fish as a Source of Economic Growth in First Century CE Galilee," *Novum Testamentum* 59, no. 2 (2017): 111–130; R. Bauckham, "Magdala and the Fishing Industry," in *Magdala of Galilee*, ed. R. Bauckham (Waco, TX: Baylor Univeristy Press, 2018), 185–268.

79. Kloppenborg, "Jesus, Fishermen, and Tax Collectors," 596. Later, on the same page, Kloppenborg insightfully notes that "if Egyptian evidence provides any guide, it does not

From the perspective of a dynamic and highly networked Galilean fishing industry, we can interpret the presence of the *telōnion* in Capernaum not as a hinderance to economic growth for local fishermen but rather as a conduit of it. Although on a different scale, an analogous type of economic relationship between local fisherman and a local *telōnion* seems to be indicated in an important inscription from Roman Ephesos (*IEph* 20 / *IK*, 11.1a-Ephesos, 20). This inscription, dated between 54 and 59 CE, was discovered, perhaps in situ, in the southeast corner of the city's ancient commercial harbor.[80] According to Ephraim Lytle, the inscription documents a business venture of a joint association of Ephesian fishermen and fish vendors (οἱ ἁλιεῖς καὶ ὀψαριοπῶλαι; line 7). In the nearly two-meter-tall stele, the joint association is said to have built from its own funds a *telōnion* for "the fish tax" (τελώνιον τῆς ἰχθυϊκῆς; line 9), a building to which a host of other donors contributed as well. Some of the donors, as Lytle mentions, contributed specific materials, such as roof tiles and bricks, or more expensive items, such as columns and Phoikaian stone to pave the open court. Furthermore, the mention of stoas (line 38) suggests that this *telōnion* served commercial purposes as well, and not merely tax collection. While there are several interpretive difficulties, Lytle argues persuasively that what we are dealing with here is a customs-house built by a joint association in the interest of streamlining the supply chain, thereby increasing the fishing association's commercial capacity. After delivering their catch to the docks, fishermen could have it brought directly to their own *telōnion* in the busy harbor, have the tax assessed on the catch immediately, and then sell the catch at wholesale to the vendors stationed in the stoas of the *telōnion*. These vendors would thus have a centralized location for their wholesale purchasing of fish and, importantly, have quick and easy access to Ephesos's Western Agora, located immediately adjacent to the harbor, where fresh seafood could hit the market and be sold at retail.

---

seem that fishermen were the impoverished lot that some scholars suggest, but instead that they enjoyed a modest income, certainly above the level of agricultural workers who were hired on a daily basis." He then goes on to offer concrete numbers from the papyri suggesting that Egyptian fishermen lived well above subsistence level.

80.   E. Lytle, "A Customs House of Our Own: Infrastructure, Duties and a Joint Association of Fishermen and Fishmongers (IK, 11.1a-Ephesos, 20)," in *Tout vendre, tout acheter: structures et équipements des marchés antiques,* ed. V. Chankowski and P. Karonis (Bordeaux: Ausonius, 2012), 213.

To be sure, Capernaum's lakeshore harbor was much smaller than the maritime harbor at Roman Ephesos.[81] Its *telōnion* was likely much smaller, too. But the social and organizational processes involved in the production and taxation of fish might not have been entirely different. Although sparse, Kloppenborg notes that there is some evidence from the Gospels that suggests fishermen in Roman Galilee were organized as occupational associations, as they certainly were in Asia Minor and Egypt. Mark's account, for example, presents pairs of brothers, Simon and Andrew, John and James with their father Zebedee, as working in a family-based enterprise with hired hands. Luke, on the other hand, envisions Simon as owning his own boat in a larger multiboat association, or "partnership" (τοῖς μετόχοις ἐν τῷ ἑτέρῳ πλοίῳ), which included the Zebedees (Luke 5:1–11).[82] The *telōnion* in Capernaum may not have been built from the funds of such a local association of fishermen, as was the case of the customs-house in Ephesos (although it could have been). But it is, indeed, quite plausible to imagine that local fishermen, who brought their catch into the Capernaum harbor to be bought and sold by market vendors, paid their customs taxes in the *telōnion* through their fishing association, which was taxed collectively on, for example, catches of fish, boat rentals, harbor maintenance, and leases on rights to fish in certain parts of the lake.[83]

---

81. See further comments on Capernaum's harbor below.

82. On the term μέτοχοι, particularly when used in the context of fishermen, as association language, see Kloppenborg, "Jesus, Fishermen, and Tax Collectors," 596 n. 93. Luke's narrative seems to present Simon and company as seine net, drag net, or as Nun suggested, trammel net fishermen, which would have required at least two boats working together and a partnership of around twenty men to bring a catch to shore (M. Nun, "Cast Your Net Upon the Waters," *Biblical Archaeology Review* 19, no. 6 [1993]: 46–49, 51–56, 70).

83. See, e.g., *O. Wilck.* 326 (100 BCE, Egyptian Thebes), which documents the common 25 percent tax on a catch of fish (τετάρτης ἁλιείων) ordered upon a person named Horos and "the partners" (τετάχαται τετάρτης ἁλιείων ιδ ἔτους Ὧρος καὶ οἱ μέτοχοι; ll. 1–2); and especially *P. Sijp.* 30 (*P. Gen.* inv. 181) (second century CE, Hermopolis), which is a long register of taxes assessed and paid (or not paid) by individuals and by various associations of fishermen and fish dealers. The document has a special focus on the taxation of boats, rented or owned. Line 52 is particularly illustrative, where the fishermen of Sinalabe were taxed 300 drachmae "according to their association, for their own boats" (Σιναλαβή, ἁλιέων κατὰ τὸ κοινόν ὑπὲρ ἰδίων πλοίων). Interestingly, the association apparently overpaid, since the tax farmers (οἱ τελῶναι) acknowledge in writing in the next line that, instead of the required 300 drachmae, 340 was actually paid. Cf. lines 49–50, in which the 280 drachmae that were supposed to be paid by an association comprised of Φαρτῆς καὶ οἱ μέτοχοι "for their own boats" had not yet

Even if taxes on fish were high, Galilean fishermen working in occupational collectives would have benefited from such organized partnerships that allowed them to increase their commercial capacity and meet high societal demand for fish products. And with a harbor front *telōnion*, Capernaum's economy, too, would have likely enjoyed a streamlined and localized supply chain that ran directly from the lake to its docks, to its customs-house, to the marketplace. Additionally, Keddie notes that since, to a certain extent, local elites depended on their tax-paying clients and a thriving commercial environment to supply their income, non-elites engaged in business and trade "had a degree of bargaining power."[84] Working within the context of a guild would have consolidated this power and provided local fishermen (and farmers) with a level of protection, for example, from tax abuse or an inability to pay. Papyrological sources show that petitions could be made to government officials to dispute instances of unjust taxation,[85] and a tax law from Roman Palmyra, discussed by Keddie, implies that vendors were sometimes allowed to postpone their payment of taxes until after they sold their goods at market; a particularly interesting tax register from second century CE Hermopolis (*P. Sijp.* 30) names several individual fishermen who had at least part of their tax burden paid for by their local fishing association.[86]

When seen in this light, the fishing industry in Capernaum may have been a more thriving and more dynamically networked economic operation than what has typically been imagined, a point which Kloppenborg has made

---

been paid. On taxes pertaining to fishing rights, see Kloppenborg, "Jesus, Fishermen, and Tax Collectors," 595.

84. Keddie, *Class and Power*, 140.

85. See, e.g., *PSI* 4.383 ll. 2–4 (third century BCE, Philadelphia), in which Zenon is petitioned by a farmer named Aristandros, who claims that although he had paid correctly the things that are due to the βασιλικόν (royal treasury), he had been wronged by those who busy themselves in the customs-house (ἠδίκηται ὑπὸ τῶν ἐπὶ τοῦ τελωνίου π[ραγ]ματευομένων). Keddie notes that by the mid-first century CE, civic councils and emperors alike are seen attempting, even if for their own political advantage, "to mitigate abuses by fixing rates, restricting surcharges, and generally lowering transaction costs and economic uncertainty" (Keddie, *Class and Power*, 140). He cites the interesting example of Tacitus's account of Nero's reforms to impede the abuses of local tax farmers (*publicani*) in *Ann.* 13.50–51.

86. *P. Sijp.* 30.31, 33–34, 39–40, 42, 46, 51, 57–58, 75. This and other elements of the document are also discussed in Kloppenborg, "Jesus, Fishermen, and Tax Collectors," 588–590.

Capernaum in the Time of Jesus   39

regarding Roman Palestine generally. Indeed, according to Mendel Nun's mappings of ancient Galilean ports, Capernaum was attached to one of the lake's largest harbor facilities, which extended some 8 km from et-Tabgha to the upper Jordan River and ran along the most productive part of the entire lake for fishing, due to the hot water currents that, from the Seven Springs/ Heptapegon (four of which are still active), flow into the lake.[87] It's not surprising then that there would have been a lakeside *telōnion* for collecting taxes on catches, boats, fishing rights, and harbor maintenance. And, while Capernaum lacked the open colonnaded space of a hellenistic agora, it most certainly did have a major north–south thoroughfare (see Locus 39 in the town plan), which ran just to the east of where the limestone synagogue and octagonal church now stand. This main street, apparently lined with shops along its eastern edge, is probably where the village's market would have been in both the early Roman and Byzantine periods.[88] The southern end of the street, in proximity to the harbor front, would have been a convenient access point for products—fish and other items—hitting the market after clearing customs. Thus, while the fishing industry in Capernaum, quite obviously, would not have been on the same socioeconomic level as the major cities of the Roman East, this does not mean that the village's fishermen were abjectly poor or barely eked out a living.[89] The village does not need to have had characteristic markers of a Greco-Roman *polis*—such as large civic buildings, a clearly delineated *cardo maximus* intersected by a *decumanus*, and colonnaded streets—for its fishermen and village merchants to have lived moderately above subsistence level.[90] In my view, when the synoptics' mention of a *telōnion* in

---

87. See Nun, "Ports of Galilee," 18–23, 25–31, 64; Kloppenborg, "Jesus, Fishermen, and Tax Collectors," 595; and De Luca and Lena, "The Harbor of the City of Magdala/Tarichaea," 177 n. 23. Nun notes that the remains of Capernaum's harbor show evidence of triangled, paired, and curved piers forming protected pools convenient for loading or unloading cargo and passengers.

88. Loffreda notes that several structures were uncovered facing outward along the eastern side of the street that lack the features of typical courtyard houses found in the village, suggesting that they be interpreted as shops. See Loffreda, *Recovering Capharnaum*, 24. See also Mattila's essays, which locate Capernaum's Byzantine shops in this strip of buildings as well.

89. Reed, *Archaeology*, 164.

90. This seems to be Reed's reasoning in *Archaeology*, 148–157 (esp. 153–155). Reed also claims that Capernaum lacked centralized planning and, rather, developed organically around

Capernaum (and perhaps also its "many tax collectors") is put within a larger socioeconomic context—of the Roman East more generally and of Roman Palestine more specifically—we might even be encouraged to think of Capernaum's fishermen as moderately prosperous, having a significant impact on local, regional, and perhaps even provincial economies.[91]

4. Conclusion
Socioeconomic Networks and the Emergence of "Jewish-Christian" Relations in Capernaum

In the introduction to his study, Kloppenborg raises the question of why fishermen and tax collectors, in particular, came to feature so prominently in the imagination of the early Jesus tradition.[92] The answer that emerges from his analysis comes down to one characteristic feature that fishermen and tax collectors seem to have shared, which allowed them to play instrumental roles in the spread of the Jesus movement: both trades were socially situated at the center of complex networks.[93] As Kloppenborg notes, fishing "generated around itself an active *network* of groups and persons connected to the

---

courtyards and domestic growth (152–153). His point of departure for this claim are the "classical Roman cities" as well as Sepphoris and Tiberias. To my knowledge, no one has argued that Capernaum was planned on a grid system to the degree of these major *poleis*. This is self-evident. However, Loffreda (with whom Reed shows no interaction) suggests that Capernaum, while not necessarily on a grid, does indeed show signs of intentional planning (Loffreda, *Recovering Capharnaum*, 24).

91. The evidence surveyed here and by other scholars, such as Kloppenborg, would seem to undermine Reed's view, derived from his interpretation of Plato, *Laws* 7.823, that fishing was considered a detestable profession and unworthy pursuit.

92. Kloppenborg, "Jesus, Fishermen, and Tax Collectors," 571–572, notes that fishing and fishermen play a significant role in stories about Jesus found in the Synoptic Gospels (Mark 1:16–20 // Matt 4:18–22; Matt 13:47–50; Luke 5:1–11), John (21:1–14), *Gospel of Thomas* (*GTh* 8), and *Gospel of Peter* (*GPet* 14:60).

93. In emphasizing the role of trade and networks in the dissemination of elective cults, including the Christ cult, Kloppenborg joins several other scholars, most notably Anna Collar, *Religious Networks in the Roman Empire: The Spread of New Ideas* (Cambridge: Cambridge University Press, 2013); Cavan Concannon, *Assembling Early Christianity: Trade Networks, and the Letters of Dionysios of Corinth* (Cambridge: Cambridge University Press, 2017); and more recently but from a different methodological angle, Eivind Heldaas Seland, *A Global History of the Ancient World: Asia, Europe, and Africa Before Islam* (London: Routledge, 2021).

industry."⁹⁴ Fishing associations were constantly entangled with other productive networks, such as those involving net-making; suppliers of tools; shippers, ship owners, ship renters, and ship makers; agents of lessors; and, of course, tax collectors and other government officials. Fishermen and tax collectors continually brought their professions and their ideas into face-to-face contact with a wide variety of other networks. These network intersections provided a necessary platform for their ideas about Christ-adherence to "jump" from one local network to another.⁹⁵ This is probably why "of the early named members of Jesus' entourage, it is only fisherman and tax collectors who are identified specifically in relation to their trade."⁹⁶

While not "upper class," fishermen in Capernaum, including the earliest Christ-followers, were probably moderately prosperous—part of an above-subsistence level working class—and would have had extensive connections with other local productive networks in a village that, for its size, boasted a vibrant socioeconomic scene. But where, in concrete spatial terms, would face-to-face contact—so crucial to both professional network building and the spread of ideas—have taken place in Capernaum? Where would fishing associations, whose members also had messianic ideas about Jesus of Nazareth, have found the necessary social platform for their ideas to "jump" from their network to others? It is certainly possible, even likely, that professional network intersections between fishermen and, for example, basalt stone craftspeople, took place in house-shops, at the harbor, in the customs office, or on Capernaum's main market-street. But if we were to imagine an institutional setting in which members of one association might, as such, engage in an attempt to persuade or influence others to accept their ideas, especially ideas that had a religiopolitical nature like a Galilean Jewish messianic movement, then the most obvious setting for such a network intersection would have been a public synagogue.⁹⁷

---

94. Kloppenborg, "Jesus, Fishermen, and Tax Collectors," 598 (italics original).

95. Here Kloppenborg is drawing from the sociological insights of Rodney Stark on the idea that elective cults travel through networks.

96. Kloppenborg, "Jesus, Fishermen, and Tax Collectors," 598.

97. Although attesting to a situation outside of Roman Palestine and so institutionally different (see chapter 2), *t. Sukkah* 4:6 is classic evidence for the importance of trade associations within synagogue contexts. According to this Tosefta passage, in the great basilica synagogue of Alexandra, people sat together according to trade: "goldsmiths were by themselves,

However, this conclusion brings us back to a question that has been debated for decades among historians and archaeologists alike: Was there a public synagogue in Capernaum during the time of Jesus in the first place? Answering this question is historiographically crucial for us, since how one answers it will have significant implications for the way one writes the history of Capernaum and "Jewish–Christian" relations, not only in the first century but also in the centuries that followed. For the issue is inherently bound up with fundamental questions about the social and institutional context of a time and place in which "Christians" were still Jews and, as members of the Jesus movement, competed for influence within broader Jewish society.[98] Thus, it is to this question we now turn.

---

the blacksmiths by themselves, the embroiderers by themselves, so that when a poor man came in he joined his fellow tradesmen, and in this way was enabled to obtain a means of livelihood" (text from Sefaria).

98. To invoke the title of Paula Fredriksen's book, *When Christians Were Jews: The First Generation* (New Haven: Yale University Press, 2018).

CHAPTER TWO

Was There a Public Synagogue in Capernaum during the Time of Jesus?

History between Texts and Archaeology

1. Introduction

ON JUNE 20, 1838, at the unenviable hour of one o'clock in the afternoon, American explorer Edward Robinson and his traveling companions came to the ruins of Tell Ḥum, a site resting just off the northwest shore of Kinneret Lake and today firmly identified as ancient Capernaum.[1] According to his

---

1. E. Robinson, *Biblical Researches in Palestine, Mount Sinai, and Arabia Petraea: A Journal of Travels for the Year 1838* (London: John Murray, 1841) 297–298. Reed, *Archaeology*, 142, says Tell Ḥum was not properly identified as Capernaum until 1866 upon the expedition of Charles Wilson. But Robinson himself noted (in Robinson, *Biblical Researches*, 300–301) that Tell Ḥum had a centuries-long tradition of being regarded as ancient Capernaum, including by some of his contemporaries, most notably John Wilson, who published his travel log in 1847, nearly twenty years before Charles Wilson (J. Wilson, *The Lands of the Bible Visited and Described*, vol. 2 [Edinburgh: William Whyte, 1847], 143). So, Reed appears to have his Wilsons mistaken. As time has shown, Robinson wrongly rejected Tell Ḥum as the site of Capernaum. Rather, he argued at length in his 1841 publication (*Biblical Researches*, 288–295) and then again in 1856 (*Later Biblical Researches in Palestine and the Adjacent Regions: A Journal of Travels in the Year 1852* [London: John Murray, 1856], 348–358), that Capernaum should be identified with the nearby site of Khirbat al-Minya. Although Robinson never lived to know it, his theory was definitively undercut in 1937, when German archaeologists Alfons Maria Schneider and Oswin Puttrich-Reignard uncovered an Umayyad mosque at Khirbat al-Minya, making it clear that the remains Robinson had seen almost a century earlier and the grand complex that Schneider and Puttrich-Reignard had been digging out since 1932 were, in fact, an early Islamic palace that rendered no pre-Islamic remains (see A. M. Schneider, "Ḥirbet El-Minje am See Genesareth," *Annales archéologiques de Syrie* 2 [1952]: 23–45; and more recently H.-P. Kuhnen, *Kalifenzeit am See Genezareth: Der Palast von Khirbat al-Minya* [Nünnerich-Asmus Verlag & Media GmbH, 2014]). This discovery made the identification of Khirbat al-Minya as Capernaum impossible and strengthened Capernaum's identification with Tell Ḥum. The most recent full-scale argument for identifying Tell Ḥum as Capernaum is in J. Laughlin, "The Identification of the Site," 191–199.

travel log, Robinson spent only twenty-five minutes there; at 1:25 he was off again to find the inflowing banks of the Jordan River. It did not take long, however, for him to recognize the special significance of Tell Ḥum's ruins. One set of remains was particularly conspicuous: "Not far off," he says, "were the prostrate ruins of an edifice, which, for expense of labour and ornament, surpasses anything we had yet seen in Palestine."[2] While, in 1838, he supposed that these white limestone ruins were either of a church or a pagan temple,[3] in May of 1852, fourteen years after his initial visit and after having seen the comparable "Jewish remains" at Kefar Bar'am and Meiron, Robinson changed his mind and became the first to conclude that the edifice at Tell Ḥum was a Jewish synagogue.[4]

Robinson's identification of Capernaum's great limestone building as a synagogue is now beyond a doubt.[5] Subsequent excavations and restorations

---

2. Robinson, *Biblical Researches*, 298.

3. Robinson, *Biblical Researches*, 299, as did John Wilson (*Lands of the Bible*, vol. 2:143).

4. Robinson, *Biblical Researches*, 346. That Robinson was the first to identify this building, as well as other buildings in the Galilee, as synagogues is noted also by H. Kohl and K. Watzinger, *Die antiken Synagogen in Galiläa* (Leipzig: J. C. Hinrichs'sche Buchhandlung, 1916), 1: "Die antiken Ruinen, deren Aufnahmen hier veröffentlicht warden, sind zuerst 1852 von Eduard Robinson auf Grund der hebräischen Inschriften und der Übereinstimmung ihrer Architektur als Synagogen bezeichnet und mit der Blüte der jüdischen Schulen in Galiläa in Zusammenhang gebracht worden."

5. A menorah inscribed on a capital and the image of a portable Torah shrine carved on a slab of limestone were found among the building's architectural remains. The structure itself was clearly a public building meant for large gatherings (C. Spigel, *Ancient Synagogue Seating Capacities: Method, Analysis, and Limits*, TSAJ 149 [Tübingen: Mohr Siebeck, 2012], 175, suggests a seating capacity of approximately 600 to 700) in a town that had a Jewish population well into the sixth century CE. On Capernaum as a predominately Jewish village in the first century, see M. Chancey, *The Myth of a Gentile Galilee*, 101–105; S. Mattila, "Capernaum, Village of Naḥum," 217–257; Cf. J. Laughlin, "Capernaum: From Jesus' Time and After," *Biblical Archeology Review* 19 (1993): 54–61, who suggests that the structure under a Roman bath (dated second to third century) uncovered in the eastern part of the village might be another Roman bath and might indicate the presence of non-Jews in Capernaum in the first century. On a Jewish population in Capernaum in the fourth century, see A. Runesson, "Architecture, Conflict, and Identity Formation: Jews and Christians in Capernaum from the First to the Sixth Century," in *Religion, Ethnicity, and Identity in Ancient Galilee*, ed. J. Zangenberg, H. W. Attridge, and D. B. Martin, WUNT 210 (Tübingen: Mohr Siebeck 2007), 231–257; B. Y. Arubas and R. Talgam, "Jews, Christians, and *Minim*: Who Really Built and Used the Synagogue at Capernaum—A Stirring Appraisal," in *Knowledge and Wisdom: Archaeological and Historical Essays in Honour of Leah Di Segni*, ed. G. C. Bottini, L. D. Chrupcala, and J. Patrich (Milan: Edizioni Terra Santa, 2014), 237–74. Epiphanius,

of the building—first only partially by Charles Wilson in the 1860s, and then more systematically by Heinrich Kohl and Carl Watzinger in 1905, Wendelin von Menden from 1906–1915, and Gaudenzio Orfali from 1922–1925— established this certainty already at an early stage, well before Franciscan archaeologists Virgilio Corbo and Stanislao Loffreda began their large-scale excavations in 1969.[6] However, although the building's identification as a synagogue is settled, at least two problems have pestered researchers since the nineteenth century and remain to this day. The first is the date of the limestone building. While some early scholarship echoed Charles Wilson's claim in 1871, that the limestone synagogue was "without a doubt the synagogue built by the Roman centurion (Luke 7:5), and one of the of the most sacred places on earth,"[7] the clear consensus today is that it surely does not date to the time of Jesus, nor is it likely to date to the second or third century as proposed by Kohl and Watzinger, but rather to sometime in the fifth or early sixth century CE.[8]

Panarion 30.11.10 indicates that, in the time of his fourth-century contemporary Joseph of Tiberius (d. ca. 356 CE), there were no non-Jews living in Capernaum (as well as in Tiberias, Sepphoris, and Nazareth). On the continued presence of Jews in Capernaum in the sixth century, see *Qohelet Rabbah* 1:8 (redacted sixth to eighth century), which, even if a rabbinic caricature, is a collective memory of an interaction between rabbinic Jews (Rabbi Joshua and his nephew) and Capernaum's *minim*, i.e., non-rabbinic Jews. See also the sixth-century donor inscription on the mosaic pavement of the synagogue at Ḥamat Gader referring to a "Yosse bar Dosti of Capernaum" (J. Naveh, *On Stone and Mosaic: The Aramaic and Hebrew Inscriptions from Ancient Synagogues* [Jerusalem: Israel Exploration Society, 1978], no. 33; G. Foerster, "Dating Synagogues with a 'Basilical' Plan and an Apse," in *Ancient Synagogues: Historical Analysis and Archaeological Discovery*, eds. D. Urman and P. V. M Flesher, 2 vols. [Leiden: Brill, 1995], 1:87–94, esp. 90–91), which suggests not only that Jews continued to live in Capernaum in the sixth century but also that some were wealthy enough to donate money to another Galilean village for the decoration of its synagogue.

6. C. W. Wilson, *The Recovery of Jerusalem: A Narrative of Exploration and Discovery in the City and the Holy Land* (London: Richard Bentley & Son, 1871), 342–345; Kohl and Watzinger, *Die antiken Synagogen in Galiläa*, 4–40; G. Orfali, *Capharnaüm et ses ruines. D'après les fouilles accomplies à Tell-Houm par la Custodie Franciscaine de Terre Sainte (1905–1921)* (Paris: Auguste Picard,1922). Although publications from the Franciscan excavations of Capernaum continue to be released, the original report on the excavations in and around the synagogue begun in 1969 was published in V. Corbo, *Cafarnao*, vol. 1: *Gli edifici della città* (Jerusalem: Franciscan, 1975).

7. Wilson, *The Recovery of Jerusalem*, 345, a theory followed and argued by Orfali, *Capharnaüm et ses ruines*, 69–86.

8. Following the theory of Kohl and Watzinger, most scholars in the early to mid-twentieth century dated the limestone synagogue to the second or third century based upon art-historical criteria and the architecture of synagogues of the "Galilean type." For discussion,

The second problem—with which I am centrally concerned in this chapter—arises from these earlier claims and pertains to whether a first-century synagogue, understood as both a purpose-built structure and a formal institution of assembly, once stood beneath the site of the later limestone synagogue.[9] Scholarship on this question over the past thirty years has been

---

see, e.g., D. Chen, "On the Chronology of the Ancient Synagogue at Capernaum," *Zeitschrift des Deutschen Palästina-Vereins* 102 (1986): 134–143; H. Bloedhorn, "The Capitals of the Synagogue in Capernaum: Their Chronological and Stylistic Classification with Regard to the Development of Capitals in the Decapolis and in Palestine," in *Ancient Synagogues in Israel: Third–Seventh Century CE*, ed. R. Hachlili (Oxford: BAR, 1989), 49–54, and his more detailed book, H. Bloedhorn, *Die Kapitelle der Synagoge von Kapernaum: Ihre zeitliche und stilistische Einordnung im Rahmen der Kapitellentwicklung in der Dekapolis und in Palaestina*, ADVP 11 (Wiesbaden: Harrassowitz, 1988); Z. Ma'oz, "The Synagogue at Capernaum: A Radical Solution," in *The Roman and Byzantine Near East*, vol. 2: *Some Recent Archaeological Research*, ed. J. H. Humphrey, JRASup. 14 (Ann Arbor, MI: University of Michigan Press, 1995), 137–148; Y. Tsafrir, "The Synagogues at Capernaum and Meroth and the Dating of the Galilean Synagogue," in *The Roman and Byzantine Near East*, ed. Humphrey, 151–161 (151–152); J. Magness, "The Question of the Synagogue: The Problem of Typology," in *Judaism in Antiquity*, part 3, vol. 4: *Where We Stand: Issues and Debates in Ancient Judaism: The Special Problem of the Synagogue*, ed. A. J. Avery-Peck and J. Neusner (Leiden: Brill, 2001), 1–48; Runesson, "Architecture," 235–237; Arubas and Talgam, "Jews, Christians, and *Minim*," 237–241; and R. Hachlili, *Ancient Synagogues—Archaeology and Art: New Discoveries and Current Research* (Leiden: Brill, 2013), 61–63, 590–593. The early dating of the building based upon art historical concerns is, today, a minority view. The dating scene shifted in 1969 when Corbo and Loffreda began their bold excavation project inside the limestone synagogue. In their first season alone, they cut seven trenches inside and around the synagogue in order to produce the first stratigraphic analysis of the building. I return to this trench-cutting operation below, but it is enough here to state that these trenches immediately provided new stratigraphic evidence that allowed the Franciscan archaeologists to date the limestone synagogue to the late fourth century. See, e.g., S. Loffreda, "The Synagogue of Capharnaum: Archaeological Evidence for its Late Chronology," *Liber Annuus* 22 (1972): 5–29. In the early 1980s, after sinking a number of additional trenches inside the building, Loffreda revised his date up to the fifth century. See, e.g., S. Loffreda, "Ceramica ellenistico-romana nel sottosuolo della sinagogoa di Cafarnao," in *Studia Hierosolymitana III*, ed. G.C. Bottini (Jerusalem: Franciscan, 1982), 273–312; and more recently, S. Loffreda, "Coins from the Synagogue of Capharnaum," *Liber Annuus* 47 (1997): 233. Magness, "Question," 21–26 has argued for a date in the sixth century. A third group of scholars have combined the art historical and stratigraphical approaches to dating the building (e.g., Bloehorn, "Capitals"; Ma'oz, "Solution"; Runesson, "Architecture"; and Arubas and Talgam, "Jews, Christians, and *Minim*"). These scholars have employed a type of *spolia* theory to explain the discrepancy between the ornamental dimensions of the synagogue, which suggest an earlier date, and the stratigraphy, which suggests a later date.

9. See section 2 below, where I present a model and definition of first-century synagogues.

Was There a Public Synagogue in Capernaum? 47

intensely divided.[10] One of the main reasons for this enduring division is that there has been very little, if any, sustained methodological reflection. Some scholars, on both sides of the debate, have emphasized certain aspects of the data while dismissing other aspects or leaving them unexplained.[11] Others have been sceptical that the question of a first-century synagogue in Capernaum can be answered at all because of the scant archaeological remains and

---

10. Scholars who reject the existence of a first-century synagogue underneath the limestone building include: H. C. Kee, "The Transformation of the Synagogue after 70 CE: Its Import for Early Christianity," *New Testament Studies* 36 (1990): 1–24; H. C. Kee, "Defining the First-Century CE Synagogue: Problems and Progress," *New Testament Studies* 41 (1995): 481–500 (495), presented again in *Evolution of the Synagogue: Problems and Progress*, ed. H. C. Kee and L. H. Cohick (Harrisburg, PA: Trinity Press International, 1999), 7–26; J. T. Sanders, *Schismatics, Sectarians, Dissidents, Deviants: The First One Hundred Years of Jewish–Christian Relations* (London: SCM Press, 1993), 38; Tsafrir, "The Synagogues at Capernaum and Meroth," 152–157 (esp. 155–56); R. A. Horsley, "Synagogues in Galilee and the Gospels," in *Evolution of the Synagogue*, ed. Kee and Cohick, 46–69 (49–50); Reed, *Archaeology*, 142–143 (although sceptical indifference is probably a better descriptor for Reed's position); Magness, "Question," 19–26; Magness, "The Pottery from the Village of Capernaum and the Chronology of Galilean Synagogues," *Tel Aviv* 39 (2012): 110–122; M. Aviam, "Capernaum I," in *Encyclopaedia of the Bible and Its Reception*, vol. 4, ed. H.-J. Klauck et al. (Berlin: De Gruyter, 2012), 944–948; M. J. Grey, "Simon Peter in Capernaum: An Archaeological Survey of the First-Century Village," in *The Ministry of Peter, the Chief Apostle*, ed. F. Judd, Jr., E. D. Huntsman, and S. D. Hopkin (Provo, UT: Religious Studies Center; Salt Lake City: Deseret Book, 2014), 27–66; and, most recently, R. Bonnie, *Being Jewish in Galilee, 100–200 CE: An Archaeological Study*, SEMA 11 (Turnhout: Brepols, 2019), 181–185. Examples of scholars who accept the existence of a first-century synagogue, with varying levels of certainty: J. F. Strange and H. Shanks, "Synagogue Where Jesus Preached Found at Capernaum," *Biblical Archaeology Review* 9, no. 6 (1983): 24–32; D. Binder, *Into the Temple Courts: The Place of the Synagogues in the Second Temple Period* (Atlanta: SBL, 1999), 186–193; L. Levine, *The Ancient Synagogue: The First Thousand Years*, 2nd ed. (New Haven: Yale University Press, 2005), 71 (although very cautious acceptance is a better descriptor of his position); Runesson, "Architecture," 237–239; S. De Luca, "Capernaum," in *The Oxford Encyclopaedia of the Bible and Archaeology*, ed. D. M. Master (Oxford: Oxford University Press, 2013), 168–180; J. Ryan, *The Role of the Synagogue in the Aims of Jesus* (Minneapolis: Fortress Press, 2017), 63; and the various publications of the excavators Corbo and Loffreda. Although I will say more about this later in the chapter, it is important to note here that not all who except the presence of a first-century synagogue in Capernaum agree as to what archaeological remains specifically constitute that first-century synagogue; even Corbo and Loffreda disagreed on this.

11. This point will become clear in the discussion of the key archaeological data in section 3 of this chapter, and it also pertains to the scholarly treatment—or lack thereof—of the textual sources from the New Testament, on which see section 4.

have thus excluded it from their historical assessment of the village's socioreligious, political, and economic environment.[12] And still other scholars have treated the issue primarily as an archaeological question and thus have either marginalized the textual evidence of the Gospels or have interpreted these texts in such a way that makes them subservient to the alleged archaeological situation: if there is no archaeological evidence for such a synagogue, it must not have existed.[13]

In this chapter, I wish to assess the question anew by providing principled methodological reflection from the perspective of Collingwoodian critical historiography. In section 2, I will briefly present some of the most important aspects of Collingwood's historical method as well as a model of first-century synagogues based upon recent synagogue scholarship. I will then use the

---

12. E.g., Reed, *Archaeology*, 143; H.-P.Kuhnen, *Palästina in griechisch-römischer Zeit*, Handbuch der Archäologie 2.2 (Munich: Beck, 1990), 191, 229; S. L. Mattila, "Revisiting Jesus' Capernaum," 82; and Grey, "Simon Peter in Capernaum," who says, "The extant synagogue remains at the site cannot be used as evidence for wealth in the first-century village and likely have no bearing on reconstructing Peter's social context" (although Grey, in the end, rejects the existence of a first-century synagogue altogether). To my knowledge, the only historians who are willing to construct the possible contribution of a first-century synagogue to the socioreligious context of Capernaum are Runesson, "Architecture," 235–239, and Ryan, *Role of the Synagogue*, 243–263.

13. See, e.g., and most recently, Bonnie, *Being Jewish in Galilee*, 181–85, where Bonnie seems to see the question as solely an archaeological matter. Also in this vein is scholarship that has followed Kee's earlier work (1990, 1995), in which synagogues in the first century are understood as informal gatherings that met in private or domestic spaces as opposed to formal assemblies that met in purpose-built public edifices (see, e.g., Carsten Claußen, "Jesus und die Versammlungen Galiläas: Zur Frage nach der Bedeutung ἡ συναγωγή," in *Jesus und die Archäologie Galiläas*, ed. C. Claußen and J. Frey, BThSt 87 [Neukirchen-Vluyn: Neukirchener Verlag, 2008], 237–238). This scholarship has looked primarily to the archaeological record before the year 2000, and, because the record at this time included very few buildings firmly identified as "synagogues," it has interpreted "synagogue" passages in the Gospels as either (1) referring to informal gatherings without public buildings, or (2) features of later redactional activity on the part of the Gospel authors (especially in the case of Luke 7:5), which reflect a later time when formal gatherings and synagogue buildings supposedly did exist. For thorough and critical discussions of this type of (now outdated) scholarship on synagogues, see the early work of A. Runesson, *The Origins of the Synagogue: A Socio-Historical Study*, CBNT 37 (Stockholm: Almqvist & Wiksell International, 2001), 169–236; and the more recent work of J. Ryan in "Jesus and Synagogue Disputes: Recovering the Institutional Context of Luke 13:10–17," *Catholic Biblical Quarterly* 79, no.1 (2017): 41–59; and Ryan, *Role of the Synagogue*, 23–36; 102–106.

method and the model to weigh the archaeological evidence in section 3 and the textual evidence of the Gospels in section 4. In section 5, I will present my conclusion. While not novel in and of itself, this conclusion will emerge from the application of a method that, I suggest, will help reset the terms of the debate over whether a first-century synagogue existed in Capernaum, and, perhaps more importantly shed further light on the social and institutional context of the early Roman village.

2. The Need for a Critical Historiography and a Model of First-Century Synagogues

The question of a first-century synagogue in Capernaum is, at its core, not an archaeological one. There are certainly archaeological questions involved; indeed, the most salient ones receive a significant amount of attention below. Nor is this question only a textual one, although the literary evidence of the Gospels must factor into our discussion as well. The question at hand, rather, is fundamentally a problem of history: Should a synagogue occupy a place in our construction of Capernaum's first-century past, and, if so, what place should it be given? This means that the evidence at our disposal is not *either* archaeology *or* texts but rather *both* archaeology *and* texts, and that the critical interrogation of these sources should lead us to ask, in the end, what the evidence, as a whole, compels us to believe. What is needed in the debate, therefore, is not scepticism but rather a critical historiography that judges and explains as much of the data as possible, and that aims at speaking not beyond the evidence but rather *between* it, filling in the gaps through a process of historical reasoning. After all, the construction of history from leftover and sometimes disparate pieces of the past is precisely what historians of antiquity do; they are not antiquarian list makers.

Scholarship in the historiographic tradition of Robin George Collingwood (1889–1943) has recognized this last point for quite some time. While Collingwood himself was a philosopher and a historian, he was also an archaeologist; his work, for example, on the archaeology of Roman Britain is still considered authoritative.[14] As W. J. van der Dussen has observed, so much of

---

14. R. G. Collingwood, *The Archaeology of Roman Britain* (London: Methuen, 1930). For an excellent review and analysis of Collingwood's career as both historian and archaeologist,

Collingwood's philosophy emerged from his thinking about the importance of archaeology as an empirical science that functioned as a precondition for doing critical history.[15] Collingwood even went so far as to assert in one of his lectures that advances in critical history rest on advances made in the archaeological sciences.[16] For Collingwood, however, history was not reduceable to the empirical, descriptive work of archaeology. While archaeology is a means to obtain historical knowledge, it is the historian's responsibility to discover materials, no matter how widely divergent in kind, that enable them to answer a particular question about the past.[17] The centrality in Collingwood's philosophy of a synthesis between archaeology and texts in the service of critical history makes it especially helpful for approaching the archaeological and textual questions about a first-century synagogue in Capernaum from a historical perspective.

There are three inherently connected conceptual categories in Collingwood's historical method that I wish briefly to present here, and which will

---

see W. J. van der Dussen, *History as a Science: The Philosophy of R.G. Collingwood* (The Hauge: Martinus Nijhoff, 1981), 201–253. As van der Dussen notes, Collingwood's impact on archaeological scholarship was not so much through actual field excavation—although he did direct a few of his own—as it was through close engagement with professional archaeologists on issues of method. See, e.g., R. G. Collingwood, "Hadrian's Wall: 1921–1930," *Journal of Roman Studies* 21 (1931): 36–64, which, in large part, had to do with methodological problems involved in excavating the wall.

15. Van der Dussen, *History as Science*, 213.

16. R. G. Collingwood, "Outlines of a Philosophy of History," 69 pp. (lecture given in April 1928), 50; van der Dussen, *History as Science*, 214. The importance Collingwood assigned to archaeology in the practice of critical history is no doubt the reason that his historical method has been used so effectively in the work of J. Ryan, especially in his *Role of the Synagogue*. The archaeology of ancient synagogues is a major feature in Ryan's historical work on Jesus. While the present article is not a work on the historical Jesus, it has certainly been inspired by Ryan's application of Collingwood's method. Although not devoted to any significant extent to archaeology, J. Bernier's recent works have also drawn deeply from the well of Collingwoodian historiography. See his Aposynagōgos *and the Historical Jesus in John: Rethinking the Historicity of the Johannine Expulsion Passages*, BibInt 122 (Leiden: Brill, 2013), and *The Quest for the Historical Jesus after the Demise of Authenticity: Toward a Critical Realist Philosophy of History in Jesus Studies*, LNTS 540 (London: T&T Clark, 2016).

17. R. G. Collingwood, "Lectures on Philosophy of History," 38 pp. (lecture given Trinity Term 1929), 38; R. G. Collingwood, "Lectures on the Philosophy of History," 75 pp. (lecture given January 1926), 30.

frame the way I approach the data from Capernaum:[18] they are evidence, inference, and the historical imagination.[19]

For Collingwood, history is not only critical but also, and necessarily, constructive.[20] It is not enough for a historian to judge through critical interpretation whether a datum is trustworthy or not; critical interpretation must also involve the application of that datum (e.g., a statement in a text, an eyewitness testimony, a material artifact) as evidence within the historian's picture of the past. History is not the rote gathering and arranging of historical data but rather the *interpretation* of that data and the *application* of them as evidence in relation to some definite historical question or problem.[21] The concept of evidence, therefore, is defined as data that are interpreted and mobilized for the purpose of constructing history.[22] While, as Collingwood notes, everything in the perceptible world, in principle, can potentially be evidence for the historian depending on the question they are asking: "historical knowledge comes mainly through finding *how to use as evidence this or that kind of perceived fact* which historians have hitherto thought useless to them."[23] This is an important point to make, because it highlights the fact that the question of a first-century synagogue in Capernaum stems not really from a problem with the data but rather from a problem with the interpretation of the data, that is, with how the data should be mobilized and applied to construct a historical argument.

---

18. Much of what follows comes from Collingwood's principal work *The Idea of History*, rev. ed., ed. J. van der Dussen (Oxford: Oxford University Press, 1994 [orig. 1946]), 231–263; see also the helpful presentation in J. Ryan, "Jesus at the Crossroads of Inference and Imagination: The Relevance of R.G. Collingwood's Philosophy of History for Current Methodological Discussions in Historical Jesus Research," *Journal for the Study of the Historical Jesus* 13 (2015): 66–89.

19. Collingwood, of course, has had his readers and critics over the past century. However, virtually all of the core principles of his philosophy of history have remained influential in contemporary historiography. His notion of history as "re-enactment" and his association with the school of British Idealism are the two issues for which he is most often critiqued. On this, see the discussion in Ryan, "Jesus at the Crossroads," 68–76.

20. Collingwood, *Idea of History*, 240.

21. Collingwood, *Idea of History*, 281; see also Ryan, "Jesus at the Crossroads," 80.

22. Ryan, "Jesus at the Crossroads," 80; Collingwood, *Idea of History*, 281.

23. Collingwood, *The Idea of History*, 247 (italics added).

Perhaps the most important methodological point to make for the current study derives from Collingwood's emphasis on the inferential nature of history. History involves the study of, for example, events, places, and people that are not accessible to our observation.[24] While archaeology is an empirical science, the study of the past is not; we cannot observe the past first hand as onlookers in a laboratory. Thus, history's objective is to study events and things not accessible to the senses "inferentially, arguing to them from something that is accessible to our observation, and which the historian calls 'evidence' for the events in which he is interested."[25]

Evidence, however, does not come as "ready-made historical knowledge, to be swallowed and regurgitated by the historian's mind."[26] Historical knowledge must be constructed from evidence, which always and only exists in pieces. The historian's picture of the past, therefore, involves the construction of a metaphorical web composed of nodes of evidence with threads of inference spun and stretched between them. The historian's task, to switch metaphors, is to organize the evidence like dots plotted on a piece of graph paper, and then to connect these dots by inferring historical knowledge from and between the points of evidence, an act that Collingwood calls "interpolation."[27] While the act of interpolating constructive historical information in the gaps between nodes of evidence is "essentially imagined"—it is an act that takes place in the historian's mind—it is not "arbitrary or merely fanciful;"[28] it is the production of historical knowledge based on an appeal to evidence. This notion of the "historical imagination," so central in Collingwood's philosophy, is not akin to the work of a historical novelist, but rather is a fundamental, even structural, part of doing any kind of history.[29]

The nodes of evidence in a historian's web are, therefore, responsible for the strength and viability of a historical construction. More and stronger evidence will result in more robust connections and imaginative threads

---

24. Collingwood, *The Idea of History*, 251–252.

25. Collingwood, *The Idea of History*, 251–252.

26. Collingwood, *The Idea of History*, 246.

27. Collingwood, *The Idea of History*, 240.

28. Collingwood, *The Idea of History*, 240–241.

29. Collingwood, *The Idea of History*, 241; see on this page the example Collingwood gives of this kind of evidence-based "historical imagination."

between those points of evidence. The plausibility of a web of imaginative construction is derived from the strength of its evidence and the interweaving and connectivity of the threads between the nodes. The historian must ask whether these connections form any kind of pattern, and then extrapolate from this pattern of evidence to construct a picture of the past that is plausibly coherent and logically permissible. This last point is worth underlining. Inductive historical reasoning, unlike methods from the natural sciences, does not and cannot lead to conclusions about the past that are logically compulsory. There is nothing in the pattern formed by a historian's observations that can obligate others to interpret the data and extrapolate from them in a particular way or even at all.[30] There are no algorithms, no formulas, and very rarely any smoking guns in the construction and representation of ancient history. In other words, evidence can never *prove* a historian's construction; it can only *justify* it.[31]

Applying these aspects of Collingwoodian historiography to the question of a first-century synagogue in Capernaum is not merely a good idea but is, I suggest, necessary if we are to make any discernible and principled progress in the debate. The situation of the Capernaum data is a good example of Collingwood's axiom that evidence does not come as "ready-made historical knowledge." The data are fragmentary and disparate. If we are to produce historical knowledge related to our question, that is, if we are to construct a picture of Capernaum's past that has any justifiable relation to what we might call "historical reality," we need to organize, interpret, and apply the relevant data as evidence, inferring from them and interpolating between them. Only then can we provide an answer to our question from the perspective of history.

If this is our historical method then we now need a historical model, one that includes a clear definition of the type of synagogue we are asking about in this chapter. As eminent social historian Peter Burke notes, historians use models—whether consciously or unconsciously—to simplify the pool of data in order to understand it and to "emphasize the recurrent, the general, and the typical, which it presents in the form of clusters of traits or attributes."[32]

---

30. Collingwood, *The Idea of History*, 254–255.

31. See also Collingwood, *The Idea of History*, 261, where he draws a distinction between "compulsive" proof, as in the exact sciences, and "permissive" proof, as in the inductive sciences, including critical history.

32. P. Burke, *History and Social Theory* (Ithaca, NY: Cornell University Press, 1992), 28.

This means that, if we are to provide an answer to our question, we need an evidence-based model of first-century synagogues that will help us interpret the data related to Capernaum, both archaeological and textual.

One of the major developments in recent historical scholarship on ancient synagogues has been just such a model. It presents the theory that synagogues in and around the first century seem to have existed as two types of institutions, both of which could be referred to by a variety of Hebrew, Greek, and even Latin terms.[33] On the one hand were the Jewish association-type "synagogues." As scholars like Peter Richardson, Philip Harland, Richard Ascough, Anders Runesson, and Richard Last have shown, this type of assembly was organizationally modeled upon the kinds of membership networks seen in Greco-Roman associations, such as *collegia*, *thiasoi*, and *hetaeriae*.[34] These types of synagogues—which will feature more prominently in the following chapter—could meet in a variety of public or private spaces and were defined by reference to, for example, shared occupations, social practices, neighborhoods, geoethnic connections, or shared ideology, such as the devotion to a particular cult or philosophy.[35]

---

33. On the variety of terms used to refer to synagogues, see A. Runesson, D. Binder, and B. Olsson, *The Ancient Synagogue from its Origins to 200 CE*, AJEC 72 (Leiden: Brill, 2008), 328 (hereafter *ASSB*). This two-type theory, articulated below, was first put forth by Runesson in his *Origins of the Synagogue*. One of its major benefits, as one will note below, is that it refrains from positing a strict definition of what a "synagogue" must be to be a synagogue. Rather, it focuses on the nature of the institution of assembly under consideration and describing its socioreligious characteristics instead of applying a set of rigid criteria by which to measure whether one is or is not a synagogue.

34. P. Richardson, "Early Synagogues as *Collegia* in the Diaspora and Palestine," in *Voluntary Associations in the Graeco-Roman World*, ed. J. S. Kloppenborg and S. G. Wilson (London: Routledge, 1996), ch. 6; P. Richardson, *Building Jewish in the Roman East* (Waco, TX: Baylor University Press, 2004), 111–134, 207–221; P. Harland, *Associations, Synagogues, and Congregations: Claiming a Place in Ancient Mediterranean Society*, 2nd rev. ed. (Kitchener, ON: Philip Harland, 2013); R. Ascough, "Paul, Synagogues, and Associations: Reframing the Question of Models for Pauline Christ Groups," *Journal of the Jesus Movement in its Jewish Setting* 2 (2015): 27–52; and R. Last, "The Other Synagogues," *Journal for the Study of Judaism* 47 (2016): 330–363; Runesson, *Origins of the Synagogue*, 213–231, *et passim*; Runesson, "Synagogues without Rabbis or Christians? Ancient Institutions beyond Normative Discourses," *Journal of Belief and Values* 38, no. 2 (2017): 159–172.

35. See Harland, *Associations*, 28–53; Runesson, "Synagogues without Rabbis or Christians?" 165. Association-type synagogues certainly existed in the land of Israel. The synagogues (συναγωγαί) of the Essenes mentioned by Philo (*Prob.* 80–83) and the synagogue of the Libertines in Jerusalem mentioned in the book of Acts (Acts 6:9–10; for discussion,

On the other hand, there were synagogues of a fundamentally different institutional nature than the associations, which filled municipal roles related to town or village civic politics. As Runesson has observed, synagogues of the public/civic type could only exist in places where Jews had control of public administration.[36] These synagogues, therefore, represented the socio-religious center of local Jewish society throughout the land of Israel.[37] The archaeological record from first-century sites in the Galilee, such as Gamla and (more recently) Magdala,[38] and sites in Judea, such as Umm el-Umdan and Kiryat Sefer,[39] suggests that such civic assemblies in both the pre-70 CE and post-70 CE periods, through at least 200 CE, could gather in purpose-built public edifices:[40] these buildings were designed with characteristic features of

---

see *ASSB* no. 18) are good examples. However, they were, by nature, more prominent throughout the Mediterranean Diaspora, in contexts where Jews were not politically autonomous and were more tightly integrated with their non-Jewish neighbours. Some examples: Richardson has compared the archaeological remains from the first phase of the Ostia synagogue to the remains of Ostia's Association of the Housebuilders (Richardson, *Building Jewish*, 213–215); a decree preserved by Josephus in *Ant.* 14:213–216 from Gaius Caesar to the Jewish community either in Delos or Parium calls the Jewish assembly there a *thiasos*, a "religious guild"; and in *Vita Contemplativa*, Philo describes the Therapeutae, a Jewish philosophical association in Alexandria, as gathering together on the seventh day in a *semneion*, some sort of room in a private house set apart for special use. The basic point to make here, then, is that in this model, association-type assemblies were not public institutions serving civic functions.

36. Runesson, *Origins of the Synagogue*, 237–387; Runesson, "Synagogues without Rabbis or Christians?" 164.

37. Ryan, *Role of the Synagogue*, 31–32.

38. S. Guttman, "The Synagogue at Gamla," in *Ancient Synagogues Revealed*, ed. L. Levine (Jerusalem: Israel Exploration Society, 1982), 30–34; D. Avshalom-Gorni and A. Najar, "Migdal: Preliminary Report," *Hadashot* 125 (2013) www.hadashot-esi.org.il/report_detail_eng.aspx?id = 2304&mag_id = 120 (last accessed on 5 April 2021).

39. A. Onn and S. Weksler-Bdolah, "Horbat Umm el-'Umdan—A Jewish Village with a Synagogue from the Second Temple Period at Modi'in." *Qadmoniot* 130 (2005): 107–116 (Hebrew); Y. Magen and Y. Zionit, "Kiryat Sefer—A Jewish Village and Synagogue from the Second Temple Period," *Qadmoniot* 117 (1999): 25–32 (Hebrew).

40. On the continuity of public synagogues in all their major aspects (spatial/architectural, liturgical, non-liturgical [i.e., political], institutional [i.e., leadership and organization]) from the pre-70 period to ca. 200 CE, see A. Runesson and W. V. Cirafesi, "Reassessing the Impact of 70 CE on the Origins and Development of Palestinian Synagogues," in *The Synagogue in Ancient Palestine: Current Issues and Emerging Trends*, ed. R. Bonnie, R. Hakola, and U. Tervahauta, FRLANT 279 (Göttingen: Vandenhoeck & Ruprecht, 2021), 37–57. The

Image 2.1. Gamla synagogue.

Photo by Anders Runesson. Used with permission.

Greco-Roman public architecture, with columns and stepped benches lining all four walls.[41] The spatial focal point in these buildings was clearly the center, which made their design conducive to deliberative-style assemblies.

Public synagogues housed regular ritual performances, the most important being the reading of Jewish ancestral writings,[42] but they also functioned

---

Mishnah provides literary evidence for continuity in the function of public synagogues during the second century CE (as buildings and formal gatherings): *Ber.* 7:3; *Ter.* 11:10; *Bik.* 1:4; *'Eruv.* 10:10; *Pesaḥ.* 4:4; *Sukkah* 3:13; *Rosh Hash.* 3:7; *Meg.* 3:1–3; 3:4–4:10; *Ned.* 5:4–5; 9:2; *Shebu.* 4:10; *Mak.* 3:12; *Neg.* 13:12; *Sotah* 7:7, 8; *Yoma.* 7:1.

41. On the institutional and architectural comparison of public synagogues and the Greco-Roman *bouleuteria* and *ekklesiasteria*, see Runesson, "Synagogues without Rabbis or Christians?" 162–163.

42. E.g., Luke 4:16–31; Acts 15:21; Josephus, *Ant.* 16:42–43. See Runesson, *Origins of the Synagogue*, 193–253; Runesson, "Synagogues without Rabbis or Christians?" 162–163, where he suggests the centrality of Torah reading in public synagogues based upon the archaeology

Image 2.2. Magdala synagogue.

Photo used with permission from Israel Antiquities Authority.

as civic spaces for hearing legal disputes, executing punitive sentences, and conducting political debates.[43] Furthermore, there is solid evidence that early public synagogues could be highly institutionalized (n.b. not uniform). That is, they could have a well-defined, although not necessarily fixed, leadership structure, with scholars increasingly suggesting that priests, not the Pharisees or rabbis, had a, if not the most, significant role within them.[44] Sources do, however, attest to a variety of officials within public synagogues: besides

---

and architecture of first-century synagogues in the land of Israel. On the historical plausibility of Luke 4:16–31, see Ryan, *Role of the Synagogue*, 172–183.

43. E.g., OG Sus 28; Matt 10:17, 23:34; *m. Mak.* 3:12; Josephus, *Vita* 276–281, 294–295.

44. L. Levine, "The Nature and Origin of the Palestinian Synagogue Reconsidered," *Journal of Biblical LIterature* 115.3 (1996): 425–448 (440–41); Binder, *Into the Temple Courts*, 355–60; E. P. Sanders, *Judaism: Practice and Belief 63* BCE–*66* CE (Philadelphia: SCM Press, 1992) 171–173; M. Grey, "Jewish Priests and the Social History of Post-70 Palestine" (PhD diss., University of North Carolina, 2011).

town elders and village scribes, the most widely attested functionary is the ἀρχισυνάγωγος/ראש הכנסת.⁴⁵ The mention of rabbis, on the other hand, is almost, if not entirely, absent; the evidence for rabbis as leaders within synagogues does not appear until the fourth or perhaps even as late as the fifth century CE.⁴⁶ Therefore, when we speak of synagogues in and around the first

---

45. Who, as evidenced by the Theodotos Inscription (*CIJ* 2.1404), could also be a priest. There is an abundance of research available on the role and status of the *archisynagogos*. The most helpful presentations of the data are T. Rajak and D. Noy, "Archisynagogoi: Office, Title and Social Status in the Greco-Jewish Synagogue," *JRS* 83 (1993): 75–93; Binder, *Into the Temple Courts*, 348–352; and Levine, *The Ancient Synagogue*, 415–427. Note that Binder does not draw the same distinction I do between public and association synagogues. Thus, our handling of the sources is slightly different. To this pre-70 CE list of synagogue leaders we should add the *archon* and almost certainly the *ḥazzan*, the "attendant," whose position seems to be analogous to the Greek *neōkoros*—the attendant of a Jewish prayer hall mentioned in a documentary papyrus from third-century Ptolemaic Egypt (*CPJ* 1.129)—and the Greek term *hypēretēs*, which is mentioned in relation to the Nazareth synagogue in Luke 4:20. The title *ḥazzan* does not only appear in rabbinic sources (on which see Levine, *The Ancient Synagogue*, 438–439; *ASSB* nos. 23, 24, 25, 86). Two inscriptions in Aramaic appear on a recently published first-century ossuary with an unknown provenance, although the editors of the inscriptions suggest the ossuary may have been discovered south of Jerusalem's Old City in the Silwan neighborhood. The inscriptions identify the ossuary's occupant as "the daughter of Samuel the priest, the hazzan of the synagogue of Apamea" and "the mother of Hanana the priest, the hazzan of the synagogue of Palmyra" (*CIIP* 1.2:494–496 [nos. 1119–1120]). The inscriptions, therefore, identify two priests—the father and the son of a woman nicknamed Ima—who were functionaries in two different synagogues in central and western Syria. As Levine, *The Ancient Synagogue*, 435–438 notes, *ḥazzanim* were clearly not the most powerful or influential functionaries in the synagogue. *Hazzanim* were do-it-all attendants. They apparently facilitated the mechanics of synagogue gatherings, such as the details of the Torah reading or, as in the Great Alexandrian synagogue, signaling to the congregation with handkerchiefs when it was time for the people to respond to the Torah benedictions (*t. Sukk.* 4:6). This, of course, does not mean *ḥazzanim* were without honor; it simply means that they, even if priests, took a distinctly backseat to those with more authority within the synagogue, in particular the *archisynagogos* or *rosh ha-knesset*. The *archisynagogos/rosh hakneset* and the *ḥazzan* retain their multifaceted social and religious character in second and early third-century sources (e.g., *m. Yom.* 7:1; *m. Sotah* 7:7–8; *m. Mak.* 3:12; *t. Meg.* 3:21; *t. Ter.* 2:13). Justin Martyr (*Dial.* 137) also mentions *archisynagogoi*, who he says teach Jews to scoff at Jesus "after the prayer" (μετὰ τὴν προσευχήν). However, Justin's text very well may not be representative of the situation in Roman Palestine in the second century.

46. D. Schwartz, "Was 70 CE a Watershed in Jewish History?" in *Was 70 CE a Watershed in Jewish History? On Jews and Judaism before and after the Destruction of the Second Temple*, ed. D. R. Schwartz and Zeev Weiss, AJEC 78 (Leiden: Brill, 2012), 13–14. On the early rabbinic movement in the land as small disciple circles, see C. Hezser, *The Social Structure of the Rabbinic Movement in Roman Palestine*, TSAJ 66 (Tübingen: Mohr Siebeck, 1997).

century, we must not envision the rabbinic institution of later centuries. To do so would be grossly anachronistic.[47]

This two-type model, which presents the first-century synagogue as a diverse yet formal socioreligious institution of assembly that could, indeed, gather in formal public buildings, strongly suggests that the older model of scholars like Kee, Horsley, White, and Claußen is no longer tenable.[48] At this point, then, we can now move on to interpret the Capernaum data, asking *if* and *how* it measures in relation to this typology. In the remainder of this article, I wish to do two things, which involve "plotting our dots," that is, mobilizing the data and establishing the nodes of evidence that will, in the end, make up my "web of historical construction." The first is to plot as many dots from the archaeological data as possible. Indeed, I will spend the majority of my time here, since it is the most complicated and contested element of the question at hand. After this, I will briefly but necessarily discuss the evidence of the written sources from the Gospel narratives, and then conclude with an assessment of the strength of our "web of construction" and whether we should picture a "synagogue" in Capernaum's first-century past.

---

47. In my view, the tendency toward historical anachronism is precisely what hinders the study of Lidia Matassa, *Invention of the First-Century Synagogue*, Ancient Near Eastern Monographs 22 (Atlanta: SBL, 2018). Her study seeks fundamentally to question the identification process of first-century synagogues, since she believes there is a lack of the kind of explicit evidence that we have in later periods when synagogues possessed features such as *bemot*, Torah shrines, inscriptions, and mosaics depicting biblical scenes and menorot (p. 4). In other words, for first-century synagogues to be identified as synagogues, Matassa wants them to look like—or at least have similar features to—these later buildings. This leads to her intense scepticism that first-century synagogues existed. As noted below, however, buildings such as the one found in 2009 in Magdala, make the existence of first-century synagogues, including synagogue buildings, nearly a foregone conclusion.

48. As articulated in Kee, "Transformation"; Kee, "Defining"; Horsley, "Synagogues in Galilee"; L. M. White, *The Social Origins of Christian Architecture,* vol. 1, *Building God's House in the Roman World: Architectural Adaptation among Pagans, Jews, and Christians* (Baltimore: Johns Hopkins University Press, 1990), 61; C. Claußen, *Versammlung, Gemeinde, Synagog: Das hellenistisch–jüdische Umfeld der frühchristlichen Gemeinden*, StUNT 27 (Göttingen: Vandenhoeck & Ruprecht, 2002), 298 and 304, although Claußen sees the idea of a first-century synagogue building in Capernaum as a distinct possibility: "So lassen archäologische und literarische Argumente gemeinsam mit dem zu beobachtenden Konservatismus in bezug auf synagogale Bauplätze die Identifizierung und Datierung der älteren Gebäudereste als Synagoge des 1. Jh.s n.Chr.—und damit in die Zeit Jesu und seiner Jünger—durchaus möglich erscheinen" (p. 181).

3. Interpreting and Mobilizing the Archaeological Data

Our discussion of the relevant archaeological data must start with the massive trench cutting operation begun by Corbo and Loffreda in 1969. This operation involved opening a total of twenty-five trenches in and around Capernaum's limestone synagogue over a span of twelve years, with the last of the trenches cut in 1981.[49] For our purposes, the most important of the trenches are the five that were made in the central nave of the main hall (trenches 1, 20, 22, 24, and 25), the five that were made in the eastern, western, and northern side aisles (trenches 2, 14, 17, 19, and 21), and the two that were made along the outer side of the synagogue's western wall (trenches 3 and 15).[50]

The trenches cut in the central nave of the main hall revealed three basic strata.[51] Stratum C, the layer immediately underneath the pavers of the central nave, consisted of a 30-cm layer of mortar. Beneath this, Stratum B, was a one-meter sealed layer of fill consisting of basalt stones, dirt, pottery, and some architectural fragments.[52] Together, Strata C and Strata B comprised an artificial podium upon which the limestone synagogue was built. Coins and pottery found beneath the pavers in these upper strata have led Loffreda to suggest that the construction of the synagogue was carried out over the course of nearly a century, beginning with the main hall in the early fifth

---

49. For a convenient list of which trenches were cut each year, see S. Loffreda, *Cafarnao V: Documentazione fotografica degli scavi (1968–2003)* (Jerusalem: Franciscan, 2005), 14–15. For documentation of the trenches that were cut in the first season in 1969 (trenches 1–7), see V. Corbo, *La Sinagoga di Cafarnao dopo gli scavi del 1969* (Jerusalem: Franciscan Printing Press, 1970), 11–60.

50. Trench 3 is not immediately visible on the plan shown above; see Corbo, *Sinagoga di Cafarnao*, 35–41.

51. The following description of the stratigraphy is drawn from several publications by Corbo and Loffreda, focusing especially on later ones, since, naturally, their interpretation of the remains evolved as seasons of excavation continued: V. Corbo, "Resti della sinagoga del primo secolo a cafarnao," *Studia Hierosolymitana III*, ed. G. C. Bottini (Jerusalem: Franciscan Printing Press, 1982), 313–357; Loffreda, "Ceramica ellenistico-romana," 273–312; Loffreda, *Recovering Capharnaum*, 41–49; Loffreda, "Coins," 223–244. These three basic strata were found more or less the same throughout the entire area underneath the limestone synagogue, although, as will be described below, the contents of these strata differed.

52. On the architectural fragments found in Strata B, see Corbo, "Resti della sinagoga," 339. I will comment further on the significance of these architectural fragments below.

Was There a Public Synagogue in Capernaum?   61

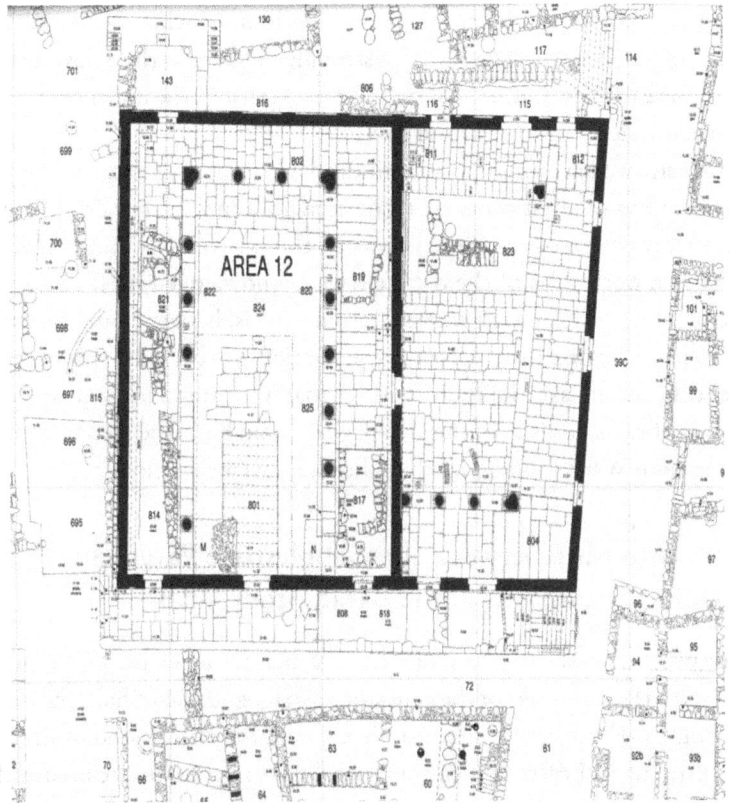

Image 2.3. Plan of the fifth-to-sixth-century limestone synagogue. Earlier structures are beneath it in the areas of the side aisles (trenches 814, 821, 819, and 817).

Adapted from the plan presented in B. Callegher, *Cafarnao IX* (Jerusalem: Franciscan, 2007), 16–17. Reproduced here with permission.

century until the eastern courtyard in the last quarter of the same century.[53] Beneath these layers, in what the excavators designated Stratum A, a large basalt cobblestone pavement—which they call massicciata A—was found in the area of the central nave, on top of which were pottery and coins dating from the first through the fifth century CE.[54] Underneath this floor, however,

---

53. Loffreda, "Coins," 233.

54. On the coins, see Corbo, "Resti della sinagoga," 316; Loffreda, "Coins," 226–230. On the ceramics, see Loffreda, "Ceramica ellenistico-romana," 284–290; and Loffreda's

only material from the Hellenistic period was found, including another pavement designated massicciata B.[55] This strongly suggests, as the excavators do, a date in the early first century for massicciata A, that is, the upper cobblestone pavement underneath the central nave.[56]

Already we have an important, indeed a key, piece of data: a large pavement dated to the first century in the area underneath the central nave of the limestone synagogue. The existence of this pavement is uncontroversial; scholars on both sides of the debate have acknowledged it. The two more difficult issues pertain to its interpretation, that is, how it should be applied as evidence. The first issue concerns the relationship between this pavement under the central nave and the structures that were found beneath and along the areas of the side aisles of the synagogue's main hall. The second concerns the question: What kind of building did this pavement belong to?

The Relationship between the Cobblestone Pavement, the Domestic Areas, and the Basalt Stone Walls

Let us take the first of these issues first. When trenches 14, 17, 19, and 21 were cut in the side aisles of the limestone synagogue's main hall, the excavators found a very different situation from what they had found underneath the central nave. Loffreda recounts that, here underneath the artificial fill of the podium, several structures were found, most of which dated from the Hellenistic through late Roman period, that is, until ca. 350 CE.[57] These remains consisted of superimposed stone pavements, walls, doorways, fireplaces, an oven, staircases, and water channels. In other words, these were

---

comprehensive study in *Cafarnao VI: Tipologie e contesti stratigrafici della ceramica (1968–2003)* (Jerusalem: Edizioni Terra Santa, 2008), esp. at 268–274.

55. E.g., a coin from the third to second century BCE was found in trench 1 (Corbo, "Resti della sinagoga," 316). On the Hellenistic pottery discovered below the first-century cobblestone pavement, see Loffreda, "Ceramica ellenistico-romana," 284–289.

56. Loffreda, "Ceramica ellenistico-romana," 311–312. Concomitantly, as noted by Binder (*Into the Temple Courts*, 190 n. 61), this data also severely undermines the theory of J. T. Sanders (*Schismatics,* 38), that the floor was laid in the second or third century.

57. For the excavators, the Hellenistic period runs from 332 to 63 BCE, while the late Roman period runs from 270 to 350 CE. The following description of the structures found in the side-aisle trenches comes largely from Loffreda, *Recovering Capharnaum,* 44–45; and his more recent comments in Loffreda, *Cafarnao V,* 15–16.

clearly the remains of private houses embedded in the areas of the side aisles. Similar remains were also found in the areas of the southern porch (trench 9) and eastern court (trench 23). Strikingly, no such remains were found in the area of the central nave. In addition to these domestic structures, the excavators found directly beneath the four peripheral walls of the main hall and beneath a portion of the stylobates of the limestone synagogue another set of walls made of basalt stone blocks. The interpretation of these basalt stone walls and their relationship to the limestone walls above, the domestic structures in the side aisles, and the large cobblestone pavement under the central nave lies at the center of the debate over whether there was a first-century synagogue in this location. Indeed, most, if not all, arguments made *against* such an idea have focused largely on undermining the connection of these walls to the first century.[58]

Corbo saw a direct relationship between the first-century cobblestone floor and the basalt stone walls.[59] Although he does not marshal any specific data, his evidence for this interpretation seems to be that the basalt walls reach down to "livelli molto antichi, (ultimo period ellenistico, primo period romano nelle trincee 1, 2, 11, 14, 15, 17, e 18."[60] For Corbo, the basalt walls and the large cobblestone pavement together form the basic structure of a first-century public building, upon which the later monumental synagogue was built. From this he inferred that this first-century public building was, indeed, a synagogue, the one built by the Roman centurion and the one in which Jesus taught, as mentioned in the Gospel accounts.[61] Concomitantly, Corbo dated the remains of the private houses in the area of the side aisles to the Hellenistic and early Roman periods, suggesting that they were destroyed at this time to make way for the first-century building.[62]

---

58. See, most recently, Bonnie, *Being Jewish in Galilee*, 181–185. For other examples, see the publications cited in footnote 10.

59. See, e.g., Corbo, "Resti della sinagoga," 316: "Da notare che il pavimento A a metri 1,80 sotto il pavimento della sinagoga è molto ben connesso con il muro di basalto."

60. V. Corbo, "Edifici antichi sotto la sinagoga di Cafarnao," in *Studia Hierosolymitana I: Studi Archeologici*, eds. E. Testa, B. Bagatti, and G. C. Bottini (Jerusalem: Franciscan, 1976), 175.

61. Following Corbo's interpretation are, e.g., Strange and Shanks, "Synagogue Where Jesus Preached," 25; and Binder, *Into the Temple Courts*, 188.

62. Corbo, "Edifici antichi," 171–174; Corbo, "Resti della sinagoga," 339.

Loffreda, however, disagrees with Corbo's interpretation. He sees much more discontinuity between the basalt walls and the first-century cobblestone pavement; and he has significantly stronger evidence to justify his interpretation:

> D'altra parte mi sembra impossibile associare "il muro di basalto" MB a quei pavimenti e datarlo di conseguenza nel primo secolo. Ecco i motivi: (1) In L802 il muro MB3 poggia sulla massicciata A a quota 10.82 con ceramica databile fino al tardo periodo romano (DF 263s). Questa a sua volta é preceduta dalla massicciata B a quota 10.62 con ceramica del periodo romano medio; (2) anche il muro MB 4 poggia sulla massicciata A con ceramica del tardo periodo romano (DF 264s); (3) in L817 il muro MB 1 (DF 279:2) poggia su un livello di degrado (DF 279:3) di strutture rimaste in uso fino al periodo romano tardivo; nella medesima area, il muro MB 5 (DF 277:12) poggia sul muro M107 (DF 277:8) che taglia un forno associato ad uno strato di occupazione formatosi sopra la massicciata A con ceramica tardo romano; (4) nell'area L825 lo stesso muro MB5 (DF 283:3) poggia sulla massicciata A (DF 283:1) che fu in uso fino al periodo romano tardivo e che è preceduta dalla massicciata B del periodo romano antico (DF 283:1); (5) in L803 il "muro di basalto" MB 2 poggia su uno strato di occupazione dove furono rinvenute due monete del terzo secolo. In base a questi dati, il "muro di basalto" non può essere riferito ai pavimenti surriferiti.[63]

Loffreda shows that the basalt stone walls were built on top of layers of occupation that were put out of use *no earlier* than the third or fourth century, making the construction of these walls coterminous with the demolition of the domestic structures in the area of the side aisles. This provides strong nodes of evidence that the basalt walls are, in fact, *not* connected to the first-century cobblestone floor and thus could not have formed part of a first-century building, since they were constructed no earlier than the late Roman period (ca. 270–350 CE).

---

63. Loffreda, *Cafarnao V*, 15 (the references in the quotation to "DF" are the "documentary photographs" available in *Cafarnao V*). See also a less detailed version of Loffreda's view presented in English in "Coins," 239.

Was There a Public Synagogue in Capernaum?   65

At this point we must consider two more issues of historical method. First, while the large cobblestone pavement under the central nave is our only datum dating to the first century, it is not the only archaeological material relevant for addressing the question of whether there was a first-century synagogue in this location. We must also consider the remains of later periods. In other words, we need to spin *diachronic* threads of inference between later periods and the first century.

Second, at the same time, and perhaps more importantly, we must spin *synchronic* threads of inference as well. This process of constructive interpolation involves three tasks:

1. We need to establish the nature of the cobblestone pavement and the type of building it belonged to by comparing it to the data of other floors in the village, particularly those of private houses, and the data of other first-century synagogues more broadly.
2. We must then determine whether there is anything in this comparison that blocks a verdict of *plausibility* regarding the inference that the cobblestone pavement belonged to a first-century synagogue. That is, we must ask: Is there anything in our comparison that makes such an inference *impossible*?[64]
3. If we are allowed a verdict of plausibility, we must go further and ask how *probable* it is that the cobblestone pavement was the floor of a first-century synagogue? At this point, we would need to consider the full range of evidence, not just the archaeological material, and thus, at last, include the textual sources within our web of historical construction.

The Nature and Function of the Cobblestone Pavement

What is the nature of the first-century cobblestone pavement? When Corbo and Loffreda first began their soundings in the late 1960s and early 1970s, they thought that the pavement underneath the area of the central nave

---

64. As a comparative example of answering such a question, consider the private houses in the areas of the limestone synagogue's side aisles that were in use until the third or fourth century, and thus block us from inferring that the basalt stone walls functioned as part of a first-century synagogue.

belonged to a residential section of the village dating back to the first century but still in use until the mid-fourth century.[65] After all, they had found the remains of private houses in trenches they had already sunk along the interior (trench 2) and exterior (trench 6) of the northern wall and underneath the southern porch (trench 9). Loffreda even published this view in a short article in the *Israel Exploration Journal* in 1973. In the same year, however, then Editor-in-Chief Michael Avi-Yonah became the first to suggest that the cobblestone pavement underneath the central nave might not be the floor of a residential area, since, he believed, the vast majority of houses excavated at Capernaum had much smaller floors made of beaten earth and not basalt cobblestone. About this cobblestone pavement, Avi-Yonah said, "This would be a much larger and better paved structure than any other private dwelling in Capernaum. Indeed, would it not be possible to conclude that these were the remains of a public building (preferably a synagogue) which existed before the present one?"[66]

The excavators were initially resistant to Avi-Yonah's suggestion, pointing out that, in fact, the pavements of *most* houses and courtyards in Capernaum were made of basalt cobblestones.[67] Furthermore, in the mid-1970s, as they sunk more trenches in the western and eastern side aisles of the limestone synagogue (trenches 14, 17, 19, 21), they continued to uncover the remains of private houses. Therefore, they continued with their initial interpretation for nearly a decade. However, in 1981, the year Corbo and Loffreda sank four additional trenches in the area of the central nave (trenches 20, 22, 24, 25), their picture of the evidence changed. While they were never able to fix its precise dimensions, they were able to determine that the cobblestone pavement ran the entire width of the central nave from stylobate to stylobate, and apparently the entire length of the central nave as well. And, as noted earlier, no domestic structures were uncovered here.[68] While Corbo and Loffreda ended up interpreting the pavement's connection to the basalt walls differently,

---

65. See, e.g., S. Loffreda, "The Late Chronology of the Synagogue of Capernaum," *Israel Exploration Journal* 23, no.1 (1973): 37–42.

66. M. Avi-Yonah, "Editor's Note," *Israel Exploration Journal* 23, no. 1 (1973): 43.

67. Which, as time passed, were renewed with superimposed cobblestones that sealed the oldest layers of occupation. See V. Corbo, *Cafarnao I*, 177.

68. Loffreda, "Ceramica ellenistico-romana," 311–312.

both were compelled to change their minds and infer that the first-century pavement was too large to have belonged to a private house or a courtyard but rather, more likely, belonged to a public building.[69]

There is diachronic and synchronic evidence that justifies the excavators' inference. First the diachronic. Public buildings (note the plural) seem to have stood on this site well after the first century. The clearest evidence for this, of course, is the limestone building itself. More controversial is the idea that an intermediate public building, one associated with the basalt walls and representing an expansion of the first-century building, stood in the late Roman period before the limestone synagogue.[70] While strong arguments have been put forth on both sides of this debate, Loffreda makes four points that ultimately and convincingly argue that the basalt walls belong to an intermediate public building, probably dating to the fourth century rather than to the original construction phase of the limestone building.[71] First, the basalt walls are not continuous under the eastern and western stylobates, and they are altogether missing under the northern stylobate. Second, the eastern court rests independently on an entirely different and

---

69. Loffreda made the mistake of reprinting his older view, originally published in 1973 in *Israel Exploration Journal* (see note 65), again in Loffreda, "The Late Chronology of the Synagogue of Capernaum," 52–56, the same year he concluded differently that the first-century floor belonged to a public building (in Loffreda, "Ceramica ellenistico-romana"). This became a problem among New Testament scholars when, writing in 1995, Kee drew upon Loffreda's old view republished in 1982 to support his thesis that the later limestone synagogue in Capernaum was built on top of a private house ("Defining," 495). He used this idea to support his larger theory that synagogues as formal institutions with public buildings developed out of private domestic spaces. Although Loffreda is partly to blame for republishing an older view in the same year he published his newer view, Kee is ultimately responsible for not keeping track of the evolving nature of Corbo's and Loffreda's interpretation of the remains as they excavated more in early 1980s.

70. Strong opponents of this view are, e.g., Tsafrir, "The Synagogues at Capernaum and Meroth;" and Magness, "Question." Strong advocates for this view are, e.g., Bloedhorn, "Capitals"; Runesson, "Architecture"; and De Luca, "Capernaum," 174–176.

71. See Loffreda, *Capharnaum*, 47–49. Bonnie, *Being Jewish in Galilee*, 183, mischaracterizes these four points as evidence used by "adherents of an early first-century synagogue" to argue that the basalt walls "belonged to a preexisting building that was later reused as the foundation for the limestone synagogue." Some scholars, indeed, have done so; but Loffreda and others, including the current author, believe these points justify the inference that there was a pervious building beneath the limestone synagogue but that this building postdated the first century.

Image 2.4. The black basalt wall running underneath the western wall of the white limestone synagogue.

Photograph by the author.

much better built foundation made of finely cut blocks; the obvious question is: Why the difference? This question is particularly revealing in light of Loffreda's more recent conclusion based on developments in the numismatic record from the site, that the entire limestone building—the main hall, the eastern courtyard, and the southern porch—represented one single building project.[72] Even if the project took many years to complete, it is difficult to

---

72. Loffreda, "Coins," 231–233. On p. 231, he states: "This evaluation of the strictly archaeological data, with which I concur completely, brings us to the conclusion that the synagogue not only is a project which was a single unit from the beginning, but was also effectively 'inaugurated' after all its component parts were already completed: prayer room, eastern courtyard, side-room on the north, entrance balcony on the south. In other words, it is inconceivable that there was a prayer room already functioning before the construction of the eastern courtyard and—obviously—before the construction of the entrance balcony." This means, for example, that the eastern court can longer be interpreted as simply a later addition (*pace* Bonnie, *Being Jewish in Galilee*, 185).

imagine the builders choosing an entirely different method of construction for the foundation of the eastern court.[73] Third, there is a slight shift in axiality along the western wall, indicating discontinuity between the basalt courses and the beginning of the limestone courses. Fourth, and perhaps most telling, the builders of the limestone synagogue compensated for the north–south slope of the western basalt wall that was apparent due to the topography of the site by tapering the limestone blocks of the first course. Architecturally, if the basalt walls were first laid as the foundation of the limestone synagogue, compensation for this sort of topographic issue would have been made there at the foundation level, that is, the level of the basalt wall and not the level of the first course of limestone. This is not how one builds upon a freshly laid foundation; it is, however, how one accommodates for and incorporates the blemishes of an earlier building.[74]

Furthermore, Corbo mentions that some elements characteristic of public architecture, such as column drums and two types of elegant cornice molding, were discovered in the fill of Stratum B under the central nave.[75] While he did not present archaeological data from the trenches to connect these elements to the first century,[76] he did draw an architectural comparison between one of the cornice moldings and a similar type found in the Franciscan excavations at Magdala, which he describes as "molto arcaico."[77] Although these fragments cannot function in our web of historical construction as evidence for a first-century building, they should not be excised from our web altogether. If we can assume—and I think we should—that the architectural elements did not find their way into the fill from afar, then they add to our picture of the evidence for a public building that predated the limestone building. The

---

73. See Loffreda, *Cafarnao V*, 174–175 (DFs 287–291) for very clear documentation (in trench 18) of the discontinuity between the foundation of the main hall versus that of the eastern court, with, on the other hand, continuity between the upper limestone courses of both.

74. I thank Uzi Leibner for discussing this architectural issue with me in private conversation. However, the responsibility of the interpretation presented above and any errors are entirely my own.

75. Corbo, "Resti della sinagoga," 339. This information seems to have gone generally unaccounted for in the debate. See, however, Grey, "Simon Peter in Capernaum;" and Strange and Shanks, "Synagogue Where Jesus Preached," 31.

76. This is a criticism raised by Grey in "Simon Peter in Capernaum."

77. Corbo, "Resti della sinagoga," 339. Cf. V. Corbo, "La città romana di Magdala," in *Studia Hierosolymitana I* (Jerusalem: Franciscan Printing Press, 1976), 365–368.

fragments reinforce the inference that there was a diachronic pattern of public buildings in this location, which makes good sense in light of (1) the location being the physical center of the village,[78] and (2) the fact that, in antiquity, newer public buildings (particularly ones with a religious bent) were often built on top of the remains of older ones.[79]

It is true that no walls, doorways, or benches have been found that are clearly connected to the first-century pavement.[80] But the stones of walls, doorways, and benches of earlier buildings are easily and often dismantled and reused in the construction of new buildings.[81] Thus, although they differed on the date, Corbo and Loffreda were both convinced that the basalt structures beneath the limestone synagogue belonged to an earlier public building that

---

78. On the synagogue's place at the center of the village, see Loffreda, *Capharnaum*, 32. The most pressing issue that challenges the existence of an intermediate public building of the third to fourth century is the lack of a pavement floor connected to this period. That is, the only stratum in which discernable pavements were found was Stratum A. See Loffreda, "Coins," 239.

79. D. Chen, "Chronology," 134–143 (143); Binder, *Into the Temple Courts*, 191–192. The building of new synagogues on top of the remains of preexisting ones is the topic of a recent paper by Uzi Leibner and Benjamin Arubas, "Invisible Synagogues from the Second Temple Period" (paper presented at *Les prèmiers synagogues en Galilée*, Lausanne University, Switzerland, April 9–11, 2019). Sites are discussed such as Khirbet Wadi Hamam, Arbel, Gush Halav, Hamath Tiberias, and Capernaum. We could add to this the synagogues at Nabratein and Umm el-Qanatir. See E. M. Meyers and C. L. Meyers, *Excavations at Ancient Nabratein: Synagogue and Environs* (Winona Lake, IN: Eisenbrauns, 2009); and Y. Dray, I. Gonen, and C. Ben David, "The Synagogue of Umm el-Qanatir: Preliminary Report," *Israel Exploration Journal* 67, no. 2 (2017): 216, although the authors do not explicitly claim that the earlier building was a synagogue. The inference that a public building—specifically a synagogue—stood in Capernaum prior to the erection of the limestone synagogue in the fifth or sixth century is further supported by Egeria's testimony in the late fourth century (see J. Wilkison, *Egeria's Travels* [London: SPCK, 1971], 196, although note that there is a textual problem in this portion of the Egeria tradition, which is preserved only by the twelfth century librarian of Montecassino known as Peter the Deacon).

80. Noted by Chen, "Chronology," 143; Grey, "Simon Peter in Capernaum"; Bonnie, *Being Jewish in Galilee*, 183–184. Corbo does note, however, that the remains of two passageways were found in the (later) inner basalt walls toward the central area of the building ("Resti della sinagoga," 339). He infers that these passageways may have functioned as an entrance. This information does not allow us to say anything directly about the first century, but it does again suggest diachronic continuity.

81. As an example, stones used for benches in the Magdala synagogue show clear evidence of being in secondary use, which suggests the building had at least one prior phase of existence.

had been "radically dismantled to place the new building on top of it."[82] If the public building represented by the basalt walls was dismantled circa the fifth or sixth century to make way for the limestone synagogue, then there is nothing that keeps us from inferring that the first-century building had been similarly dismantled as part of an expansion project in the fourth century. In other words, the absence of benches, doorways, and walls directly connected to the first-century pavement does not make the inference that the pavement belonged to a public building *impossible*.

Now we turn to the synchronic evidence from within Capernaum itself and to the broader context of first-century public synagogues. What distinguishes the cobblestone pavement as belonging to a public building rather than a private house or peristyle courtyard is its size. While its precise dimensions are impossible to determine due to the limits of the trenches, if we estimate based on the dimensions of the central nave, then the cobblestone pavement would measure around twenty meters long by eight meters wide, or about 160 m^2.[83] The vast majority of the floors of Capernaum's private houses

---

82. Corbo, "Resti della sinagoga," 339; Loffreda, *Cafarnao V*, 15–16.

83. These are the dimensions given in De Luca, "Capernaum," 174. Bonnie, *Being Jewish in Galilee*, 184, uses the imprecision involved in this estimate as an argument to cast doubt on the supposed large size of the cobblestone floor. He then attempts to establish a connection between the floor and the walls of the earlier houses found in the side aisles: "A more plausible explanation is that the cobblestone floor exposed in several trenches beneath the limestone synagogue is related to the wall remains of the earlier houses. This is evidenced by the fact that at several spots it can be seen that the cobblestone floor runs up to these wall remains. While scholars have rejected this possibility on the basis that the cobblestone floor was too large in size to belong to houses, it should be acknowledged that the size of the cobblestone floor cannot really be estimated from the few trenches dug beneath the floors of the limestone synagogue" (184). In my view, this argument does not hold weight. First, the fact that, in certain places the cobblestone pavement runs up to the walls of the private houses, is dubious. It simply suggests that in these places the walls of the houses abutted the public building. The more important observation is that no remains were found of walls or any other domestic structures whatsoever in the area of the central nave. This absence is conspicuous. If the cobblestone floor was directly related to a domestic structure or larger housing complex, surely evidence of this sort would have turned up, as it did in trenches 14, 17, 19, and 23. Second, it is true that there is an element of imprecision in the estimation of the size of the first-century cobblestone floor. However, such imprecision is a common reality for all archaeologists, who often must draw conclusions based on even less precise data than what Corbo and Loffreda had to work with. Third, concomitantly, Bonnie mischaracterizes the extent of the trench cutting operation

and courtyards, while built similarly and of similar material, were much smaller. The only floor from early Roman period Capernaum that comes close to this size is that of Court 67, the "grande cortile" of *insula* 2, which originally measured at fifteen meters by seven meters.[84] This area, in contrast to the area of the cobblestone pavement under the limestone synagogue, shows the signs of typical domestic uses for which peristyle courtyards were so well known: the remains of three ovens and a grinding stone were found there.[85] Furthermore, Court 67 was at a later period apparently broken up into smaller houses (nos. 42–44) and reduced to a smaller courtyard measuring 5.8 meters by 5.85 meters.[86] This suggests the area was perceived in later periods to have a fundamentally different character and function within the village than the cobblestone pavement, which occupied a large central space for centuries. On the whole, therefore, the evidence from Capernaum itself justifies the inference that the large first-century cobblestone floor belonged to a public building.

If the cobblestone pavement is sufficiently distinguished from the floors of private houses and courtyards in Capernaum, then how does it compare to the floors of first-century public synagogues in general? Two observations here. First, some scholars have tried to cast doubt on such a comparison, noting that none of the synagogue buildings known from the first century were built with cobblestone pavements; rather, they consisted of pavement stones and/or packed earth.[87] If belonging to a synagogue, the cobblestone pavement in Capernaum would, therefore, represent a unique case. Singularity, however, is not evidence that blocks a judgment of plausibility. After all, the

---

in the area of the central nave; more than just "a few" trenches were sunk. As noted above, altogether, twenty-five trenches were cut throughout the entire building, with five being sunk in the area of the central nave alone, running both north–south and east–south. The data rendered was significant. The excavator's inference that the first-century cobblestone floor extended the entire length and width of the area of the central nave is, therefore, justified by the evidence.

84. Corbo, *Cafarnao I*, 181–182.

85. See village plan in Loffreda, *Cafarnao V*; see also Loffreda, *Capharnaum*, 21 on the typical courtyards uncovered in Capernaum.

86. Corbo, *Cafarnao I*, 184.

87. Bonnie, *Being Jewish in Galilee*, 184; Grey, "Simon Peter in Capernaum," 47.

counterevidence is that, according to Corbo and Loffreda, *most* floors in Capernaum were constructed with basalt cobblestone, making it the preferred building technique in the village.

The size of the cobblestone pavement under the central nave (not the entire area encompassed by the basalt walls) puts the pavement into the realm of other known first-century public synagogues. For example, the main assembly room alone of the nearby Magdala synagogue measures 120 m^2;[88] the building at Khirbet Qana measures ten meters by fifteen meters (150 m^2); the Gamla synagogue, the largest, is about tewenty meters by sixteen meters (320 m^2); further south, the Umm el-'Umdan synagogue is about ten meters by twelve meters (120 m^2); Kiryat Sefer, the smallest, is 9.6 meters by 9.6 meters (92.16 m^2); the building at Herodion measures 15.15 meters by 10.6 meters (ca. 160 m^2); and the Masada synagogue measures about fifteen meters by twelve meters (180 m^2). Some have argued, specifically targeting Corbo's view, that it is difficult to imagine a small subsistence-level farming village like Capernaum in the first century being home to a synagogue that would have been larger (24.5 meters by 18.7 meters) than the one at Gamla.[89] However, if we follow Loffreda's view, that the cobblestone pavement in Capernaum belonged to a building encompassing only the area under the central nave, then the building would have been significantly smaller and thus would not have been abnormally large in comparison to these other synagogues or in proportion to the modest population and moderately prosperous economy of the village.[90] While a roughly twenty meter by eight meter building would have still been large—and particularly narrow—it would not have been as large as the Gamla synagogue and not that much larger than some of the other synagogues mentioned above.

Where has this discussion landed us? In sum, there is nothing in the archaeological data, synchronic or diachronic, that necessarily blocks us from justifiably inferring that the first-century cobblestone pavement belonged to a

---

88. According to the floor plan kindly provided by Jordan Ryan and Marcel Zapata-Meza, the entire area of the Magdala synagogue, including its western ancillary chamber, is almost three hundred square meters. The measurements for the other sites listed above are taken from *ASSB*, s.v.

89. See, e.g., Bonnie, *Being Jewish in Galilee*, 184; Grey, "Simon Peter in Capernaum," 46–47.

90. On the moderate economic prosperity of Capernaum in the early Roman period, see chapter 1.

public synagogue building. Loffreda himself puts the situation well when he says: "Prove archeologiche in senso assoluto e irrefutabile non ci sono, ma non esistono neppure prove in contrario."[91] Historiographically, we are still forced to speak in terms of *plausibility* rather than *probability*. Our web cannot yet hold the weight of a robust imaginary construction. For it to do so, it needs more nodes of evidence.

4. Interpreting and Mobilizing the Textual Data

We now only very briefly need to consider how the relevant textual data fit within our web of historical construction. A major hurdle for scholars who have argued against the existence of a first-century "synagogue" in Capernaum is the fact that the existence of such an institution is directly attested in three independent Gospel traditions: Mark 1:21–28; 3:1–6; Luke 4:33; 7:5; and John 6:59 all mention a συναγωγή in the town. While all of these texts *could* be referring to a physical building, it is true that the only text that refers *unequivocally* to Capernaum's "synagogue" as a built structure is Luke 7:5 (ἀγαπᾷ γὰρ τὸ ἔθνος ἡμῶν καὶ τὴν συναγωγὴν αὐτὸς ᾠκοδόμησεν ἡμῖν).[92] Some scholarship produced especially in the 1990s, which hypothesized the nonexistence of synagogue buildings before 70 CE,[93] dismissed Luke 7:5 as an anachronistic anatopism, reflective of a post-70 Diaspora context rather than a pre-70 setting in the land of Israel.[94] John

---

91. Loffreda, "Ceramica ellenistico-romana," 311. Bonnie's statement that "Loffreda's new suggestion creates the difficult problem that the identification of a first-century synagogue rests solely on the presence of a cobblestone floor" (*Being Jewish in Galilee*, 184) betrays the fact that he is approaching the question only from the perspective of the archaeological sciences rather than from the perspective of critical history. He is certainly right, that the key archaeological datum for a first-century synagogue is the cobblestone floor. But there is other relevant data, archaeological and, crucially, textual, that must be part of any historical construction as well. While, admittedly, Bonnie's study intends to focus on the archaeology of early synagogues, the study, at the same time, leaves the reader with the impression that a historical argument has been made. But a critical argument about history that altogether ignores the relevant textual data is not, in fact, history.

92. Luke 7:5: ἀγαπᾷ γὰρ τὸ ἔθνος ἡμῶν καὶ τὴν συναγωγὴν αὐτὸς ᾠκοδόμησεν ἡμῖν.

93. See footnote 13.

94. See discussion in Ryan, *Role of the Synagogue*, 102–106. Binder argues that, although the Matthean parallel (Matt 8:5–13) does not mention a synagogue, the Lucan version better preserves the underlying tradition (see *Into the Temple Courts*, 93–96). Further, the

Kloppenborg's study of the Theodotos Inscription (*Corpus Inscriptionum Judaicarum* 2.1404)—which was found during the Raimund Weill excavations in 1913–1914 just south of the Temple Mount on the eastern ridge of the lower City of David and which explicitly mentions the construction of a synagogue building (ᾠκοδόμησε τὴν συναγωγὴν; ll. 3–4)—effectively killed this "nonexistence hypothesis."[95] Kloppenborg demonstrated on basis of the stratigraphy of the find site and the inscription's palaeography that it was likely cut in the Herodian period, not in the second or third century CE as Kee had argued.[96] Furthermore, the recent excavation of an early Roman building at nearby Magdala in 2009 whose identification as a synagogue is beyond a doubt—a decorated stone with a menorah on its façade was found *in situ* in the main hall—suggests that the "nonexistence hypothesis" should stay dead. It also justifies applying Luke 7:5 as evidence of a first-century synagogue building in Capernaum.

The text from Luke, however, certainly does not demand that we interpret all the other Gospel texts the same way.[97] But it does, perhaps, encourage us to do so. It is quite natural, for example, to read Mark 1:29 as a report that Jesus and his disciples had left one built structure (ἐκ τῆς συναγωγῆς ἐξελθόντες) only to enter immediately another built structure (ἦλθον εἰς τὴν οἰκίαν Σίμωνος καὶ Ἀνδρέου).[98] A similar parallelism might be indicated in John 18:20, where the Johannine Jesus claims to have always taught publicly "in a synagogue and in the temple" (ἐν συναγωγῇ καὶ ἐν τῷ ἱερῷ). If the text envisions τὸ ἱερόν here as the built public space of the Jerusalem temple courts,[99] then it likely envisions συναγωγή in a similar way. Of course, the only place in John in which Jesus actually teaches ἐν συναγωγῇ is Capernaum. Thus, as Birger Olsson has argued, followed recently by Ryan, there is no real reason to doubt that ἐν συναγωγῇ in

---

phenomenon of Gentiles contributing financially to the building of Jewish synagogues is attested in inscriptions. See, e.g., *ASSB* no. 103.

95. See J. S. Kloppenborg Verbin, "Dating Theodotos (*CIJ II 1404*)," *Journal of Jewish Studies* 51, no. 2 (2000): 243–280.

96. See Kee, "Transformation," 7.

97. A point duly noted by S. K. Catto, *Reconstructing the First-Century Synagogue: A Critical Analysis of Current Research*, LNTS 363 (London: T&T Clark, 2007), 195.

98. See also Luke 4:38: Ἀναστὰς δὲ ἀπὸ τῆς συναγωγῆς εἰσῆλθεν εἰς τὴν οἰκίαν Σίμωνος.

99. See the interesting translation choice of the New English Translation, where ἐν τῷ ἱερῷ is rendered "in the temple courts."

John 6:59 is meant as a reference to an assembly held in Capernaum's public synagogue building.[100]

Regardless of their worth as evidence for the historical Jesus, the Gospel narratives present a picture of the Capernaum "synagogue" that coheres well with the model of public synagogues discussed earlier in this article. Taken together, they present it as a public institution, governed by local administrative officials, and as a place for Torah interpretation and dispute. The "synagogue" is open to any of Capernaum's residents, including people with sickness and "unclean spirits" (Mark 1:23, 3:1; Luke 4:33), and thus it appears to belong to the majority of the Jewish population of the village. While associations seem to have participated in its affairs (e.g., the Pharisees in Mark 3:6), it is not controlled by any particular religiopolitical interest group.[101] Luke 7:3 supports this judgment: here the "elders of the Jews" (πρεσβυτέρους τῶν Ἰουδαίων), that is, the public officials representing the Jews of Capernaum, assert that the centurion had built the synagogue "for us" (ἡμῖν).[102] Torah teaching and halakhic debate are seen as the central activities of the synagogue (Mark 1:21-22, 3:1-6; Luke 4:31; John 6:25-71). In Mark 3:1-6, the Pharisees are portrayed as losers in a sharp dispute with Jesus over Sabbath halakha. In John's narrative, a nondescript crowd (ὄχλος) gathers in the synagogue to hear Jesus give a midrashic sermon drawn from the Torah and the Prophets (Exod 16; Num 11:4-9; Isa 53:14 [cited in John 6:45]).[103] Dispute over his interpretation ensues, both between Jesus and the crowd and among the crowd itself (John 6:41; 6:52).[104] The marks of an institution of public assembly are

---

100. B. Olsson, "'All My Teaching Was Done in Synagogues...' (John 18,20)," in *Theology and Christology in the Fourth Gospel: Essays by the Members of the SNTS Johannine Writings Seminar*, eds. G. van Belle, J. G. van der Watt, and P. J. Martin (Leuven: Peeters, 2005), 221-222. Olsson is followed by Ryan, *Role of the Synagogue*, 247. Both scholars rightly note that the lack of an article in a prepositional phrase is not surprising and thus does not undermine the translation of ἐν συναγωγῇ as "in the synagogue."

101. Cf. *m. Ned.* 5:5.

102. Noted by Ryan, *Role of the Synagogue*, 32. On the role of elders in synagogues, see, e.g., Philo, *Hypoth.* 7:13; *CIJ* 2.1404 ll. 9-10; *m. ʿEruv.* 10:10; *t. Meg.* 3:21; *t. Sukk.* 4:6.

103. On John's presentation of Jesus's teaching in the Capernaum synagogue as a midrashic "synagogue homily," see the still relevant and convincing work of P. Borgen, *Bread from Heaven: An Exegetical Study of the Concept of Manna in the Gospel of John and the Writings of Philo*, NovTSupp 10 (Leiden: Brill, 1965).

104. On the Johannine Capernaum episode, see Ryan, *Role of the Synagogue*, 243-263.

all over the accounts of the Capernaum synagogue, and it is reasonable to infer from this evidence that a public building is also included.

Even if the Gospel material does present a portrait of Capernaum's "synagogue" as both a formal institution of assembly and a purpose-built structure, it is possible that all three independent strands of Gospel tradition are simply literary inventions of their respective authors. But the question for us concerns how likely this is to be the case in light of the evidence marshaled above. To be sure, as was discussed earlier, evidence can never prove a historical construction true as in the observable sciences; it can only justify the historian's judgment. An imaginative historical construction is only true in so far as it represents the best explanation of the relevant data. Therefore, in my judgment, the explanation that seems to explain the data best and require the least amount of speculation is that the Gospels offer historically reliable evidence for the existence of a first-century synagogue in Capernaum, understood as both a public institution and a building.

5. Conclusion

In conclusion, it is historiographically simpler and thus preferable to spin one final thread of inference that posits a connection and mutually clarifying relationship between the archaeological and the textual data. As "azzardoso e utopistico" as it might sound (to use Loffreda's words),[105] the picture of Capernaum's early Roman past that I have constructed, based upon the methodological framework presented in section 2 above, includes a first-century public synagogue. Certainly, the picture is not perfect; a few more pixels would be preferable, and there is always the possibility that some or all of the points of data will need to be revised in the future as they receive more criticism from scholars. But currently there is enough evidence that justifies the inference, and what is more, there is enough visible in this picture to suggest that historians should make use of the institution of Capernaum's public synagogue in their historical constructions of other social and cultural aspects of the first-century village as well.

The setting of the public synagogue would have been an important platform for local network intersections and thus an ideal context for new ideas to

---

105. Loffreda, "Ceramica ellenistico-romana," 311.

"jump" from one network to another.[106] In it, religiopolitical interest groups like the Pharisees and members of messianic movements like the earliest Christ-followers would have jostled face-to-face for influence and new recruits. If we take the accounts of the Gospels into consideration, the first followers of Jesus seem to have been socially positioned at the intersection of two networks that apparently populated the synagogue: Christ-followers and fishermen. That is, as fishermen—a trade, as we saw in chapter 1, that was often organized into guilds and highly networked—their ideas about Jesus and his movement had a natural "jumping off" point, with the synagogue providing the concrete space and institutional infrastructure needed to facilitate direct social encounters. In other words, adding a public synagogue to our portrait of early Roman Capernaum reinforces the argument that it was a village of connections, and that it experienced not only the movement of people and goods in and out of its vicinity but also the spread of ideas. For a small Galilean village, Capernaum had a robust economy that was linked to its equally robust social landscape, the center of which would have certainly been its public synagogue.

The public synagogue was Capernaum's central institution during a time when Jewish–Christian relations in the village was a primarily—if not exclusively—intra-Jewish affair. True, the Capernaum centurion mentioned in Luke's account was a gentile, but his attraction to Jesus is entirely couched within his broader attraction to the Jewish people. That is, Luke does not present him as a Christian, since, after all, Christianity as something distinct from Judaism did not exist yet.[107] It was a time when all Christ-followers were either Jews or Jew-*ish*, that is, gentiles who behaved Jewishly but retained their non-Jewish ethnic identity ("Judaizers"). But what happened to Jewish Christ-followers in Capernaum after the first generation? Did they disappear, as many scholars suggest? Or did Jewish Capernaum continue as a place for an association of Jesus-oriented Jews who continued to participate in village life and seek influence within the public assembly? These questions will occupy us next.

---

106. On social networks and the spread of new ideas, see the discussion at the end of chapter 1.

107. On the anachronisms "Christian" and "Christianity" for this period, see A. Runesson, "The Question of Terminology: The Architecture of Contemporary Discussions on Paul," in *Paul within Judaism: Restoring the First-Century Context to the Apostle*, ed. M. D. Nanos and M. Zetterholm (Minneapolis: Fortress Press, 2015), 53–78.

CHAPTER THREE

Jewish Christ-Followers in Capernaum before the Fourth Century

Reconsidering the Texts, Archaeology, and Institutional Context of Jewish–Christian Relations in Capernaum before Constantine

1. Introduction

THE HISTORICAL LIKELIHOOD that local Jesus-oriented Jewish groups were present in the Galilee between the late first and early fourth centuries was, until the early 1990s, a widely accepted view.[1] The most influential force behind it was, perhaps, the work of two Franciscan archaeologists, Bellarmino Bagatti and Emmanuele Testa, who themselves had built their historical perspectives largely upon the contemporary work of Jesuit theologian Jean Daniélou as put forth in his *Théologie du judéo-christianisme*.[2] Over the course

---

1. I prefer the terms "Jesus-oriented Jews" and "Jewish Christ-followers" to the more frequently used terminology of "Jewish Christians" or "Jewish Christian sects." On the problems inherent to the terminology of "Jewish Christian" and "Jewish Christianity," see M. Jackson-McCabe, "What's in a Name? The Problem of 'Jewish Christianity,'" in *Jewish Christianity Reconsidered: Rethinking Ancient Groups and Texts*, ed. M. Jackson-McCabe (Minneapolis: Fortress Press, 2007), 7–38, and now more comprehensively in M. Jackson-McCabe, *Jewish Christianity: The Making of the Christianity-Judaism Divide* (New Haven: Yale University Press, 2020); D. Frankfurter, "Beyond 'Jewish Christianity': Continuing Religious Sub-Cultures of the Second and Third Centuries and Their Documents," in *The Ways That Never Parted: Jews and Christians in Late Antiquity and the Early Middle Ages*, ed. A. H. Becker and A. Y. Reed (Minneapolis: Fortress Press, 2007), 131–143; O. Skarsaune, "Jewish Believers in Jesus in Antiquity—Problems of Definition, Method, and Sources," in *Jewish Believers in Jesus: The Early Centuries*, ed. O. Skarsaune and R. Hvalvik (Peabody, MA: Hendrickson, 2007), 3–21; J. C. Paget, "The Definition of the Terms *Jewish Christian* and *Jewish Christianity* in the History of Research," in Skarsaune and Hvalvik, *Jewish Believers in Jesus*, 22–52.

2. B. Bagatti, *The Church from the Circumcision: History and Archaeology of the Judaeo-Christians*, trans. E. Hoade (Jerusalem: Franciscan, 1971 [repr. 1984]); Bagatti, *Ancient*

of the middle decades of the twentieth century, Bagatti and Testa erected a grand hypothesis—known today by many by the clever title "The Bagatti-Testa hypothesis"—that many of the Christian sites in Palestine, especially in the Galilee, are authentic holy places because small groups of Judaeo-Christians from the first until the fourth century had identified and preserved locations that they believed were particularly significant to the ministry of Jesus.[3] These sites were then appropriated by non-Jewish Christians when Constantine began establishing Christian churches in Palestine. For Bagatti and Testa, these Judaeo-Christians represented a distinct branch of early Christianity, had a distinct sectarian theology divergent from both emerging (rabbinic) Jewish and (gentile) Christian orthodoxy, and their histories were firmly traceable through archaeological remains and literary sources, such as the polemics against *minim* in rabbinic literature and patristic treatments of heterodox Jesus-oriented Jewish groups like the Nazoraeans and Ebionites.[4]

The scholarly situation is much different today, as the Bagatti-Testa hypothesis has been subjected to nearly three decades of intense criticism. While Franciscan scholars in general continue to affirm the hypothesis,[5] others have argued that neither rabbinic nor patristic sources render reliable historical evidence for Jesus-oriented Jewish groups in second- and third-century Galilee, and that the pre-Constantinian archaeological evidence for such groups at sites like Nazareth and Capernaum is tenuous at best.[6]

Christian Villages of Galilee (Jerusalem: Franciscan, repr. 2001); E. Testa, *Il simbolismo dei giudeo-cristiani* (Jerusalem: Franciscan, 1962); Testa, *The Faith of the Mother Church: An Essay on the Theology of the Judeo–Christians*, trans. P. Rotondi (Jerusalem: Franciscan, 1992); J. Daniélou, *Théologie du judéo-christianisme* (Paris: Cerf, 1958 [Eng. trans., 1964]).

3. See, e.g., Bagatti, *Church from the Circumcision*, 3–29.

4. See, e.g., the discussion in Bagatti, *Church from the Circumcision*, 30–65.

5. Notable non-Franciscan scholars who, nevertheless, are generally more favorably disposed toward the hypothesis, particularly the basic element of a presence of Jewish Christ-followers in the Galilee before the fourth century, are: S. Mimouni, *Les fragments évangéliques judéo-chrétiens apocryphisés: Recherches et perspectives* (Paris: Gabalda, 2006); and A. Runesson, "Architecture, Conflict, and Identity Formation," 231–257.

6. E.g., L. M. White, *The Social Origins of Christian Architecture*, vol. 2, *Texts and Monuments for the Christian Domus Ecclesiae in its Environment*, Harvard Theological Studies 42 (Valley Forge, PA: Trinity Press International, 1997), 156–157, 157 n. 56, 159; M. Aviam, "Christian Galilee in the Byzantine Period," in *Galilee through the Centuries: Confluence of Cultures* (Winona Lake, IN: Eisenbrauns, 1999), 281–300 (283–284), where he states very

According to a recent essay by Jürgen Zangenberg, while the Galilee was certainly the geocultural matrix of the historical Jesus, post–New Testament sources are mainly silent on the development of early Christianity in the region before the fourth century.[7]

The major impetus for this pendulum swing was Joan Taylor's work in the late 1980s and early 1990s. In her book *Christians and the Holy Places* (1993), Taylor heavily criticized the Bagatti-Testa hypothesis for its propagation of a distinct Judeo–Christian branch of early Christianity, its historical overreaching, and its fragile methodological foundation.[8] Taylor emphasized repeatedly—and correctly, we might add—that there is little, if any, direct archaeological evidence that ties local Jewish Christ groups

---

clearly that "there are no archaeological remains in the Galilee of Christianity before the fourth century CE," but yet goes on to admit that "it is very clear that some of the first Judaeo–Christian groups were located in Jewish Galilee during the second and third centuries CE." See also G. Snyder, *Ante-Pacem: Archaeological Evidence of Church Life before Constantine*, 2nd ed. (Macon: Mercer University Press, 2003), 134–137; E. Adams, *The Earliest Christian Meeting Places: Almost Exclusively Houses?*, rev. ed. (London: T&T Clark, 2016), 105–107; J. Zangenberg, "From the Galilean Jesus to the Galilean Silence: Earliest Christianity in the Galilee until the Fourth Century CE," in *The Rise and Expansion of Christianity in the First Three Centuries of the Common Era*, ed. C. K. Rothschild and J. Schröter (Tübingen: Mohr Siebeck, 2013), 75–108; and R. Hakola, "Galilean Jews and Christians in Context: Spaces Sacred and Contested in the Eastern Galilee in Late Antiquity," in *Space in Late Antiquity: Cultural, Theological, and Archaeological Perspectives*, ed. J. Day et. al. (London: Routledge, 2016), 161-164. On the historical unreliability specifically of Epiphanius's treatment of the Nazarenes as a heretical group, see P. Luomanen, *Recovering Jewish–Christian Sects and Gospels*, VC 110 (Leiden: Brill, 2012), 241–242. It is important to note that Hakola, and to a lesser degree Zangenberg, cites Luomanen's work to support a *general* distrust of the literary sources on the historical existence of Jewish Christ-groups in the Galilee. Luomanen, however, makes no such generalizing claim. The only source, according to Luomanen, that is essentially invented *ex nihilo* is Epiphanius's on the heresy of the Nazarenes. In fact, Luomanen argues positively for the historical existence of a Jewish Christ-group in the Syro-Palestinian region as reflected by the Hebrews of the *Gospel of the Hebrews* (see p. 242). Further, Hakola asserts that "the archaeological shortcomings of this so-called Bagatti-Testa hypothesis have repeatedly been exposed" (p. 161). In my view, this is not an accurate representation of the state of the question. The problems with the Bagatti-Testa hypothesis have not revolved around archaeological shortcomings but rather around the *interpretation* of the archaeological data. In other words, it is less a problem of data and more a problem of interpretation.

7. Hence the title of Zangenberg's essay, "From the Galilean Jesus to the Galilean Silence."

8. J. Taylor, *Christians and the Holy Places: The Myth of Jewish–Christian Origins* (Oxford: Oxford University Press, 1993).

to Galilean locations,[9] and even if there was such evidence, it would not immediately follow that these are authentic sites from the time of Jesus.[10] She also forcefully argued a point, today taken for granted, that historians should not take at face value, as Bagatti and Testa did, the ideological and inventive portrayal of Jewish Christ groups in Christian heresiologies such as Epiphanius's *Panarion*.[11] Taylor made a similar point with regard to the rabbis, who were heresiologists in their own right, and she stressed that not every appearance of *minim* in rabbinic literature should be understood as a reference to Jesus-oriented Jews.[12] For Taylor, the Bagatti-Testa school went much too far in its historiography of Christian holy places; indeed, it created a "myth of Jewish–Christian origins."

The question I wish to raise, however, is whether, as a result of Taylor's critique, the pendulum has swung too far, and whether "myth" is really a fair term to describe the situation of the evidence. Some scholars have recently acknowledged the importance of Taylor's critique, but, at the same time, have indicated that it may have been too harsh and overly sceptical.[13] And, while it is certainly true that both the literary and archaeological sources are enigmatic and firm conclusions are difficult to come by, enigmatic sources are not silent sources.

In this chapter, I reconsider the question of Jewish Christ-followers in the Galilee, although in a more restricted manner by focusing solely on the case of Capernaum. Capernaum rests at the center of the scholarly debate, and it

---

9. Taylor's book treats not only Christian holy places in the Galilee but all over Palestine, including the Golan.

10. For the sake of clarity, the current discussion is not interested in the question of the authenticity of holy sites.

11. Epiphanius's treatment of the Ebionites, for example, as a "heretical" Jewish Christ-group active in the Galilee during his day is given in *Panarion* 30.

12. The more recent works of Zangenberg, "Galilean Silence," and Hakola, "Galilean Jews and Christians" are highly indebted to Taylor's criticism of the Bagatti-Testa hypothesis.

13. M. Bockmuehl, "Syrian Memories of Peter: Ignatius, Justin, and Serapion," in *The Image of the Judaeo-Christians in Ancient Jewish and Christian Literature*, eds. P. J. Tomson and D. Lambers-Petry, WUNT 158 (Tübingen: Mohr Siebeck, 2003), 125; J. F. Strange, "Archaeological Evidence of Jewish Believers?" in Skarsaune and Hvalvik, *Jewish Believers in Jesus*, 729; Runesson, "Architecture"; R. Riesner, "What Does Archaeology Teach Us about Early House Churches," *TTK* 78, no. 3–4 (2007): 174–178. Some early reviews of Taylor's book leveled similar criticisms, e.g., O. Irshai (*JRS* 84 [1994]: 264–265) and S. Borgehammar (*CH* 63 [1994]: 253–254).

has rendered some of the most intriguing—and difficult to interpret—literary and archaeological materials as well. To be clear, I am not reconsidering here whether in pre-Constantinian Capernaum there lived a marginal Jewish Christian sect with a distinct theological outlook and desire to preserve an authentic site from the time of Jesus. My question is more modest and, perhaps, more basic: Was there, simply, a presence of ethnic Jews in Capernaum between the late first and early fourth centuries whose identities also included some level of adherence to Jesus?[14] Additionally, similar to the previous chapter, I am interested in exploring how we should go about answering this question. Thus, in the first section below (section 2), the central issue of historical method will be addressed again, especially as it pertains to the relationship between texts and archaeological data. Section 3, then, will consider the relevant sources and offer an assessment of their value as evidence and, more importantly, what they are evidence for. While some other materials are referenced, central to the discussion of sources is the midrashic text *Qohelet Rabbah* 1:8 and 7:26, which recounts an encounter between a rabbinic figure and a group of *minim* in Capernaum, and the archaeology of Room 1—the so-called "sala venerata,"

---

14. One might note here that my definitional approach to the terms "Jewish Christ-followers" and "Jesus-oriented Jews" is broad and avoids specific halakhic and/or theological elements. In so doing, I hope to circumvent at least some of the methodological problems Taylor rightfully identified in the works of Bagatti and Testa. My methodological starting point is summed up in statement by Karin Hedner Zetterholm: "The recent insight that Jewish self-identity in antiquity seems to have been fluid enough to have allowed for adherence to Jesus as an option *within* Judaism has opened up new avenues for exploring the existence and nature of non-rabbinic varieties of Judaism by reading texts, previously considered the products of 'heretical' Christians (or 'Jewish Christians'), or as 'Christian' appropriation of Jewish traditions, as *Jewish* texts and as evidence of diversity within Judaism." See K. H. Zetterholm, "Alternate Visions of Judaism and Their Impact on the Formation of Rabbinic Judaism," *Journal of the Jesus Movement in its Jewish Setting* 1 (2014): 127–153 (127–128). In other words, what it meant to be Jewish and Christ-following were both perspectival and, despite the boundaries constructed by heresiologists, noncontradictory. For the sake of the current chapter, I approach "Jewishness" as an ethnogeographical category, that is, as a category applicable to local residents of Capernaum, which, according to various sources (e.g., the New Testament, Epiphanius, and the material culture), seems to have been predominately, if not exclusively, a village inhabited by Jews from the first to fourth century CE. Similarly, I approach "Christ-adherence" as a fluid and nonexclusive category in this period and as a term applicable to any expression of Jesus orientation. For the purposes of this chapter (as well as chapter 4), I take the act of commemoration—the material, spatial, and meaning-making processes inherent to remembering a person or event—to count as one such expression of Christ adherence.

which both ancient and modern tradition has associated with the house of the apostle Peter mentioned in the Gospels.[15] In section 4, I will exercise the historical imagination to argue that, while the sources give us little, if any, justification for constructing specifics, such as theological identities or ritual practices, they do grant a picture, even if somewhat vague, of the institutional identity and socioreligious setting of the village from the late first to fourth century.

2. The Problem of Method, Again

As James F. Strange rightly observed, the fundamental problem in the debate over the presence of Jewish Christ-followers in Capernaum (and other ancient Palestinian sites) is that of method.[16] In 1985, Graydon Snyder criticized Testa's work on alleged Judaeo–Christian symbols as an example of the enduring effect of the so-called Roman School of early Christian archaeology.[17] What Snyder meant by this was that Testa's approach was prone to "harmonizing the literary tradition with the archaeological data, or more pointedly, producing archaeological data that will confirm presupposed, later traditions."[18] Taylor followed and expanded upon Snyder's criticism, linking adherents of the Bagatti-Testa hypothesis to nineteenth-century biblical archaeologists who sought to "'prove the Bible true' by science,"[19] and for whom archaeology was simply biblical history's handmaiden. According to Taylor, Bagatti and Testa similarly used archaeology to prove their view of the Judaeo–Christian beginnings of Christian holy places.

As a critical response to this approach, Taylor formulates her methodological program—or at least one important part of it—by way of invoking Roland de Vaux's two-step principle, that literary and archaeological material must first be evaluated separately, and then they can be used together to construct history.[20] This, of course, is a sound and important methodological principle,

---

15. Matt 8:14; Mark 1:29; Luke 4:38.
16. Strange, "Archaeological Evidence of Jewish Believers?" 740–741.
17. Snyder, *Ante Pacem*, 11.
18. Snyder, *Ante Pacem*, 11.
19. Taylor, *Christians and the Holy Places*, 3.
20. Taylor, *Christians and the Holy Places*, 4. See R. de Vaux, "On the Right and Wrong Uses of Archaeology," in *Near Eastern Archaeology in the Twentieth Century*, ed. J. A. Sanders (Garden City, NY: Doubleday, 1970), 64–80.

since, as a first step, it aims at maintaining the autonomy of individual sources, and thus cautions the historian against forceful harmonization. Taylor implements this step meticulously. However, the second step mentioned by de Vaux is just as important for the historian: the literary and archaeological sources need to be evaluated together to construct history. On this point, Taylor's approach is, in my view, noticeably weaker.

Taylor's methodological tendency is three-fold: first, to isolate the sources from each other; second, to highlight the lack of clarity and the interpretive difficulty that each source on its own presents; and third, to draw conclusions in the negative, that is, that the sources do not provide positive support for the presence of Jewish Christ-followers. An example of this is while traditional interpretation of the Capernaum *minim* in *Qoh. Rab.* 1:8 and 7:26 has understood the texts as references to a group of second-century Jewish Christ-followers,[21] Taylor stresses that the term *minim* in rabbinic literature does not always refer to Christians—or, more specifically, to Jesus-oriented Jews—and so we cannot simply assume that the term, appearing as it does in a late midrash (ca. sixth century), refers to such an earlier historical group.[22] Taylor likewise casts uncertainty on the archaeological data related to the earliest phases of Room 1, which some have interpreted as a Christ-oriented assembly space that was in use as early as the late first or early second century (see section 3.2). She notes that even if these remains are dated before the fourth century—a point which she highly doubts—there is nothing that positively indicates that the room was a special gathering space for Jewish Christ-followers in this period.[23]

Taylor's problematizing of the referent of *minim*, her skepticism regarding the historical value of *Qohelet Rabbah*, and her doubts arising from the ambiguity of the archaeology, while in many ways commendable, form an entirely deconstructive argument that morphs throughout her work into a

---

21. E.g., Robert Herford, *Christianity in the Talmud and Midrash* (1903; repr. New York: Ktav, 2007), 215; B. Visotzky, "Overturning the Lamp," *JJS* 38 (1987): 72–80; A. Schremer, *Brothers Estranged: Heresy, Christianity and Jewish Identity in Late Antiquity* (Oxford: Oxford University Press, 2010), 210 n. 9; M. Hirshman, *Midrash Kohelet Rabbah 1–6: Critical Edition based on Manuscripts and Genizah Fragments, with an Introduction, References, Variant Readings and Commentary* (Jerusalem: Schechter Institute of Jewish Studies, 2016), 79, 122–123, 123 n. 358 (Hebrew).

22. Taylor, *Christians and the Holy Places*, 25–30 (esp. p. 30).

23. Taylor, *Christians and the Holy Places*, 284.

kind of historical dogma of its own. It brackets out that each datum can, and has been, justifiably interpreted differently (the term *minim* sometimes *can* refer to Jesus-oriented Jews in rabbinic literature);[24] the presentation of the Capernaum *minim* story in *Qoh. Rab.* 1:8 could *both* reflect a sixth-century polemical setting *and* preserve a tradition about a second-century rabbinic encounter with Jewish Christ-followers;[25] and the ambiguity of the archaeology of Room 1 is not evidence against its interpretation as a special gathering space for Jewish Christ-followers. Taylor's approach offers little by way of what the Capernaum sources are evidence *for*, if not for the presence of Jewish Christ-followers before Constantine. It confuses the deconstructive argument with the total task history.

As we discussed in the previous chapter, modern historiography in the philosophical tradition of Robin Collingwood has recognized for a long time that history is not only deconstructive but also, and necessarily, constructive.[26] While I will not recount that entire discussion here, I want to recall briefly two points that were made, which are methodologically pertinent to the topic and aims of this chapter.

First, we should remember that it is not enough for a historian to judge through critical interpretation whether a historical datum is trustworthy or not; critical interpretation should also involve the application of that datum as evidence within the historian's picture of the past. History is not the rote gathering and arranging of historical data but rather the *interpretation* of that data and the *application* of them as evidence in relation to some specific historical question or problem.[27] The concept of evidence, therefore, is defined as data that are interpreted and mobilized for the purpose of constructing history.[28]

---

24. A point made by Oded Irshai in his review of Taylor's book: "Review of 'Christians and the Holy Places: The Myth of Jewish-Christian Origins', by Joan E. Taylor," *Journal of Roman Studies* 84 (1994): 264. See also, more recently, P. Schäfer, *Jesus in the Talmud* (Princeton, NJ: Princeton University Press, 2007), and the discussion on Talmudic *minim* stories by M. Bar-Asher Siegal, *Jewish–Christian Dialogues on Scripture in Late Antiquity* (Cambridge: Cambridge University Press, 2019), 1–42.

25. This is Hirshman's position, noted recently in his critical edition (*Midrash Kohelet Rabbah 1–6*, 57–58, 58 n. 95).

26. See my earlier discussion of Collingwoodian historiography in chapter 2, section 2.

27. Collingwood, *Idea of History*, 281; see also J. Ryan, "Jesus at the Crossroads," 66–89 (80).

28. Ryan, "Jesus at the Crossroads," 80; Collingwood, *Idea of History*, 281.

This is an important point here because it highlights that the question of Jewish Christ-followers in pre-Constantinian Capernaum stems not really from a problem with the data but rather from a problem with the *interpretation* of the data, that is, with how the data should be mobilized and applied to construct a historical argument.

Second, and perhaps the most important methodological point to make for the current chapter, derives from the Collingwoodian tradition's emphasis on the inferential nature of history. History involves the study of, for example, events, places, and people that are not accessible to our observation.[29] Thus, history's objective is to study events and things not accessible to the senses "inferentially, arguing to them from something that is accessible to our observation, and which the historian calls 'evidence' for the events in which he is interested."[30] Evidence, however, does not come as "ready-made historical knowledge, to be swallowed and regurgitated by the historian's mind."[31] Historical knowledge must be constructed from evidence, which always and only exists in pieces. The historian's picture of the past, therefore, involves the construction of a metaphorical web composed of nodes of evidence with threads of inference spun and stretched between them. These nodes of evidence are responsible for the strength and viability of a historical construction. More and stronger evidence will result in more robust connections and imaginative threads between those points of evidence. The plausibility of a web of imaginative construction is derived from the strength of its evidence and the interweaving and connectivity of the threads between the nodes. The historian must ask whether these connections form any kind of pattern, and then extrapolate from this pattern of evidence to construct a picture of the past that is plausibly coherent and logically permissible. Inductive historical reasoning, unlike methods from the natural sciences, does not and cannot lead to conclusions about the past that are logically compulsory. There is nothing in the pattern formed by a historian's observations that can obligate others to interpret the data and extrapolate from it in a particular way or even at all.[32] There are no algorithms, no formulas, and very rarely any smoking guns in the

---

29. Collingwood, *Idea of History*, 251–252.
30. Collingwood, *Idea of History*, 251–252.
31. Collingwood, *Idea of History*, 246.
32. Collingwood, *Idea of History*, 254–255.

construction and representation of ancient history. In other words, evidence can never *prove* a historian's construction; it can only *justify* it.[33]

This last point brings us to what is, in my view, the defining methodological issue concerning the topic of this chapter. One of the major pillars upon which some scholars have built their criticisms is the lack of "direct evidence" and "incontrovertible proof" of the presence of Jewish Christ-followers in Capernaum.[34] Such demands, however, raise questions about the expectations we put on pre-fourth-century data and what, precisely, would constitute direct evidence for Jesus-oriented Jews in the first place. After concluding that "there is no literary evidence of Jewish–Christians living in Palestine from the middle of the second century onwards," Taylor pivots to the archaeological evidence:

> If one is to identify archaeological remains as being specifically Jewish-Christian, it would be necessary to argue that these remains show incontrovertible proof of Jewish praxis being maintained by the community which left them. Symbols and strange graffiti would have to be such that no other interpretation is possible. One would need to find examples of Hebrew language, or symbols in which Jewish iconography alone is used to propound a Christian message, or inscriptions which mention Jewish customs and festivals and give a clear indication of Christian belief.[35]

Three points can be made here. First, from my perspective, Taylor has asked for the impossible. Very rarely, if ever, do historians of antiquity deal by way of incontrovertible proof and material for which there is only one valid interpretation. Second, Taylor has asked for the impossible *for this period*. Direct material evidence that gives a clear indication of Jewish Christ-followers before the fourth century expects too much of archaeology.[36]

---

33. See also Collingwood, *Idea of History*, 261, where he draws a distinction between "compulsive" proof, as in the exact sciences, and "permissive" proof, as the inductive sciences, including critical history.

34. E.g., Taylor, *Christians and the Holy Places*, 46 (see also p. 41). See also what seems to be a similar expectation in Zangenberg, "Galilean Silence," 107; Hakola, "Galilean Jews and Christians," 161.

35. Taylor, *Christians and the Holy Places*, 46.

36. As noted by E. M. Meyers and J. F. Strange, *Archaeology, the Rabbis, and Early Christianity* (London: SCM Press, 1981), 125: "It has long been a truism in the study of early

As classical historian Jonathan Hall notes, the absence of a discernable "archaeological culture" should not be taken by historians as commensurate with the absence of a people group.[37] Third, the criterion that discernably Jewish materials (iconographic or inscriptional) would need to propound at the same time a "Christian message" or "give a clear indication of Christian belief" assumes (1) that, in a village like Capernaum, there was already a clear distinction between what was Jewish and what was Christian before the fourth century; (2) that this distinction should have left a clear impression in Capernaum's pre-fourth-century archaeological record, with something like a sign affixed to Room 1 reading in Hebrew, "Jews who keep sabbath and the other holy days also worship Jesus the Christ here"; and (3) that the earliest architectural remains from Room 1 cannot themselves be expressions of Christ-belief, even though, admittedly, they do not participate in the same kind of discursive activity as written texts or inscriptions.[38]

To sum up this section, then, my historiographic goal in this essay is not to produce an incontrovertible picture of the past but rather one that is justified through critical reexamination of the sources. The aim is to construct a web composed of nodes of evidence with threads of inference spun between them. Of course, the act of inferring involves imaginative interpretation, and interpretation by its very nature involves subjectivity. But as Collingwood

---

Christianity that if we were to depend solely on archaeological evidence we might conclude that Christianity sprang full-grown from the head of Constantine in the fourth century CE. In other words, the problem of methodology is particularly acute here, as is the question of proper interpretation."

37. See J. M. Hall, *Ethnic Identity in Greek Antiquity* (Cambridge: Cambridge University Press, 1997), 128–129, 136. Hall questions the capacity of archaeology to identify ethnic groups, and so problematizes methods that have assumed that "archaeological cultures" (which he defines as "complexes of regularly associated traits") are simply "the material expression of what today would be called a people." In other words, the relationship between archaeology and an identifiable group of people is complex and not straightforward.

38. Architecture, however, most certainly represents discursive activity, as it plays an important role in the social processes of meaning-making within a particular culture, every bit as much as do written texts. On this, see L. Findley, *Building Change: Architecture, Politics, and Culture Agency* (London: Routledge, 2005). As it relates to Capernaum specifically, see J. F. Strange, "The Archaeology of Religion at Capernaum, Synagogue and Church," in *Religious Texts and Material Contexts*, ed. J. Neusner and J. F. Strange, Studies in Ancient Judaism (Lanham, MD: University Press of America, 2001), 43–63.

observed a long time ago, while all history is inferential, the more a historian can root inferences in evidence, the more compelling the web of imaginative historical construction will be.

3. The Sources

Literary Sources

As Zangenberg notes, there is no doubting that the historical Jesus made the Galilee the geographical matrix of his activity; however, the development of the Jewish Jesus movement in the Galilee after his death and whether there was any continuity in the transmission of tradition between the time of this movement and the early fourth century are questions that are more difficult to answer.[39] While the archaeological discovery of an indisputably Christ-oriented building from third-century Kefar ʿOthnay now falsifies any claim that Christ-followers in general were absent from the Galilee before the time of Constantine,[40] a sizable amount of scholarship has looked to various literary data to argue that Jesus-oriented Jews, indeed, also lived in the region during this period. For example, an increasing number of scholars have located the Gospel of Matthew within the context of postwar Galilee, and thus have taken it as evidence for the presence there of Jewish Christ-followers toward the end of the first century.[41] Similar suggestions have been

---

39. This point has been well articulated by Zangenberg, "Galilean Silence."

40. For a discussion of this building as an architectural reception of the Jesus tradition in the third century, see A. Runesson and W. V. Cirafesi, "Art and Architecture at Capernaum, Kefar ʿOthnay, and Dura Europos," in *The Reception of Jesus in the First Three Centuries*, vol. 3, *From Celsus to the Catacombs: Visual, Liturgical, and Non-Christian Receptions of Jesus in the Second and Third Centuries CE*, ed. Chris L. Keith (London: T&T Clark), 175–182.

41. On the Galilean provenance of Matthew, see, e.g., A. J. Saldarini, "The Gospel of Matthew and Jewish–Christian Conflict in the Galilee," in *The Galilee in Late Antiquity*, ed. Lee I. Levine (Cambridge, MA: Harvard University Press, 1992), 23–38, here 26–27; J. Andrew Overman, *Church and Community in Crisis: The Gospel According to Matthew* (Valley Forge, PA: Trinity Press International, 1996), 16–19; Ekkehard W. Stegemann and Wolfgang Stegemann, *The Jesus Movement: A Social History of Its First Century* (Minneapolis: Fortress Press, 1999), 223–225; L. M. White, *From Jesus to Christianity: How Four Generations of Visionaries and Storytellers Created the New Testament and Christian Faith* (New York: HarperSanFrancisco, 2004), 240; A. Runesson, "Rethinking Early Jewish–Christian Relations: Matthean Community History as Pharisaic Intragroup Conflict," *JBL* 127.1 (2008): 95–132; J. Kampen, *Matthew within Sectarian Judaism* (New Haven: Yale University Press, 2016),

made with reference to the Gospel of Mark. Cilliers Breytenbach has noted that the textual world of Mark evinces knowledge of Galilean Jesus traditions,[42] and Christopher Zeichmann has recently argued that Mark might have even been composed in Capernaum itself.[43] Many, including Taylor, have understood the well-known passage from *t. Ḥul.* 2:20–24—which presents two rabbinic encounters with a *min* named Jacob of Kefar Sekaniah/Sama set in second-century Sepphoris—as a reflection of memories about the presence of Jesus-oriented Jews in the region, whether or not they were resident in Sepphoris specifically.[44] While F. Stanley Jones has suggested that *Rec.* 1:27–71 is a distinct source authored by a Jewish Christ-follower in early 3rd century Judea,[45] Albert Baumgarten has located this source (and the rest of the Pseudo-Clementine material) in the Galilee, since it demonstrates such close engagement between ideas found among rabbinic Jews and Jewish

---

6. For a discussion and critique of the Galilee as a place of origin for Matthew, see David C. Sim, "The Gospel of Matthew and Galilee: An Evaluation of an Emerging Hypothesis," *ZNW* 107, no. 2 (2016): 141–169, who advocates for Syrian Antioch as the most likely candidate.

42. C. Breytenbach, "Mark and Galilee: Text World and Historical World," in *Galilee through the Centuries: Confluence of Cultures*, ed. E. Meyers (Winona Lake, IN: Eisenbrauns, 1999), 75–85.

43. C. Zeichmann, "Loanwords or Code-Switching? Latin Transliteration and the Setting of Mark's Composition," *Journal of the Jesus Movement in its Jewish Setting* 4 (2017): 42–64; C. Zeichmann, "Capernaum: A 'Hub' for the Historical Jesus or the Markan Evangelist?" *JSHJ* 15 (2017): 147–165.

44. E.g., Taylor, *Christians and the Holy Places*, 29; S. Miller, "The Minim of Sepphoris Reconsidered," *HTR* 86.4 (1993): 377–402 (380); J. Schwartz and P. J. Tomson, "When Rabbi Eliezer Was Arrested for Heresy," *JSIJ* 10 (2012): 149–153, 162–164; Siegal, *Jewish–Christian Dialogue*, 11. Taylor is willing to admit that *t. Ḥul.* 2:20–24 reflects a memory concerning the activity of a Jewish Christ-follower in Sepphoris, since Sepphoris lacks a traditional Christian holy site; that is, she argues that just because a Jewish Christ-follower was active in Sepphoris does not mean that large groups of Jewish Christ-followers established the holy sites in Capernaum, Nazareth, Bethlehem, and other places.

45. F. S. Jones, *An Ancient Jewish Christian Source on the History of Christianity: Pseudo-Clementine Recognitions 1.27–71* (Atlanta: Scholars Press, 1995), 3, 140, 154–155. While there is no debate concerning its "Jewish Christian" character, there is some debate over whether *Recognitions* 1.27–71 should be identified with the so-called "Ascents of James," a Jesus-oriented Jewish document that Epiphanius asserts was used by the Ebionites (*Pan.* 30.16.7) and shares a number of themes also found in *Recognitions* 1.27–71. See R. Bauckham, "The Origin of the Ebionites," in *The Image of the Judaeo-Christians*, ed. Tomson and Lambers-Petry, 164–171). I am not as concerned with whether the source is Ebionite as I am with its pre-fourth-century date and its potential provenance in the Galilee.

followers of Jesus.[46] And Richard Bauckham has interpreted some of the patristic data from, for example, Julius Africanus (*Letter to Aristides apud* Eusebius, *Hist. eccl.* 1:7:14), Eusebius (*Onom.* 172), and Epiphanius (*Pan.* 30:2:7–9) as evidence for the activity of early Jewish Christ-followers in Galilean locations such as Nazareth and Kokhaba.[47]

However, at the center of the debate about Jewish Christ-followers in Capernaum specifically are two other literary sources, which are the focus of the discussion below—one from Epiphanius, which does not need very much attention, and the other, as already mentioned, a midrashic text from *Qoh. Rab.* 1:8. In *Pan.* 30:11:9–10, Epiphanius reports that a certain Jewish convert to imperial Christianity named Joseph of Tiberias (ca. 285–356) had been commissioned by Constantine to build churches in Jewish cities and towns throughout the Galilee, "especially at Tiberias, Diocaesarea, Sepphoris, Nazareth, and Capernaum," since these towns had no "Greeks, Samaritans, or Christians among the populations."[48] It was, according to Epiphanius, a kind of rule in these places not to have non-Jews living among them (φυλάσσεται <τὸ> παρ' αὐτοῖς [τοῦ] μὴ εἶναι ἀλλόεθνον).

Taylor is quite right to conclude that there is nothing in the literary sources or the archaeological record to suggest that Epiphanius's assertion was wrong, that Capernaum was anything other than an entirely Jewish town before the fourth century.[49] The problem, however, is that Taylor seems to take Epiphanius's reference to there being "no Christians" in

---

46. J. E. Burns has floated the idea—admittedly speculative—that *Rec.* 1.27–71 functioned as an addendum to the Gospel of Matthew (see *The Christian Schism in Jewish History and Jewish Memory* [New York: Cambridge University Press, 2016], 155 n. 175), although he emphasizes the speculative nature of this hypothesis. I thank Karin Hedner Zetterholm for alerting me to the scholarship on *Rec.* 1.27–71. On the idea that *Rec.* 1.27–71 contains receptions of the Gospel of Matthew, see Zetterholm's essay, "Israel and the Nations in the pseudo-Clementine *Homilies* and *Recognitions* 1.27–72: Receptions of the Gospel of Matthew," in *Matthew within Judaism*, ed. A. Runesson and D. Gurtner, ECL (Atlanta: SBL, 2020), 399–426.

47. R. Bauckham, *Jude and the Relatives of Jesus in the Early Church* (Edinburgh: T&T Clark, 1990), 60–68, and, more recently, in "James and the Jerusalem Community," in *Jewish Believers in Jesus*, ed. O. Skarsaune and R. Hvalvik, 55–95 (esp. 77–81). See Bauckham, *Relatives of Jesus*, 62–66 on the identity of the place name "Kokhaba"; the data is simply a mess to sort through in light of several locations having similar names mentioned by different authors.

48. F. Williams, trans., *The Panarion of Epiphanius of Salamis: Book I (Sects 1–46)*, 2nd rev. exp. ed. (Leiden: Brill, 2009), 140.

49. Taylor, *Christians and the Holy Places*, 288.

locales like Capernaum to mean *all kinds* of Christ adherents, including Jews; an entirely Jewish town with no Christians means, for Taylor, no Jewish Christians. But Epiphanius's claim in this passage is more restrictive. His reference to Christians appears last in a list of other ἀλλοεθνεῖς, "other nations," that is, Greeks and Samaritans. His point is that there are no gentiles in these places.[50] By "Christians," therefore, he must have in mind specifically Christ-followers from non-Jewish ethnic groups, that is, Byzantine Orthodox Christians who, like him, are aligned with the aims of imperial Christianity.[51] This is in keeping with Epiphanius's use of the term throughout the *Panarion*; he never uses the term "Christian/s" to describe Jesus-oriented Jewish groups, which for him, without exception, fit the category of heresy. Even Joseph of Tiberias is, for Epiphanius, no longer a Jew but an anti-Arian Χριστιανὸς ὀρθόδοξος (*Pan.* 30.5.5). Thus, that Capernaum was among those towns that had "no Christians" does not undermine the hypothesis that Jewish Christ-followers were present before the fourth century.

Qohelet Rabbah is, in my view, more difficult to deal with.[52] Its apparently late date (sixth to eighth century) and complex redactional tendencies have made historians of early rabbinic Judaism and Jewish–Christian relations somewhat allergic to it.[53] Two passages from the midrash, 1:8 and 7:26, explicitly mention *minim* and *minut* in Capernaum (כפר נחום)—the former in the context of a story about R. Joshua's susceptible nephew, Ḥanina, and his encounter with Capernaum's *minim*, and the latter in the context of R. Issi of Caesarea's interpretation of *Qoh.* 7:26 as relating to the *minut* of, among others, the "sons of Capernaum." For our purposes, *Qoh. Rab.* 1:8 is more

---

50. Hence Williams's translation of *Pan.* 30:11:10: "The <rule> of having no gentiles among them is observed especially in Tiberias, Diocaesarea, Sepphoris, Nazareth, and Capernaum" (*The* Panarion, 140).

51. See also comments made by D. Boyarin, "Rethinking Jewish Christianity: An Argument for Dismantling a Dubious Category (to which is Appended a Correction of my *Border Lines*," *JQR* 99.1 (2009): 7–36 (esp. p. 18).

52. The following analysis is based upon the Socino edition of *Qohelet Rabbah* with recourse to Hirshman's critical edition of the Hebrew and Aramaic text.

53. For example, Schwartz and Tomson, "Rabbi Eliezer," 148–149 n. 9 note a number of scholars who, while focusing on its appearance in the Tosefta and Bavli, pass over or ignore the tradition of the arrest of R. Eliezer for heresy as it is represented in *Qohelet Rabbah*.

important, although we will have reason to reference 7:26 as well. The major interpretive issues facing *Qoh. Rab.* 1:8 are twofold. The first issue has to do with the identity of the Capernaum *minim*, that is, are they Jewish Christ-followers, non-rabbinic Jews, or non-Jewish Christians? Second, is the passage purely the literary creation of the redactors in the sixth century, or might it also preserve some memory of a second-century rabbinic encounter?[54] Let us tackle these in turn.

There are three points of evidence that justify understanding the Capernaum *minim* as Jewish Christ-followers rather than simply non-rabbinic Jews or non-Jewish Christians. First, the Capernaum *minim* story follows immediately on the heels of the stories about the *min* Jacob of Kefar Sekaniah and his encounters with Rabbi Eliezer ben Hyrcanus and Rabbi Eliezer ben Dama, which are also preserved in the Tosefta and the Bavli. While the historical situation of *Qohelet Rabbah* is significantly different than the Toseftan and Bavlian versions, Jacob of Kefar Sekaniah is, nevertheless, surely depicted as a Jesus-oriented Jew.[55] The reader of the midrash is, therefore, primed to read the *minim* of Capernaum within the same frame of reference as Jacob the *min*.[56]

Second, the Capernaum episode does not end with the story of Ḥanina and Rabbi Joshua. Rather, it extends to the following story of Rabbi Jonathan and his deserting disciple, which is connected though a small but important

---

54. See Taylor, *Christians and the Holy Places,* 30; Miller, "The Minim of Sepphoris Reconsidered," 385 n. 31; Hakola, "Galilean Jews and Christians," 161, 161 n. 99.

55. To Rabbi Eliezer ben Hyrcanus, Jacob tells "a word in the name of Jesus son of Pandera." In the story with Rabbi Eliezer ben Dama, Jacob tries to heal him after ben Dama is bitten by a snake for his attraction to Jacob's *minut*. Parallel versions are in *t. Ḥul.* 2:22–24; *y. Avodah Zarah* 2:2; *y Shabb.* 14:4; *b. Avodah Zarah* 16b–17a, 27b. Note the interesting manuscript situation of instances of Jesus's name in *Qoh. Rab.* 1:8, whereas the MSS Vatican 291, Oxford 164, Pesaro 1519, and Constantinople 1520 all read "He [i.e., Jacob of Kefar Sekaniah] told me a word in the name of Jesus son of Pandera." The Vilna MS has an empty space after "in the name of" and the Jerusalem MS reads "in the name of so-and-so." The Socino edition of *Qoh. Rab.* for some reason follows the Jerusalem MS.

56. Miller, "The Minim of Sepphoris Reconsidered," 385 n. 31 downplays context as an indicator of the referent of *minim* in the Capernaum episode because of the apparent "composite" nature of the excerpt. In my view, the composite nature of the excerpt, a natural result of editorial activity, does not, however, make the placement of these stories meaningless. There are clearly thematic threads that tie the stories together, especially the stereotyped charges brought against the *minim* (magic and sex; see below).

linguistic detail: "One of R. Jonathan's students fled to *them*."⁵⁷ While the next lines identify the "them" here as, once again, *minim*, the use of the anaphoric pronoun to start the story suggests it is, specifically, the Capernaum *minim* that are still in view.⁵⁸ This means, as Burton Visotzky noted over thirty years ago, that the Rabbi Joshua and Rabbi Jonathan stories combine to create a stereotyped charge against these *minim* that was commonly brought against Christ-followers by both Jews and pagans in the second and third centuries⁵⁹ and by the rabbis in Talmudic literature.⁶⁰ The story of Rabbi Joshua and the bewitching of Ḥanina brings them up on charges of sorcery (especially on the Sabbath), while the story of Rabbi Jonathan and his wayward student accuses them of sexual deviancy, specifically wife-sharing. The midrash has the Capernaum *minim* then cite to R. Jonathan Prov. 1:14 ("Cast in your lot among us; we will all have one purse") as justification for engaging in wife-sharing, which clearly plays on the late first- or early second-century self-understanding of some early Christ groups as having "all things in common" (Acts 2:44). Furthermore, reading the Rabbi Joshua and Rabbi Jonathan stories together clarifies that Capernaum's *minim* are meant to be understood as Jews and not gentile Christians or pagans; upon witnessing many men occupying themselves with one woman, Rabbi Jonathan cries: "Is this the way for Jews to behave!"⁶¹

A third point of evidence that the *minim* in Capernaum refer specifically to Jesus-oriented Jews lies in Rabbi Joshua's response to Ḥanina after

---

57. רבי יונתן ערק חד מן תלמידוי לגביהון. (text from Hirshman's edition, p. 76).

58. This detail is not mentioned by Miller or Taylor in their respective treatments, and so both scholars appear to have only the Hanina and Rabbi Joshua episode in mind when they consider the identity of the Capernaum *minim*.

59. E.g., Justin, *Dial.* 10; Origen, *Contra Celsum* 6:27, 40. See Visotzky, "Overturning the Lamp," *JJS* 38 (1987): 72–80.

60. On rabbinic charges against Christ-followers and characterizations of Jesus using the tropes of sorcery and illicit sex, see also Schäfer, *Jesus in the Talmud, et passim.*

61. Socino ed. This would undermine Miller's suggestion that the Capernaum *minim* could very likely be pagans. To Miller's credit, a short story of a pagan woman who approaches Rabbi Eliezer to be made a proselyte directly precedes the introduction of the Capernaum *minim*. This woman is accused of incest, which leads Rabbi Eliezer to reject her request. She then goes to Rabbi Joshua who welcomes her. Although she, too, is portrayed with the stereotype of sexual misdeeds, she never speaks *minut* and the story never calls her a *min*, which clearly distinguishes her from characters such as Jacob of Kefar Sekaniah and the *minim* of Capernaum.

the *minim* had cast a spell on him and forced him to ride on a donkey on the Sabbath: "Since the ass of that wicked person has roused itself against you, you are not able to reside in the land of Israel." Herford believed that Ḥanina's Sabbath-day donkey ride and the phrase "the ass of that wicked person" (חמרא דההוא רשיעא) were unmistakable references to Jesus, not least because of the association of an ass with Jesus in other rabbinic literature and in pagan sources, such as the Alexamenos Graffito.[62] Taylor, however, dismisses the phrase "the ass of that wicked person" as a reference to Jesus in *Qoh. Rab.* 1:8, saying:

> The reference is quite clearly to Balaam. "The ass of Balaam" is a standard epithet in rabbinic Judaism. Balaam was the Gentile accuser of Israel (Num. 22–4) whose ass saw the angel of the Lord on the road before Balaam was able to do so (Num. 23:21–35). Balaam in rabbinic literature mouths blasphemous arguments in general, but never specifically Christian ones.[63]

Taylor's interpretation has a lot going for it, but it might create a false dichotomy. That is, she overlooks the point, reasserted recently and quite persuasively by Peter Schäfer, that in rabbinic literature the work, identity, and fate of Balaam are often closely linked with that of Jesus and vice versa.[64]

---

62. Herford, *Christianity in the Talmud and Midrash*, 146–154, 214–215. Herford's association of an ass with Jesus is largely based upon his interpretation of the story of Imma Shalom, her brother Rabbi Gamliel, and their attempt to trick a certain Christ-following "philosopher" into taking a bribe in *b. Shabb.* 116a–b by offering him a donkey. As Herford and Visotzky both showed, the story is full of allusions to the Gospel of Matthew. The Alexamenos Graffito (ca. 200 CE; Rome) depicts (in caricature form) a crucified figure with the head of a donkey apparently being worshipped by a man who might be dressed as a Roman guard. An inscription below the crucified figure reads: "Alexamenos, worship the god" (see Snyder, *Ante Pacem*, 60). According to Tertullian, *Apol.* 16:1–2, Jews were mocked as worshipping a god that took the form of an ass, an idea Tertullian says Tacitus put into the minds of Romans with his account of the origins of the Jews in book 5 of his *History*. Tertullian also says that, because Christians and Jews are so near to each other with respect to their obligations to their deity, Christians, too, were associated with the worship of a god having an ass's head.

63. Taylor, *Christians and the Holy Places*, 25.

64. Schäfer, *Jesus in the Talmud*, 31–33, 84–87, 89–92. In *b. Ber.* 17a–b, Jesus takes Balaam's places among the list of "bad companions" who will not have a portion in the world to come (see the original mishnah it is based on in *m. Sanh.* 10:1), as he joins Ahitophel, Doeg, and Gehazi. In *b. Git.* 55b–57a, Jesus is grouped together with Balaam in their punishment in hell.

Jewish Christ-Followers in Capernaum 97

Schäfer goes so far as to say that, especially in the Bavli, Jesus himself is presented as "the new Balaam."[65] Thus, the phrase "the ass of that wicked person" in *Qoh. Rab.* might very well be Balaam language, as Taylor claims, but the phrase appears immediately juxtaposed to stories that mention Jesus and report the activity of Jacob of Kefar Sekaniah, a Jewish Christ-follower who, like Jesus and Balaam, is guilty of leading the people astray. It seems to me, then, that Herford (and those who have followed in his wake)[66] was

---

There is a third figure among them, the Roman general Titus, but, as the one who destroyed the Temple, he suffers a greater and longer punishment than the other two. Perhaps the most interesting examples of this close relation in rabbinic thinking is found in *b. Sanh.* 106b, where a certain *min* tests Rabbi Hanina on how old Balaam was when he died. Rabbi Hanina responds by citing Ps 55:24: "'Bloody and deceitful men shall not live half their days,' [indicating he was] thirty-three or thirty-four years old." The *min* replies: "You have spoken well; I myself saw the notebook [פנקסיה] of Balaam and it was written therein: Balaam the lame was thirty-three years old when Pinehas the highwayman killed him." Louis Feldman (*Judaism and Hellenism Reconsidered*, 588 n.8) says that the view asserting Balaam is Jesus in this story has been "generally rejected." While we certainly need to be careful with taking vague references and names as symbolic stand-ins for Jesus, the use of Balaam in *b. Sanh* 106b might be worth rethinking. An almost sure allusion to Mary, Jesus's mother, appears before it, in *b. Sanh.* 106a, and Jesus himself is mentioned explicitly three times in a rather long story about his interaction with Rabbi Yehoshua ben Perahya in *b. Sanh.* 107b. Furthermore, while Balaam's age of death could be entirely coincidental, the fact that the *min* mentioned in the story derived this knowledge from having personally seen "the notebook of Balaam" is interesting. Nowhere in the biblical narratives is a book or written chronicle associated with Balaam. Some have seen this as a reference to Gospel material, although none of the Gospels give thirty-three as the age of Jesus's death. The question must remain open. According to István Czachesz, the *Acts of Thomas* brings together motifs from the biblical Balaam narrative and Jesus's entry into Jerusalem in its episodes involving asses (*AThom.* 39, 69). See Czachesz, "Speaking Asses in the *Acts of Thomas*: An Intertextual and Cognitive Perspective," in *The Prestige of Balaam in Judaism, Early Christianity, and Islam*, ed. G. H. van Kooten and J. van Ruiten (Leiden: Brill, 2008), 275–286.

65. Schäfer, *Jesus in the Talmud*, 111. We should also note that, while in the unpublished version of his critical edition of *Qohelet Rabbah* (his 1983 PhD dissertation), Marc Hirshman translates the Aramaic homonym חמרא (wine or ass) with the modern Hebrew חמור (ass), he is clearly drawn to the earlier interpretation of Saul Lieberman, who apparently took the Aramaic חמרא in *Qoh. Rab.* 1:8 to mean the Hebrew יין (wine) rather than חמור, and thus as a veiled reference to the Eucharist. See Hirshman, *Midrash Kohelet Rabbah 1–6*, 79 (Hebrew). On these discrete meanings of חמרא, see Jastrow, *s.v.* Hirshman's affinity for interpreting חמרא as "wine" is followed by Visotzky, "Overturning the Lamp," 76–77, and both seem to favor the idea that it is meant as a reference to the Eucharist.

66. For example, besides the works of Bagatti and Testa, see A. Cohen in his Socino translation of *Qoh. Rab.*; Vsotzky, "Overturning the Lamp;" Hirshman, *Midrash Kohelet Rabbah*, 79.

right to conclude that *Qoh. Rab.* represents the *minim* of Capernaum as Jesus-oriented Jews.

We have yet to say anything, however, about the midrash's relationship to history. One interpretive option, which some scholars have indeed chosen, is to assign *Qoh. Rab* 1:8 no historical value at all, whether for an earlier (second century) or later (sixth century) period. This position, in my view, is overly skeptical. The story locates the *minim* in a small Galilean town known from the historical record but otherwise unmentioned in other Jewish literature from late antiquity. *Minim* stories do not require specific locations, and Capernaum, relatively small as it was, does not appear to have accrued in the Jewish world any particular cultural or symbolic currency—positive or negative—that would make it an ideal place to represent a fictive encounter between rabbinic Jews and Jewish Christ-followers for purely ideological reasons. If the story does not intend to reflect any historical information, even on a general level, about such an encounter that took place at some point in the town's history, the glaring question that arises is: Why did these redactors choose *Capernaum* for this story? Further, as will be discussed below, there is an archaeological record that, while perhaps difficult to interpret in its earliest phases, clearly shows in its later phases (fourth to sixth century) that Jews and Christians interacted in Capernaum; a limestone basilical synagogue and an octagonal Byzantine church sit only twenty-five meters apart from each other.[67] A better position, then, is to conclude that the midrash preserves at least some historical tradition about a conflict between rabbinocentric Jews and Jewish Christ-followers that took place in the town. After all, although she does not think that the *minim* in the story are Jewish Christ-followers, even Taylor in the end allows for the possibility that *Qoh. Rab.* 1:8 "preserves some folk memory of the Capernaum population of the second century being resistant to rabbinic authority."[68]

To my mind, the more difficult question to address is to which time period this historical tradition belongs: Does *Qoh. Rab.* 1:8 preserve an earlier tradition about an encounter that belongs to the second century based on its use of rabbinic figures known from that period, or does it preserve a later tradition that reflects the sixth-century polemical setting of its redactors? The most challenging part to answering this question is that since the story has no parallels

---

67. On this, see Runesson, "Architecture."
68. Taylor, *Christians and the Holy Places*, 30.

in other rabbinic literature, its redactional history cannot be traced, as can be, for example, the story of Rabbi Eliezer's arrest.

The Rabbi Eliezer tradition has the good fortune of being found in three versions, which appear in three different redactional contexts: *t. Ḥul.* 2:24 (ca. third-century Palestine), *b. Avodah Zara* 16b–17a (ca. fourth to sixth century Babylonia), and *Qoh. Rab.* 1:8 (sixth century Palestine). Joshua Schwartz and Peter Tomson have produced a thorough study of the story's redaction history.[69] They note with reference to the version persevered in *Qoh. Rab.* That while the midrash collection as a whole is set within the very different social and religious milieu of Byzantine Palestine, "in the case of the Rabbi Eliezer tradition, it clearly builds upon the Tosefta and very probably the additional material of the Bavli."[70] In other words, the Rabbi Eliezer tradition in *Qoh. Rab.* is certainly influenced by the Bavli and its own Byzantine environment,[71] but the midrash is unquestionably working with a second-century tradition preserved in the Tosefta. This is all to suggest that it might be possible to posit the redactional tendencies evinced in *Qohelet Rabbah*'s version of the Rabbi Eliezer tradition as a model for understanding the prehistory and composition of the Capernaum *minim* story. We might conclude, for example, that the Capernaum story was composed within the sixth-century polemical setting of the redactors and shows signs of Bavlian influence—the use of Balaam language as an allusion to Jesus, the caricature of Jewish Christ-followers as sorcerers and sex addicts—but that it also built, as did the Rabbi Eliezer tradition, on an earlier tradition about two named rabbis from the second century that had encounters with Jewish Christ-followers.

The obvious problem with this conclusion is that unlike the Rabbi Eliezer tradition, which is preserved in the Tosefta, we have no knowledge of an actual earlier tradition for the Capernaum story; while possible, it is completely hypothetical and thus does little to anchor a historical judgment in evidence. On the other hand, if the Capernaum story is understood strictly as a polemical feature of its redactors, this too is an important datum that we must interpret, as the story would then be understood to reflect an encounter between rabbinic Jews and Jewish Christ-followers in sixth-century Capernaum. The question

---

69. Schwartz and Tomson, "When Rabbi Eliezer Was Arrested for Heresy."
70. Schwartz and Tomson, "When Rabbi Eliezer Was Arrested for Heresy," 167.
71. For examples of these influences, see Schwartz and Tomson, "When Rabbi Eliezer Was Arrested for Heresy," 167–168.

that follows from this observation is whether, historiographically, it is better to posit—or to use Collingwood's terminology, "interpolate"—continuity or discontinuity in the presence of Jewish Christ-followers in the town leading up to the sixth century. That is, is it more likely that *Qoh. Rab.* polemicizes against a group of Jewish Christ-followers who had arrived in Capernaum only sometime between the fourth and sixth centuries, or does it address a group that had been there since at least the second century and continued to be there in the sixth century, until the time in which Jewish–Christian polemics reached their zenith in the anti-Jewish legislation of Justinian?[72] In my view, Benjamin Arubas and Rina Talgam are right to assert that it is easier to imagine continuity in the presence of Jewish Christ-followers in the village from the second to the sixth century.[73] Generally speaking, Jesus-oriented Jews were a small minority in Palestine, especially by the time of Justinian, and as Jewish and Christian heresiologists indicate, they were not particularly liked by rabbinic Jews or Byzantine Christians. The idea of a Jewish Christ-group moving into Capernaum sometime during the fourth to sixth centuries when it had already become occupied by Byzantine colonizers is unlikely. Equally unlikely is the notion that Jesus-oriented Jews had altogether left Capernaum in an earlier period; as Arubas and Talgam remark: "Otherwise there was no point in mentioning them in *Qohelet Rabbah*."[74] Continuity of presence seems to be the best interpretation.

In sum, it is certainly possible to mobilize the literary data in a way that justifies the inference that Jewish Christ-followers were present in pre-fourth-century Capernaum, but the web of historical construction they constitute on their own is, admittedly, not very strong. However, we have not interpreted and mobilized all the relevant data yet; the archaeological data must now be considered.

The Archaeological Sources

While there is, today, no real debate surrounding the identification of the ancient site of Capernaum,[75] a decades-long disagreement continues over the

---

72. On Justinian's anti-Jewish policies, see S. Bowman, "Jews in Byzantium," in *The Cambridge History of Judaism*, vol. 4, *The Late Roman–Rabbinic Period*, ed. S. T. Katz (Cambridge: Cambridge University Press, 2006), 1048–1051.
73. Arubas and Talgam, "Jews, Christians, and '*Minim*,'" 272 n. 98.
74. Arubas and Talgam, "Capernaum," 272 n. 98.
75. For short discussion, see Chapter 2 footnote 1.

Image 3.1. Ariel view of Capernaum, with the octagonal church and limestone synagogue in center view. Picture taken August 16, 1972.

From Loffreda, *Cafarnao V*, 38 (DF 3). Image used with permission.

interpretation of the archaeological remains it has left behind. In the center of the town, separated by a mere twenty-five meters, stand what would have been in the fifth and sixth centuries two rather imposing structures. To the north are the remains of a large limestone synagogue, probably built in the late fifth or early sixth century.[76] To its south are remains of a Byzantine church, constructed in the shape of three concentric octagons,[77] erected in the early to mid-fifth century to commemorate the traditional site of St. Peter's house, where, according to the Gospels, Jesus spent a significant amount of time and

---

76. I acknowledge here that the date of the limestone synagogue's original construction is hotly debated. For discussion, see Runesson, "Architecture," 235–239.

77. The octagon is a common feature in Christian architecture in late antiquity. One can note the octagonal designs of the Golden Church in Antioch (begun in 327 CE and dedicated 341 CE), the basilica of San Vitale in Revenna (north Italy; sixth century), the double concentric octagonal Church of the Theotokos (late fifth century), and, perhaps the most important comparator, the triple concentric octagonal apse in the Church of the Nativity in Bethlehem (ca. fourth century).

Image 3.2. Ariel view (looking northeast) of *insula* 1 (*insula sacra*), with the location of Room 1 (*sala venerata*) marked at the center of the octagon.

From Loffreda, *Cafarnao V*, 46 (DF 26). Image used with permission.

performed miracles (Matt 8:14–15 // Mark 1:29–35 // Luke 4:38–39).[78] The presence of two contemporaneous monumental buildings set in such proximity

---

78. Scholars seem to agree on the fifth-century date of the octagonal building. See, e.g., V. Corbo, *Cafarnao I*, 64; Taylor, *Christians and the Holy Places*, 269; L. M. White, *Social Origins of Christian Architecture*, 158; R. Riesner, "What Does Archaeology Teach Us," 174. G. Foerster, "Recent Excavations at Capernaum," *IEJ* 21 (1971): 207–211, suggested a sixth-century date based upon a comparison with the Church of the Theotokos on Mt. Gerizim, which was built in the last decade of the fifth century, and which he believes predates the octagonal church at Capernaum. Taylor is sympathetic to Foerster's view but does not clearly endorse his dating. J. F. Strange, "The Capernaum and Herodium Publications (Part 1)," *BASOR* 226 (1977): 68, on the other hand, suggests the octagon was finished in the mid-fifth century but began in the late fourth to early fifth century.

is a treasure trove for the study of Jewish–Christian relations in Palestine in late antiquity. However, here I will focus on the site of the octagonal church, *insula* 1 (the so-called *insula sacra*), and the issue of its prior phases and uses.

The first archaeologists to conduct systematic excavations of the site, Virgilio Corbo and Stanislao Loffreda, identified three major phases to *insula* 1.[79] Phase 1 ran from the first century BCE to the fourth century CE, during which the *insula* consisted mainly of private houses. From the late Hellenistic period to the first century CE, there were several occupational layers, which were made from successive beaten-lime floors mixed with fragments of domestic vessels. The housing complex in *insula* 1 was of the same general design as other houses in the village—small rooms with tiled roofs assembled around a large courtyard.

According to the excavators, in the second half of the first or early second century, a twelve square meter area of beaten-lime floor in the northeast side of Room 1 (which was in total ca. 41 m^2) was then paved with at least six superimposed layers of white plaster.[80] Fragments of painted plaster from the room's walls were also found in these superimposed layers. The superimposed layers of floor and wall plaster appear to have been kept "scrupulously clean," in contrast to previous strata, and free from the presence of any domestic vessels.[81] Small pieces of Herodian oil lamps were found along the inner walls of the room and embedded not only within the beaten lime floor but also within the white plaster pavements overlaying the lime floor. These Herodian lamp fragments strongly support the excavators' date of the alterations to Room 1 to the late first or early second century.[82] Taylor,

---

79. See Loffreda, *Capharnaum*, 52–66; Corbo, *Cafarnao*, 1:59–106. Scholars appear to have generally accepted the basic chronology of these three major phases. As we shall see shortly, however, the sharp disagreement centers on the date of the apparent changes made to one of the rooms within the late Hellenistic or early Roman house complex, namely Room 1, the *sala venerata*, which became the central architectural focus of the later building phases.

80. Loffreda, *Capharnaum*, 57; Corbo, *Cafarnao*, 1:78–98 discusses the stratigraphy of Room 1 with pictures. See pp. 105–106 for a summary of the room's chronology.

81. Loffreda, *Capharnaum*, 57; Corbo, *Cafarnao*, 1:106: "[S]opra lo strato di occupazione surriferito, sono stati individuati tre pavimenti in battuto di calce con assenza di ceramic casalinga."

82. Loffreda, *Capharnaum*, 57; Corbo, *Cafarnao*, 1:106 says "minutissimi frammenti di lucerne erodiane furono raccolti nei sottili strati di pavimenti in calce. In base a questi ritrovati non ci sembra azzardato concludere che a partire dalle ultime decandi del primo secolo d.C., l'ambiente 1 fu trasformato in *domus-ecclesia*."

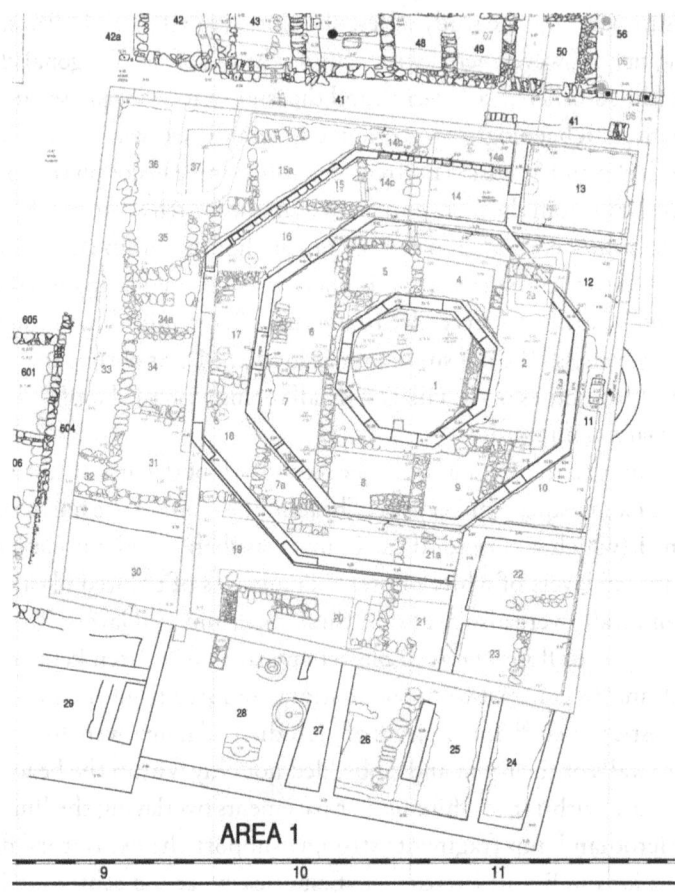

Image 3.3. Detail of the town plan, focusing on *insula* 1.

From Loffreda, *Cafarnao V*, 247. Used with permission.

however, has argued that dating these changes to Room 1 based upon tiny pieces of Herodian lamps found in the plaster of beaten-lime floors is highly contentious.[83] She suggests instead that the plastering may have been done in the third or even the fourth century,[84] and she speculates that the first or

---

83. Taylor, *Christians and the Holy Places*, 282–283. True, most of the fragments were very small. However, there was one complete lamp and one entire lower half of a lamp that were found as well (see note below).

84. The reason Taylor gives for this suggestion is that Loffreda apparently identified pottery with a date range of the first to third century on top of Bed of Stones B (first century) and

second century Herodian lamp fragments could have found their way into the fourth-century plaster mix if the mix was made in a refuse dump outside the city. With reference to what these alterations mean, she says that the most we can say is that "the family who occupied this house were slightly more wealthy than the rest."[85]

Strange is right to judge Taylor's argument as difficult to accept. "It is simpler," he says, "to argue that the lamp fragments date the plaster than to argue that the lamp fragments were kept around for two or even three centuries and then used in the plaster."[86] The excavators' dating of the first alterations to Room 1 appears sound. As Taylor notes, it is possible that these renovations simply indicate the unique wealth of its Jewish occupants. The question, however, is why this particular room was plastered, painted, and

---

beneath Bed of Stones A (fourth century) and thus between where the superimposed layers of plaster pavements are. Thus, Taylor argues that the unique layers of plastering of Room 1 could not have happened before the third century and likely not until the fourth. Taylor, however, does not give a citation of Loffreda on this point, and I have not been able to find Loffreda's own words on this third-century pottery in any of his Italian or English publications. This is what he says in his original publication of the Capernaum ceramics data about floors plastered over Bed of Stones B: "Fra la massicciata A e la massicciata B compare una serie di pavimenti in batturo di calce. Questi si sono preservati specialmente nel settore orientale dell'ambiente. L'unica testimonianza del livello di occupazione è data da una trentina di frammenti minutissimi di lucerne erodiane inglobati nei sottili strati di calce. Questo fatto sta ad indicare che i suddetti pavimenti furono mantenuti scrupolosamente puliti. Appartengono al medesimo strato due lucerne erodiane ritrovate fra i blocchi di basalto del muro orientale e un frammento di misura in pietra dolce. La lucerna n. 6093 [. . .] è completa, mentre dell'altra [. . .] si é preservato soltanto il fondo." See S. Loffreda, *Cafarnao II: La ceramica* (Jerusalem: Francescan, 1974), 116. Giving Taylor the benefit of the doubt, that Loffreda does say what she says he says, it would seem that Taylor has mistaken Loffreda's first- to third-century date range (probably more specifically 70–270 CE; see Loffreda, *Cafarnao VI*, 265, specifically table 14, where he dates the pottery types found in Locus 1.5, the layer above Bed of Stones B [first century] and below Bed of Stones A [fourth century]) to mean that he found specific pieces of pottery actually dating from the first, second, and third centuries. This is why Taylor seems shocked to find fragments of Herodian oil lamps in plaster that she assumes must have been laid *after* the third century. But Loffreda was likely referring to pottery that, within his typology of ceramics, could fit *anywhere between* the first and third centuries. The fragments of Herodian oil lamps, which cannot date any later than the early second century, thus allowed Loffreda to date the pottery and the superimposed layers of lime plaster pavements between Bed of Stones B (first century) and Bed of Stones A (fourth century) to the late first or early second century.

85. Taylor, *Christians and the Holy Places*, 284.
86. Strange, "Archaeological Evidence of Jewish Believers?" 729–730 n. 77.

kept meticulously clean and absolutely no other room in the house or in the entire ancient village. It seems easier to infer that Room 1 was set apart from the rest of the housing complex from the time of the late first or early second century for special use by some of Capernaum's local Jewish villagers.[87]

The question, of course, is what this "special use" was. It is abundantly clear that, in Phase 2 of its history (late fourth to mid-fifth century), the room, having been converted into a so-called *domus ecclesia*,[88] was used as a gathering space by Christ-followers, certainly by pilgrims but likely by locals as well.[89] The

---

87. Capernaum in the first and early second centuries was entirely Jewish. M. Chancey, *The Myth of a Gentile Galilee*, 101–105, includes Capernaum among those villages in the Galilee that have very little evidence of a non-Jewish presence. Jewish stone vessels were discovered around the areas of the synagogue and the "House of Peter," demonstrating that Jewish purity was a concern for at least some of the town's inhabitants. Chancey argues throughout his book that non-Jews were a small minority in the Galilee, especially before the First Revolt. See also S. L. Mattila, "Capernaum, Village of Naḥum," 217–257. Cf. J. C. H. Laughlin, "Capernaum: From Jesus' Time and After," 54–61, who suggests that the structure under a Roman bath (dated second to third century) uncovered in the eastern part of the village might be another Roman bath and indicate the presence of non-Jews in Capernaum in the first century. However, (1) Roman-style baths do not immediately indicate the presence of non-Jews, and (2) even if there was a non-Jewish population, the evidence, as of now, continues to suggest a sizable Jewish majority in Capernaum. See also A. Killebrew who distinguishes between Greco-Roman cities with populations of pagans and Jews, and Jewish villages, which "tended to be more homogenous in their social, economic, and religious make-up, usually comprising large extended families with strong kinship ties." A. Killebrew, "Village and Countryside," in *The Oxford Handbook of Jewish Daily Life in Roman Palestine*, ed. C. Hezser (Oxford: Oxford University Press, 2010), 189–209 (194–195).

88. Phase 2 involved some major architectural changes within *insula* 1. First, the *insula* was set apart from the rest of the village by a quadrilateral enclosure wall with a perimeter of 112.25 meters. The focal point of this quadrilateral structure is clearly Room 1. Second, while three original walls from Phase 1 were left standing, the room itself was given a new polychrome pavement, a plastered arch that ran north to south and divided the room into two subunits, and a new roof. Notably, no benches or columns were added, which might suggest, along with the enclosure wall, that the space was not public in nature during Phase 2. The kind of architecture indicated here seems to stand somewhere between the public and the private/domestic, perhaps similar to the sort of architecture that could be used by Greco-Roman associations in antiquity. Third, a variety of colors and geometric shapes were used to decorate the room's plastered walls. These changes suggest that the formal status of Room 1 as a gathering space had increased significantly by the late fourth century. For the architectural description, see Loffreda, *Capharnaum*, 58 and my discussion in chapter 4.

89. The late fourth-century building, like other analogous Christian buildings such as in Dura Europos and Kefar 'Othnay, remained embedded in the local landscape, and there is nothing to suggest that it was used only by pilgrims. The fact that we see non-local expressions of Christ-belief from pilgrims to Capernaum (see note below) does not immediately exclude the idea that local Christ-followers also used the building. The interaction between local and

Jewish Christ-Followers in Capernaum

Image 3.4. Some fragments of the wall graffiti from Room 1.

From Loffreda, *Cafarnao V*, 67 (DF 60). Image used with permission.

testimony of Egeria[90] and fragments of wall graffiti inscribed with expressions of Christ-belief root this claim in evidence.[91] The issue that remains is, again,

---

nonlocal expressions of religion is quite the case today in contexts where famous churches attract pilgrims from around the world yet simultaneously serve a local worshiping community. On Capernaum in comparison to Dura Europos and Kefar 'Othnay, see Runesson and Cirafesi, "Art and Architecture," 151–200.

90. Egeria apparently visited the site while on her travels throughout Palestine (ca. 380 CE). She says, "In Capernaum, however, out of the house of the chief apostle an *ecclesia* was made, whose walls are still standing today as they were" (translation mine; Latin reads: *In Capharnaum autem ex domo apostolorum principis ecclesia facta est, cuius parietes usque hodie ita stant, sicut fuerunt*; *CSEL* 39:112–13). Egeria is discussed further in the next chapter.

91. Testa identified 151 fragments in Greek, thirteen in Syriac, nine in Aramaic (depending, of course, on whether one accepts Taylor's rereading and basic dismissal of these fragments; see below), and two in Latin. See Loffreda, *Capharnaum*, 60. While all 175 fragments are

whether we should interpolate continuity in the room's use between Phase 1 and Phase 2 or discontinuity. While they will be considered in more detail in the next chapter, taking a closer look at the wall graffiti might help us here as well.

Corbo, Loffreda, and Testa based their theory that Room 1 was used as a Christ-oriented gathering space already in Phase 1 (ca. late first to early second century) largely on their interpretation of the wall graffiti. Critics of their theory, however, have assumed with little to no argument that all the "Christian graffiti" date only to the fourth century.[92] Taylor does not appear to reckon with the date of the graffiti at all;[93] Snyder claims that "an examination of the graffiti, many left by pilgrims, indicates that all are later than the 'peace,'" although there is no "examination" to be found in the two paragraphs he devotes to the Capernaum remains;[94] and L. Michael White asserts inaccurately that "all the graffiti analyzed by Testa point to a fourth-century date."[95] While Testa did, indeed, assign many of the graffiti, especially those employing *nomina sacra*, to the fourth century (and after), he also assigned some to the third century, using especially the epigraphic data from Dura Europos for comparison, and he even assigned some to as early as the late second century.[96] Admittedly, dating inscriptions such as these is notoriously

---

difficult to interpret, some inscriptions are, indeed, clearer than others, and there is at least a portion that seems to reflect Christ-oriented language and so demonstrate the room's use by Christ-oriented groups. Among them there are, according to Testa's reconstruction and analysis, a number of interesting portrayals of Jesus. For example, he appears to be addressed as Χ(ριστ)Ε Θ(εέ), "Christ, god" in no. 44, a graffito that Testa puts within the trajectory of similar *nomina sacra* usage in the fourth and fifth centuries. Testa also reads graffito no. 89 as an address to Κ(ύρι)Ε Ι(ησού)Σ Χ(ριστ)Ε, "Lord Jesus Christ," favoring a comparison with third-century *NOMINA SACRA* found at Dura Europos. And he has "no doubt" that graffito no. 94 should be read as a pilgrim's dedication ΥΨΙΣΤ(Ω) ΧΟ ΣΩΤ(ηρι), "to the Most High, to Christ, Savior." Strange, "Archaeological Evidence of Jewish Believers?" 730, confirms.

92. White, *Texts and Monuments*, 156–157, 157 n. 56, 159; Taylor, *Holy Places*, 293–294; Adams, *Earliest*.

93. Both in her book (Taylor, *Holy Places*, 284) and her earlier article ("Capernaum and its 'Jewish–Christians': A Re-Examination of the Franciscan Excavations," *BAIAS* 9 [1989–90]: 7–28 [19]), she introduces the graffiti as "the graffiti found on the plaster of the walls of the '*domus ecclesia*' [. . .]," which seems to imply that she takes all the graffiti as a product of the fourth century or later.

94. Snyder, *Ante Pacem*, 136.

95. White, *Texts and Monuments*, 157 n. 56. White's mistake is noted by Riesner, "Early House Churches," 177. Unfortunately, White's error is repeated in Adams, *Earliest*, 107.

96. For example, with reference to some of the Greek graffiti, Testa, *Cafarnao*, 4:81: "L'analisi delle iscrizioni ci ha messo di fronte una scritta del periodo imperiale, dal II secolo

difficult, and it, of course, does not mean that Testa's dating is necessarily correct. In my view, however, historians should take his dating as their point of departure until evidence can be marshaled that suggests those dates must be revised. While Taylor's work and Strange's review of Testa's volume have shown that there is plenty of reason to doubt some of Testa's specific reconstructions and interpretations, no arguments have been presented that undermine his dating of the graffiti.[97]

On the basis of the late first and early second century renovations to Room 1 and, now, the earliest graffiti, we have reason to believe that Room 1 was used as a gathering space for Christ-followers beginning sometime in the second century. But what about the question of specifically *Jewish* Christ-followers? Particularly important to the Bagatti-Testa approach to this question was Testa's identification of nine Aramaic graffiti, which he supposed confirmed that local Jewish Christ-followers used the building. In arguing against Testa's theory, Taylor follows up on comments first made by Strange in his review of Testa's volume, that some of the graffiti identified by Testa as Aramaic could very well be misread *Greek* when turned upside down or read backwards.[98] Taylor goes further and suggests that "most of the alleged Aramaic graffiti are quite clearly Greek, and among those that are doubtful, it would be presumptuous to suggest that they are Aramaic purely because of their obscurity."[99] The significance of this is that, for Taylor, the use of Greek demonstrates that Room 1 was visited by "those from afar" rather than local Aramaic Jewish Christ-followers.[100] However, in his most recent engagement

---

avanzato alla prima metà del IV, con il suo *floruit* nel III" (italics original); and Corbo, *Cafarnao*, 1:106: "le iscrizioni piu antiche affidate alle pareti intonacate della sala venerata, vanno datate fra la fine del secondo e gli inizi del terzo secolo." I am thus uncertain why Loffreda asserts in *Capharnaum*, 60, that the oldest graffiti are dated to the third century.

97. Even Strange, "Capernaum and Herodium (Part 2)," 64–69, in his tough criticism of Testa's work on the graffiti, never explicitly disputes Testa's dating. For example, while Strange disputes the specific transcription and interpretation Testa gives of fragment no. 105, Strange seems to accept Testa's dating of it between 165 CE to the mid-third century.

98. J. F. Strange, "The Capernaum and Herodium Publications (Part 2)," *BASOR* 233 (1979): 63–69 (66–67). Pages 64–69 provide extensive criticism of Testa's entire volume: E. Testa, *Cafarnao IV: I graffiti della casa di S. Pietro* (Jerusalem: Franciscan, 1972).

99. Taylor, *Christians in the Holy Places*, 287.

100. Taylor, *Christians and the Holy Places*, 274, followed by Zangenberg, "Galilean Silence," 106. This assertion, that the use of Greek immediately implies visitation from non-Jewish Christians "from afar" is strange. As has been known for quite some time, there is an abundance of evidence that shows that Jews from the Second Temple period through

with the Capernaum graffiti (in 2007), Strange himself argues that Taylor went too far: "Taylor dismisses most of the Aramaic as mis-read Greek. That is possibly true—maybe even certainly true in a very few cases, but not for Nos. 100 and 103."[101] The two fragments referenced here by Strange (considered by him to be in Hebrew, not Aramaic) were dated by Testa to the second to third century and reconstructed to read צפראת ("Sepphorean")[102] and גשה אמשך

---

late antiquity used Greek. Examples: Greek inscriptions from the Second Temple period (e.g., *CIJ* 2.1402; *CIJ* 2.1400; Jerusalem); second-century Greek papyri from the Judean desert (e.g., *P. Yadin* *52 [also known as 5/6 *Hev* 52 and *SB* VIII]; *P. Yadin* 18; *P. Hev/Se* gr 60; *P. Hev/Se* gr 63); Greek inscriptions on mosaic floors in synagogues in late antiquity; Greek inscriptions naming rabbis from Bet She'arim; and, not least, a Greek donor inscription on a column in Capernaum's limestone synagogue (ca. fifth or sixth century) (there is an Aramaic inscription from the Byzantine period on another of the synagogue's columns). There is a similar assumption pertaining to the use of Syriac in some of the graffiti, that is, that the use of Syriac must imply that the user was a non-Jewish Christian from abroad. While Syriac was used by Palestinian Christians (a dialect known as Christian Palestinian Aramaic, with a script almost identical to Estrangelo) starting in the fifth century CE, there is a possibility that some Palestinian Jews had adopted Syriac as their dialect of Aramaic one or two centuries before this (see M. Morgenstern "Christian Palestinian Aramaic," in *The Semitic Languages*, ed. S. Weninger [Berlin: De Gruyter, 2012], 628–37). In *b. Sotah* 49b, Rabbi Judah (second to third century) says that Jews in the land of Israel should not speak "Syriac" (סורסי) but rather Hebrew or Greek, whereas Rav Yosef rules that Jews in Babylonia should not speak "Aramaic" (ארמי) but rather Hebrew or Persian. It is hard to know precisely what languages (and accompanying scripts) are being referred to in this text from the Bavli. If סורסי here refers generally to "Aramaic" (Jastrow, *s.v*) one might ask why, after centuries of use by Jews in the land of Israel (and in the Tanak), Rabbi would suddenly object to its use. Additionally, סורסי here seems distinguished from ארמי, a term that can also simply refer to "Aramaic" (Jastrow, *s.v.*). I suggest, then, that סורסי in this passage is referring specifically to Syriac as a distinct dialect of Aramaic. Jews appear to have spoken or at least been familiar with other dialects of Aramaic spoken in Syrian regions (e.g., Palmyrene [*CIIP* no. 1120]). While Syriac quickly emerged as the dialect of Syrian Christianity, it must have also been an attractive dialect for Jews, perhaps including Jewish Christ-followers, in the Syro-Palestinian region. Why else would Rabbi Judah make such a ruling against its use by Jews in the land? It is possible, then, that *b. Sotah* 49b represents a ruling that Jews in the land should not use Syriac precisely because of its particularl associations with the Jesus movement, including Jewish Christ-followers. All of this is to say, simply, that associating the Syriac graffiti from Room 1 with non-Jewish "pilgrim Christianity" is an assumption that could be viewed differently. On Judaism's close interactions with the Syriac Jesus movement, see M. Bar-Asher Siegal, "Judaism and Syriac Christianity," in *The Syriac World*, ed. D. King (London: Routledge, 2018), 146–157.

101. Strange, "Archaeological Evidence of Jewish Believers?" 731.

102. Testa, *Cafarnao IV*, 97, 100. If Testa (and Strange) is right, then an inscription left in Hebrew or Aramaic by a Sepphorean Christ-follower in Capernaum is indeed an interesting connection between the two towns.

("Come near [and] I may touch you"), respectively. While these reconstructed words and phrases, and their meaning, are certainly debatable since they are so hard to read, Strange is right to raise the question of why Hebrew letters appear among the graffiti *at all*. "The simplest response," he says, "is that these are a few people for whom Hebrew and perhaps Aramaic are mother tongues. The presence of Hebrew or Aramaic graffiti tends to confirm the hypothesis of a Jewish Christian presence among the pilgrims at Capernaum."[103] Indeed, the presence of Hebrew or Aramaic would even meet one of Taylor's criteria for identifying Jewish Christ-followers as noted above.

Summary of the Sources

The textual and archaeological sources, when taken together, leave us with the following nodes of evidence, established (in Collingwood's terms) as "relatively fixed" points within our web of construction:

1. Literary evidence from *Qoh. Rab.* 1:8 present a story about Capernaum's Jewish Christ-followers in a sixth-century polemical setting but that might very well reflect a historical tradition about a second-century encounter.
2. A room in a house—Room 1—uniquely renovated in the late first or early second century, kept free of all domestic objects, and very likely used by local Christ-followers, which is supported by the diachronic evidence from Phase 2.
3. Christ-oriented graffiti from Room 1, which, according to Testa, emerge in the second to third century onward. At least two fragments contain Hebrew or Aramaic characters, which suggests Jewish identity.

Surely there is no smoking gun, no slam-dunk piece of evidence that allows one to make an absolute argument about the presence of Jewish Christ-followers in Capernaum before Constantine. Taylor's work and the work of others have appropriately cautioned us against this. But, in my view, the sources are not "silent" and the evidence, as circumstantial as it might be, is strong enough that the hypothesis should not be characterized as a "myth."

---

103. Strange, "Archaeological Evidence of Jewish Believers," 731.

While, in the approach taken in this essay, we are justified in inferring from the data that Jesus-oriented Jews were present in the town before the fourth century, we are not justified, as Taylor demonstrated so well, in inferring anything about them as a "sect" with a particular theological outlook. On the other hand, I suggest that the data especially from the early archaeology of Room 1 does indeed allow us to infer constructively some things about Capernaum's Jewish Christ-followers regarding not their "sectarian" identity but rather their institutional setting. To this construction I now turn.

4. Constructing Capernaum's Institutional and Socioreligious Setting

When Room 1 was renovated in the late first or early second century, it no longer functioned strictly as domestic space, although it remained architecturally connected to a private housing complex; this is suggested by the complete absence in the room of domestic vessel remains.[104] These renovations evidently converted the room, as argued above, into an assembly area for Christ-followers, perhaps analogously to the Christ-oriented assembly halls set within altered domestic spaces at Dura Europos and Kefar 'Othnay.[105] On the other hand, as an altered domestic space, Room 1 was clearly not designed in this period to be a public building or the socioreligious center of Capernaum's village life.[106] That role was filled by Capernaum's synagogue just twenty-five meters to the north.

As discussed in chapter 2, there is solid combined archaeological and literary evidence to justify the historical claim that, underneath the limestone

---

104. Noted by Meyers and Strange, *Archaeology*, 129.

105. Adaptation of private homes to allow for semipublic gatherings was common in the Roman world, as L. Michael White has argued in *Building God's House in the Roman World: Architectural Adaptation among Pagans, Jews, and Christians* (Baltimore: Johns Hopkins University Press, 1990), and more recently in "Early Christian Architecture: The First Five Centuries," in *The Early Christian World*, 673–696. On Dura Europos and Kefar 'Othnay, see Runesson and Cirafesi, "Art and Architecture." While, in its first phase, Room 1 did not yet have the kind of formalized architecture of assembly that these other structures had (e.g., arch with pilasters, fixed installations), already in the late-first- or early-second-century Room 1, as a room set apart for special gathering for ritual activity, was certainly of the same genre of meeting space.

106. I would suggest that Room 1 never obtained this status, even in its transformation into an octagonal church in the fifth or sixth century.

synagogue from the fifth or sixth century, there was a public synagogue that stood in the early decades of the first century, which was then expanded sometime in the late third or fourth century. This synagogue would have been the meeting space of the popular assembly in Capernaum, just like any other Jewish town or village in Roman Palestine. It would have operated as the sociospatial setting for a variety of administrative and socioreligious activities, such as adjudication on legal matters, execution of punitive sentences like floggings,[107] Torah reading and its interpretation,[108] and political disputes.[109] In principle, it could have also functioned as the village's treasury and its library. Yet, the central point is that such synagogues were controlled by the people of a village, the village masses, and, as such, they did not belong to a particular group.[110] Rather, public synagogues were precisely the settings where people competed for influence within Jewish society.

We should recall, however, that, on the other hand, were the Jewish "association synagogues," which were organizationally modeled upon the kinds of membership networks we see in Greco-Roman associations.[111] This type of synagogue was not a public institution but rather was defined by reference to, for example, shared occupations, social practices, neighborhoods, geoethnic connections, or shared ideology, such as devotion to a particular cult or philosophy. A particularly interesting example in light of our discussion of Room 1 in this chapter is Philo's description of a Jewish religiophilosophical association called the Therapeutae in his *De vita contemplativa* 25–33.[112] Here Philo

---

107. E.g., OG Sus 28; Matt 10:17; 23:34; *m. Mak.* 3:12.

108. E.g., Luke 4:16–31; Acts 15:21; Josephus, *Ant.* 16:42–43. See Runesson, *Origins of the Synagogue*, 193–253; Runesson, "Synagogues without Rabbis or Christians?" 162–163, where he suggests the centrality of Torah reading in public synagogues based upon the archaeology and architecture of first-century synagogues in the land of Israel. On the historical plausibility of Luke 4:16–31, see J. Ryan, *The Role of the Synagogue*, 172–183.

109. Josephus, *Vita* 276–281, 294–295.

110. See, again, Josephus, *Vita* 277–303; Luke 4:16–31; *m. Meg.* 3:1.

111. P. Richardson, "Early Synagogues as *Collegia*," ch. 6; Richardson, *Building Jewish*, 111–134, 207–221; P. Harland, *Associations, Synagogues, and Congregations*; R. Ascough, "Paul, Synagogues, and Associations," 27–52; and R. Last, "The Other Synagogues," 213–231, *et passim*; Runesson, "Synagogues without Rabbis or Christians?"

112. On this text as evidence for association synagogues, see *ASSB* no. 160. For a thorough critical review of scholarship on Philo's description of the Therapeutae, see R. S. Kraemer, *Unreliable Witnesses: Religion, Gender, and History in the Greco-Roman Mediterranean* (Oxford: Oxford University Press, 2011), 57–116.

describes individual rituals performed in what he calls a "sanctuary" (σεμνεῖον), apparently some sort of room within each private house that was set apart for special nondomestic use (*Contempl.* 25). Into these spaces, he says, group members bring nothing of daily life, such as food, drink, or anything else that supports the needs of the body. Instead, they devote themselves completely to the study of the laws, the prophets, and the hymns in order to grow in knowledge and piety. Then, every seventh day, there is a common gathering of the association in a κοινὸν σεμνεῖον, a larger double-chambered structure composed of two houses separated by a single wall, which divided men and women (*Contempl.* 32–33).

Because, beginning in the late first or early second century, Room 1 seems to have been altered to accommodate a gathering of local Jewish Christ-followers, and because the public synagogue across the street would have met the sociopolitical and civic needs of Capernaum, Runesson is, in my view, right to suggest that Room 1 had become the assembly space of a Jesus-oriented Jewish association, perhaps along similar lines as the situation of Philo's Therapeutae. Yet, drawing a distinction between Room 1 and the public synagogue on the basis of institutional function does not mean that we should assume that Capernaum's Christ association did not participate in the public assembly just twenty-five meters away. Indeed, we have evidence from Greco-Roman and Jewish antiquity that associations could do just this. For example, Peter Rhodes has shown that clubs and associations could work, sometimes rather hard, to sway the political agenda of a city's public assembly to fall in line with their own.[113] In Roman Palestine, some Jewish associations, such as the Pharisees, could work closely with public officials such as archons and chief priests to influence popular assemblies in Jerusalem.[114] According to the Gospels, while Jesus and his earliest followers had their own association gatherings, they also interacted with other Jews in public synagogues.[115]

---

113. P. Rhodes, "Demagogues and Demos in Athens," *Polis* 33, no. 2 (2016): 264. Cf. also Acts 19:23–41.

114. See, e.g., the story in Josephus, *War* 2:411.

115. On Capernaum, see Mark 1:29 and 2:1–2, where Jesus and his followers are depicted as moving between the public synagogue and their own gathering, which met in the house of Peter and Andrew.

These interactions in civic spaces between Jesus-oriented Jews and non-Jesus-oriented Jews continued well into the first centuries of the Common Era.[116] Eventually they involved competitive engagements between Jewish Christ-followers and members of the emerging rabbinic movement "over how 'Judaism' should best be defined and lived."[117] Thus, in my view, despite the possibility of opposition from members of the early rabbinic movement—still very much a marginal movement in these early centuries with no demonstrable authority in public synagogues—Capernaum's Jewish Christ-followers were still active in public village life. As such, they would have had access, as all other Jews in town, to their village's public institution. As Christ-followers, however, they would have formed an association *within* the larger public assembly and sought to influence it in accordance with their socioreligious views.

The point to make here, then, is that an association was not a "sect" in the sense of a secluded group disconnected from the public politics of village life. Indeed, associations could be quite influential, were they able to accrue the right kind of social capital. If, for example, the Gospels of Matthew and Mark do indeed reflect a Galilean context of a segment or two of the postwar Jesus movement,[118] and if the comment in Acts 9:31 that claims Christ-groups had "multiplied" throughout the Galilee is not Luke's mere narrative embellishment, then it might be possible to claim that Jewish Christ-associations in the region were actually making headway in their attempt, in competition with non-Jesus-oriented Jews, to influence the larger Jewish community by means of their activity in the public assembly. Such a socioreligious setting would also make sense for the story of the Capernaum *minim* in *Qoh Rab.* 1:8: the second-century tradition that the redactors are building upon reflects a rabbinic polemic against a Christ-association that was influencing—or from the rabbis' perspective, *enticing*—the Jewish popular assembly of the town.

---

116. On interactions between Jesus-oriented Jews and rabbinic Jews in the first few centuries CE, see Zetterholm, "Alternate Visions of Judaism"; and A. Runesson, "What Does It Mean to Read New Testament Texts 'within Judaism'?" *NTS* 69 (2023): 299–312 (304–305).

117. Runesson, "New Testament Texts," 305.

118. See note 41 above.

5. Conclusion

Whereas scholars have been right to push against the Bagatti-Testa model of isolated "Jewish Christian" sects with distinct theological characteristics roaming about the Galilee, some scholars, in my view, have gone too far in suggesting that the only type of early Christianity we have evidence for is of a non-Jewish "international" or "pilgrim" type that begins after Constantine. When the pre-fourth-century texts and archaeology are coordinated, the historical web, the imaginative picture of the past that has emerged in this study is one of an association of Jewish Christ-followers who were engaged in the life of Capernaum's Jewish public assembly. This, of course, does not preclude the idea of an increasing flow of non-Jewish Christian pilgrims into the village; indeed, we will see this phenomenon at play in the following chapter. But this type of Christ-orientation—the gentile pilgrim—was not the predominate one in pre-fourth-century Capernaum. In this period, Jesus-oriented Jews were the main category of Christ-follower and thus Jewish–Christian relations in Capernaum were still a mainly intra-Jewish affair.

CHAPTER FOUR

Architecturalizing Jesus in the Fourth Century

Jewish–Christian Relations and the Capernaum Christaeum

1. Introduction

AT THE TIME of Constantine the Great's conversion to Christianity in the year 312, Room 1 of Capernaum's *insula sacra* was still, and rather simply, a room in a house. To be sure, it was a room set apart. It had been renovated in the late first or early second century, painted with layers of white plaster, and kept free from all domestic vessels. In the third century, it was decorated with painted plaster on its inner walls and emerged as a tourist site for a few nonlocal pilgrims, perhaps especially from Syria.[1] But, by the start of the fourth century, Room 1 had been embedded, cloaked, and camouflaged within a domestic context for the better part of two centuries. For over two hundred years, it had spatialized local memories of Jesus tradition by shaping and conditioning these memories visually through its vernacular architecture.[2]

The rise of Constantinian Christianity did not change this situation, at least not immediately. Indeed, from the archaeological record, Corbo and

---

1. On the decorated plaster of the inner walls of Room 1 in the third century, see S. Loffreda, *Recovering Capharnaum*, Studium Biblicum Franciscanum Guides 1 (Jerusalem: Franciscan, 1993), 58–60.

2. Paul Oliver defines "vernacular architecture" as the following: "Vernacular architecture comprises the dwellings and all other buildings of the people. Related to their environmental contexts and available resources, they are customarily owner- or community-built, utilizing traditional technologies. All forms of vernacular architecture are built to meet specific needs, accommodating the values, economies, and ways of living of the cultures that produce them" (*Built to Meet Needs: Cultural Issues in Vernacular Architecture* [Oxford: Architectural Press, 2006], 30). On the interpretation of the history of Room 1 as the reception of a Jesus tradition, see A. Runesson and W. V. Cirafesi, "Art and Architecture," 151–200.

Loffreda paint a picture of continuity in the material and spatial character of Room 1 between the late first and fourth centuries.[3] As Corbo notes, even as Room 1 grew into a cultic gathering space, in the following centuries the larger *insula* that encompassed it "continued to throb with the ordinary life of men."[4] In other words, by the early fourth century, Room 1 had not yet developed into a public attraction for early Christian travelers. It was still, and simply, a room in a house, with the cultic and the mundane existing side-by-side. The fact that Room 1 was still, toward the end of Constantine's life (d. 337), couched or even, perhaps, hidden within domestic space might explain why the earliest Christian pilgrim account, the Bordeaux Pilgrim (ca. 333), makes no mention of Capernaum, and why, perhaps, Eusebius says nothing about churches or even a Christian presence in his entry on Capernaum in his *Onomasticon* (ca. 326–330).[5] Furthermore, Capernaum in this period remained a predominately Jewish town. Thus, while Room 1 seems to have continued primarily to serve as the gathering place of a local Jewish Christ association, we might, at the same time, reasonably assume that *insula* 1 continued to be occupied by houses owned by members of the local Jewish population. In other words, before and after the turn of the fourth century, Jewish–Christian relations in Capernaum remained an intra-Jewish affair.

However, sometime in the fourth century—Corbo (mid-fourth century) and Loffreda (late fourth century) have differed in their dating—the architectural and social context of Room 1 began to change. This chapter explores these changes and interprets them historically within the broader context of the fluid and unstable nature of Jewish–Christian relations in the late Roman and early Byzantine East. My main argument here is that the fourth century architectural changes to Room 1 and its larger *insula* reflect the intersection of local Jewish "vernacular" modes of remembering Jesus, on the one hand, with the need to accommodate the rise of non-Jewish Christian pilgrimage to Capernaum on the other.[6] I will suggest that the evolution of Room 1 in

---

3. Loffreda, *Recovering Capharnaum*, 58; V. Corbo, *The House of Saint Peter at Capharnaum* (Jerusalem: Franciscan, 1972), 54.

4. Corbo, *House of Saint Peter*, 54.

5. It should be noted, however, that, in *Onomasticon*, Eusebius is generally sparse in his remarks on Christianity and says very little about Constantine's building projects in fourth-century Palestine.

6. See further discussion below. For now, on vernacular and official modes of cultural memory, and their coming together in the construction of "public memory," see J. Ryan,

Architecturalizing Jesus in the Fourth Century

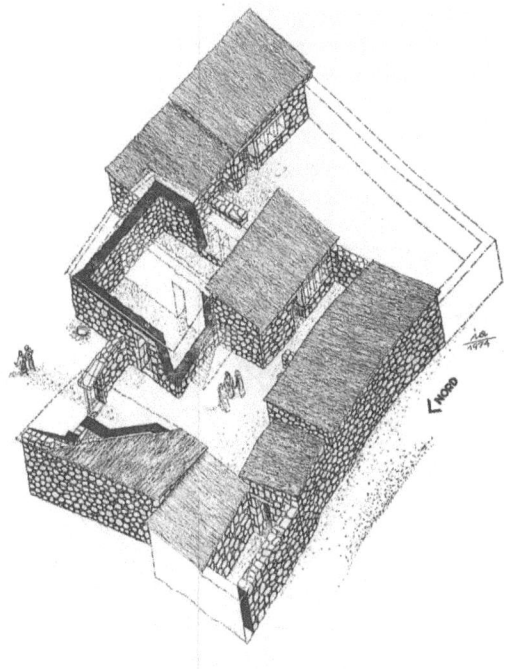

Image 4.1. Reconstruction of *Insula* 1 in the early Roman period (first to second century CE).

Image from Corbo, *Cafarno I*, Tavola X. Used here with permission.

the fourth century gave rise to the entanglement of an emerging non-Jewish Christian identity in the village with the town's Jewish past and present—an entanglement that only became problematic for Byzantine elites in later centuries.

2. *Insula* 1 as Vernacular Architecture

"Following an unbroken sequence of occupation," Loffreda says, "the insula sacra underwent major changes in the late fourth century AD."[7]

From the Passion to the Holy Sepulcher: Memories of Jesus in Place, Pilgrimage, and Early Commemorative Churches over the First Three Centuries, The Reception of Jesus in the First Three Centuries 7 (London: T&T Clark, 2021), 12–14, 185–195 (on Capernaum specifically).

7. Loffreda, *Capharnaum*, 58. I note again here that Loffreda and Corbo (*Cafarnao I*, 71–73) have differed in their dating of these changes, and neither archaeologist provides a detailed enough stratigraphy of Room 1 for the historian to draw a hard and fast conclusion. The

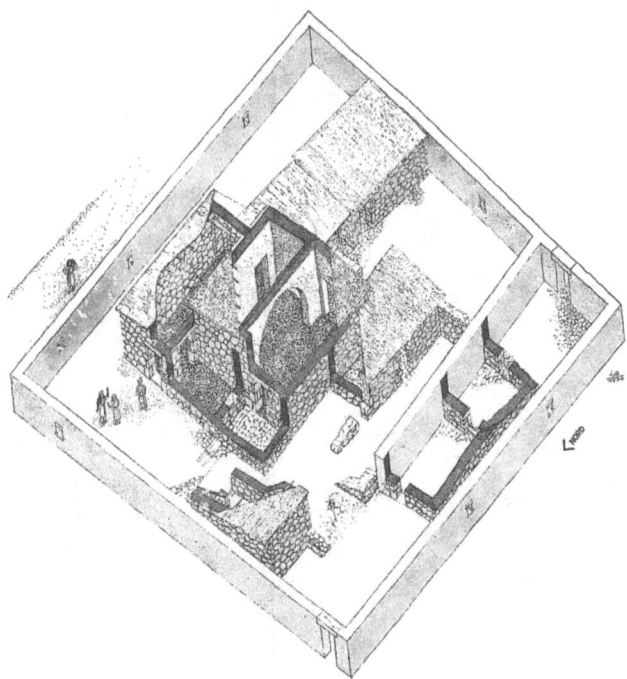

Image 4.2. Reconstruction of *Insula* 1, after renovations in the mid- to late fourth century CE.

Image from Corbo, *Cafarno I*, Tavola VIII. Used here with permission.

While interpreting these material and spatial changes will be crucial for our understanding of social change in the village, it is, in fact, just as important to consider what did *not* change at this point the history of *insula* 1. Three of Room 1's original walls were left standing (the southern, eastern, and western walls),[8] and no fixed benches, columns, or interior furniture were added. Unlike the early Christ-oriented buildings at Dura

---

mid- to late fourth century is the best we can do at this point, but it will not affect greatly the main argument of this chapter.

8. The fourth-century pilgrim Egeria, who visited Capernaum ca. 380 CE, seems to have known about these original walls when she said, "In Capernaum, however, out of the house of the chief apostle a church was made, whose walls are still standing today as they were" (Latin reads: *In Capharnaum autem ex domo apostolorum principis ecclesia facta est, cuius parietes usque hodie ita stant, sicut fuerunt*; CSEL 39:112–113). There are some critical issues with this text that will be dealt with later in the chapter. The

Europos (third century) and Kirk-Bizzeh (early fourth century) in Syria, and Kefar 'Othnay in Palestine (third century), there is no evidence in the Capernaum building of specifically Christian ritual architecture such as a baptistery, eucharist table, ambo, or cathedra. While, as we will see shortly, Room 1 did, indeed, transform into a more focalized assembly space, the fourth-century renovators, nevertheless, embedded these changes within the existing built environment. *Insula* 1 continued to encompass occupied dwellings, although it is difficult to know precisely how many, and Room 1 continued to relate spatially and materially to its domestic context, being far from the public monumental structure that would stand in its place in the 5th and 6th centuries. As an expression of a link with the domestic environment, which constituted local age-old memories about the life of Jesus in a Jewish house in a Jewish town, the building that emerges here in fourth-century Capernaum was not enclosed in public monumental form. That is, the fourth-century changes to *insula* 1 were not about creating a unique edifice that was meant to break visually, spatially, and culturally from its built environment. Rather, they were about rearticulating and expanding the vernacular architecture of Room 1.

This rearticulation and expansion involved both artistic and spatial elements.[9] Room 1, measuring 5.8 meters by 6.45 meters, was given a new polychrome pavement, and a variety of colors and geometric shapes were used to decorate its plastered walls. Unlike the fifth- or sixth-century octagonal church, the decorative program of the fourth-century building did not include human or animal representations.[10] The northern wall of Room 1 was rebuilt, and a plastered arch spanning from north–south divided the room into two subunits and supported a new roof made of strong mortar. The piers of this central arch, which were found *in situ*, received two superimposed layers of plaster. Immediately to the east of Room 1, an atrium with white plastered pavement and a northeastern side chamber were added. However, perhaps the most significant

---

question of how Egeria came to know that the walls were original to the ancient house will also be addressed.

9. The following description of the fourth century changes to *insula* 1 and Room 1 come from Loffreda, *Capharnaum*, 58–63; Corbo, *House of Saint Peter*, 53–74; and Corbo, *Cafarnao I*, 59–74.

10. The central ring of the later octagonal church features a mosaic pavement that encloses the image of a peacock. This mosaic will be discussed in the following chapter. For a description, see Corbo, *House of Saint Peter*, 14–15.

change occurred when *insula* 1 was set apart from the rest of the village by a quadrilateral enclosure wall having a perimeter of 112.25 meters. This enclosure wall had a roughly square plan and was entered from two doorways, one in the southwestern corner and another in the northwestern corner. When the wall was constructed, some houses along the western and northern sides of the *insula* were destroyed, but others to the south remained, with Room 1 clearly becoming the spatial focal point of the reorganized *insula*.

What did these changes mean on a spatial level? While the renovations to *insula* 1 and its central room did not transform them into public space—certainly not the type of space expressed in the architecture of the Constantinian basilica and concentric churches[11]—neither did they allow them to remain as they were in their earlier phase (ca. second to mid-fourth century) as a domestic space, albeit already altered in this phase. Thus, terminologically, neither "house" nor "church" adequately captures the nature of the space. The closest parallels to *insula* 1 from the late Roman world, conceptually if not architecturally, are domestic complexes that encompassed an assembly hall for a cult association. For example, *mithraea* from the second to fourth century have been found embedded in residential areas in Rome,[12] and, closer geographically to Capernaum, the buildings in Dura Europos (renovated house) and Kefar 'Othnay (purpose-built hall in a residential area) were assembly spaces for Christ groups.[13] While there are, of course, differences among them, these buildings belong, analytically speaking, to the same category of institution. That is, they all emerged within altered domestic environments and, somehow or another, functioned as the gathering spaces of associations whose members were socially connected through devotion to a particular cult.[14]

---

11. On which, see chapter 5.

12. S. L. Dyson, *Rome: A Living Portrait of an Ancient City* (Baltimore: Johns Hopkins University Press, 2010), 285–286.

13. For discussion of the Christ-oriented buildings at Dura Europos and Kefar 'Othnay, see Runesson and Cirafesi, "Art and Architecture." On the practice of adapting private houses for semipublic gatherings, see L. M. White, *Building God's House*.

14. On the architecture of public and semipublic (association) institutions in antiquity, specifically with reference to synagogues, see A. Runesson, "Synagogues without Rabbis or Christians?" 159–172. Cf. P. Richardson, "An Architectural Case for Synagogues as Associations," in *The Ancient Synagogue: From Its Origins until 200 CE*, ed. B. Olsson and M. Zetterholm, CBNTS 39 (Stockholm: Almqvist & Wiksell, 2001),

It is for this reason that Anders Runesson and I have proposed the term *christaeum* to describe the Kefar 'Othnay building,[15] and that I wish to apply it also to Room 1 at Capernaum. The term *christaeum* allows us to avoid certain assumptions that often accompany terms such as "church," "*domus ecclesia/* house-church," and "prayer hall," such as the ethnic identities of its users, their beliefs, and their rituals.[16] It also, more positively, captures several important facets of the room. It describes the character of Room 1 as an assembly space for a Christ cult, akin to other cult associations, such as *mithraeum* for Mithras or *sarapaeum* for Sarapis, but it further communicates that the room had gained certain architectural elements in its fourth-century iteration that distinguished it from its previous phase, making it no longer a usual house. While, earlier, Room 1 was set apart from the rest of the housing complex by means of its excessive plastering and its conspicuous absence of domestic objects, in its fourth-century phase the addition of the quadrilateral enclosure, the eastern atrium, and the north–south arch bifurcating the room into two subunits had set it apart spatially, transforming the entire *insula* into focalized cultic space.

Admittedly, Room 1 lacked physical features found in other cultic buildings, such as the peripheral benches and fixed central altars typical of Roman *mithraea*, or the Christian ritual architecture found at Dura Europos and Kirk-Bizzeh. But neither of these Christ-oriented buildings nor the Roman *mithraea* found in residential settings commemorated a specific spot in which the nature of the building itself was fundamental to the type of cult offered.[17] The absence of furniture and other ritual architecture in Room 1, I suggest, was intentional and served to shape one's experience of the room not simply

---

90–117. While, as noted by Taylor (*Christians and the Holy Places*, 274), *insula* 1 shows no signs of specifically Christian architecture, its function as a Christ-oriented cultic space by this time (fourth century) is clearly demonstrated by the proliferation of graffiti found in the plastered walls of Room 1. As mentioned elsewhere in this book, while the texts of the graffiti fragments are very difficult to discern—perhaps even impossible in most cases—the simple point is clear: there were graffiti etched on these walls and, in light of the diachronic history of Room 1, they are best interpreted as the markings of Christ cult devotees.

15. Runesson and Cirafesi, "Art and Architecture," 179–180.

16. Note that Taylor is also hesitant to use the term "house church" to describe Room 1 in this phase, albeit for her own reasons (see *Christians and the Holy Places*, 274).

17. See a similar argument presented in Ryan, *Memories of Jesus*, 191–192.

as a cultic space but, more specifically, as a cultic space set within its "original" historical environment, that is, as the original house of the apostle Peter. This is precisely Egeria's experience in ca. 380 CE, when she specifically mentions that the actual walls of Peter's house were still standing and were functioning as part of the building she visited. For her, there was something important about experiencing the space as authentic, as original, and as directly and tangibly tied to the time of Jesus.

The creation of a spatial experience of authenticity is not unlike when we, today, visit the houses of famous people of the past, which, while no longer real houses because they have been transformed into history museums, are nevertheless meant to be experienced as that person's "original house." Such "house museums" are carefully curated, and they methodically restrict and control the movement of their consumers (read: pilgrims), who, while walking along a preordained path, offer the "cult of commemoration" to a valorized hero(ine) from a time long ago.[18] In these spaces, memories are not simply encountered as fossilized objects but are, instead, produced, institutionalized, and take on their own social agency.[19] More will be said about Room 1 as a commemorative space below, but here we can say that in the fourth century, the room, like these house museums, was intended to be experienced as a historic house, with the use of a focalized built space carefully facilitating the movement of its users, the production of cult, and the experience of authentic sacred space. Indeed, Loffreda notes that the fourth-century additions to the *insula* shaped it into a tripartite structure comparable to the Jerusalem temple[20]: the structure moved its users in an east–west direction, from the open-air space created by the enclosure wall,[21] to entry through the eastern atrium

---

18. It is worth connecting this point to one made by Sarah Maza in her survey of the debate among modern historians about the role of heritage in historiography. She notes that some historians have argued that heritage studies often work with the goal of presenting the past as it really was, which, to the demise of history, is a way to control, hegemonize, and hierarchize a society's memory, understanding, and access to the past. See the discussion in S. Maza, *Thinking about History* (Chicago: University of Chicago Press, 2017), 130–131.

19. On the notion of the "cult of commemoration," see the discussion below on the Capernaum *christaeum* and commemoration.

20. Loffreda, *Capharnaum*, 63.

21. Taylor, *Christians and the Holy Places*, 274 has interpreted the open-air space created by the enclosure wall as "surely to accommodate the horses and donkeys of travellers, and indeed the travellers themselves." I certainly do not deny that the open-air space may have

and the eastern subunit of Room 1, through the vaulted arch, and into the western subunit of Room 1, which was the cultic focal point, as evidenced by the many graffiti fragments found in this area. But whether the renovators had the Jerusalem temple in mind, the point to make is that *insula* 1 in this period was a rearticulated house that functioned as a cult assembly hall expressed in non-monumental, vernacular architecture.

3. *Insula* 1 and the Intersection of Space and Identity

Who was responsible for the fourth-century renovations to Room 1, and who were its primary users? Loffreda's suggestion, that the spatial arrangement of *insula* 1 was designed to evoke the Jerusalem temple, is directly tied, of course, to his and the rest of the Bagatti-Testa school's view of the Judeo–Christian origins of Room 1. In this view, local Jewish Christ-followers were responsible for the first alterations to the room in the late first or early second century, having set it apart as a "venerated room" (*sala venerata*) remembered for its association with events from the life of Jesus. Nearly three centuries later, in the last quarter of the fourth century, Jewish Christ-followers local to Capernaum were likewise responsible for converting *insula* 1 into a house church and were the building's primary users.

Scholars have heavily criticized the Bagatti-Testa view on the fourth-century building. The main criticism has been that, just as there is no positive evidence that Jewish Christ-followers used Room 1 as a venerated space *before* Constantine (see chapter 3), neither is there positive evidence that Jewish Christ-followers used Room 1 as a venerated space *after* Constantine. The basic conclusion of most critics has been two-fold: (1) Christian veneration of the place began *ex nihilo* in the fourth century; and (2) *insula* 1 was built and used

---

had this practical function. But, while I am not necessarily convinced by Loffreda's interpretation that *insula* 1 was designed to evoke the Jerusalem temple, his interpretation has the benefit of seeing the space as part of a larger spatial focalization program that was meant to be experienced as a whole. Furthermore, it is not clear to me why travelers to the village would have needed wall-enclosed space such as this to accommodate their possessions. Contrary to some interpretations of this enclosure, it was clearly not a fortification wall in any period of its existence. It would have afforded no real protection from aggressors or thieves. This point, coupled with Loffreda's interpretation, leads me to suggest that the wall was never meant to keep people out but rather to create a spatial experience for people within.

exclusively as a pilgrimage center for non-Jewish Christians coming from afar. The first was the topic of chapter 3; here we need to discuss further the second, the question of the function of the renovated *insula* and the identities of its users, for this question gets to the heart of my historical construction of the building's place in Jewish–Christian relations in the fourth-century village.

There are two nodes of data pertaining to Capernaum in the fourth century, upon which scholars appear generally to agree. The first is that Capernaum remained an entirely Jewish village, just as it had been in centuries prior.[22] The second is that *insula* 1 in this period was the site of an increasing amount of Christian pilgrimage activity, which is evidenced by the presence of multilingual wall graffiti and Egeria's travel report. However, what historians have failed to agree upon is how to bring these two nodes together to construct a justifiable picture of the past: How could a Christian building be allowed to exist and operate in an entirely Jewish town at a time when anti-Jewish legislation and other types of Christian antagonism toward Jews was, in general, on the rise? As Taylor rightly mentions, there is very little evidence that fourth-century Christian authorities exercised absolute power over Jewish towns in the Galilee. The Roman church was hardly consolidated enough to govern its own constituency, let alone control the on-the-ground practices of non-Christian groups that had populated the empire for centuries.[23] True, the Palestinian Jewish community may have suffered a dreadful blow in the wake of the revolt against Gallus Caesar (351–352 CE),[24] but the Jewish Patriarchate remained intact, perhaps even quite powerful, and the Jewish community continued to be populous and influential, despite its emerging minority status.[25] Furthermore, the anti-Christian reign of Julian, although brief (361–363 CE), exemplifies Roman Christianity's fragility in

---

22. Taylor, *Christians and the Holy Places*, 288.

23. On the instability of the category of Christianity and the Roman church, especially in the fourth century, see further discussion below.

24. It should be noted, however, that the historical circumstances of the Gallus Revolt are currently shrouded in a good deal of mystery. What we can say about its causes, scope and scale, and impact on Jewish communities in Palestine in the mid-fourth century is actually quite limited. See D. Goodblatt, "The Political and Social History of the Jewish Community in the Land of Israel, c. 235–638," in *The Cambridge History of Judaism*, vol. 4, *The Late Roman–Rabbinic Period*, ed. S. T. Katz (Cambridge: Cambridge University Press, 2006), 404–431; H. Sivan, *Palestine in Late Antiquity* (Oxford: Oxford University Press, 2008), 137 n. 102, 319, and 319 n. 69.

25. See Goodblatt, "Jewish Community."

the mid-fourth century. Thus, the question for us is: If Capernaum's Jewish community had considerable autonomy at this time, why did it not mount any significant opposition to the transformation of Room 1 into a *christaeum*?

One proposal has been to suggest that Joseph of Tiberias built it. According to Epiphanius (writing in ca. 374 to 375), Joseph was a prominent Jewish man who was close to the Patriarch's circle of power until he converted to "orthodox" Christianity.[26] Sometime after his conversion, he apparently came to Emperor Constantine's notice, received the rank of *comes*, and was granted permission "to build Christ's churches in the Jewish towns and villages where no one had ever been able to found churches, since there are no Greeks, Samaritans or Christians among the population."[27] Epiphanius singles out places like Tiberias, Diocaesarea (Sepphoris), Nazareth, and Capernaum as locations that were especially strict with regard to keeping gentiles out, and we should recall from the previous chapter that when Epiphanius says that there were no Christians in these towns, he does not mean to include Jesus-oriented Jews but rather specifically has in mind non-Jewish "orthodox" Christians. After all, as Goranson has observed, Epiphanius did not consider Jewish Christ-followers as Christians in the first place.[28] Nevertheless, Epiphanius apparently names these places as the intended targets of Joseph's building activity. Yet, Tiberias is the only place about which he says anything in detail; absolutely nothing is mentioned about Joseph's actual work in Capernaum.

There are, indeed, some interesting reasons to believe that Joseph of Tiberias was responsible for the fourth-century renovations to the Capernaum *christaeum*.[29] On Corbo's dating (ca. mid-fourth century), it is possible that

---

26. For the most thorough critical discussion of the historical credibility of Epiphanius's Joseph of Tiberias story, see Stephen C. Goranson, "The Joseph of Tiberias Episode in Epiphanius: Studies in Jewish and Christian Relations" (PhD diss., Duke University, 1990), 73–125. Goranson offers a balanced appraisal, noting that, while there are certainly legendary aspects of Epiphanius's story, the basic scenario of Joseph's building activities in the Galilee is plausible and generally credible. See also Ryan, *Memories of Jesus*, 186 n. 9, who agrees.

27. *Pan.* 30.11.9–10 (trans. Williams).

28. See his extensive argument in Goranson, "Joseph of Tiberias," 73–99. Goranson is quite convinced that the *minim* mentioned in various rabbinic stories about Sepphoris, Tiberias, and Capernaum are, indeed, Jesus-oriented Jews, and that other Jesus-oriented Jewish groups were active in Galilean sites like Nazareth.

29. Oddly enough, Corbo and Taylor—who, in the end, reach wildly different historical conclusions—both posit Joseph of Tiberias as the builder of the Capernaum *christaeum*. See Corbo, *Cafarnao I*, 71–72; Taylor, *Christians and the Holy Places*, 288–290.

the renovations and Josephus's building activity were coterminous.[30] Taylor makes the potential connection between the abundance of lime plaster found in the pavement and walls of Room 1 and Epiphanius's mention that Joseph set up as many as seven lime kilns on the outskirts of Tiberias in preparation for his project.[31] A further possible connection between Epiphanius's account and the archaeology of Room 1, mentioned neither by Corbo or Taylor, is Joseph's opportunistic use of preexisting structures. According to Epiphanius, the citizens of Tiberias were trying to convert the city's old *Hadrianaeum*, which was currently unfinished, into a public bath.[32] When Joseph saw this, he "took the opportunity" to use four preexisting walls that stood to an unknown height as the starting point for his church. If Joseph was the architect of Capernaum's fourth-century *christaeum*, then his material opportunism might explain why three original walls of Room 1 were left in place during the renovations.

For Corbo, the fact that Joseph himself was a Judeo-Christian explains why the Jewish community of Capernaum mounted no serious opposition to his building. By the fourth century, Jewish Christ-followers were a sizeable group with a sizeable influence in the village and thus likely welcomed Joseph and his building project.[33] Taylor, in contrast, points out that Joseph had become, according to Epiphanius, an "orthodox" Christian, and that "a Jew who became an orthodox Christian was not, however, a Jewish-Christian by definition."[34] Thus, if anything, his "orthodox" identity would have put him at strict odds with Capernaum's Jewish community. Moreover, there is no evidence that Jesus-oriented Jews were present in the village to welcome Joseph in the first place. There must have been some reason other than Joseph's Jewish parentage that explains the apparent lack of opposition from the Jewish population at Capernaum, as well as at other locations Joseph allegedly built

---

30. It is likely that Joseph's building activity was over before ca. 355. According to Goranson, Epiphanius had met Joseph between 355–360, when Joseph was already an old man ("Joseph of Tiberias," 138). Epiphanius mentions that Joseph was already at least seventy years old when he met him in Scythopolis (*Pan.* 30.5.1).

31. *Pan.* 30.12.4. Taylor, *Christians and the Holy Places*, 288.

32. *Pan.* 30.12.2–3.

33. See Corbo, *Cafarnao I*, 71–72. While Loffreda does not think Joseph of Tiberias built the fourth-century *christaeum*, he does believe, based on the reference in *Qoh. Rabb.* 7:26, that Jesus-oriented Jews represented a sizeable portion of the Capernaum community. See Loffreda, *Recovering Capharnaum*, 30–31.

34. Taylor, *Christians and the Holy Places*, 276.

churches.³⁵ For Taylor, an economic benefit is the mostly likely explanation. Joseph had the support of the Empire, including its financial backing. Thus, she thinks it is "probable" that Joseph bought the entirety of *insula* 1 sometime before Constantine's death (ca. 337) and converted the space exclusively into a Christian pilgrimage center—not a church for active worship and instruction, and certainly not a place for Jewish Christ adherence—with perhaps a few clergy employed for its upkeep.³⁶ Joseph likely struck a deal with the Jewish authorities in the village, convincing them that the *christaeum* would not be a threat to the larger community and would, in fact, boost town revenue due to the increased foot traffic from Christian travelers.³⁷ According to Taylor, while Joseph was able to persuade the Jewish community of Capernaum that there was, indeed, something "in it for them," Joseph's hidden agenda was to Christianize Capernaum using the medium of pilgrimage.

There are, on the other hand, several obstacles to both Corbo's and Taylor's overarching historical constructions and the claim that Joseph of Tiberias built the Capernaum *christaeum*. If, for the moment, we allow that Joseph was, in fact, associated with the building of the Capernaum *christaeum*, there are three important aspects to reconsider. First, Taylor is right to point out that, at least as Epiphanius's presents him, Joseph was, by the time of his building, an "orthodox" Christian. But she overstates what this must have meant for Joseph's perception of his own Jewish identity and what it must have implied about his relationship to Capernaum's Jewish community. Taylor approaches the category of "orthodox" Christian as an inherently stable one and reifies the clear boundaries between "orthodox" Christian and "Jewish" that are ideologically constructed in Epiphanius's heresiological framework. The result is that her historiography is shaped around the assumption of hard and fast social–historical dividing lines between the two. Thus, for Taylor, Joseph embodied the supersessionist ideal: he was an "orthodox"

---

35. Taylor, *Christians and the Holy Places*, 290.

36. Taylor, *Christians and the Holy Places*, 275–276, 293.

37. Taylor's historical construction is not entirely dissimilar to that of Arubas and Talgam. But whereas Taylor's proposal is more limited to the suggestion that Joseph of Tiberias built the fourth-century Capernaum *christaeum* and was allowed to do so by Capernaum's Jewish community because of the economic benefit it brought to them, Arubas and Talgam suggest further that Joseph as a representative of Christian Rome was also directly responsible for funding the building of the limestone synagogue across the street. This hypothesis will be discussed in the next chapter.

Christian, and, therefore, no longer considered himself Jewish in any meaningful way, and his commitment to Christian "orthodoxy" must have meant that he encountered opposition from Jews to all of his building projects. If he did not, then there must have been some external factor (e.g., financial benefit) that mitigated the opposition.

However, when Epiphanius is read against the grain and in the context of the fluidity that marked the socioreligious landscape of the empire in the mid- to late fourth century, we arrive at quite a different characterization. "Christianness"—and the dividing line between it and "Jewishness"—hardly existed as a neat and tidy category in the fourth century, even in the eyes of the emperors, which is precisely why Epiphanius and other heresiologists in his day, both Christian and Jewish, were writing in the first place. Joseph may have been, for Epiphanius, an "orthodox" believer, but even in his Joseph story, which presents "orthodox" Christianity as the winner in all scenarios, we get the hint that if we read between the lines, Epiphanius's polemical impulse may very well have been due to the fact that the boundary between Jewish and Christian identities was, for him, uncomfortably porous, and that Christians and Jews had long been interacting quite closely and in mutually influential ways that created unfeigned social and political anxiety for Christian elites like him.[38] Indeed, as Ryan has pointed out, the alterations to Capernaum's Room 1 in the fourth century were done "*without* the construction of new imperial monuments."[39] That is, in contrast to other fourth-century sites, such as the early Church of the Annunciation in Nazareth, we get no sense from the Capernaum remains that early imperial (read: "orthodox") Christianity had attempted to map itself onto the local landscape. Rather, memories of Jesus's life had been attached to a "previously existing *Jewish* structure,"[40] suggesting that whoever was responsible for the construction intended to see the fourth-century building in basic continuity with its Jewish past and was not necessarily concerned with championing what would be in this time a fledgling and fragile imperial (again, read: "orthodox") Christian identity.

Second, it is not quite the case that there is no evidence whatsoever for opposition to the construction of the Capernaum *christaeum*. Epiphanius is, indeed, mute on this point, and there is nothing to be gleaned from the

---

38. Note here where in the Joseph story this "hint" is coming from.

39. Ryan, *Memories of Jesus*, 194 (italics original).

40. Ryan, *Memories of Jesus*, 194 (italics original).

archaeological record. But, as we discussed in chapter 3, there is some rabbinic evidence that, depending on one's interpretation, could indicate that some rabbinocentric Jews around the fourth century conflicted with the Jesus-oriented Jewish community in Capernaum and, thus, the building of the village's *christaeum*. *Qohelet Rabbah* 7:26 constructs a memory about Rabbi Issi of Caesarea (fourth century) and his distain for Capernaum's *minim* and their *minut*. If the refence to *minim* in this text is to Jesus-oriented Jews, which I think it is (see discussion in chapter 3), then Rabbi Issi's complaint against them for their separatism from the rabbinic community (*minut*) amounts to opposition in the form of a rhetorical critique. In this portion of the midrash, Rabbi Issi partitions the Jewish community into those who are "good," with their associated rabbis, and those who are "sinners," with the *bnei kfar Nahum* squarely within this latter social grouping.[41] It is conceivable that the builder of the Capernaum *christaeum*—whether or not it was Joseph of Tiberias—experienced some type of resistance from such rabbinocentric Jews, even if it was left on the rhetorical level.

In my view, this is probably the type of Jewish group that Epiphanius envisions as having opposed Joseph's work in Tiberias.[42] Tiberias was not only the seat of the Jewish Patriarchate but also home to a historic and substantial Jewish aristocracy; both were deeply entangled with the emerging influence and authority of Palestinian rabbis.[43] Even though Epiphanius's narrative is

---

41. The midrash's heresiological aim—social partitioning—is not unlike Epiphanius's, although on a smaller scale.

42. *Pan.* 30.12

43. See Sivan, *Palestine in Late Antiquity*, 23–24. For an excellent survey of various historical-critical issues surrounding the nature of the Patriarchate in the fourth century, its relationship to the rabbis, and the extent of its power, see Goodblatt, "Jewish Community," 416–423. Sivan sees Epiphanius's presentation of Joseph's "triumph" in Tiberias, if historical, as having multiple meanings: "It provided a most trenchant statement of Constantine's equation between kingdom and creed. It affirmed the constitution of the new imperial creed with the substitution of Christ and Constantine for Hadrian and the Hadrianeum. And it demonstrated the superiority of Christian over Jewish 'magic' since the sign of the cross repeatedly achieved what other faith symbols failed to accomplish" (23). Thus, she says, "the location of Joseph's main recorded activity, Tiberias, was carefully calculated to enhance the exploit in the full flow of nascent Christian imperialism" (24). While Sivan is right to highlight that, as presented by Epiphanius, the competitive nature of Joseph's encounter with Tiberian Jews reflects nascent "orthodox" or imperial Christianity's conflict with Judaism, she overstates Joseph's, and thus Christianity's, triumph in Epiphanius's account. While it could be said that Joseph is, in the end, the winner in the

likely mistaken on some historical details and draped in the rhetoric of ancient stereotypes, he does seem to know that Tiberias was a particularly prestigious place in the Jewish world. Epiphanius rightly reckons that a Jewish city with resources, a substantial rabbinic community, and the power of the Patriarchate, could, indeed, challenge the building plans even of a *comes* commissioned by Constantine himself. Despite his rhetorically charged, anti-Jewish language and ideological aims, Epiphanius is willing to grant that the Jewish opposition was still *somewhat* successful, and that Joseph was able to finish only a "small church" (*Pan.* 30.12.4, 9).

The socioreligious situation in Capernaum was obviously different than Tiberias. True, Tiberias likely also had a presence of Jesus-oriented Jews, whom the rabbis encountered and debated,[44] but rabbinic influence in the city seems to have been much stronger. In contrast, while the *minim* of Capernaum are constructed as an object of rabbinic criticism, there is no evidence indicating that rabbis or rabbinocentric Jews held great power in the fourth-century village. The synagogue—in use during the first century, renovated and expanded sometime in the third or fourth century, and then transformed into the monumental limestone synagogue in the fifth or sixth century[45]—suggests that Capernaum still had a Jewish public assembly at this time, and that it was, perhaps, growing spatially in competition with the growth of the contemporaneous *christaeum* across the street. Capernaum's public assembly would have continued to be open to Jewish villagers of all stripes, including Jewish members of the Christ association, which arguably had a presence in the village since the late first or early second century.[46] The institutional situation of Capernaum's *minim* in the fourth century would,

---

scenario, Epiphanius portrays him as being only marginally successful. He says that the Jewish community continued to harass Joseph and that he eventually furnished out of the *Hadriaeum* only a "small church." This could hardly have been considered a triumph for Joseph. What this episode seems to indicate is that, regardless of Joseph's feelings of success and actual relationship to his orthodox identity, the Tiberian (rabbinocentric) Jewish community was perceived to be autonomous and powerful enough to oppose a significant imperial Christian intrusion onto their landscape.

44. Even though dated, see Reuven Kimelman, "Rabbi Yohanan of Tiberias: Aspects of Social and Religious History of Third Century Palestine" (PhD diss., Yale University, 1977), 187, 202.

45. See discussion in chapter 2, especially on the so-called "multiple synagogues theory."

46. See discussion in chapter 3.

therefore, have been similar to centuries past and quite like the situation recounted in *Pesikta de Rav Kahana* 18.5. This Palestinian midrash, redacted in the fifth or sixth century, tells a story about Rabbi Yohanan of Tiberias's contentious encounter with a *min* set *within* the context of the Great Synagogue of Sepphoris. In commenting on this midrash, Goranson notes, "one of the most remarkable things about this story is that having a *min* appear in the Sepphoris synagogue causes no surprise; Jerome, after all, said, with some hyperbole, that the *minim* were found '*per totas Orientis synagogas.*'"[47] In other words, at least some *minim*, despite being constructed as separatists from the rabbinic community, were understood as continuing to participate in the ongoings of the public assembly. But while this midrash, indeed, sheds light on rabbinic perceptions of *minim*, it sheds an equal amount of light on the nature of public synagogues in the days of Rabbi Yohanan and, perhaps, also the midrash itself. What made public synagogues such an important institution to Jewish society was not that they condensed and consolidated Jewish identity under a singular authoritative interpretation. Rather, it was precisely the opposite. For centuries, public synagogues functioned as a concrete and conceptual space for the proliferation of diverse interpretations of Jewishness, providing a context in which competition, debate, and popular opinion decided society's winners and losers, leaders and followers. It was their capacity to accommodate ideological, ethnic, and cultural difference, to bend and flex but not quite break, that make it entirely *un*remarkable to find a *min* in this type of space, despite Goranson's otherwise eloquent observation.

Thus, when we think about Capernaum's social landscape at the time of the construction of the *christaeum*, we need to envision multiple orientations of Jewish identity, as well as the likelihood that some or even many of Capernaum's Jews had no attachment to an association at all—rabbinic, Jesus-oriented, or otherwise. Jesus-oriented Jews in the village may have been considered *minim* separatists by certain rabbis and, perhaps, would have fallen into one of Epiphanius's *haerases*, but it is possible that average everyday Capernaum assembly-goers did not draw such conclusions—or even care to. We ought not get swept away by the polemical aims of rabbinic and Christian heresiological rhetoric. In my view, it makes good historical sense to say that,

---

47. Goranson, "Joseph of Tiberias," 103, working largely from the observations made by Kimelman, "Rabbi Yohanan of Tiberias," 187–188.

as members of the Jewish community, Jewish Christ-followers continued to have access to and seek influence within the public assembly, and as members of a Christ-association, they continued to offer cult in the village's *christaeum*. These two institutional identities did not compete with one another because they were of two fundamentally different types.

Third, the proposal that economic factors—rooted in Joseph's alleged promise of increased wealth brought to the village by pilgrim foot traffic—were the main reason that Capernaum's Jewish community allowed Joseph to erect a Christian building in the fourth century runs up against several challenges. Perhaps the biggest is that there is no evidence that Joseph ever predicted such wealth or made such a promise, whether to the Capernaum community or to any other community he supposedly built in. Furthermore, while, as Sharon Mattila has shown, there seems to have been general continuity in Capernaum's relative economic prosperity from the Hellenistic period to the Byzantine period, material indicators of wealth brought to the village specifically by Christian travelers do not appear, really, until the fifth and sixth centuries, long after the time of Joseph.[48] It is in these centuries that Late Roman Fine Wares, stamped with crosses and imported from locations such as Cyprus and North Africa, appear in great numbers in Capernaum.[49]

This material record accords well, chronologically, with the historical evolution of Christian pilgrimage to Palestine more broadly. While Christian tourism to the region was taking place already in the fourth century, and arguably before then,[50] it was, during that time, not even close to the major industry it would become in the fifth and sixth centuries, when the production and consumption of "pilgrimage commodities" forcefully propelled the cultural, political, and ideological colonization of Palestine by the Byzantines. While the Constantinian era certainly initiated the groundwork, it was not

---

48. S. Mattila, "Capernaum, Village of Naḥum," 217–257.

49. For descriptions, including dates, of the over one-hundred fragments of LRFW stamped with crosses found in Capernaum, see S. Loffreda, *Cafarnao VI*, 107–110. Images are presented in S. Loffreda, *Cafarnao VII: Documentazione grafica della ceramica (1968–2003)* (Jerusalem: Edizioni Terra Santa, 2008), 65–69.

50. For different historical perspectives on the development of Christian pilgrimage to Palestine, see the essays in R. G. Ousterhout, ed., *The Blessings of Pilgrimage* (Champagne-Urbana: University of Illinois Press, 1990).

Image 4.3. Late Roman Fine Wares stamped with crosses found in Capernaum, mostly dated to the fifth and sixth centuries.

Photo by the author.

until the time of Byzantine emperors, namely Theodosius II (408–450) and Justinian I (527–565), that Palestine became a commodified object and crystalized politically into a Christian, though no less Roman, "Holy Land."[51] In other words, in the fourth century, the economic benefit of Christian travel to Capernaum would have been meagre at best. The economic market for Christian tourism did not exist yet, and neither Joseph nor anyone else could have predicted that it would emerge any time soon. Recall that the so-called Bordeaux Pilgrim, writing ca. 333, does not even mention Capernaum, and the first to do so is not until Egeria in the 380s. To be sure, the existence of wall graffiti in Room 1 from the fourth century, and perhaps even before, suggests that Capernaum saw more Christian travelers on its streets than just Egeria; however, neither the graffiti nor Egeria's testimony is evidence that such visits translated into economic gains in this period. Indeed, such gains belong to a century or so later in the village's history, when Christians not only traveled to Capernaum for religious tourism but emigrated there to take up permanent residence.[52]

---

51. See R. L. Wilken, *John Chrysostom and the Jews: Rhetoric and Reality in the 4th Century* (Berkley, CA: University of California Press, 1983), 16–17. This point in some ways coincides with Doron Bar's argument, that imperial Christianity did not achieve any real momentum in the Galilean hinterland until the fifth and sixth centuries. See D. Bar, "The Christianisation of Rural Palestine during Late Antiquity," *JEH* 54.3 (2003): 401–421.

52. This will be discussed in chapter 6.

To this point, I have used the Joseph of Tiberias hypothesis as a way into discussing some of the broader historical issues that are relevant to Capernaum's fourth-century past and whether or not Joseph was actually associated with the building of the *christaeum*. Now we can more directly address the question: Was Joseph the builder? One reason that he might not have been concerns the date of the fourth-century renovations to Room 1. While, as mentioned earlier, Corbo dated the alterations to around the mid-fourth century, Loffreda has stated that the renovations occurred in the *late* fourth century.[53] If Loffreda is right, then the construction of the *christaeum* would have postdated the life of Joseph.[54] Goranson, whose study of the Joseph of Tiberias tradition remains the most thorough, thinks that Joseph was likely familiar with Capernaum, and that it would not be surprising if he had wanted to influence the Christ-believing community there. Nevertheless, in the end, Goranson concludes that "we have no evidence specifically linking him to any of the expansions of the Capernaum house church."[55] After all, Epiphanius never explicitly states that Joseph built a church in Capernaum. While he does list Capernaum among the exclusively Jewish towns of the Galilee in which Joseph was authorized to build, he only says that Joseph completed buildings in Tiberias, Sepphoris, and "certain other towns."[56] Although the connection between Joseph and Capernaum remains possible, any picture of the past that places the connection at its center is bound to be blurry.

If neither Joseph the person nor the idea of increased wealth-flow from non-Jewish Christian pilgrimage adequately explains how a Christian building could have been successfully erected in an entirely Jewish town

---

53. Loffreda, *Recovering Capharnaum*, 58.

54. This observation is also made by Ryan, *Memories of Jesus*, 190.

55. Goranson, "Joseph of Tiberias," 115. In my view, it might be worth rephrasing Goranson's statement here that we have "no evidence" to read something like "weak evidence" or "not enough evidence." Both Corbo and Taylor do provide some arguments with some evidence for Joseph's involvement, but, in my view, they hold very little weight, which renders their respective historical constructions quite frail.

56. Goranson mentions the suggestion by Bargil Pixner in 1985, that the "church" Epiphanius is often understood as saying Joseph built in Capernaum was actually located in nearby Tabgha, where excavations uncovered a burial inscription apparently mentioning a certain "Joseph." Goranson, however, provides strong evidence for why this Joseph should not be identified with the Joseph of Tiberias known from Epiphanius's account. See Goranson, "Joseph of Tiberias," 135–139.

in fourth-century Capernaum, then what does? In my view, it is better to imagine that, not only were Jesus-oriented Jews resident in the village, but they also had a noteworthy level of influence in the public assembly. The use of vernacular strategies in the architectural renovations of *insula* 1, to my mind, makes it more likely that the changes were carried out by locals. However, even if they were funded and executed by an outside patron, like Joseph, and even if that patron had an association with "orthodox" imperial Christianity, like Joseph, a building constructed, unlike other fourth-century churches in Palestine, to maintain *continuity* architecturally with its Jewish past may have been perceived as altogether unthreatening to the larger Jewish community and especially advocated for by those who participated in the village's Christ cult. The capacity of Capernaum's Jewish Christ-followers to sway the popular assembly to allow the construction of the *christaeum* may also have been bolstered by one of humanity's most powerful emotions: apathy. Even though there is no positive evidence for it, our historical imagination must include space for the fact that everyday human experience is often marked by a blinding indifference towards the Other that populates our social landscape. To put it bluntly, Capernaum's non-Christ-following Jews simply may not have cared all that much about the *christaeum*, or at least not enough do anything about it. There was no opposition to it because there was no need for opposition. The ongoings of the Capernaum Christ cult did not, in the fourth century, affect their everyday lives in any significant manner. As Taylor has rightly argued, in the fourth century, the Jewish community in Capernaum would have had a high level of autonomy; it was not under absolute Christian rule.[57] Indeed, even more broadly, Jewish communities throughout the Galilee and the late Roman East, continued their vibrant existence as a social and cultural force to be reckoned with. The force of the impact of a politically and ideologically consolidated Christian empire was yet to be felt, and the social anxiety spawned by members of the Jewish community who were attracted to the Jesus movement was still the concern of relatively small, albeit growing, circles of rabbis and their followers.

To be sure, by the fourth century, and even long before it, many wells of ink had run dry from the amount of anti-Jewish supersessionist literature penned by the Christian literary elite. And, as Ryan has argued, such

---

57. Taylor, *Christians and the Holy Places*, 293.

anti-Jewish ideology certainly did impress itself on the remains of some fourth-century imperial churches, such as the Church of the Holy Sepulcher and the early Church of the Annunciation, to name just two.[58] But these hostile pens and oppressive monuments do not—nor could they, nor do they necessarily intend to—reflect the whole situation of Jewish–Christian relations in the fourth century. In Capernaum, the architectural, and therefore ideological, situation of the *christaeum* is fundamentally different than those monuments. Because the changes to *insula* 1 were dressed in vernacular form, constructed with local resources and embedded in the local landscape to engender continuity with the site's Jewish past, it is difficult to see, in this period, an ideology of non-Jewish Christian supersessionism at work among its remains. Indeed, as we will see in chapter 5, such an ideology is *precisely* what is at work in the following centuries, with the construction of Capernaum's octagonal church. But, just as in the time *before* Constantine, local Jewish–Christian relations *after* Constantine remained a primarily intra-Jewish affair. However, with the growth of non-Jewish Christian travel to Capernaum in the mid- to late fourth century—which, as we might recall, is one of the relatively fixed nodes of data in our web of historical construction—Jewish–Christian relations in the village also took on a *non-local* dynamic. What this dynamic entailed brings us, again, to the topic of Capernaum's relationship to the phenomenon of Christian travel and to the question of why the fourth-century renovations to *insula* 1 were introduced in the first place.

4. *Insula* 1 and the Growth of Christian Travel to Capernaum

Why was *insula* 1 renovated by Capernaum's Jewish Christ-followers in the mid- to late fourth century? The answer to this question is almost certainly not monocausal, but, as Paul Oliver has said, all vernacular architecture—which he associates inherently with domestic buildings—is designed in some way or another to meet the various social and cultural needs of local communities.[59] Thus, the question posed here has to do with constructing a portrait of at

---

58. See, e.g., Ryan, *Memories of Jesus*, 214–215.
59. Oliver, *Built to Meet Needs*, xxi–xxviii.

least some of the needs that the rearticulation and expansion of the vernacular architecture of *insula* 1 may have met, especially those that pertained to evolving relations between Christians and Jews—including Jesus-oriented ones—in the village.

One of the few points of agreement among scholars is that Capernaum experienced a noticeable uptick in Christian tourism in the mid- to late fourth century. Egeria's report about her trip in the 380s would seem to indicate as much, but it is the multilingual wall graffiti fragments dated to the period of the *christaeum*, mainly appearing in Greek but also in Syriac and possibly Latin, which have led scholars to conclude that non-Jewish Christian travel to the village began to blossom in this period. This conclusion is, in general, correct, and I will argue below that it was the driving force behind the changes made to *insula* 1. As my entry point into making this argument, I want to reconsider briefly three assumptions that have undergirded some recent scholarly interpretations of the Capernaum graffiti, which have led scholars, wrongly in my view, to draw the further conclusion that the graffiti are, *in toto*, a witness to non-local Christian visitors who performed their cult of commemoration independently of, and perhaps with antagonism toward, Capernaum's local Jewish Christ-following community. The first two assumptions I will engage have to do, specifically, with the Greek and Syriac graffiti and the identities of their inscribers, while the third assumption concerns the function of graffiti as a social act.

It is useless to say much, if anything, about the actual content of the graffiti, since they are so fragmentary and, beyond individual letters, so difficult to decipher. Thus, my comments will assume Testa's linguistic identifications among the graffiti and focus more abstractly on them as a social phenomenon. My argument here will be that we need to allow for the possibility that Jews themselves could have also inscribed some of the Greek and Syriac graffiti, and that non-local, non-Jewish Christian travel to Capernaum could just as well be seen through the historical lens of Christian attraction to Judaism in the context of the late-fourth-century Roman East. It is, I will suggest, the steady increase in Capernaum of non-local Christian attraction to Judaism, in particular Jewish ways of remembering Jesus, that provided the impetus for the architectural changes made to *insula* 1. These changes met the needs of Capernaum's local Jewish Christ-followers to shape and control how these memories were constructed by mediating the experience of travelers spatially through a building that stood architecturally in direct continuity with its Jewish past and, demographically, in an entirely Jewish village.

Some scholars have assumed that, since most of the Capernaum graffiti is apparently in Greek, this must mean that *insula* 1 was primarily visited by non-local, non-Jewish Christians.[60] While this might be true, it is, nevertheless, an assumption, and it reflects a misunderstanding about the use of Greek among Jews at this time. There is an abundance of evidence that Jews in the land of Israel used Greek not only in the days of the Second Temple period but also during late antiquity.[61] Thus, while it is, indeed, possible that the Greek graffiti were inscribed by non-local, non-Jewish Christians, it is just as possible that some were inscribed by Jews local to Capernaum. After all, a donor inscription on a column from the later Capernaum limestone synagogue was inscribed in Greek.

On the other hand, the presence of Greek-speaking non-Jewish Christians from abroad in Capernaum does not necessarily imply the absence or exclusion of the village's Jewish Christ-followers from the ongoings of the *christaeum*. Almost forty years ago, Robert Louis Wilken, and now more recently Paula Fredriksen, have noted that Christian identity in the fourth century was inherently unstable, for Christianity had had very little impact on the social fabric of Roman cities, which continued to operate on the basis of the political and cultural legacy of their Hellenistic past.[62] The traditions of Greek education, social custom, literature, art and architecture, myths and legends—including the gods—continued to shape the values of a city's citizens and the character of its public leaders. Furthermore, vibrant Jewish communities

---

60. Taylor, *Christians and the Holy Places*, 274; R. Hakola, "Galilean Jews and Christians in Context," 161–164; Zangenberg, "Galilean Silence"; Ryan, *Memories of Jesus*, 189, seems also to suggest this.

61. For example, there are Greek inscriptions from the Second Temple period (e.g., *CIJ* 2.1402; *CIJ* 2.1400, both from Jerusalem); Greek papyri from the Judean desert from the second century CE (e.g., *P. Yadin* *52 [also known as 5/6 *Hev* 52 and *SB* VIII], *P. Yadin* 18, *P. Hev/Se* gr 60; *P. Hev/Se* gr 63); Greek tomb inscriptions from the fourth to fifth century CE Bet She'arim in the Galilee; and Greek inscriptions in synagogues in late antiquity, such as at Hammath Tiberias and in Capernaum itself (e.g., *CIIP* V 1 nos. 6415 and 6651). Admittedly, no Jewish literature from late antiquity seems to have been penned in Greek. But see the discussion below of *b. Sotah* 49b, which concerns the question of whether Jews in the land of Israel should be permitted to learn Greek; the Gemara suggests that both earlier and later sages permitted it.

62. Wilken, *Rhetoric and Reality*, 24; P. Fredriksen, *Augustine and the Jews: A Christian Defense of Jews and Judaism* (New York: Doubleday, 2008).

existed throughout the Empire, engaging thoroughly with their non-Jewish neighbors in commerce and culture yet, in many cases, maintaining an identity discernably Jewish and often attractive to Christian churchgoers.[63] Social and cultural identities were highly fluid, with Christians, pagans, and Jews not only living together in confined spaces but also interacting in culturally complex and mutually influential ways. Hence, as Wilken highlighted, the phenomenon of non-Jewish Christian attraction to Jewish life—including specific Judaizing behaviors such as synagogue attendance and participation in ritual festivities—was pervasive in the fourth-century Roman East.[64]

The textured portrait that Wilken and Fredriksen paint of porous social and cultural boundaries in the fourth century should not at all be surprising; well before, during, and after the advent of the Jesus movement, boundaries between Jews and non-Jews had gone unpoliced in many parts of the Greek and Roman worlds. Thus, it is possible that the Greek (and Latin) graffiti found in Capernaum—that is, in a Jewish town and in a building materially connected to its Jewish past—reflect the unstable boundaries of this period and a type of Christian attraction to remembering Jesus within a Jewish space.[65] Indeed, we should not forget the observation of James F. Strange, mentioned in the previous chapter, that among the very same graffiti fragments were found other fragments apparently with Hebrew letters inscribed on them, directly suggesting Jewish coparticipation in the Capernaum *christaeum*.

In a similar vein, we should not be hasty to conclude that the presence of Syriac among the graffiti, inscribed in Estrangelo, points strictly to Christian pilgrimage activity severed from the Jewish community of Capernaum. It seems, from a variety of sources, that Jews and Syrian Christians had especially close contact in both the Roman province of Syria-Palestina and Sasanian Persia, the cultural setting of the later Babylonian rabbis.[66] Certainly, this contact could be hostile, but it also could be marked by mutual attraction.

---

63. On such a situation in Antioch, specifically, see Wilken, *Rhetoric and Reality*, 34–65.

64. Wilken, *Rhetoric and Reality*, 66–94.

65. As I will argue in the next chapter, this type of Christian remembering of Jesus in fourth-century Capernaum contrasts sharply with that of the fifth and sixth centuries, when Byzantine Christians were explicit about remembering Jesus within the context of supersessionist Christianity.

66. See M. Bar-Asher Siegal, "Judaism and Syriac Christianity," 146–156.

Sources from fourth-century Syria, such as Ephrem's anti-Jewish liturgical poetry (written in Syriac), John Chrysostom's virulent homilies against Jews and Judaizers (written in Greek), and some early versions of eastern canon law likely compiled in Antioch provide evidence of both—strong antagonism towards Jews and Judaism from the literary and theological elite but, when read against the grain, strong attraction to Judaism and participation in Jewish life on the part of everyday Syrian Christians.[67]

There is also a passage from the Bavli that seems to suggest awareness that some Jews in Palestine were interested in speaking Syriac. The passage is from *b. Sotah* 49b, paralleled in *Bava Kamma* 82b–83a, and appears in a larger discussion about whether the Mishnaic sages thought it was appropriate for Jews to learn and teach their children Greek and Greek wisdom. The Gemara questions whether the sages really opposed learning Greek. The Gemara reasons by reporting that even the great Rabbi Judah Ha-Nasi had supported the use of Greek, ruling that it was preferable for Jews in the land of Israel to speak it or Hebrew rather than "Syriac" (סורסי). A parallel is then drawn to Rav Yosef's ruling that it was better for Jews in Babylonia to speak Hebrew or Persian rather than "Aramaic" (ארמי). The main point of the Gemara seems to be that, while Hebrew is the language preferable to all—it is, for the rabbis, the *lishon haqodesh*—Jews should be permitted to speak the language of their respective political overlords, whether Greek (Roman Palestine) or Persian (Sasanian Babylonia).

But why do Bavlian sources allege that Rabbi Judah shunned the use of סורסי by Jews in Palestine? Passages from the Yerushalmi express precisely the opposite view, asserting that the use of סורסי should not be despised (e.g., *y. Sotah* 7.2.3; *Meg.* 1.9.3). The reason for this difference might be that the two Talmuds are referring to two different sociolinguistic phenomena. "Syriac" in the Yerushalmi is probably used as a name for the Aramaic spoken by Jews in Palestine (i.e., what scholars call Jewish Palestinian Aramaic [JPA]), while "Syriac" in our Bavli text probably does not refer to JPA but rather a Palestinian Aramaic particularly associated with Syrian Christianity, having an alphabet based on northern Syrian Estrangelo script.[68] In late antiquity, the growth and

---

67. C. Shepherdson, *Anti-Judaism and Christian Orthodoxy: Ephrem's Hymns in Fourth-Century Syria*, NAPSMS 20 (Washington, DC: Catholic University of America Press, 2008); Wilken, *Rhetoric and Reality*; and Siegal, "Judaism and Syriac Christianity," 146–56.

68. See M. Morgenstern "Christian Palestinian Aramaic," 629.

development of the Aramaic language, in its various dialects, created a point of contact between Christians and Jews in the East, including in Babylonia. This might explain Rav Yosef's supposed, and otherwise surprising, aversion to Babylonian Jews speaking ארמי, "Aramaic," a language the Jewish people had been using for centuries, including in their own sacred writings.[69] But, by the late fourth and fifth centuries, Christians in Palestine and Babylonia were now speaking Aramaic, too. Thus, for the Bavli redactors, it was, at this point, preferable for Jews to speak Persian rather than a language that had increasingly become associated with Christianity. From this perspective, the Bavli expresses a desire to construct a boundary marker between Jews and Christians that ran along sociolinguistic lines. But, again, when these rulings are read against the grain, they suggest that a much more fluid situation existed on the ground: not only were some Syrian Christians attracted to Jews and Judaism as mentioned above, but also some Jews were attracted to speaking a language associated with Syrian Christianity.

The Greek and Syriac graffiti from Room 1, taken in tandem with the witness of Egeria, probably testify to some level of non-Jewish Christian travel to Capernaum in the fourth century. However, beyond the possibility that some of the graffiti could have, in principle, been inscribed by local Jews themselves,[70] the point that Capernaum was an entirely Jewish village at this time must, in my view, have a greater impact on our interpretation of what non-local Christian travelers understood themselves to be doing as they visited the village and offered their cult of commemoration in the *christaeum*. Rather than focus exclusively on the non-local dimension reflected in the graffiti in favor of seeing an "international," "global," or "pilgrim" type of Christianity at work in the village, we need to see both local and non-local elements in dynamic relation to one another. That is, we must recognize that the graffiti—in all of their linguistic manifestations—were not inscribed in a sociospatial vacuum. They were performed in relation to their immediate spatial environment, namely, the built space of Room 1, and within the larger

---

69. On the chronological development of Syriac and geographical grouping of dialects, see the essays by Holger Gzella and Aaron Michael Butts in King, ed., *The Syriac World*. Also note in Jastrow, *s.v.* the comment that ארמי was sometimes used by the rabbis as a euphemistic substitute for the terms "Roman" and "Christian."

70. Recall the mention of Hebrew lettering found among the graffiti, which would already suggest the activity of Jews in the *christaeum*.

social setting of a Jewish village.[71] Thus, the non-local component expressed in the graffiti intersected and entangled itself with the local component expressed concentrically in (1) the rearticulated vernacular architecture of Room 1, and (2) the broader demographic context of Capernaum. In other words, when non-Jewish Christian travelers like Egeria entered the *christaeum*, they knew—perhaps because they were told, as Egeria seems to have been about the still-erect walls of Peter's original house—that the spaces in which they were constructing their memories of Jesus, building and village, stood in continuity with and *within* a Jewish past.

Travelers to Capernaum would have also known that they were entering into, and therefore participating in, the assembly space of a Christ-association. Egeria calls the place an *ecclesia*, but she is probably using the Latin term loosely, not as a reference to a public Christian building but simply to a place where she knew Christ-followers gathered. Jennifer Baird has shown that graffiti were a common practice in association contexts, including cultic associations, as sources especially from Dura Europos indicate, where graffiti were found in the *mithraeum*, in the Christ-oriented building, and in the synagogue.[72] And Ryan is surely right to assert that the graffiti from the Capernaum *christaeum* are indicative of commemorative activity; indeed, the primary ritual performed within its walls was the construction of memories about Jesus and his apostles that created not simply a sacred space but, more specifically, a sacred *spot*.[73] But the presence of commemorative graffiti does not necessarily mark the *christaeum* exclusively as a pilgrim destination. Graffiti

---

71. On the importance of interpreting ancient graffiti within their spatial environment, see J. A. Baird, "The Graffiti of Dura-Europos: A Contextual Approach," in *Ancient Graffiti in Context*, ed. J. A. Baird and C. Taylor (London: Routledge, 2011), 49–68.

72. Baird, "The Graffiti of Dura-Europos," 64. On the graffiti from the *mithraeum* in Dura Europos, see E. D. Francis, "Mithraic Graffiti from Dura-Europos," in *Mithraic Studies*, ed. J. R. Hinnells (Manchester: Manchester University Press, 1971), 2:424–445. On the Jewish graffiti from Dura-Europos, see K. B. Stern, *Writing on the Wall: Graffiti and the Forgotten Jews of Antiquity* (Princeton, NJ: Princeton University Press, 2018), *et passim*.

73. Ryan, *Memories of Jesus*, 189–190. On the material and social significance of "devotional graffiti" in early Christianity, see A. M. Yasin, "Prayers on Site: The Materiality of Devotional Graffiti and the Production of Early Christian Sacred Space," in *Viewing Inscriptions in the Late Antique and Medieval World*, ed. A. Eastmond (Cambridge: Cambridge University Press, 2015), 36–60; E.-M. Butz and A. Zettler, "Pilgrim's Devotion? Christian Graffiti from Antiquity to the Middle Ages," in *Travel, Pilgrimage, and Social Interaction from Antiquity to the Middle Ages*, eds. J. Kuuliala and J. Rantala (London: Routledge, 2020), 141–164.

commemorating special days and rituals were present in the various cultic associations in Dura Europos, including the *mithraeum*, which also clearly housed local assemblies of local attenders. This might mean that Christian travelers to Capernaum understood themselves, and their memory-making activity, as participating in a local Jewish Christ-association that was, by the fourth century, accessible to non-Jews from elsewhere. Such a constructed scenario for fourth-century Capernaum could be seen, generally, in continuity with earlier periods of Greco-Roman antiquity, in which the participation of non-Jews in Jewish associations was not abnormal,[74] and local associations of various types could be accessible to non-locals who nevertheless shared some type of social connection. As Richard Ascough has noted, translocal links would have been particularly common among associations of traders who, by definition, were "on the move."[75] Thus, translocal social networking is another way of understanding the intense entanglement of the local and non-local elements at work in the Capernaum *christaeum*. Non-local travelers to the village would have had access to a Jewish association by means of their Christ-group connection, a situation not dissimilar to some modern houses of worship today that cater to both locals and visitors simultaneously.

This leads us to a final point to consider here about the function of the Capernaum graffiti, *as such*. The main assumption from most scholars—an assumption that is not necessarily incorrect—has been that the Capernaum graffiti are pilgrim graffiti, which are the result of participants offering their cult of commemoration. That the graffiti have to do, on some level, with commemorative activity is a foregone conclusion. But there is more to be said. Indeed, as scholars like Jennifer Baird, Claire Taylor, Karen Stern, and others have emphasized, ancient graffiti are a type of everyday writing activity that defy monolithic interpretation.[76] On the one hand, as Ryan has pointed out on a theoretical level, the act of commemoration itself has

---

74. On the presence of non-Jews in associations that offered cult to the Jewish god, see R. Last, "The Other Synagogues," 330–363.

75. On translocal relationships among associations in Greco-Roman antiquity, see R. Ascough, "Translocal Relationships among Voluntary Associations and Early Christianity," *JECS* 5, no. 2 (1997): 223–241 (esp. 229–230).

76. For theoretical and methodological discussions of the concept of "graffiti," especially pertaining to definition and identification (in antiquity and today), see J. A. Baird and C. Taylor, "Ancient Graffiti," in *The Routledge Handbook of Graffiti and Street Art*, ed. J. I. Ross (London: Routledge, 2016), 19–21; J. A. Baird and C. Taylor, "Ancient Graffiti in Context,"

less to do with the notion of distilling, encapsulating, and preserving static memories than with social and cultural processes of identity formation. When individuals and communities "remember," they construct relationships with the past in ways that answer questions such as "Who am I?" "Who are we?" and "To whom or what do we belong?" That is, commemoration is a type of heritage history, whose purpose it is to construct the past in a way that orients itself towards "us" rather than "all."[77] Thus, the act of commemoration is an expression of power that creates, shapes, and exerts a group's social identity as inheritors of a particular history by destabilizing the boundary between the past and present, sometimes even dissolving it entirely; the question "Who are we?" is answered by conflating it with claims about "who they were."

On the other hand, the use of graffiti, specifically, as a material medium reinforces the identity-forming function of commemoration as a social act and the power dynamics inherent to it. Stern's work on the Dura Europos graffiti in their comparative context is instructive on this point.[78] Stern interprets some of the most common forms among the nearly fourteen-hundred graffiti found in the third-century city—whether in the synagogue, the Christ-oriented building, the Temple of Aphlad, or the *mithraeum*—as prayer petitions, many of which contained requests on the part of the inscriber to be "remembered for good." These prayer petitions probably had multiple functions, including documenting a person's attempt to initiate contact with a deity, but perhaps even more important was their social function. According to Stern, such graffiti were not displayed privately; rather "people deliberately and clearly drew them to be accessible to audiences of passersby;"[79] hence, their clustering in some of the most easily visible spaces of assembly buildings, such as doorways. In some settings, such as the Dura *mithraeum* and synagogue, the graffiti even reflect a sense of competition among the inscribers, suggesting that

---

in *Ancient Graffiti in Context*, ed. A. Baird and C. Taylor (London: Routledge, 2011), 1–17; Baird, "Graffiti of Dura-Europos," 49–51.

77. On heritage studies as an approach to history—not always looked upon favorably by modern historians—see Maza, *Thinking about History*, 131.

78. See K. Stern, "Prayer as Power: Amulets, Graffiti, and Vernacular Writing in Ancient Levantine Synagogues," in *The Synagogue in Ancient Palestine: Current Issues and Emerging Trends*, ed. R. Bonnie, R. Hakola, and U. Tervahauta, FRLANT 279 (Göttingen: Vandenhoeck & Ruprecht, 2021), 237–239.

79. Stern, "Prayer as Power," 237.

"supplicants wanted their names and remembrance requests to be more visible than others as they vied for sacred real estate."[80] The point of these graffiti, Stern says, was to entreat visitors to the respective space, including non-local ones, to view and, if literate, to vocalize the prayer petition on behalf of the inscriber, with the result that the request for memorialization could be "activated" for their benefit.[81] In other words, graffiti such as these are not simply declarative writings but rather "dialogical and coercive;" they work as active agents in the inscriber's effort to gain the good favor of a deity, with readers' responses to them determining the efficacy of the writing.[82]

There are obvious differences between the Dura and Capernaum graffiti. Perhaps the most significant is that many of those from Dura, studied by both Baird and Stern, are legible, whereas most of those from Capernaum are not. Thus, I am not claiming here that the Capernaum graffiti necessarily fit the genre of prayer petitions (although they might) or that they served precisely the same social functions as those at Dura. But there are aspects of Stern's analysis that, I suggest, are transferable here. First, the graffiti from Capernaum are apparently restricted in their distribution to the walls of Room 1, that is, the focalized and, therefore, the most visible and traversed area of *insula* 1. This could be due to the accidence of preservation, but, in my view, is more likely due to the same reason Stern identifies for the clustering of graffiti inscribed in the doorways of buildings at Dura and in ancient synagogues more broadly: it offered the best access to an intended audience. Second, this restriction in distribution suggests that the Capernaum's graffiti—which span mainly the third to the early fifth century—indicates a growing chorus of written voices that not only wished to be heard from on-high but also intended to invoke audiences of passersby whom they sought to involve in their acts of commemoration. Whether and in what way these voices in Capernaum competed over "sacred real estate" would seem impossible to know in light of the challenge of the graffiti's decipherment. However, the very presence of graffiti, as such, in multiple languages, accumulated over a long period of time, suggests a historical process in which non-Jewish Christ-followers who traveled to Capernaum increasingly asserted their agency in a way that claimed

---

80. Stern, "Prayer as Power," 237.

81. Stern, "Prayer as Power, 238. Stern mentions the non-local reader/vocalizer component inherent to the social function of graffiti on p. 239.

82. Stern, *Writing on the Wall*, 51.

the commemorative space of the *christaeum* as their own, in collaboration with those who came before and enlisting the help of those who would come after. From this perspective, we can see in the graffiti a gradual and accumulative growth of non-Jewish commemorative practice in Capernaum. While this practice first took shape before and after the turn of the fourth century squarely within the Jewish material and conceptual space of Room 1, it grew as a powerful yet still highly unstable cultural force during the course of the post-Constantinian fourth century, akin to the growth of non-Jewish Christianity throughout the Roman Empire.

In my view, such a slow and unsteady growth in the representation and influence of non-Jewish Christian voices at Capernaum—which mimicked slow-moving provincial currents propeling the Christianization of Palestine more broadly—provides an explanation for at least one of the major needs driving the rearticulation and expansion of *insula* 1's vernacular architecture. To be sure, the need to *remember* was fundamental to the renovations—the new focalized architecture of *insula* 1 was, as Ryan asserts, commemorative in nature—but the need to remember *in a certain way* as a response to the growth of non-local and non-Jewish identities in Capernaum was even more pressing. Lisa Findley, whose work we will encounter in more depth in the next chapter, has noted that commemorative architecture—the spatialization of a community's collective memory—is directly related to the exercise of power and the establishment of cultural hierarchies. Such architecture does not function simply as a repository for the preservation of a community's static memory about the past but rather dynamically conditions, controls, and crystalizes its memory in the present.[83] Memory can be constructed in architecture through various spatial strategies: external form and internal layout, such as elevation (e.g., monumental steps, raised platforms); focalization (central or axial); exclusive or surveilled access (e.g., walls, gates, fences); constriction; and scripted spatial movement are all mechanisms used to construct hierarchical space in which certain cultural narratives are stamped with normative interpretations. These types of spaces put restrictions on the agency of their actors and function to legitimize a particular cultural identity (or a collective of identities), activating the agency of insiders and curtailing the agency of outsiders. In contrast, nonhierarchical space employs multiple focal points or none at all. Such space allows for a wider range of actors, non-normative interpretations of culture, and expressions of

---

83. Findley, *Building Change*, 124–165.

subjective experience in the construction of cultural memory. The strategic use of empty, dilated, or ambiguous space, nonscripted spatial movement, and open access entry ways are examples of how architecture can, spatially, work against social hierarchies.

The expansion of the architecture of *insula* 1 in the mid- to late fourth century was an expression of hierarchical space that prioritized and reasserted an interpretation of Jesus within the local cultural framework of Capernaum's—and thus Jesus's—Jewish heritage. Several of the spatial strategies mentioned by Findley can be identified in the renovations: conscious attention was apparently given to external form (domestic building), focalization (centrality of Room 1), surveilled access (enclosure wall),[84] constriction (Room 1 divided into two subunits by a central arch), and scripted spatial movement. The construction of hierarchical space was an attempt to control the construction of non-local memories of Jesus by putting material limits on the exercise of non-Jewish Christian imagination. As non-local participation in Capernaum's Christ-association grew, the architecture of the *christaeum* intended to condition how non-Jewish travelers constructed their Christian identities in this particular space, that is, it mediated how they were to answer the question "Who are we?" It provided a spatial arrangement that communicated the message that non-Jews were being allowed, or perhaps invited, to participate in a Jewish Christ-association. Whatever cultural, ethnic, and linguistic inflections were scribbled on its walls as answers to this question, the *christaeum*—which spatialized the memory of the apostle Peter's house as it really was, in a Jewish house in a Jewish town—was meant to preempt cultural narratives that excluded Jesus-oriented Jews and curtailed their agency.

5. Conclusion
The Demise of the Capernaum Christaeum

From the point of view of the historical construction presented in this chapter, the rearticulated vernacular architecture of *insula* 1 was ultimately a failure, though not of any fault of its own. While certainly a valiant attempt to meet

---

84. As mentioned earlier in this chapter, the enclosure wall was not a fortified wall and thus, in my view, was not primarily intended for protection or to keep people out. Nevertheless, it did bottleneck the flow of traffic by nature of its having only two entrances. A slower pace of traffic would have, of course, been easier to control and to surveille.

the needs of Capernaum's Jewish Christ-association—such as the need for cultural visibility and the reassertion of the Jewish memory of Jesus—non-Jewish memory-building came to outweigh and outgrow the *christaeum*'s walls and marginalize, although not necessarily displace, its Jewish users. We can see this process beginning to happen already in the writing of Egeria in the late fourth century. Egeria says nothing negative about Jews in her travel log entry on Capernaum, and she does mention seeing "the synagogue where the Lord cured a man possessed by the devil,"[85] which might mean that she was brought into sympathetic contact with Jewish Christ-followers in the town. On the other hand, Egeria actually says nothing *at all* about Jews of any persuasion, *as Jews*. And her silence is telling. Wilkinson has observed that Jews are mentioned as Jews only once among the authentically Egerian texts, and it is in a passage where she expresses open antagonism based on her memory of an otherwise unknown story in which "the Saviour" curses a synagogue and its local Jewish community.[86] Thus, as Ryan and Jacobs have noted, unless serving as a negative example or facilitating a memory of Jesus, Jews were altogether "invisible" to Egeria.[87]

Of course, Jewish communities in Roman and Byzantine Palestine, were not invisible, and many were apparently thriving, asserting their cultural agency, and attracting the participation of non-Jews, both around the time of Egeria and afterward. Indeed, as we will explore in chapter 6, Capernaum's Jews could very well have constituted that kind of community. But the growth in Capernaum of non-Jewish modes of commemorating Jesus, of which Egeria's writing is a representation, must have had a diminishing effect on the cultural and institutional agency of the town's Jewish Christ-followers. After all, by the middle of the fifth century, non-Jews were not only visiting but also emigrating to Capernaum, and the *christaeum* had met its physical demise, being obliterated and buried, when the octagonal church was erected over top of it. Thus, from around the time of Egeria's trip in the 380s to about 450, the cultural agency of Capernaum's Jewish Christ-association gradually faded

---

85. Wilkinson, *Egeria's Travels*, 196.

86. See Wilkinson, *Egeria's Travels*, 200. On Egeria's attitude towards Jews in general, see pp. 296–297.

87. A. Jacobs, "Visible Ghosts and Invisible Demons: The Place of Jews in Early Christian Terra Sancta," in *Galilee Through the Centuries: Confluence of Cultures*, ed. E. M. Meyers (Winona Lake, IN: Eisenbrauns, 1999), 359–376.

until it became entirely invisible. This certainly does not mean that Jewish Christ-followers as historical actors in the village vanished completely from Capernaum's social landscape. But it does mean that their institutional setting had changed. As two monumental buildings came to dominate the village's skyline between the fifth and sixth centuries, Jewish Christ-followers were left to ponder and puzzle over the messages communicated through their architecture about the security of Jewish and Christian identities. They now stood among the mix of Byzantine Christians from areas around the eastern Empire and the broader Jewish community, squeezed somewhere in the middle, and having to compete to regain a voice that their beloved *christaeum* had once granted them.

CHAPTER FIVE

Architecturalizing Power and Resistance
Capernaum's Octagonal Church and Limestone Synagogue

What we now call "monumental architecture" is first of all the expression of power, and power exhibits itself in the assembly of costly building materials and of all the resources of art.[1]

1. Introduction

IN THE MID-FIFTH century, buried beneath a fill of dirt and stones, Capernaum's *christaeum* and its vernacular architecture met their end.[2] Gone was the spatial manifestation of a type of commemorative imagination that envisioned Jesus at home, in his Jewish place. Gone, too, was the cultural and institutional agency of Capernaum's Jewish Christ-followers, a group that probably did not vanish from the village,[3] but, alas, whose spatial presence bore the brunt of the winds of social change that blew in more and more non-Jewish Christians from around the Byzantine Empire. The previous

---

1. L. Mumford, *The City in History* (New York: Harcourt, Brace, and World, 1961), 65.

2. Loffreda, *Recovering Capharnaum*, 64–67.

3. Runesson, "Architecture, Conflict, and Identity Formation," 251, where he suggests that three distinct social groups inhabited Capernaum in the fifth century: Byzantine Christians, Christ-believing Jews, and non-Christ-believing Jews. For my view on the continued presence of Jewish Christ-followers in Capernaum, even into the sixth century, see chapter 4. Stated briefly here, I follow Marc Hirshman's view of *Qohelet Rabbah*—a rabbinic midrash redacted sometime between the sixth and eighth centuries, which includes stories about *minim* in Capernaum who are quite possibly Jesus-oriented Jews—that while reflecting a polemical situation in Capernaum in the sixth century, it probably also preserves local memories of rabbinic encounters with Jewish Christ-followers in the village around the second or third century. Thus, in my view, we should envision continuity in the presence of Jewish Christ-followers rather than rupture, despite the otherwise shifting demographics in Capernaum during the fifth and sixth centuries.

century had been one of great socioreligious instability, in Capernaum just as throughout the late Roman–Byzantine world. Pagan traditionalists continued in the legacy of their Hellenistic past, debates over Christian orthodoxies and heresies proliferated, and Jewish communities continued, generally, to prosper under Roman law and attracted various kinds of sympathy from their non-Jewish neighbors. The idea, argued in the previous chapter, that non-Jewish Christian travel to Capernaum in the fourth century began as an outworking of such an attraction to Jewish life, and, in particular, Jewish ways of remembering Jesus, fits intimately well with the parallel notions of a "practically pluralistic" and "comfortably chaotic" fourth-century Roman East.[4] While the slow growth of non-Jewish émigrés to the village and non-Jewish memory-building would have minoritized Room 1's Jewish users, we have at least some reason to believe that such a comfortable chaos continued to characterize Capernaum into the fifth century, as Jews, Jewish Christ-followers, and non-Jewish Christians populated its streets.

But, as Paula Fredriksen has noted, it is precisely in the socioreligious flux and fluidity of the late fourth to fifth century that anti-Jewish rhetoric and imperial legislation bloomed, intensified, and culminated in repressive laws like Emperor Theodosius II's ban on the construction of new synagogues in 423 (*CTh* 16.8.25) and in other laws aimed not only at Jews but also pagans, heretics, and groups generally considered by the imperial church to be religious deviants and thus dangerous to the well-being of the Empire.[5] However, Fredriksen also mentions that the reason for this

---

4. Paula Fredriksen, drawing on Christine Shepardson's work, calls the unstable context of the (late) fourth century "comfortably chaotic." The term "practical pluralism" is also from Fredriksen. See P. Fredriksen, "Divinity, Ethnicity, Identity: 'Religion' as a Political Category in Christian Antiquity," in *An End to Antisemitism!*, vol. 3, *Comprehending Antisemitism through the Ages: A Historical Perspective*, ed. A. Lange et al. (Berlin: Walter de Gruyter, 2021), 111, 111 n.37, 114. See also C. Shepardson, "Between Polemic and Propaganda: Evoking the Jews of Fourth-Century Antioch," *Journal of the Jesus Movement in its Jewish Setting* 2 (2015): 151–182.

5. Fredriksen, "Divinity, Ethnicity, Identity," 101–102, 111. On heresiology in the *Codex Theodosianus*, see R. Fowler, "'The Insanity of Heretics Must Be Restrained': Heresiology in the Theodosian Code," in *Theodosius II: Rethinking the Roman Empire in Late Antiquity* (Cambridge: Cambridge University Press, 2013), 172–194. For a historical analysis of the impact of Theodosius II's anti-Jewish legislation on Jewish communities throughout the diaspora, see R. S. Kraemer, *The Mediterranean Diaspora in Late Antiquity: What Christianity Cost the Jews* (Oxford: Oxford University Press, 2020), 188–239.

growth in Christian anti-Jewish invective "had nothing to do with real Jews and everything to do with imperial efforts to define, mandate, and control 'orthodoxy.'"[6] That is to say, socioreligious chaos might have been comfortable in the everyday lives of those buying and selling in marketplaces, chatting on the *cardines*, or even attending both church and synagogue (see chapter 6), but it was perceived by Christian elites in the early decades of the fifth century, from the palace to the pulpit, to be a threat to the stability of an ever-unstable Roman social system.[7] The legal and ideological definition of "orthodoxy" and the concomitant invention of the idea of "illegal religion" were deployed as political tools to consolidate Christian, and thus *imperial*, Roman identity.

There is no denying—nor should we want to—some type of connection between the virulent anti-Jewish rhetoric of the Christian literati and the real violence committed against real Jewish communities in various regions of the empire during the time of Theodosius II and after. As Ross Shepard Kraemer has recently narrated in painstaking detail, the destruction of synagogues, forced conversions of Jews to Christianity, and the denial of Jews to serve in civic offices did, indeed, happen; and the legal situation of Jews in the eastern empire appears to have only worsened in the sixth century under Justinian I.[8] But, as many scholars have noted, constructing social history from law codes, liturgies, and rhetorical texts is a tricky business. Our histories need to

---

6. Fredriksen, "Divinity, Ethnicity, Identity," 111. Fredriksen's view is similar to the one expressed by R. L. Wilken in his *John Chrysostom and the Jews*.

7. On the internal and external challenges to Theodosius II's rule and Roman stability, see A. D. Lee, *From Rome to Byzantinum AD 363–565: The Transformation of Ancient Rome* (Edinburgh: Edinburgh University Press, 2013), 81–198; C. Kelly, "Rethinking Theodosius," in *Theodosius II: Rethinking the Roman Empire in Late Antiquity* (Cambridge: Cambridge University Press, 2013), 1–64.

8. See Kraemer, *Mediterranean Diaspora*, 188–314, pages which include two chapters on the time of Theodosius II and one on Justinian; and, earlier, S. Schwartz, *Imperialism and Jewish Society, 200 BCE to 640 CE* (Princeton, NJ: Princeton University Press, 2001), 186. For a helpful survey of Jews and Jewish life during the time of Justinian, see N. de Lange, "Jews in the Age of Justinian," in *The Cambridge Companion to the Age of Justinian*, ed. M. Maas (Cambridge: Cambridge University Press, 2005), 401–426. On synagogue destruction in Palestine, as well as Jewish liturgical attitudes toward Christians and Christianity around the sixth century, see S. Fine, "Non-Jews in the Synagogues of Late-Antique Palestine: Rabbinic and Archaeological Evidence," in *Jews, Christians, and Polytheists in the Ancient Synagogue: Cultural Interaction During the Greco-Roman Period*, ed. S. Fine (London: Routledge, 1999), 204–207.

resist monocausal explanations and grand metanarratives that represent the hostile attitudes of religious specialists, Jewish and Christian, as immediately equivalent to on-the-ground social realities. We cannot assume, for example, that anti-Jewish homilies from Christian preachers always, or even often, motivated the actual behavior of churchgoers,[9] or that imperial laws were enforced consistently everywhere or even at all.[10] Similarly, within Jewish social contexts, anti-Christian attitudes expressed in the liturgical poetry of the *piyyutim* cannot be taken as descriptions of Jewish thinking about Christians and Christianity *in toto*. A more well-rounded historiography of Jewish–Christian relations will take into account the fact that social conditions differed from region to region, between cities and villages, and were not always marked structurally by conflict and violence. While Jewish communities surely found themselves increasingly marginalized in the legal realm, Judaism, as Schwartz and Fredriksen have reminded us, was never actually outlawed as an "illegal religion," as were the *pagani* and *hereitkoi*, and Jews seem to have remained highly culturally engaged.[11] Indeed, in fifth- and even sixth-century Palestine, Syria, and Asia Minor, there is ample evidence, especially from synagogue archaeology (see below) and ecclesiastical law (see chapter 6), that at least some Jewish communities flourished, continued to have popular pull among Judaizing Christians, and were well-integrated within Roman society.[12] Sources like these make it all the more important for historians to reckon with the fact that Jewish and Christian practices of

---

9. See two studies by Ramsey MacMullen: "The Historical Role of the Masses in Late Antiquity," in his *Changes in the Roman Empire: Essays in the Ordinary* (Princeton, NJ: Princeton University Press, 1990), 250–276 (esp. 271–273), where he argues that churchgoers were usually not propelled into action by sermons and preaching; and "The Preacher's Audience (AD 350–400)," *JTS* 40.2 (1990): 510, where he concludes that churchgoers in major cities, that is, in contexts like John Chrysostom's Constantinople, were actually a quite small selection of the population.

10. Schwartz, *Imperialism*, 186; de Lange, "Jews in the Age of Justinian," 407.

11. Schwartz, *Imperialism*, 186; Fredriksen, "Divinity, Ethnicity, Identity," 111.

12. See the discussion in de Lange, "Jews in the Age of Justinian," 415–418. In my view, one of the best examples of a Galilean Jewish village community thriving in as late as 564 CE comes from the Nabratein (Kefar Nevoraia) synagogue, where a beautifully decorated lintel was inscribed and dated with the following: "According to the counting of four hundred and ninety-four years to (from) the destruction of the Temple (lit. "House"); built during the public service of Ḥanina son of Lizar and Luliana son of Yudan." Translation from *CIIP* V/1 no. 6081.

textualization in late antiquity—liturgical, literary, or legal—had little to do with the aim of representing the "real world" and mostly to do with the concern for ordering specialist knowledge, for power, and for the intracommunity construction of "orthodox" identity.

Literary and homiletical texts, however, were not the only media for shaping and creating religiopolitical ideologies. The boom in monumental architecture, also a kind of "text" in the structuralist sense, reflects an expansion of the rhetorical repertoire of religious providers in late antiquity.[13] In this period, monumental architecture became a spatial and visual tool to mobilize ideology and, alongside words, to order knowledge about the socioreligious and political realms. Capernaum is a prime example of this use of architecture. Sometime during the fifth to sixth century, two monumental buildings, an octagonal church and a basilical synagogue, were erected approximately twenty-five meters away from each other. Each of them is a rhetorical *tour de force*; neither of them can be understood apart from the other. In this chapter, I explore the rhetorical dimensions of these buildings, asking what messages their architectures might have communicated about space and power, and about the making, defining, and controling of Jewish and Christian identity in the village. This analysis will be followed up in chapter 6, in which I will "read" these architectural messages skeptically and against the grain of Capernaum's broader built landscape, with the goal of constructing some aspects of the social history of Jewish–Christian interaction in the fifth- and sixth-century village.

The current chapter has three main movements. First, I provide a brief theoretical discussion that frames my approach to the discursive nature of monumental architecture as a social practice and its inherent connection to public displays of power and cultural agency. The emergence of the octagonal church and limestone synagogue visually and tangibly transformed Capernaum's built landscape. This observation is obvious enough. What we need, however, is a mechanism to interpret *how* these buildings contributed to this transformation and *what* their architecture might have meant within the larger cultural, discursive context of Jewish–Christian relations in this region of the

---

13. Victor Buchli, *An Anthropology of Architecture* (London: Bloomsbury, 2013), 17, mentions that the "material register of built form" can be understood in different ways, such as "text, sign system, as embodied experience; visually, tactilely, aurally, and so on." Hagith Sivan's notes that architecture came alongside words in the expression of violence between Christians and Jews in Palestine in late antiquity. See H. Sivan, *Palestine in Late Antiquity*, 24.

Byzantine Empire.[14] The second and third movements of the chapter represent my interpretations of the architectures of the octagonal church and limestone synagogue. My primary aim in these sections is not to settle debates about the dating and typologies of these buildings, debates which have characterized much of the discussion about the limestone synagogue in particular. Rather, I am interested in how each building represents a strategic answer to questions about the nature of "Jewishness" and "Christianness," and thus how, together, they represent a dialectical discussion of sorts.[15]

2. Architecture and Power

Monumental architecture has always been a form of cultural production linked intimately, even subserviently, to political, cultural, and economic power.[16] Lisa

---

14. The basic principle that architecture conveys meaning beyond its formal and technical qualities was developed methodologically in the mid-twentieth century by Richard Krautheimer in his study of medieval Christian architecture. It has been recently—and, in my view, successfully—applied in Jordan Ryan's study of early Christian architecture. See J. Ryan, *From the Passion to the Church of the Holy Sepulchre*, 15–16.

15. My use here of the terms "strategic," "question and answer," and "dialectical discussion" are technical methodological concepts. In using them, I am not presupposing that the buildings represent a single, essentialized "answer" to a corresponding single, essentialized "question" about Jewish and Christian identities. Rather, "question and answer" is a type of logical framework that features in Robin Collingwood's epistemology and guides his approach to historical thinking. See especially the excellent treatment of this aspect of Collingwood's philosophy in two articles by Christopher Fear: "The Question-and-Answer Logic of Historical Context," *History of the Human Sciences* 26, no. 3 (2013): 68–81; "Collingwood's Logic of Question and Answer: Against the Relativization of Reason," in *Other Logics: Alternatives to Formal Logic in the History of Thought and Contemporary Philosophy*, ed. A. Skodo (Leiden: Brill, 2014), 81–100. In short, all sources of historical construction—written documents, material remains, and the like—are assertions, answers to preexisting questions that confronted the authors and makers of the sources in their particular culturally and historically conditioned contexts. For Collingwood, historical knowledge does not consist wholly of these assertions, of these "answers." To think that would equate to a "crude empiricism" in which "to know and to assert are identical" (R. G. Collingwood, *Speculum Mentis, or The Map of Knowledge* [Oxford: Clarendon, (1924) 1963], 77; cited in Fear, "Collingwood's Logic of Question and Answer," 86). In other words, history is not identical to its sources, and sources do not hold absolute sovereignty over our thinking about the past. Instead, historical knowledge involves the historian's seeking to understand as much as possible the questions for which a source is offering an answer. It is in this "dialectical discussion"—the logic of "question and answer"—that knowledge emerges and history is constructed.

16. See T. Markus, *Buildings and Power: Freedom and Control in the Origin of Modern Buildings* (London: Routledge, 1993).

Findley, whose work I introduced in the previous chapter, has written at length about how, as a spatial practice, architecture gives physical form to ideology, communicating messages about power relationships and the construction of identity.[17] Architecture, then, is related to the larger entanglement of power with the control of space; it is the occupation of space through building, and, as such, it is a means deployed by power to transform, circumscribe, and control a landscape as well as those who inhabit it.[18] Architecture visibly declares the presence of power in the current moment, and it establishes a spatial legacy that is neither neutral nor innocent but rather that embodies the attitudes, cultural practices, and ideologies of the power that produced it. In other words, architecture emerges as a direct spatial consequence of power—the ability of an individual or group to act on their own behalf, to exercise and impose their agency—with power and space joined at the proverbial hip, a point made over forty years ago by Michel Foucault when he presumed that writing the history of spaces would be a task one and the same with writing the history of powers.[19] Buildings, therefore, are material signposts of power, of political, economic, and cultural agency.

Architecture locates power in time and place, deploying various visual and spatial strategies intended to mediate relationships, for example, between people, between people and knowledge, and between people and things.[20] Architecture, thus, spatializes on a smaller scale the social and epistemological systems that make up larger political and cultural contexts. Changes in these larger contexts are often accompanied by changes in spatial organization at various scales, from individual bodies to buildings, neighborhoods, and entire nations. For example, Findley discusses in detail the devastating large-scale and long-lasting spatial impact that European colonialism brought upon the landscapes of African and Pacific regions, and the use of architecture as a spatial

---

17. Here, and in this section generally, I am dependent on Findley's theoretical insights presented throughout her book *Building Change: Architecture, Politics, and Cultural Agency*.

18. The relationship between space, power, and (colonial) control over landscapes is a topic of particular interest in postcolonial analysis and can be seen already as a major theme in Edward Said's *Orientalism* (New York: Random House, 1978).

19. M. Foucault, *Power/Knowledge: Selected Interviews and Other Writings 1972–1977*, ed. Colin Gordon (New York: Pantheon Books, 1980), 149.

20. Markus, *Buildings and Power*, 39.

strategy for transforming these landscapes.[21] Building was, and continues to be, a strategy used to inscribe onto colonized landscapes Eurocentric values and, simultaneously, to erase the cultural and political autonomy of indigenous populations.

On the other hand, a major theme in Findley's work is to show that architecture can also play a subversive role in the endeavor to critique and resist power. Just as buildings can be expressions of the agency of the powerful—those with access to political, economic, and cultural capital—they, too, can function to empower oppressed social groups, proclaim their presence, and promote social change. Buildings small and large have the capacity to function pragmatically and symbolically as material participants in the reoccupation of space and to provide a spatialized framework for the reclamation and restoration of a marginalized group's cultural agency and visibility. Thus, one of the most effective responses to power is to do as power does: transform space. Just as larger scale changes in political and cultural contexts influence the spatial landscape, so too do smaller scale changes in a building's architectural organization influence the social and epistemic meanings of a built space. When space is occupied differently, dynamics of power, transmission of knowledge, and modes of acting and being acted upon are likewise transformed.

As Findley notes, perhaps the most basic and nearly universal expression of spatial power occurs when social hierarchies, including their economic and cultural components, are translated into physical spatial hierarchies.[22] Social hierarchies are the building blocks of power. They are constructed using a range of socially expedient mechanisms of classification (e.g., race, ethnicity, gender, class) and function to stratify social groups according to levels of authority, status, and access to resources. Such hierarchies impact the spatial landscape at various scales. Buildings that occupy the space of a city center or the axis of a major road signal their position of political power; entire cities

---

21. Findley's analysis of space and colonial power is scattered throughout her book, and she is in frequent touch with the work of other postcolonial theorists, including Edward Said's work mentioned above.

22. Findley, *Building Change*, 9; see pp. 11–27 for her discussion of other spatial strategies of power: marginalization, segregation, and larger-scale, longer-term mechanisms of spatial transformation, such as apartheid, colonialism, and globalization.

have been spatially arranged to marginalize and segregate groups of people perceived to be at the bottom of the racial hierarchy, as many cities indeed were in the American South during the Jim Crow era and in South Africa during Apartheid.[23]

The architecture of a single building, by means of its external design and internal spatial organization, can reify or resist hierarchies that exist within a larger society, doing so in a carefully circumscribed space. Ancient temples, with their monumental external design and proclivity to stratify internal space according to levels of proximity to the divine, are prototypical examples of this point. Today, too, large buildings constructed, for example, with advanced technologies and expensive, rare, or non-local materials, speak an architectural language that communicates a powerful economic presence and control of material resources. Buildings designed in a neoclassical style or with so-called "stripped classical" art and architecture—like many political buildings were in Europe and the United States beginning in the mid-eighteenth century—invoke classical antiquity to visibly mark the ideology of European cultural hegemony in the modern world. In buildings such as museums, libraries, schools, and cultural centers, architecture plays a major role in the construction—or deconstruction—of cultural hierarchies, as built space physically locates and materially mediates the production of knowledge and memory.

As we approach Capernaum's monumental landscape, this complex relationship between built space and the exercise of power is kept central. Like their spatial predecessors from the Greco-Roman past and their multitudinous descendants in the contemporary world, churches and synagogues of late antiquity, in their various architectural forms, were not simply religious buildings that facilitated communication between heaven and earth. They were assertions of presence and agency, sites of epistemological and cultural production, and makers of social hierarchies. They set the spatial script for the performance and control of orthodox knowledge and identity. But, within the colonial context of the Byzantine East, monumental architecture also

---

23. On the specific case of Montgomery, Alabama, see C. E. Barton, "Duality and Invisibility: Race and Memory in the Urbanism of the American South," in *Sites of Memory: Perspectives on Architecture and Race*, ed. C. E. Barton (New York: Princeton Architectural Press, 2001), 1–12.

provided, particularly for Jewish communities, a playbook for the spatial resistance of power and new expressions of cultural identity. As we will see, many of these spatial dynamics were at work in fifth- and sixth-century Capernaum.

3. Architecturalizing Power
The Death of the Christaeum *and the Birth of the Octagon*

The material end of Capernaum's *christaeum*—Room 1 and all the structures of its larger *insula*—was not the result of natural disaster, human accident, or slow and steady decay. Rather, being intentionally buried under a fill,[24] the building was "killed," a term used by some architectural historians and anthropologists not only to describe the destruction and disembodiment of a building but also to capture the intense animacy of built forms and their inherent effect on social relations.[25] Victor Buchli notes that "because buildings as such are extensions of individual and collective minds, when they are destroyed, much more than the individual or the building is killed."[26] That is, architectural forms shape social structures not only by means of their presence but also by means of their absence, by means of their destruction and disposal.[27] For, when buildings die, opportunities are generated to rethink social order and continuity. Indeed, buildings arguably acquire *more* meaning, or what Buchli describes as "excess meaning," when they are killed; they take on an added significance by reconfiguring epistemological frameworks and producing new social effects.[28] The death of a building is inextricably bound to the meaning of that building's life and of the bodies that once supplied it with life-sustaining practices. But the divestment and disembodiment of a building—its becoming "lifeless"—also produces meaning for the object that "re-places" and "re-presences" the absence that once occupied the space. From this perspective, the act of "re-presencing" a

---

24. Loffreda, *Recovering Capharnaum*, 64–66.

25. See the discussion, from an anthropological perspective, on the concepts of the animacy, destruction, and ruination of built forms in Buchli, *Anthropology of Architecture*, 243–258.

26. Buchli, *Anthropology of Architecture*, 249.

27. Buchli, *Anthropology of Architecture*, 233.

28. Buchli, *Anthropology of Architecture*, 245–247.

killed building—building in place of, building over, rebuilding—leads, at the least, to the fracturing of collective memory, if not to the willful forgetting of the past and its erasure.[29]

To understand the birth of Capernaum's octagonal church in the mid-fifth century,[30] we need to appreciate its connection to the death of Capernaum's *christaeum*. The *christaeum* was neither razed to the ground nor pulled apart limb from limb; rather, it was filled in, filled up, and built over, with the concentric octagon then being erected on a raised platform. The foundations of the inner octagon were set directly upon the walls of Room 1.[31]

There are many examples from ancient pagan, Jewish, and Christian contexts of religious buildings being erected over top of preexisting structures or being variously incorporated into a new build. But it is often difficult to interpret the message being communicated when one building dies so that another might live. Is it one of social continuity or discontinuity? Of antagonism and suppression, or friendship and rapport? Or perhaps the message is more mundane: the previous building had run the course of its material life, a new one was needed to serve daily social needs, and it was simply easier to build on top of older remains. Seen in isolation, neither the octagon's "re-presencing" function nor its architectural form is able to answer this question with any texture; after all, octagonal churches were fairly commonplace in Christian architecture in late antiquity, being especially associated with martyria, that

---

29. Buchli, *Anthropology of Architecture*, 250–251, discusses the reconstruction of the Frauenkirche in Dresden, which was destroyed by Allied bombs during the Second World War and the site left empty until the end of communism. Buchli, summarizing the work of architectural historian Adrian Forty says, "The church was rebuilt to forget socialism and the memory of wartime trauma. Forty observes how the rebuilding, then, paradoxically silenced two distinct memories in the experience of twentieth-century history" (251).

30. Scholars seem generally to agree on the fifth-century date of the octagonal building. See, for example, Corbo, *Cafarnao I*, 54–56; Loffreda, *Recovering Capharnaum*, 64; Taylor, *Christians and the Holy Places*, 269; L. M. White, *The Social Origins of Christian Architecture*, 158; Riesner, "What Does Archaeology Teach Us," 174. Foerster, "Recent Excavations at Capernaum," 207–211, suggested a sixth-century date based upon a comparison with the Church of the Theotokos on Mt. Gerizim, which was built in the last decade of the fifth century, and which he believes predates the octagonal church at Capernaum. Taylor is sympathetic to Foerster's view but does not clearly endorse his dating. Strange, "The Capernaum and Herodium Publications (Part 1)," 68, on the other hand, suggests the octagon was finished in the mid-fifth century but began in the late fourth to early fifth century.

31. Loffreda, *Recovering Capharnaum*, 64, 66. See also the earlier description given in Corbo, *The House of Saint Peter*, 20.

Image 5.1. Aerial view (looking south) of the octagonal church and limestone synagogue. From Loffreda, *Cafarnao V*, 47 (DF 27). Used here with permission.

is, with shrines devoted to the commemoration of either a holy site or an early Christian hero (see further discussion below).[32] Thus, the key to answering this question, in my view, is to approach the Capernaum octagon diachronically and contextually.

Vered Shalev-Hurvitz notes that what made the Capernaum octagon unique was not its shape or technological production—although those, too, are important for its understanding—but rather its construction in a Jewish

---

32. On Byzantine round and octagonal churches, see the authoritative study of Vered Shalev-Hurvitz, *Holy Sites Encircled: The Early Byzantine Concentric Churches of Jerusalem* (Oxford: Oxford University Press, 2015). Pages 267–273 contain her treatment of the Capernaum octagon, which I will discuss further below.

Image 5.2. Looking southeast. Central octagon set on the walls of *sala venerata*.

Image from Loffreda, *Cafarnao V*, 56 (DF 38). Used here with permission.

village.³³ However, it was erected at a time of discernable growth in the presence of non-Jewish Christians who had emigrated from other regions of the Roman East, such as Asia Minor, Cyprus, Syria, and North Africa.³⁴ Eventually, the demographics of the village shifted toward a non-Jewish majority,

---

33. Shalev-Hurvitz, *Holy Sites Encircled*, 272, who contends that Capernaum remained predominately Jewish well into the fifth century.

34. See Mattila, "Capernaum, Village of Naḥum," 246, 251. The emergence of the octagon parallels the influx of Late Roman Fine Wares from Cypress and North Africa with stylized crosses that flowed into the village along with the hands that carried them. Fifth-century coinage from around the eastern Mediterranean found in Capernaum also suggests foot traffic from abroad and an increasingly globalized economy in the village.

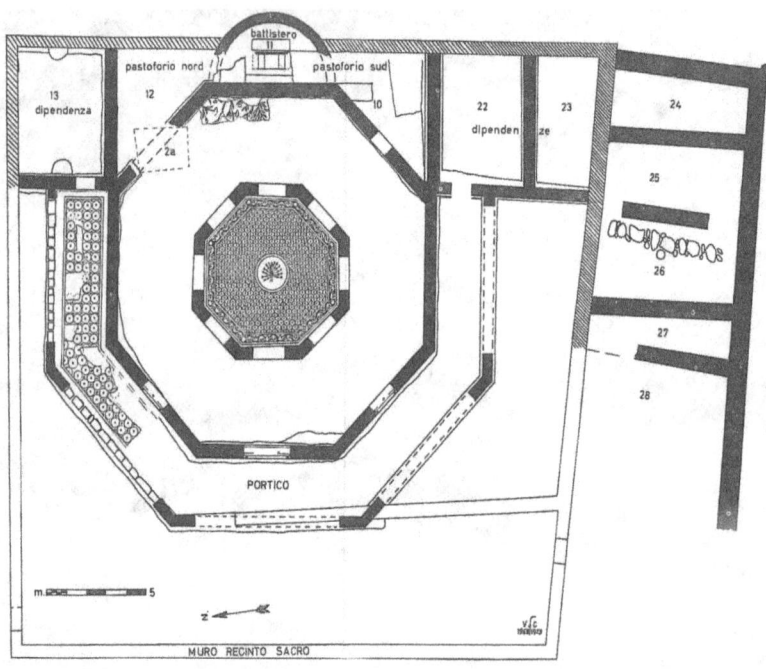

Image 5.3. Plan of a mid-fifth-century octagonal church.

Image from Corbo, *Cafarnao I*, Tavola IV. Used here with permission.

but it, nevertheless, seems to have retained a strong-voiced Jewish minority (see Section 4 below).[35] The plan of the octagon represents a stark departure

---

35. Runesson, "Architecture," 250–251 notes that, in fifth- and sixth-century Capernaum, non-Jewish Christians were "certainly in control." While I agree that, population-wise, non-Jewish Christians probably held the majority by this time in the village, it is quite another thing to argue that this group "controled" the village, if by "control" one means power over local political and administrative governance. Christian material culture in Capernaum— which Runesson points to in his observation about such control—certainly gives us solid evidence for a strong Christian cultural presence. However, it does not say much, if anything, about political and administrative control in the village. Indeed, this type of Christian power would not have had a seat in Capernaum itself, which was still a rather small rural town in the fifth and sixth centuries, and which lacked a building for imperial administration. While the Capernaum octagon was certainly a political building, it likely did not serve civic administrative purposes; as I will suggest below, it was a building that curated a "cult of saints," that is, the cult of the apostle Peter. Capernaum, instead, would have been governed administratively from either the provincial capital by the *hegemon* of *Palaestina Secunda* (Scythopolis/Beth Shean) or perhaps by a council of local elites from Scythopolis or, more likely, Tiberias,

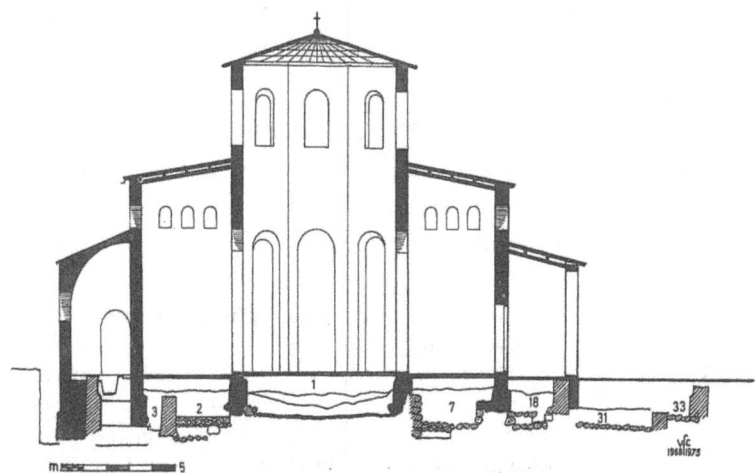

Image 5.4. Hypothetical reconstruction of the mid-fifth-century octagonal church.

Image from Corbo, *Cafarnao I*, Tavola V. Used here with permission.

from the spatial arrangement of *insula* 1 in its three earlier phases, all of which were characterized by a local vernacular architecture, even if rearticulated and enlarged as in the case of the *christaeum*.

The concentric octagon transformed Capernaum's spatial landscape by re-presencing the vernacular architecture of Room 1—which had, since the late Hellenistic period, been rooted in the material culture tradition of Jewish Galilean houses—with a monumental form strongly reflective of non-local Roman-Byzantine cultural identity.[36] The *christaeum* had been designed to facilitate a tactile cultic commemorative experience that was predicated

---

whose main responsibility it was to enforce imperial wishes both in the city and in the rural areas adjacent to the city, especially regarding public infrastructure and taxation. How well and evenly these local councils of elites enforced imperial mandates, particularly beyond the collection of taxes, is a significant question, the answer to which is: probably not very evenly, especially in rural areas. See P. Filipczak, *An Introduction to the Byzantine Administration in Syro-Palestine on the Eve of the Arab Conquest*, Byzantina Lodziensia 26, trans. A. Mękarski (Lodz: Wydawnictwo Uniwersytetu Łódzkiego, 2015), 79.

36. See Shalev-Hurvitz, *Holy Sites Encircled*, 8–11, 20–24, 168–195 on the Greco-Roman origins and Byzantine adaptation of round and octagonal buildings. Shalev-Hurvitz mentions no Jewish settings in which such architectural forms were employed. This does mean Jewish communities were unfamiliar with such architecture, only that currently we have no examples of Jewish groups employing the round or octagonal form in their building activity.

upon Room 1's direct visibility, its accessibility, and its incorporation of earlier "original" parts of the early Roman residence. Like a museum, it was meant to mediate and construct memories of Jesus in the apostle Peter's historical house, as it really was back then. While the octagonal building continued the commemorative tradition of Peter's house in Capernaum,[37] it fundamentally reconfigured and reordered this memory by rejecting the site's material past through a strategy of nonincorporation and invisibility, of erasure.[38] The

37. In around the year 570, the anonymous Piacenza Pilgrim wrote, rather tersely, in a travel log: "Then we came to Capernaum and the house of blessed Peter which is now a basilica." English translation is by Andrew S. Jacobs (http://andrewjacobs.org/translations/piacenzapilgrim.html). The Latin reads: *Item veniemus in Capharnaum in domo beati Petri, quae est modo basilica* (*CSEL* 39:163). There is some debate over the pilgrim's use of the term *bisilica* and whether what the pilgrim refers to coincides with the octagon that was excavated by Corbo and Loffreda. See Taylor's presentation of some of the relevant questions in *Christians and the Holy Places*, 272–273. She concludes, rightly in my view, that *basilica* was a loose term for the pilgrim and need not necessarily refer to another building. See also Shalev-Hurvitz, *Holy Sites Encircled*, 269 n.322, who concurs with Taylor's view.

38. Shalev-Hurvitz suggests that the octagon was built over a (random?) fourth-century housing complex—not a Christ-oriented building—and that "the ancient walls, within a centrally planned structure, were preserved, in order to establish the authenticity of a specific old residential house as a historical 'house', which had been Jesus' residence while he was active in the village, and, contrary to the excavators' view, this could be done only while building the octagonal church, not previously" (*Holy Sites Encircled*, 271). In my view, there are a number of problems with Shalev-Hurvitz's suggestion here. First, she argues that the octagon in the mid-fifth century is the first indication of Christian veneration in Capernaum, dismissing the earlier evidence for Christ-worship and (what I have called) the *christaeum*. Shalev-Hurvitz seems to base most, if not all, of her argument on the absence in some literary sources (especially Eusebius's *Onomasticon* and Epiphanius's *Panarion*) of the mention of a House of Peter that, for her, should have been known by these authors if there was such a fourth-century church in Capernaum (270). But, as I mentioned in chapter 4, Eusebius, like his contemporary the Bordeaux Pilgrim, most likely wrote before the renovation of Room 1 into the *christaeum*; Room 1 was a heavily plastered room within a larger housing complex when Eusebius wrote the *Onomasticon*. Besides, in *Onomasticon*, Eusebius is generally sparse in his remarks on Christianity and says very little about Constantine's building projects in fourth-century Palestine. It is possible that the *christaeum* was not built even when Epiphanius wrote the *Panarion* in the mid-370s. But even if it was, the same general argument holds: the *christaeum* was still couched in the vernacular architecture of Capernaum's domestic landscape, and it was not yet the important pilgrimage center it would become a half-century later. And, in any case, Epiphanius says hardly anything about his awareness of Christian buildings anywhere. His saying nothing specific about a house of Peter that was a church is entirely not surprising. And neither is it surprising that the monk Valerius of Bierzo and Jerome fail

erection of the octagon meant that Room 1 was divested of real bodies, of tactility, of visual and spatial access, and that the local vernacular memory of the room as a Jewish house was effaced. Thus, the birth of the octagon in Capernaum as a commemorative church was also, and at the same time, a material manifestation of power through a kind of iconoclasm of memory; as it ordered knowledge about the past within its own cultural frame, it destroyed past knowledge of a building that resided outside of it. The octagon represented a type of break with *insula* 1's Jewish past characterized by colonial absorption; this past had been literally and metaphorically "built over."[39]

Within the context of this death and life material situation, the form of the octagonal building itself now deserves further consideration. Recalling Findley's study, the external design and internal organization of a building are inherently connected to the power relations it attempts to construct. The formal, functional, and ideological origins of concentric churches are debated,

---

to mention it. One the other hand, while Shalev-Hurvitz points to the absence of evidence in several early Christian literary sources, she dismisses the evidence of Peter the Deacon's (twelfth century) description of the house of Peter, which might preserve the missing section of Egeria's diary that describes her visit to Capernaum. The authentically Egerian character of Peter the Deacon's description has been debated for quite a long time; Shalev-Hurvitz is not alone in her rejection of it, but she fails to interact with John Wilkinson's argument, which I find persuasive: while Peter the Deacon's editorial hand is discernable, it is likely that he preserves an Egerian "core." The passage he preserves can, therefore, be used as support for a fourth-century Christ-oriented building that was already at that time associated with the memory of St. Peter's house. Second, Shalev-Hurvitz says next to nothing about the archaeological evidence for the fourth-century building and its use for Christ-cult, which, as I have argued in chapter 4, is substantial when viewed from a critical historiographical and diachronic perspective. Third, her statement that the octagon "preserves" the "ancient walls" of the fourth-century housing structures "in order to establish the authenticity of a specific residential house as a historic 'house'" is, to my mind, somewhat of a mischaracterization. It is true, as I noted above, that the walls of the *christaeum* were not razed; rather they were completely buried. To what extent can one call the act of being buried under a fill preservation? Preservation implies continuity, of which, architecturally, we see virtually none in the transition of *insula* 1 from *christaeum* to octagon. Further, Shalev-Hurvitz is absolutely right that the architecture of *insula* 1 was used "to establish the authenticity of a specific residential house as a historic 'house,'" but this is the strategy of the fourth-century *christaeum*—a building which *did*, in fact, preserve the ancient walls of the previous housing complex—not the fifth-century octagonal church.

39. Such a discontinuity between the *christaeum* and the octagon—and the identities projected by them—is noted also by Runesson, "Architecture," 247–248.

and it is probably the case that any monogenetic explanation is destined to miss the mark.[40] The earliest concentric Christian buildings in Palestine—the Anastasis (in the Church of the Holy Sepulchre) and the Church of the Ascension in Jerusalem in the fourth century, and the Church of Mary's Tomb and the Kathisma in the first half of the fifth century—were all built over sites associated with the life of Jesus, which suggests that the Capernaum octagon took its cue from the monumental architecture of these earlier Jerusalem churches and shared a similar commemorative function.[41] On the one hand, by the middle of the fifth century, Capernaum generally and Room 1 specifically had already been a place of Christian commemoration for 350 years. On the other hand, with the raising of the octagon, the ways in which commemoration was performed spatially and, therefore, institutionally fundamentally changed.

Unlike basilicas, which were rectangular in form and generally easier to build, concentric churches were circumscribed, self-contained, and required much more sophistication geometrically and technologically.[42] They took an immense amount of theoretical knowledge, architectural skill, and generous patronage, whether from city elites or the emperor himself, and thus often spatialized class and economic hierarchies within particular social settings.[43] Spatially, rather than having a focus in the short wall of the building opposite the entrance, at the apse, the focus in a concentric structure was in the center,

---

40. Greek *heroa*, which were used to commemorate the heroes of Greece's mythological past, Roman mausolea, palace halls, and even baths are examples of some of the possible conceptual and concrete precursors of the round and octagonal churches of late antiquity. There is no doubting the general point that concentric churches were the cultural progeny of Roman architectural practice, in particular the concentric architecture of imperial family tombs and earlier domed buildings like Hadrian's grand Pantheon in Rome. See discussions in Shalev-Hurvitz, *Holy Sites Encircled*, 8–11, 169–176.

41. This is a point emphasized in Shalev-Hurvitz, *Holy Sites Encircled* and followed closely by Ryan, *Memories of Jesus*.

42. On the history and architecture of the Christian basilica, see J. R. Strange, "Christianity: The Fourth Century Christian Basilica," in *Religious Texts and Material Contexts*, ed. J. Neusner and J. F. Strange (Lanham, MD: University Press of America, 2001), 89–138; and J. R. Strange, "Does Archaeology Generate Propositions about Religion?" in *A City Set on a Hill: Essays in Honor of James F. Strange* (Mountain Home, AZ: BorderStone Press, 2014), 298–317. See also Shalev-Hurvitz, *Holy Sites Encircled*, 20–24 for her discussion of some of the major characteristics of concentric churches in general.

43. See Shalev-Hurvitz, *Holy Sites Encircled*, 169–180.

like the bullseye of an archery target. The Capernaum octagon's centripetal focus is a point of continuity with the previous spatial arrangement of the fourth-century *christaeum*, and the quadrilateral enclosure wall continued to provide a neat perimeter for the mid-fifth-century building as well.[44] The delineation of space, however, was much more pronounced and clearly hierarchical in the octagon. The building had an inner octagonal core that was segregated by one complete surrounding concentric aisle, the ambulatory, which itself was segregated by a partially surrounding aisle that formed a five-sided semioctagon; the remaining three sides were directly integrated with several eastern dependent rooms.[45] This outer aisle functioned as a portico, which, although lacking circumferential niches or small chapels like the slightly earlier Kathisma Church (Jerusalem) and the slightly later Church of the Theotokos (Mt. Gerizim),[46] did have a mosaic pavement and three doorways that granted movement eastward into the ambulatory.[47] The ambulatory does not appear to have had a mosaic pavement, but its shape allowed for the continual circulation of bodies around the inner core,[48] which was supported by eight pilasters and probably crowned by arches to allow easy visual access to the center.[49] The

---

44. While the enclosure wall maintained its basic form when the octagon was built, it did receive some modifications. According to Loffreda, the western portion of the wall was "cut down to the average level of the mosaic floor of the church" in order to create a more direct approach to the church. See Loffreda, *Recovering Capharnaum*, 64.

45. See description in Corbo, *House of Saint Peter*, 10–11.

46. Shalev-Hurvitz dates the fifth-century construction phase of the Kathisma to 431 to 439, with restoration happening in the sixth century, which included a new dome, support system, large new *bema*, and an apse (*Holy Sites Encircled*, 140). She dates the Church of the Theotokos on Mt. Gerizim to 474 to 491 (pp. 216–35). The Capernaum octagon is also significantly smaller than these other octagonal churches; indeed, it is the smallest on record (see plate 19 C in *Holy Sites Encircled* for size comparisons of concentric churches).

47. Shalev-Hurvitz, *Holy Sites Encircled*, 268, presumes that the portico had arched spans supported by Ionic columns. But she bases her assumption not on archaeological evidence—the excavators mention no such remains—but on a nineteenth-century drawing of the ruins of Capernaum, in which arched spans and Ionic columns are depicted.

48. Whereas the Christian basilica segregated space by inviting foot traffic to start at one end of the building and end at the other, the concentric church moved devotees around the object of commemoration. On the spatial arrangement of the Christian basilica, see Strange, "Christian Basilica," 105.

49. Corbo, *House of Saint Peter*, 10.

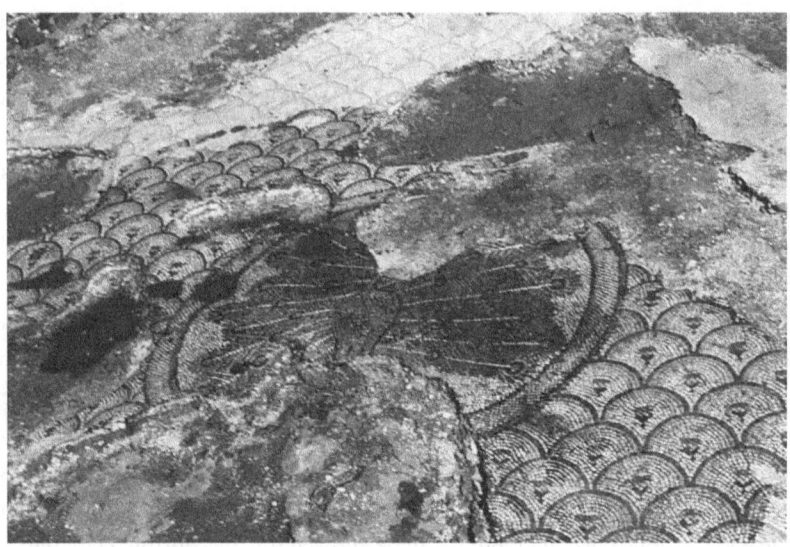

Image 5.5. Photo looking southeast of the damaged mosaic pavement containing the image of a peacock. This was the floor of the octagonal church, which, when first laid, sealed the earlier phases of Room 1 from view.

From Loffreda, *Cafarnao V*, 82 (DF 98a). Used here with permission.

inner octagon, the "holy hot spot," likely supported a wooden dome or vaulted roof covered with tiles,[50] and it had a mosaic pavement, at the center of which was the image of a peacock.

The shape of concentric churches—round and octagonal—created the perception of an architecturally incorruptible and geometrically perfect building. Shalev-Hurvitz has noted that "the inflexibility of the structure, its closed symmetrical form with one central focus and its perpetual qualities supported the notion that it represents eternity, and thus the crowning dome was frequently fashioned as heaven, as a 'firmament' (gold or starry blue) which divides the outer world and the inner, round world."[51] In Capernaum, as bodies were invited into an unending orbit around the inner octagon, eyes were directed to the center to ponder a depiction of a peacock. The peacock,

---

50. Corbo, *House of Saint Peter*, 10, 16. On the use of wood in the construction of domed buildings, se Shalev-Hurvitz, *Holy Sites Encircled*, 172–173.

51. Shalev-Hurvitz, *Holy Sites Encircled*, 22–23.

common in Roman funerary iconography, was pervasive, too, in ancient Christian art, appearing in the Roman catacombs, on sarcophagi, and, as in Capernaum, in church decoration.[52] While it has no scriptural connection, the peacock, like the phoenix and the dolphin, was associated with the ideas of fleshly resurrection and immortality, perhaps, as Robin Jensen has suggested, because of the belief that its flesh was incorruptible.[53] Thus, the art and concentric architecture of the octagon combined to spatialize knowledge about Christian perpetuity, eternity, and immortality. Together they fashioned a Christian body that was propelled into constant motion through the mind's commemoration of apostolic space and the message not only of Christ's fleshly resurrection but also the hope of one's own.

The shape of the octagon, specifically, and therefore how it spatialized knowledge, had a meaning potential that other concentric forms, such as round or tetraconchal churches, did not. Scholars have long recognized the significance of the *ogdoad*, or octave, in early Christian thought.[54] The origins of the symbolic significance of the *ogdoad* are probably to be found in ancient Egyptian creation myths, but, as Stig Frøyshov notes, many early Christians, from Justin Martyr to John Chrysostom, latched on to it as a way to express their theology of "the Lord's Day" as the first and the eighth day of the week, as the day of Christ's resurrection, and thus as a replacement and supplantation of the Jewish sabbath: "The idea of Sunday as the eighth day expresses the fundamental opposition between the Jewish cultic day and the Christian cultic day, probably within an anti-Jewish polemic."[55] Thus, the eight-sided shape of

---

52. R. M. Jensen, *Understanding Early Christian Art* (London: Routledge, 2000), 159.

53. Jensen, *Understanding Early Christian Art*, 159 and 159 n.20. For the idea of the incorruptibility of the peacock's flesh, see Augustine, *Civ. Dei* 21.4.

54. From the perspective of the history of Christian liturgy, see the important study by Stig Simeon R. Frøyshov, "The Early Development of the Liturgical Eight-Mode System in Jerusalem," *St. Vladimir's Theological Quarterly* 51.2–3 (2007):149–150. I thank Stig for our conversation about this topic and for alerting me to his article.

55. Frøyshov, "Eight-Mode System," 150. Two of the earliest texts to do this are the *Epistle of Barnabas* and Justin Martyr in his *Dialogue with Trypho*. *Ep. Barn.* 15:8–9: "Finally, he says to them: 'I cannot stand your new moons and sabbaths.' You see what he means: it is not the present sabbaths that are acceptable to me, but the one that I have made; on that sabbath, after I have set everything at rest, I will create the beginning of an eighth day, which is the beginning of another world. This is why we spend the eighth day in celebration, the day on which Jesus both arose from the dead and, after appearing again, ascended into heaven."

the octagon aligned ideologically with ancient Christian ideas about Christianity's ultimate and eternal triumph over Judaism.[56] And, as Frøyshov's article demonstrates, the supersessionist impetus of the eightfold pattern extended to the composition of Christian liturgy, in particular the liturgical and musical system of eight modes developed and used in fifth- and sixth-century Jerusalem known as the Oktoechos ("eight[fold] sound").[57]

The relationship between the *ogdoad* and the idea of Christian triumph over Judaism is especially pronounced in Capernaum. Erected on a platform and raised above street level in the middle of a historically Jewish town, the octagon projected a sociocultural hierarchy at the same time as it projected a spatial one. The external form of the octagon took the type of Christian self-definition constructed through its hierarchical internal design and commemorative content and turned it outward, into a rhetoric of spatial appropriation, of takeover and of ownership of memory. The ideology of Christian resurrection and immortality was imposed upon Capernaum's built landscape. In the context of this village, the octagonal form communicated something very similar to what the *Epistle of Barnabas* expressed

---

Justin, *Dial*. 41: "The command of circumcision, again, bidding [them] always circumcise the children on the eighth day, was a type of the true circumcision, by which we are circumcised from deceit and iniquity through Him who rose from the dead on the first day after the Sabbath, [namely through] our Lord Jesus Christ. For the first day after the Sabbath, remaining the first of all the days, is called, however, the eighth, according to the number of all the days of the cycle, and [yet] remains the first." *Dial*. 138: "For righteous Noah, along with the other mortals at the deluge, i.e., with his own wife, his three sons and their wives, being eight in number, were a symbol of the eighth day, wherein Christ appeared when He rose from the dead, for ever the first in power." Frøyshov article demonstrates in great detail that the sociotheological symbolism of the *ogdoad* was still vital in Palestinian Christianity in the fifth century and continued to influence liturgical development in the sixth century.

56. Shalev-Hurvitz, *Holy Sites Encircled*, 186–187 notes that concentric churches in general may have functioned to supplant "foreign cults," since many of them were built over previous pagan and Jewish cultic sites.

57. Frøyshov, "Eight-Mode System," 171–173. Shalev-Hurvitz, *Holy Sites Encircled*, 187–188, notes that besides the Anastasis in the Church of the Holy Sepulchre, the other concentric churches of Jerusalem seem to have served monastic communities. Frøyshov notes that the Oktoechos was a public or cathedral liturgy, not a monastic liturgy. Thus, on the one hand, we cannot assume that the eight-mode liturgical system was actually used in the Capernaum octagon. On the other hand, there is no evidence that the Capernaum octagon serviced a monastic community specifically and restrictedly. There is nothing that precludes the performance of the Oktoechos in Capernaum. Nevertheless, my basic point above is not to say that it was but rather to show how the symbolism of the *ogdoad* influenced Christian architecture and liturgy in Palestine in late antiquity more broadly.

nearly three centuries earlier regarding the replacement of the Jewish sabbath with the eighth day: "the beginning of another world" (*Ep. Barn.* 15:8). And that world was, by the mid-fifth century, ruled and ordered by politically empowered Christians.[58]

The rhetoric of Christian triumphalism spatialized in the Capernaum octagon seems to have extended to its ritual aspects as well. Sometime after its initial construction, two additions were made to the octagon: an apse was constructed on the building's eastern side, which broke through and protruded slightly beyond the earlier eastern wall of the enclosure wall, and a narrow baptistery was made with steps in the middle of the apse.[59] Shalev-Hurvitz suggests that the addition of the baptistery coincided with the sharp increase of pilgrimage to Palestine in the sixth century, and that the main purpose of the church, therefore, became missionary in nature, as it functioned primarily to offer baptism to these Christian travelers.[60] This is certainly a reasonable hypothesis, which is supported by the fact that the apsidal baptistery created a new axial focus that reduced, or at least destabilized the importance of the center.[61] It should be emphasized, however, that baptism was a deeply, even essentially, political issue in the fifth and sixth centuries; the law codes of both Theodosius and Justinian highly regulate the ritual, distinguishing between baptismal practices that are legal, and hence orthodox, and illegal, and hence heretical.[62] Thus, baptism was not simply a matter of "dying and rising with

---

58. On this, see also Runesson, "Architecture."

59. For a description, see Corbo, *House of Saint Peter*, 25–27. In its later addition of the apse, the Capernaum octagon follows the pattern of the earlier Jerusalem concentric churches, none of which had an apse initially (Shalev-Hurvitz, *Holy Sites Encircled*, 189).

60. Shalev-Hurvitz, *Holy Sites Encircled*, 272. Shalev-Hurvitz does not state her evidence for dating the addition of the baptistery to the sixth century. Indeed, Corbo himself said initially, "We do not have sufficient elements to determine when the baptistery was added to the octagonal church, thus blocking the passage between the two sacristies" (*House of Saint Peter*, 27).

61. A point noted by Shalev-Hurvitz, *Holy Sites Encircled*, 22.

62. One of the pressing concerns of both law codes is to outlaw the second baptism or rebaptism, which was practiced among heretical groups like the Montanists and Donatists (see, e.g., *CTh* 16.6; *CJust* 1.6). However, both codes also provide laws on how to handle a person who, more generally, "profanes holy baptism." For example, such people are to be "segregated from the community of all men, shall be disqualified from giving testimony, and as We have previously ordained, they shall not have testamentary capacity; they shall inherit from no person, and by no person shall they be designated as heirs. We should also have ordered them to be expelled and removed to a distance if it had not appeared to be a greater punishment to dwell among men and to lack the approval of men. But never shall they return to their former

Image 5.6. Photo (looking north) of the apsidal baptistry added sometime in the sixth century.

Image from Loffreda, *Cafarnao V*, 81 (DF 95). Used here with permission.

Christ," as the apostle Paul might have said (Rom 6:1–4), but, even more, a matter of dying and rising with the emperor, of becoming a well-ordered imperial Christian.

On February 1, 425, still about a quarter-century before the Capernaum octagon was built, Theodosius II issued a law that prohibited attendance at theaters and circuses on special Christian days—on "the Lord's Day" (i.e., Sundays), Christmas, Easter, and Pentecost—days on which it was

> status; the disgracefulness of their conduct shall not be expiated by penitence nor concealed by the shadow of any carefully devised defense or protection, since fiction and fabrication cannot protect those persons who have polluted the faith which they had vowed to God, who have betrayed the divine mystery and have gone over to profane doctrines. Help is extended to those persons who have slipped and to those who go astray, but those who are lost, that is, those who profane holy baptism, shall not be aided by any expiation through penitence, which customarily avails in other crimes" (e.g., *CTh* 16.7.4).

particularly common for people to receive "the new light of holy baptism" (*CTh* 15.5.5). Interestingly, the text of the law adds to this list of holy days "the commemoration of the Apostolic Passion, the teacher of all Christianity."[63] Fritz Graf has rightly argued that the apostles referred to here must be Peter and Paul, the cult of whom was widely popular and seems to have been imported from Rome to Constantinople during the reign of Theodosius I.[64] The day of commemoration that the *Theodosian Code* probably has in mind, therefore, is the Festival of Peter and Paul, a day which, by 425, had already been celebrated in Constantinople every June 29, the traditional date of Peter's martyrdom, for nearly twenty-five years.[65] Utilizing a grandiose and totalizing discursive strategy to describe the suffering of the apostles as the "teacher of all Christianity," the law elevated the festival to a social and legal status near, if not identical, to that of the days commemorating the life, death, and resurrection of Christ himself. By doing so, the text of the writ groups "the commemoration of the Apostolic Passion" with the other special days on which the practice of baptism was especially prevalent.

---

63. Text of *CTh* 15.5.5 here and in the following text is from Clyde Pharr, trans., *The Theodosian Code and Novels and the Sirmondian Constitutions* (Princeton, NJ: Princeton University Press, 1952), 433.

64. F. Graf, "Laying Down the Law in Ferragosto: The Roman Visit of Theodosius in Summer 389," *JECS* 22, no. 2 (2014): 234. The Theodosius referred to in the title of Graf's article is Theodosius I, whereas the one discussed on p. 234 is Theodosius II. See also the fascinating study by Gitte Lønstrup Dal Santo, "*Concordia Apostolorum—Concordia Augustorum.* Building a Corporate Image for the Theodosian Dynasty," in *East and West in the Roman Empire of the Fourth Century: An End to Unity?* ed. R. Dijkstra, S. van Poppel, and D. Slootjes (Leiden: Brill, 2015), 99–120 (esp. 100). For evidence of the widespread popularity of the cult of Peter and Paul, one only needs to do a quick search of the Cult of Saints in a late-antiquity database, which has digitally gathered a large amount of literary and archaeological sources on the topic: http://csla.history.ox.ac.uk/.

65. *Liber Pontificalis* 1 (ca. 530s, Rome): "He [Peter] was crowned with martyrdom along with Paul ... he was buried on the Via Aurelia, in the temple of Apollo, close to the place where he was crucified, and to Nero's palace on the Vatican, in the Triumphal territory, via Aurelia, the third day before the kalends of July [29 June]." Trans. R. Davis, *The Book of Pontiffs (Liber Pontificalis)*, 2nd ed., Translated Texts for Historians 6 (Liverpool: Liverpool University Press, 2000). See Lønstrup Dal Santo, "Corporate Image," 102, where she mentions that Constantinople's observance of the Festival of Peter and Paul on June 29 was in accordance with the long-established tradition of the Roman church. Eastern churches, such as in Antioch, Jerusalem, and Nicomedia celebrated the Festival of Peter and Paul on December 28. See also Graf, "Laying Down the Law," 235–236 on the likely socioeconomic motivations behind such holy day legislation, rather than the overtly religious motivations.

Altogether, the writ also has a very clear heresiological, that is, political aim: after condemning the "madness of the Jewish impiety" and the "insanity of stupid paganism," obedience to the prohibition is equated with "duty to the Emperor" and reverence to the "omnipotent God."

It is quite an intriguing idea to interpret the material ritual transformation of the Capernaum octagon, as well as the increase in Christian pilgrimage to the village from throughout the Byzantine East, against the backdrop of this Theodosian legislation and the wider growth of the cult of Peter and Paul in the fifth and sixth centuries. Indeed, one might ask, what better way to celebrate the day of the Apostolic Passion than to be baptized in the spot that commemorated the house of the blessed Peter himself? Such a backdrop would also highlight the imperialistic and heresiological rhetoric inherent to the festival's observance and the practice of baptism in a local context like Capernaum. According to the logic of the festival's observance as presented in *CTh* 15.5.5, the apostle Peter should not—in fact, *could* not—be remembered by Christians as a Jewish man in his Jewish home following a Jewish messiah; such a thing would amount to associating Christ's "chief apostle" with what the *Code* calls "the madness of the Jewish impiety." Rather, according to Theodosian writ and Constantinopolitan tradition, Peter was to be remembered as a Roman martyr, whose suffering, along with the apostle Paul's, constituted the great pedagogue of all Christianity, meaning, of course, *Roman imperial* Christianity. Seen from this angle, the addition of the apsidal baptistery could represent the material participation of the Capernaum octagon in a broader discourse of theopolitical alignment—alignment with a now de-Judaized hero from Christianity's ancient past, with *Romanitas*, and, ultimately, with the "orthodoxy" of the emperor himself. Thus, while the concept of "pilgrimage" might still be appropriate to describe the spatial semiotics of the octagon, it becomes severely impoverished if understood solely as a category of "religious" experience, divorced from its embeddedness within broader discourses of power and identity formation.[66]

---

66. This is one of my few criticisms of J. F. Strange's otherwise very insightful essay, in which he applies Christopher Tilley's theoretical concept of artifact as "solid metaphor" to the Capernaum churches (both the *christaeum* and the octagon) and the synagogue. In it he argues that the octagon (like the *christaeum* before it) were "solid metaphors" for pilgrimage, understood as a personal religious experience of the divine. See J. F. Strange, "The Archaeology of

The Capernaum octagon was an attempt to reorder spatial relations in the village and thereby create a visual expression of Christian power. While small compared to other concentric churches in Palestine, the octagon made a big statement about who was in and who was out, who was old and who was new, who was on top and who was on bottom. In the late fourth and early fifth centuries, Room 1 had been institutionally aligned with a Jewish Christ-association that hosted non-Jewish visitors and continued to complete for influence within the public synagogue standing across the street. In the mid-fifth century onward, however, the octagon—built over Room 1 and seen within the larger heresiological and political landscape of the Byzantine East—established a cult of saints curated around a Romanized apostle Peter and institutionally aligned with imperial power and the performance of orthodox identity. Its art and architecture became part of the rhetorical repertoire of Christian supersessionism in late antiquity, which already had a long history of expression from pen and pulpit. And its anti-Jewish message was especially defined in Capernaum, a historically Jewish town that still had a Jewish community inhabiting its landscape in the fifth and sixth centuries. But, despite the octagon's loud bark, the presence of this Jewish community and a magnificent synagogue from nearly the same period suggest that the octagonal church tells only one side of the rhetorical story in this period of Capernaum's history.

4. Architecturalizing Resistance
The Limestone Synagogue and the Rejection of Christian Triumphalism

Parts of the story of Capernaum's limestone synagogue were told in chapter 2—but only parts. There I argued on historical grounds for the probability that, before the construction of this monumental building, two earlier synagogues stood in the same location, one from the early Roman period (ca. first century) and another from the late Roman period (ca. third to fourth

---

Religion at Capernaum, Synagogue and Church," in *Religious Texts and Material Contexts*, ed. J. Neuser and J. F. Strange (Lanham, MD: University Press of America, 2001), 43–62. The pilgrimage-oriented function of the octagon is also the view held by Taylor, *Christians and the Holy Places*, 272.

century) that expanded upon the earlier one. Although there is virtually nothing we can say about the architecture of these earlier buildings, there is much we can say about the limestone synagogue, which represented the spatial and material apex of an architectural process that seems to have run chronologically parallel to—and was deeply entangled with—the evolution of *insula* 1.

There was a reason Edward Robinson described his first encounter with the remains of the limestone building in the summer of 1838 as surpassing anything he and his traveling companions had yet encountered in Palestine. The building was massive.[67] Portions of the outer walls as reconstructed by Corbo and Loffreda suggest that, in places, the walls reached at least twelve courses high and were probably higher. The limestone blocks, with which most of the synagogue was built, came from quarries at least ten kilometers away, perhaps from Mt. Arbel, and were finely worked.[68] According to Loffreda, the heaviest of them reached almost four tons.[69] The main hall alone measured internally 23 meters (north to south) by 17.28 meters (east to west) and accommodated somewhere between five hundred and seven hundred people.[70] It was accessed by climbing a large staircase either at the western or eastern end of the porch, which flanked the southern Jerusalem-oriented façade of the main hall. Like other synogogues of the so-called "Galilean" type in late antiquity, the interior space of the main hall was divided into a central nave and two side aisles by a U-shaped stylobate made of stone ashlars.[71] On the stylobate stood fourteen

---

67. The following description is derived primarily from Loffreda, *Recovering Capharnaum*, 49, but for more detail, see also Corbo, *Cafarnao I*, 113–170.

68. Zvi Uri Ma'oz, "The Synagogue at Capernaum," 139.

69. Loffreda, *Recovering Capharnaum*, 32.

70. C. Spigel, *Ancient Synagogue Seating Capacities*, 173–177.

71. For descriptions of similar interior architecture in the synagogues of Gush Halav, Chorazin, Nabratein, Bar'am, Meiron, and Arbel, see R. Hachlili, *Ancient Synagogues—Archaeology and Art*, 139. The Capernaum synagogue was once considered to be the classic example of the Galilean-type synagogue, one of three types comprising traditional synagogue typology, along with the Transitional/Broadhouse type and the Byzantine type. While, in general, the typology still helpfully groups together buildings with similar architectural features, recent scholarship has called into question the earlier linear approach that linked each of these types to a specific historical period (i.e., Galilean type is earliest, second or early third century; Transitional/Broadhouse type is late third or fourth century; and Byzantine type is fifth or sixth century). See discussion in L. Levine, "Diversity in the Ancient Synagogue of Roman-Byzantine Palestine: Historical Implications," in *Diversity*

large columns set on pedestals and two heart-shaped pillars supporting the northeast and northwest angular corners.[72] Two tiers of permanent benches lined the walls of the western and eastern side aisles. Off the northwest corner of the building was a side room accessible only through a doorway in the main hall; the function of this room is still unknown. Along the outer walls of the side room, two flights of steps are preserved that appear to have led to the entrance of an upper gallery.[73] The main hall communicated directly with an eastern trapezoidal courtyard by way of a pilastered doorway. This courtyard was surrounded on three sides by a roofed portico, having eleven pedestaled columns set on a stylobate shaped like an inverted C, with two heart-shaped pillars at the northeast and southeast angular corners.[74] It was accessed from the

---

and Rabbinization: Jewish Texts and Societies between 400 and 1000 CE, eds. G. McDowell, R. Naiweld, and D. Stökl Ben Ezra (Cambridge: Cambridge University Press, 2021), 1–4; Jodi Magness, "The Huqoq Synagogue: A Regional Variant of the Galilean Type," in *The Synagogue in Ancient Palestine: Current Issues and Emerging Trends*, FRLANT 279, eds. R. Bonnie, R. Hakola, U. Tervahauta (Göttingen: Vandenhoeck and Ruprecht, 2021), 161–163; and D. Milson, *Art and Architecture of the Synagogue in Late Antique Palestine: In the Shadow of the Church*, AJEC 65 (Leiden: Brill, 2007), 18–32. Cf. the recent discussion in U. Leibner, "The Dating of the 'Galilean'-Type Synagogues: Khirbet Wadi Ḥamam as a Case-Study," in *Synagogues in the Hellenistic and Roman Periods: Archaeological Finds, New Methods, New Theories*, Ioudaioi 11, ed. L. Doering and A. Krause (Göttingen: Vandenhoeck and Ruprecht, 2020), 43–69, who defends some aspects of the traditional typology, at least as it relates to the Galilean type.

72. The number fourteen derives from the reconstruction presented in Loffreda, *Recovering Capharnaum*, 34, which is based on the assumed spacing between the columns. However, as seen in the most recent plan of the village, printed in *Cafarnao IX* (p. 17), the remains of only eleven pedestaled columns were actually found.

73. While some earlier scholars interpreted this gallery as a *matroneum*, Loffreda leaves it as an open question (*Recovering Capharnaum*, 36). Spigel has argued persuasively that, rather than imagining a uniform situation in which men and women either sat together or sat separately in ancient synagogues, each seating situation needs to be taken on its own terms. See C. Spigel, "Reconsidering the Question of Separate Seating in Ancient Synagogues," *JJS* 63, no. 1 (2012): 62–83. In Capernaum, there is no evidence whatsoever—at least not yet—that the gallery functioned as a *matroneum*. Pointing to some rabbinic sources, Levine notes (*The Ancient Synagogue*, 342–343) that balconies could have functioned as a place for festive meals, as a residence for a *ḥazzan*, place of study, or possibly for litigation.

74. Again, the number eleven derives from the reconstruction presented in Loffreda, *Recovering Capharnaum*, 34, which is based on the assumed spacing between the columns. However, as seen in the most recent plan of the village, printed in B. Callegher, *Cafarnao IX*, 17, the remains of only three pedestaled columns were actually found. The two heart-shaped pillars were found as well.

outside either by climbing the large staircase on the southeast side of the porch and entering one of the two doors along the southern side, or by climbing the large staircase off the northeast corner of the courtyard, which led to another three entry options. The three openings along the eastern wall of the courtyard were not doors but windows. The courtyard itself added an internal area of over 250 square meters, raising the total internal area of the building to around 650 square meters. Thus, in contrast to the octagonal church, which was the smallest of its architectural kind,[75] the limestone synagogue was one of the largest. As Spigel notes, there is no way to know precisely the percentage of Jews living in Capernaum in the fifth and sixth centuries, but in a village with a population ranging between 1,500 and 2,700 comprising both Jews and Christians, it is quite possible that the synagogue could have held within its walls the majority of the local Jewish community.[76]

Size was not the only thing the synagogue had going for it. Its decoration represents some of the most lavish stone-carved Jewish art known from the Galilee in late antiquity and, perhaps, from all of Palestine.[77] While no mosaic carpets like those that famously adorn the floors of many Galilean synagogues were found among the Capernaum remains, many of the same artistic motifs—figural and non-figural—are attested among its carvings. Flooding the visual landscape of the building were elaborate friezes decorated with floral imagery, geometric patterns, eagles, lions, and the "peopled scrolls" motif; elegant capitals, cornices, lintels, and other architectural elements were ornamented with, for example, wreaths, conch shells, menoroth, and at least three separate depictions of Torah shrines.[78] One of the most well-known of these

---

75. Shalev-Hurvitz, *Holy Sites Encircled*, 268–269, Plate 19C.

76. Spigel, *Ancient Synagogue Seating Capacities*, 177. *Pace* Runesson, "Architecture," 253, who assumes that the synagogue would have been "much too big for the Jews of Capernaum."

77. Noted by Ma'oz, "The Synagogue at Capernaum," 139. One might also note, however, the similar decorative program of the Chorazin synagogue, although it is not on the same scale as the one at Capernaum. On the Chorazin building, see Z. Yeivin, *The Synagogue at Korazim: The 1962–1964, 1980–1987 Excavations*, IAA Reports 10 (Jerusalem: IAA, 2000) (Hebrew and English).

78. For several important art historical studies of the Capernaum synagogue, see, for example, Bloedhorn, "The Capitals of the Synagogue of Capernaum," 49–54; Ma'oz, "The Synagogue at Capernaum"; Arubas and Talgam, "Jews, Christians, and *Minim*," 237–274; and, most recently, Svetlana Tarkhanova, "The Friezes with the 'Peopled Scrolls' Motif in the Capernaum Synagogue: Dating by Stylistic Method and Some Aspects of the Reconstruction," in *The Synagogue in Ancient Palestine*, ed. R. Bonnie, R. Hakola, and U. Tervahauta,

Architecturalizing Power and Resistance

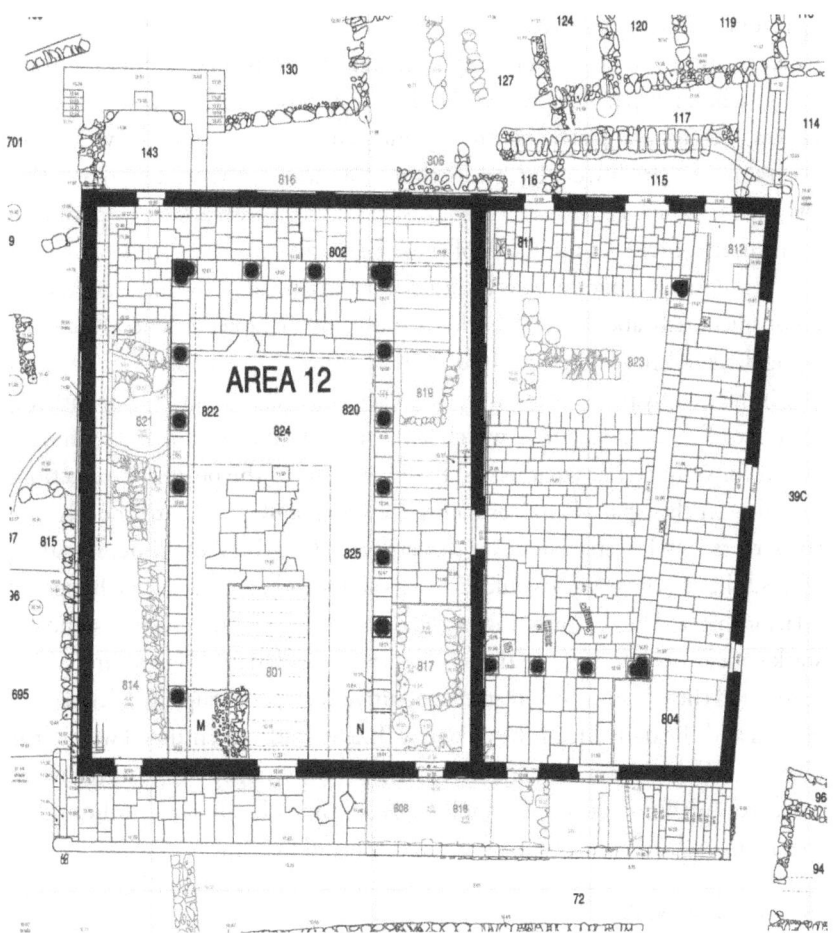

Image 5.7. Plan of the limestone synagogue.

From Loffreda, *Cafarnao V*, 247. Used here with permission.

depictions appears in a scene carved on a large slab of limestone portraying a five-columned structure supporting a gabled roof, a pediment decorated with a conch, and the paneled double doors of the Torah ark. Interestingly, this Torah shrine is pictured as being on wheels, which raises the question of whether the

---

FLRANT 279 (Göttingen: Vandenhoek & Ruprecht, 2021), 195–218. On the art and architecture of Torah shrines in ancient synagogues, see R. Hachlili, "The Niche and the Ark in Ancient Synagogues," *BASOR* 223 (1976): 43–53; and, more recently, "Torah Shrine and Ark in Ancient Synagogues: A Re-evaluation," *ZDP* 116, no. 2 (2000): 146–183 (see pp. 148, 153, 158 where she mentions Capernaum).

synagogue itself had a portable ark that wheeled the Torah scrolls into place when necessary rather than having a permanent repository for them, as some earlier scholarship had supposed.[79] However, Corbo and Loffreda's discovery of two symmetrical platforms on the southern Jerusalem-oriented wall of the central nave, which were later joined into "a more sophisticated 'teba'" that spanned the nave's entire width, suggests that the Torah ark had a permeant home in in a niche set upon one of these platforms.[80]

The entire synagogue was built upon an artificial podium, which raised it conspicuously above street level. The building occupied a central location, being flanked immediately to the east by the village's main north–south street and immediately to the south by its primary east–west street.[81] The southeast staircase of the build's porch, which led directly to its monumental entrance, rested conveniently at what would have been one of the busiest intersections in town. In this spatial environment, the synagogue pressed to the edges of the streets, casting shadows over passersby and, at the same time, signaling accessibility to those who would climb its stairs and enter its doors. Its spatial relationship to the surrounding *insulae* (i.e., *insulae* 2, 4, 5, and 6) stands in stark contrast to the octagonal church with its quadrilateral enclosure, which segregated the octagon and created a cognitive and spatial rupture between the church and the daily life of the village. While visually accentuated within the context of Capernaum's larger built landscape, the synagogue's posture toward its surroundings expresses no such rupture. Indeed, open and unbound, it speaks an architectural language of presence and integration.

---

79. Noted by Hachlili, "Torah Shrine," 147 n. 4.

80. Loffreda, *Recovering Capharnaum*, 35.

81. Ma'oz claims that the limestone synagogue was not located in the best position in the village, such as at its highest point, the centre (i.e., the market on the shore in lakeside villages), open to view, or sheltered from the wind ("The Synagogue at Capernaum," 139). This "discrepancy," as he calls it, factors into his larger theory of who built the synagogue, which will be discussed below. The point I wish to make here is that Ma'oz seems to be wrong in his general assertion that the synagogue did not occupy the best position in the village. First, according to Loffreda, the synagogue actually did occupy the "physical center of the town" (*Recovering Capharnaum*, 32). Second, the synagogue was located at the intersection of the village's two main streets, one of which (the north–south "cardo") was lined with shops on the eastern side, suggesting, indeed, that the synagogue was closely linked to a marketplace context (see chapter 6). Third, one of the functions of the artificial platform, upon which the synagogue was built, was, arguably, to make the monumental building "open to view" from anywhere in the village. Fourth, Ma'oz does not take into consideration that the location of the limestone synagogue was determined by its preexisting built environment, including the probable earlier synagogue, whose place it was taking.

Architecturalizing Power and Resistance

Image 5.8. Details of finely decorated friezes and capitals from the limestone synagogue.

From Loffreda, *Cafarnao V*, 43 (DFs 14–21). Used with permission.

How one interprets the rhetorical dynamics of the synagogue's architecture depends largely on two foundational questions, both of which have attracted significant attention from scholars but only one of which seems anywhere close to achieving something of a consensus status. Since the excavations of Corbo and Loffreda in the late 1960s, the increasingly held view of the limestone synagogue's date of completion is that it belongs in the late fifth or even early sixth century.[82] I see very little reason to dispute this view.

---

82. In the early and mid-twentieth century, the broad consensus was that the limestone building dated to the second or third century CE, a view based mainly on stylistic analysis of the synagogue's decorative program. However, in the late 1960s and early 1970s, Corbo and Loffreda challenged the consensus view in favor of a late fourth or fifth century dating based on the stratigraphic analysis that resulted from their systematic excavations underneath the synagogue in 1969 (Corbo, *Cafarnao I*, 113–169). The terms of the subsequent debate were generally bifurcated along disciplinary lines, with art historical approaches being pitted against stratigraphic ones. Despite some notable dissent (e.g., Tsafrir, "The Synagogues in Capernaum and Meroth," 151–161) and at least one attempt to reconcile the discrepancy between the artistic style and the stratigraphy of the limestone synagogue (Ma'oz, "The

The more difficult question, however, concerns the socioeconomic context of the building's construction, including the issues of who funded it and how the building was then used. How, scholars have wondered, could a church and a synagogue—two monumental buildings representing two socioreligious groups who were severely at odds with one another during this period—be allowed to stand just twenty-five meters apart?

The Synagogue's Socioeconomic Context

Over the past fifty years, several distinct theories have been proposed to answer this question.[83] The most "radical" and "stirring" among them have revolved around the idea that imperial Christians—not Jews—were, in fact, responsible for building the synagogue and that the building itself functioned, not unlike today, as a site of Christian tourism, fashioned as the synagogue of Jesus known from the Gospels. Theories that posit imperial Christian patronage for the synagogue run up against a complete lack of evidence.[84] As Runesson has noted, this dearth is explained rather simply: Byzantine Christians built *churches* to

---

Synagogue at Capernaum"), scholarship has generally favored the latter dating based on archaeological data. In 1997, Loffreda himself, in fact, revised his own dating of the entire synagogue to the last quarter of the fifth century based on a new study of the coins found in the building (Loffreda, "Coins," 232–233), and Jodi Magness has argued strongly for a date in the sixth century based on her interpretation of the numismatic and ceramic records ("The Question of the Synagogue," 22–23). Furthermore, in a recent, and in my view quite significant study, Svetlana Tarkhanova has shown that even the synagogue's decorative style—the main, and really only, data that has traditionally supported the early dating—actually *supports the later dating* suggested by the stratigraphic evidence, particularly as proposed by Magness (see "The Friezes with the 'Peopled Scrolls' Motif," 195–218).

83. For a full and up-to-date critical discussion of the main theories and approaches to the socioeconomic context of the limestone synagogue, see W. V. Cirafesi, "The Socio-Economic Context of Capernaum's Limestone Synagogue and Jewish–Christian Relations in the Late Ancient Town," *Scandinavian Jewish Studies* 32, no. 1 (2021): 49–54.

84. It is certainly true, as Arubas and Talgam assert, that imperial funds were used to build *churches* in the fourth and following centuries, but there is no evidence that imperial funds were ever directed to build *synagogues* ("Jews, Christians, and 'Minim,'" 241–246). The example they mention of the ancient synagogue in Nazareth—which, according to Egeria, was converted into a church but, according to the Anonymous Piacenza Pilgrim, continued as a synagogue frequented by Christian pilgrims and the Jewish community—is no solid comparison, since, even if we follow the testimony of the Piacenza Pilgrim (which I am not necessarily convinced we should do), there is no evidence that imperial funds were involved in its construction or preservation in any way.

commemorate Jesus, not synagogues, since they sought to remember Jesus within the framework of Christianity and not Judaism.[85]

Admittedly, the context of the Capernaum synagogue is unique; no other synagogue from the Galilee in late antiquity is situated on a site of Christian memory and so closely to a monumental church.[86] But this does not mean that Christians were responsible for the synagogue's construction, nor, conversely, that Jews were not. From a political standpoint, there is no material evidence that Christians had destroyed a previously standing synagogue—that is, the "middle synagogue"—in order to clear the way for their own building.[87] And there is very little evidence that imperial laws restricting the building of new synagogues (*CTh* 16.8) were enforced in the region in any systematic or consequential way. Indeed, in light of all the monumental synagogues built during this period, quite the opposite seems to have been the case. Additionally, often overlooked in historical scholarship on synogogues and Jewish–Christian relations in late antiquity, is that from 423 to 425 CE the second most powerful person in the entire Roman East was a man named Asclepiodotus. He was the Praetorian Prefect of the East, and not only was he apparently known to be much more sympathetic toward pagans—his family members had been recent pagan converts to Christianity—but he was also quite sympathetic toward Jews, issuing in 423 an edict ordering the restitution of synagogues.[88] While his prefecture was short—he was quickly denounced to Theodosius by Simeon Stylites—his attitude shows that a general climate of sympathy toward

---

85. Runesson, "Architecture," 253 n.84.

86. Beth Yerah (Khirbet al-Karak), on the southern shore of the Kinneret Lake about five miles south of Tiberias, had once been thought to be a site comparable to Capernaum. Scholars had once supposed Beth Yerah rendered evidence of a Byzantine church and, about fifty meters to its south, a synagogue encompassed by a Roman fort. However, recent research on the site by Donald Whitcomb has confirmed an Umayyad date for the complex and the conclusion that the supposed synagogue was actually an Umayyad palace. See D. Whitcomb, "From Pastoral Peasantry to Tribal Urbanites: Arab Tribes and the Foundation of the Islamic State in Syria," in *Nomads, Tribes, and the State in the Ancient Near East*, ed. J. Szuchman (Chicago: University of Chicago Press, 2009), 245–246.

87. While Runesson does not think Christians were responsible for the building of the limestone synagogue, he does think it "not improbable" that the previously standing black basalt synagogue was destroyed in transfer of power from local Jewish administration to Byzantine colonization ("Architecture," 251).

88. J. R. Martindale, *The Prosopography of the Later Roman Empire*, vol. 2, *A.D. 395–527* (Cambridge: Cambridge University Press, 1980), 160.

Jews penetrated even to the top political layers of Roman Christianity in the fifth century. It seems to be no wonder that the fifth century saw a boom in synagogue building in the region more broadly.[89]

From an economic standpoint, the Capernaum synagogue does not at all seem to have been a special case. Raimo Hakola has rightly argued that sites with grand synagogues from the fourth to sixth century, such as the recently excavated buildings at Huqoq, Horvat Kur, and Wadi Hamam, point to the remarkable amount of resources local Galilean Jews could pour into the making of their public buildings.[90] To these buildings we could also add other monumental synagogues from the Galilee that have been known about for quite some time, such as at Chorazin, Bar'am, Nabratein, Meiron, and Gush Halav. Seen from this angle, then, the proximity of church and synagogue in Capernaum does not imply that its Jewish community lacked the political and economic power to construct—materially and ideologically—their own sense of identity, or that they needed a Christian emperor's money to fund their public building projects. To the contrary, this assumption significantly underestimates local Jewish cultural and political agency in a time and place for which the archaeological evidence, especially related to synagogues, has increasingly suggested Jews asserted such agency frequently and vociferously.

However, the idea that local Galilean Jewish communities, such as the one in Capernaum, could boldly assert their identities in the face of a Christianizing empire does not mean that these communities were *entirely* economically self-sufficient. The comparative data from Huqoq, Horvat Kur, and Wadi Hamam, while certainly demonstrating the social and cultural vitality of these communities in late antiquity, do not render conclusive evidence on this front. While inscriptions on mosaic pavements from Horvat Kur, Wadi Hamam, and possibly Huqoq do, indeed, seem to suggest that local donors contributed

---

89. This point coheres with Jodi Magness's general argument that the Galilee did not see decline in the fifth century, as some scholars had once argued. See J. Magness, "Did Galilee Decline in the Fifth Century? The Synagogue at Chorazin Reconsidered," in *Religion, Ethnicity, and Identity in Ancient Galilee: A Region in Transition*, ed. J. Zangenberg, H. Attridge, and, D. Martin, WUNT 210 (Tübingen: Mohr Siebeck, 2007), 259–274.

90. R. Hakola, "Galilean Jews and Christians in Context: Spaces Shared and Contested in the Eastern Galilee in Late Antiquity," in *Spaces in Late Antiquity: Cultural, Theological, and Archaeological Perspectives*, ed. Juliette Day *et al*. (London: Routledge, 2016), 141–165; Hakola, "Galilean Synagogues as Local Responses to Cultural Globalization in Late Antiquity," in *The Synagogue in Ancient Palestine*, ed. R. Bonnie, R. Hakola, and U. Tervahauta, FLRANT 279 (Göttingen: Vandenhoeck & Ruprecht, 2021), 271–288.

to parts of the synagogues, these inscriptions are far from evidence that the total economic weight of these buildings was borne at the local level.[91] In my view, we should think similarly about the case of the Capernaum synagogue. On the one hand, receiving very little attention in historical scholarship are two donor inscriptions that were found on individual columns belonging to the period of the limestone building.[92] While one was carved in Greek (*CIIP* V 1: no. 6415) and the other in Aramaic (*CIIP* V 1: no. 6416), both have similar donor formulae, which mention (at least) three family generations and the contribution of a column to the synagogue.[93] A man named Herod and his son Justus are the primary donors in the Greek inscription; Ḥalfu/o is the donor named in the Aramaic inscription. Additionally, a donor inscription found on the mosaic pavement of the sixth-century synagogue at Hamat Gader names, among other people from around the Galilee, a certain "Yosse bar Dosti

---

91. At Ḥorvat Kur, a short Aramaic inscription mentioning a certain 'El'azar son of Yudan son of Susu (or Qoso / Qusu)' is set above the remains of what was likely a depiction of a menorah (J. K. Zangenberg, "The Menorah on the Mosaic Floor from the Late Roman/Early Byzantine Synagogue at Ḥorvat Kur," *Israel Exploration Journal* 67 [2017]: 114). Nothing in the inscription is said specifically about a contribution from this person, but Zangenberg is right that it is plausible that the individual "had contributed to the community, its synagogue, or the floor and was honored with this inscription" (114). Of course, if this individual was a donor, he almost certainly did not fund the entire building but rather, as was more common, donated to a specific architectural element within the synagogue (see Levine, *The Ancient Synagogue*, 86–87 for examples). The mosaic panel with the menorah seems to be the most likely candidate. Analogously, the donor inscription in Panel 11 in the western aisle of the Wadi Hamam synagogue states: "The sons of Simon made [i.e., donated] this panel from their own [means]" (translation from U. Leibner and S. Miller, "A Figural Mosaic in the Synagogue at Khirbet Wadi Hamam," *JRA* 23 [2010]: 249). An inscription found in the "Commemorative Panel" in the Huqoq synagogue might also function to bless those who made charitable donations to the construction or repairs of parts of the synagogue (see J. Magness et al., "The Huqoq Excavation Project: 2014–2017 Interim Report," *BASOR* 380 (2018): 96–97). No named individuals seem to be mentioned. However, as Magness et al. say, "the mosaic and its inscription are fragmentary and difficult to interpret, so no firm conclusions can be drawn at this point."

92. Informing my approach to these inscriptions are studies by H. Lapin, "Palestinian Inscriptions and Jewish Ethnicity in Late Antiquity," in *Galilee through the Centuries: Confluence of Cultures*, ed. E. Meyers (Winona Lake, IN: Eisenbrauns, 1999), 239–267; and Schwartz, *Imperialism*, 276, 280 ff.

93. The Greek inscription reads: "Herod, son of Mo[ni]mos, Justus his son, together with the children, erected this column." The Aramaic inscription reads: "Ḥalifu/o son of Zebidah, son of Yoḥanan, made this column. May he be blessed" (trans. slightly adapted from V. Tzaferis, "Capernaum," in *NEAEHL* 1:294).

from Capernaum" as a monetary contributor to that building.[94] There is no reason to doubt that all of these donors were Jewish and that they and their families were local to Capernaum.[95] We are, therefore, on rather solid ground in claiming that segments of Capernaum's local Jewish population possessed a level—perhaps even a significant level—of internal wealth, some of which could have been directed toward the construction of the synagogue.

But was there enough local wealth to sustain a building project that, according to Loffreda, lasted nearly three-fourths of a century from start to finish?[96] The theory that the synagogue also received some type of external financial support has circumstantial evidence in its favor, evidence that has been bolstered by a recent archaeological discovery. First, even if Hamat Gader was a special attraction in the region due to its hot springs, the inscription on the floor of its synagogue mentioning donors from all around the Galilee, indeed, shows that local Jewish communities, and specifically Jews from Capernaum, had socioeconomic networks in place from which to draw and to which to contribute. The flow of money and resources, human and material, does not appear to have been confined to isolated towns and villages but was, rather, dynamic, relatively diffuse, and operated with a strong sense of

---

94. On the sixth century date of the mosaic pavement of the Hamat Gader synagogue, see G. Foerster, "Dating Synagogues," 87–94, esp. 90–91.

95. On the high probability that these donors were local, see L. Levine, *The Ancient Synagogue*, 373, where he says: "As might be expected, donors were almost always members of the local community." Interestingly, he lists the donor inscription from Hamat Gader as an exception, in which non-local Jews donated to the synagogue building, with these donors being specifically labeled as hailing from Sepphoris, Arbel, Capernaum, Emmaus, and Kefar 'Aqavia. The fact that the characteristic blessing—"May the King of the Universe extend a blessing upon their works"—comes after the mention of the donors and the sums of their contribution, to my mind, severely hinders Arubas and Talgam's theory (Arubas and Talgam, "Jews, Christians, and *Minim*," 246) regarding this Yosse bar Dosti from Capernaum. They suggest that the Hamat Gader inscription is inconsistent with the *minim* texts of *Qohelet Rabbah* 1:8 and 7:26, since "no synagogue would accept the donation of a heretic (or at least the heretic would attempt to hide his identity in some way)." They conjecture that Yosse bar Dosti's donation may have been so large that the Hamat Gader community could not have refused it, or that the donation was made in the attempt to clear Capernaum's bad name. It seems to me that Arubas and Talgam wrongly allow the highly ideological midrash to dictate the interpretation of the inscription, for it is just as or even more likely that Capernaum's Jews were simply not considered *minim* (as some rabbis asserted) by other (non-rabbinic) Jews.

96. See Loffreda, "Coins," 232–233.

translocal social connectivity.⁹⁷ In other words, Jews in the Galilee of late antiquity did not live in a rural backwater. As Sharon Mattila has recently shown—and as will be discussed in more detail in chapter 6—villages and villagers were engaged in high levels of market exchange, with relative sophistication and access to wealth.⁹⁸ The intense rise of Christian pilgrimage to the region in the fifth and sixth centuries certainly contributed to this general state of economic prosperity, but it would be a mistake to say Christian pilgrimage was the *only* factor generating this wealth.⁹⁹ Village life, as Mattila puts it, was a much more "diverse and complex phenomenon."

Second, in 2015 Runesson's theory that the Capernaum synagogue was financed by wealthy Jews in Tiberias received a boost.¹⁰⁰ During excavations

---

97. For example, the same craftspeople and artisans could work in multiple towns and on multiple synagogues. Levine (*The Ancient Synagogue*, 373) notes a father and son pair who laid the mosaic floors in the synagogues of Beth Alpha and Beth Shean, and another artisan who worked in 'Alma and Bar'am in the Upper Galilee. Town marketplaces (called in rabbinic literature the *shuk*) could bring in a significant level of out-of-town foot traffic and generate notable economic gain. Note what Cynthia Baker says about the *shuk* in late ancient Galilee: '[It was] the chief locale for commerce in goods, services, and information of all sorts. It is . . . that place where all manner of people of local, distant, and foreign origin had access to one another, as well as to goods that were similarly of local, distant, and foreign origins' (C. Baker, *Rebuilding the House of Israel: Architectures of Gender in Jewish Antiquity* [Stanford: Stanford University Press 2002], 105). Capernaum's *shuk* comprised of house shops that lined the major north–south road (see L39 in figure 3). See Mattila, "Capernaum," 224 (her figure D).

98. S. Mattila, "Inner Village Life in Galilee: A Diverse and Complex Phenomenon," in *Galilee in the Late Second Temple and Mishnaic Periods*, vol. 1, *Life, Culture, and Society*, ed. D. A. Fiensy and J. R. Strange (Minneapolis: Fortress Press, 2014), 312–345.

99. Noted in Sivan, *Palestine in Late Antiquity*, 46–47.

100. Runesson, "Architecture," 252–253. While I am, in general, quite sympathetic toward Runesson's theory about the involvement of Tiberian Jews in the project, we differ on three key points here. First, the evidence of wealth internal to Capernaum is not accounted for by Runesson. Thus, Runesson's external funding theory, while not necessarily wrong, is incomplete. Second, Runesson seems to wed his view to Günter Stemberger's view that, specifically, the house of the Jewish patriarch was behind the Capernaum project, as was the growing political influence of the rabbis, which might explain the "conservative" architecture of the synagogue (by which they appear to mean lack of figural art). But (a) as Levine has noted (*The Ancient Synagogue*, 463–465), there is very little evidence to support seeing a relationship between the patriarch and synagogues in general, and there is no evidence at all of patriarchal involvement in Capernaum specifically; (b) not only would I question Stemberger's (and thus Runesson's) conceptualization of the art and architecture of the Capernaum synagogue as

at Kursi Beach,[101] led by Haim Cohen and Michael Artzy of the University of Haifa, a marble slab with a dedicatory Aramaic/Hebrew inscription dating to ca. fifth century was discovered on the floor of a synagogue. The inscription was first published in 2016 in the *Journal of the Jesus Movement in Its Jewish Setting*.[102] Not only does the inscription confirm the existence of a local Jewish population in Kursi contemporaneous with a Christian one, but it also seems to confirm that building materials could, indeed, be imported by Jews from an external Jewish source.[103] Although fragmentary in places, the inscription clearly mentions a donation to the Kursi synagogue from an individual "from Tiberias" (דמן טיבריה). The statement in lines 2 to 3 of the donor (name is fragmentary/indiscernible) "who contributed marble (מרמריה)[104] for the honor of (this) holy [place]"[105] does not appear to be a reference merely to the marble tablet itself but to a general contribution of marble that was, perhaps, used in architectural elements throughout the synagogue. As the excavators judiciously note, since the synagogue has not been fully excavated, it is impossible to know this with any certainty.[106] But, regardless, marble—a high-demand

---

"conservative," but I would also question the idea that the rabbis themselves had a unified view on what constituted allowable art in synagogues (see Levine, *Visual Judaism in Late Antiquity*, 272, where he cites rabbinic evidence for the allowance of figural art); and (c) Levine has recently noted that the "conservativism" that Stemberger and Runesson sense in Capernaum is characteristic of most synagogues in the Upper Galilee and thus is probably due to the regional factor ("Diversity," 8). Third, one of Runesson's reasons for seeing external financial support is that the limestone building was probably much too large for the Jews of Capernaum. But this is an assumption and might not necessarily have been the case, as noted above.

101. Kursi is an archaeological site on the eastern shore of the Lake of Galilee near the foothills of the Golan Heights. Since the fifth century, it has been known as a Christian pilgrimage location and as home to Galilee's largest monastic complex.

102. Open access to the publication can be found at jjmjs.org. See H. Misgav, M. Artzy, and H. Cohen, "The Synagogue Inscription from Kursi," *Journal of the Jesus Movement in its Jewish Setting* 3 (2016): 167–169.

103. *Pace* Ma'oz's assumption that, because the limestone blocks from which the synagogue was constructed were imported from outside Capernaum, imperial Christians must have been the ones who did it ("The Synagogue at Capernaum," 139).

104. Jastrow, *s.v.* מרמירא.

105. Translation by the excavators in Misgav, Artzy, and Cohen, "Synagogue Inscription," 168.

106. Misgav, Artzy, and Cohen, "Synagogue Inscription," 169.

yet non-natural resource in Palestine—was quarried and imported from all over the Mediterranean world to the major cities of the region.[107] It was apparently masoned by associations of marble cutters in these cities, including in Tiberias,[108] but it took individuals with financial means—like the Tiberian mentioned in the Kursi synagogue inscription—to fund the transport of dressed marble to local villages. Thus, no matter the actual extent of the marble's use in the Kursi synagogue, the inscription encourages us to imagine a dynamic socioeconomic network in place during the fifth and sixth centuries, a network that both connected Jewish communities to one another and involved them in the broader complex currents of commercial activity throughout the Byzantine Empire.

The Capernaum synagogue was, therefore, probably the result of *both* internal *and* external streams of financial support. From this perspective, we can imagine a socioeconomic scenario in which the local Jewish community partnered with Jews from around the Galilee—individuals, families, and perhaps also trade associations—to launch what Uzi Leibner has called "a struggle of monuments,"[109] a grand building project that, beyond its function for public use by local Jews, could ideologically compete with, and even outperform, the octagonal church just to its south.

The Synagogue's Architectural Language in Its Discursive Setting

We are now in a position to return to the question of the rhetorical dynamics of the synagogue's architecture. While these dynamics likely were pluriform and shifted over the course of the building's decades-long construction process, my approach will be to explore them in the context of the building's completion in the late fifth to early sixth century. And this context is, potentially,

---

107. M. L. Fischer, "Marble Imports and Local Counterparts: Luxury Business in Roman Palestine," *Topoi: Orient—Occident* 8 (2007): 249.

108. See Levine, *The Ancient Synagogue*, 373 n. 285, where he cites an inscription from Tiberias that states "may God's grace be with Abraham the marble-cutter." Y. Hirschfeld, *Roman, Byzantine, and Early Muslim Tiberias: A Handbook of Primary Sources* (Bloomington, IN: Indiana University Press, 2005), 34, notes that this inscription was found engraved on the capital of a synagogue pillar.

109. Leibner, *Settlment and History*, 403.

highly illuminative. Not only was this the time when the Christianization of Palestine, especially in rural areas, took full flight, seeing sharp increases in Christian tourism and the building of churches,[110] but it is also the time when the concept of "the synagogue" reached its apex as an ideological Other in Christian polemical literature. The fifth-century anonymous work *Altercatio ecclesiae et synagogae*, or *The Dispute between Church and Synagogue*, is perhaps the best example of this.[111]

The *Altercatio* presents two women, Ecclesia and Synagoga, arguing in a fictional courtroom over who has the right to possess the world. The work has a clear polemical agenda, which is laid out in the introduction by the anonymous author, who describes Synagoga as a poor, disgraced, and adulterous woman on the one hand, and Ecclesia as a chaste and deserving matron on the other. The *Altercatio* employs normativizing rhetoric to demonstrate the utter superiority of Ecclesia over Synagoga; the latter not only loses the court case, but she is also stripped of all her integrity and virtue as well. But the aim of the *Altercatio* is not simply to fill the sails of Christian triumphalism with hot air, although it does do that. Rather, its aim is to construct and affirm Jewish–Christian *difference*, as "the church" and "the synagogue" are pitted against each other as diametrically opposed institutions of two diametrically opposed religions. That is, the allegory of Ecclesia and Synagoga means to create and control the boundary between a consolidated imperial Christianity—Ecclesia, after all, has the explicit and exclusive support of Augustan law (*augustali iure*; ed. Oehl, line 19)—and a Judaism that functions as an all-too-familiar Other, which was never outlawed but was classified by the roughly contemporaneous Theodosian Code (438 CE) as among the "religious deviants" of the Empire (*CTh* 16).[112]

---

110. See D. Bar, "The Christianisation of Rural Palestine during Late Antiquity," *JEH* 54.3 (2003): 401–421, who argues that the Christianization of rural Palestine did not achieve real momentum until the fifth and sixth centuries. See also Runesson, "Architecture," 252 and 252 n.79. Cf. J. Patrich, "The Early Christianization of the Holy Land—The Archaeological Evidence," *Studi di Antichità Cristiana* 66 (2016): 265–293.

111. For an introduction, translation, and historical study of the work, see B. Oehl, "Die Altercatio Ecclesiae et Synagogae: Ein antijudaistischer Dialog der Spätantike" (PhD diss., Universität Bonn, 2012).

112. Fredriksen, "Divinity, Ethnicity, Identity," 102. On "religious deviance" in antiquity, see J. Rüpke, *Religious Deviance in the Roman World: Superstition or Individuality?* trans.

Any non-Jewish Christian who came to Capernaum in the late fifth to early sixth century and whose ideas about "the synagogue" had been informed by the likes of the *Altercatio* would have been immediately challenged by a very different picture. There, towering above street level, they would have seen a synagogue, not poor and dilapidated like Synagoga from the *Altercatio*, but spectacularly decorated and glistening white against the backdrop of its black basalt surroundings. Indeed, one could read the grandeur of the Capernaum synagogue as a direct rebuttal of the *Altercatio*'s claims and as engaging in its own reifying of difference but from a Jewish perspective. Of course, we have no idea whether the *Altercatio* specifically or other texts like it diretly provoked those who built the limestone synagogue. But, in my view, it is quite likely that the supersessionist ideology of the octagonal church was. An interpretation of the synagogue's architecture—its function as built space—must take into consideration this discursive setting, a setting in which competing identities were being, quite literally, carved in stone. That is, the material, visual, and spatial design of the limestone synagogue needs to be seen, in some way, as a *response* to the octagonal church.

Scholars have long noted that Jews throughout the Byzantine Empire found various ways to shape their identities in reaction to Christian

---

D. M. B. Richardson (Cambridge: Cambridge University Press, 2016). To be sure, the (non-Jewish) Christian discursive practice of totalizing and dichotomizing Judaism and Christianity by subsuming them under the concepts of "the synagogue" and "the church" predates the fifth century. The seeds of it appear already in the second century, in Justin Martyr's *Dialogue with Trypho* and it becomes widespread in the fourth century with the rise of a politically empowered Christianity. See A. Runesson, D. Binder, and B. Olsson, *The Ancient Synagogue*, 1–4, and nos. 210–217; J. Lieu, "The Synagogue and the Separation of the Christians," in *The Ancient Synagogue: From Its Origins until 200 CE*, ed. B. Olsson and M. Zetterholm, CBNTS 39 (Stockholm: Almqvist & Wiksell International, 2003), 189–207 (esp. 195–197); and L. V. Rutgers, "The Synagogue as Foe in Early Christian Literature," in *"Follow the Wise": Studies in Jewish History and Culture in Honor of Lee I. Levine*, ed. Z. Weiss et al. (Winona Lake, IN: Eisenbrauns, 2010), 449–468. I note above that this dichotomizing discourse via the language of "the synagogue" versus "the church" is a specifically *Christian* practice, because, while rabbinic literature certainly has its own heresiological impulse and boundary-making strategies, it never, as far as I know, uses the institutions of synagogue (בית כנסת) and church (בית רשות) to accomplish these ideological aims. Lastly, it might be interesting to note that no such discursive practice is evident in New Testament literature, despite Rutgers's claim that the anti-Jewish practice of Christian polemicizing against "the synagogue" in later centuries is traceable to New Testament authors, especially Paul.

imperialism.[113] As it relates specifically to synagogues, Jodi Magness and Magnus Zetterholm have each interpreted the construction of monumental synagogues in relation to the growing colonial power of Christianity.[114] But Runesson's study is currently the only one to apply similar insights to the architecture of the Capernaum synagogue. While his is not a full analysis, Runesson makes the intriguing suggestion that the limestone building represented "a defiant act of defence against the colonizers, a reclaiming of a place in a town the Jews saw as theirs."[115] Although, as I will discuss further in the next chapter, I disagree with Runesson that this "defence theory" accurately explains the sphere of everyday relations between Jews and Christians in the village, the theory is, indeed, worth developing as we move to consider *how* the limestone synagogue represented spatialized resistance to the ideology of Christian triumphalism.

Returning to the synagogue's use of imported limestone is a good place to start. As Ma'oz has mentioned: "The import of building material from outside sources is not recorded at any other Galilean synagogue, and it is extremely rare even in the excavated areas of Tiberias."[116] What should we make, then, of this unique feature in Capernaum? In her work, Findley notes that the material expression of a building is not a neutral matter but is, rather, deeply political and can be used as a critical tool to involve a building's architecture in social change.[117] Beyond the obvious point that it can be a representation of status and wealth, a building's materials demonstrate access to resources and are associated with innovation, can symbolize an ability to control and activate systems of production, and are statements of relative position in regard to other people, cities, and nations. Thus, there is a direct line of connection between construction materials and their ability to supply a building with symbolic presence and cultural agency.[118] This is

---

113. For example, Irshai, "Confronting a Christian Empire," 179–289 (chs. 6–10).

114. J. Magness, "The Date of the Sardis Synagogue in Light of the Numismatic Evidence," *AJA* 109 (2005): 467; and M. Zetterholm, "A Struggle among Brothers," 101–103.

115. Runesson, "Architecture," 252.

116. Ma'oz, "The Synagogue at Capernaum," 139. Ma'oz presumed this point supported his overall theory of Christian imperial involvement in the construction of the limestone synagogue, but as discussed above, this theory has no basis in actual evidence.

117. Findley, *Building Change,* 208.

118. Findley, *Building Change,* 56.

seen especially in contexts in which a local building industry has a limited range of materials—such as in Capernaum with its abundance of basalt stone—and *outside* resources are imported and deployed to create the desired symbolic value.

Being constructed out of a large number of large blocks of imported limestone coming from at least ten kilometers away—rather than locally found black basalt—the Capernaum synagogue expressed many of the political dynamics described by Findley. Not only is it a statement about wealth and status, but, perhaps even more importantly in the colonial context of Byzantine Palestine, it also showed control over natural resources and an ability to assemble and mobilize a manual and skilled labor force. In combination with the building's elevated spatial position in the center of the town, the imported limestone was a proclamation of Jewish agency in the village vis-à-vis the octagon's message of Christian triumphalism. It functioned as a demand to be seen, as a reassertion of Jewish presence and, even more, as a projection of Jewish space resistant to Christian appropriation.

Concerning the space itself, it is widely understood that many synagogues from Byzantine Palestine were modeled on the architecture of the Christian basilica, itself an adaptation of the Roman civic basilica, which had been in use since around the second or first century BCE.[119] Basilica-type synagogues, as Levine notes, usually included an atrium, narthex, rows of columns, a large central nave and side aisles, with a *bēma* or apse in the Jerusalem-oriented wall.[120] This modeling, according to Levine, is particularly clear in those synagogues, such as the one in Capernaum, that are found in proximity to the lake of Galilee, in Bet Shean, and in the coastal and Judean regions, that is, in areas with a larger Christian population.[121] But, while the Christian basilica is often framed as a cultural influence on Jewish building practices, it can just as well be framed as a site of Jewish resistance. That is, the appropriation of Christian architecture by Jews, especially in Capernaum, could have been a strong critique of Christian

---

119. For example, Y. Tsafrir, "The Byzantine Setting and Its Influence on Ancient Synagogues," in *The Synagogue in Late Antiquity*, ed. L. I. Levine (Philadelphia: ASOR Press, 1987), 147–157; Levine, *The Ancient Synagogue*, 246, 325, 341–342, 355, 617; and Milson, *Art and Architecture of the Synagogue*.

120. Levine, *The Ancient Synagogue*, 325.

121. Levine, *The Ancient Synagogue*, 246.

cultural imperialism. The many fragments of Late Roman Fine Wares with stamped crosses scattered throughout the village remind us that, in the fifth and sixth centuries, Capernaum was being flooded not only with Christian bodies but with Christian materiality. Taking a Christian architectural form and "Judaizing" it would have been a strong push against the expansion of Christian cultural hegemony.

The Capernaum synagogue "Judaized" the basilica form through both its interior design and exterior decoration. Byzantine churches typically had chancel screens separating the apsidal altar where the clergy officiated from the central nave where the congregation gathered. The spatial ordering of people and knowledge was fundamentally hierarchical in nature. Levine mentions that such hierarchical division was absent in synagogue worship, although the remains of chancel screens have been found at just a handful of synagogue sites.[122] In Capernaum, like in many other Galilean synagogues, there were, indeed, ritual and social focal points: the Jerusalem-oriented southern entrance wall with two flanking *bēma* platforms, one of which likely contained a Torah ark, provided the ritual focus,[123] and the donor inscriptions on columns, which highlighted the euergetistic prominence of a few individuals and their families, provided the social focus. But the space itself, and therefore the people that occupied it, were not physically and visually segregated from the rest of the central nave. For example, there is no evidence of special seating, such as the railing found in the synagogue at Sardis, which apparently separated the benches reserved for leaders from the rest of the congregation. The entire main hall of the Capernaum synagogue, as well as the eastern courtyard, speak a communitarian language, a language of "we," not entirely unlike the relational language of public synagogue architecture from the Second Temple period. This language not only set the limestone building apart from the Christian basilica in general, but, more specifically, it contrasted starkly with the deeply hierarchical ordering of space in the octagonal church a few meters away. While the language there is of restriction and control—of both knowledge and bodies—the internal organization of space in the synagogue, particularly its inward facing benches along the two side aisles of the main hall, functions to relinquish control and to open the space up to multiple interpretations of tradition.

---

122. Levine, *The Ancient Synagogue*, 341–342.

123. See Strange, "The Archaeology of Religion at Capernaum," 50–52, where he argues that a Torah ark was the main feature on one of these platforms.

Architecturalizing Power and Resistance 199

The exterior decoration of the limestone synagogue would have made it impossible for someone passing on the street to mistake it for a pagan temple. Such a mistake apparently did happen frequently enough in other contexts for some rabbis to discuss its halakhic implications (*b. Shabb.* 72b; *b. Sanh.* 61b). But, in contrast to the modest exteriors and relatively rich interiors of synagogues from the Lower Galilee and nearby urban centres, the Capernaum synagogue's exterior was the ornamental focus.[124] Its monumental entranceway and extensive stone carvings on its doors, window areas, capitals, lintels, doorposts, friezes, pilasters, gable, and arch sent powerful outward-facing messages about the cultural identity of the building.[125] To be sure, this focus on the building's exterior was not unique to Capernaum; it was, in general, typical of synagogues from rural Upper Galilee.[126] But the sheer lavishness of the decoration and Capernaum's rapidly Christianizing context, I suggest, activated social meanings in the iconography of the synagogue's exterior that were not nearly as strong as in other synagogues from the region.[127]

5. Conclusion

In his carefully argued study, Schwartz has said that synagogues from Palestine in late antiquity played a central role in the construction of an "ideology of self-enclosure," a shared and inwardly directed vision of the local Jewish community as, and as participating in, the "biblical people of Israel."[128] Schwartz's claim—which I find mostly persuasive—derives largely from language used in many synagogue inscriptions invoking concepts such as *qahal*

---

124. Levine, *The Ancient Synagogue*, 246.

125. Levine, "Diversity," 8; Levine, *The Ancient Synagogue*, 246.

126. Levine, *The Ancient Synagogue*, 246; cf. Schwartz, *Imperialism*, 280, who sees, rather, a fundamental similarity between synagogues in urban settings (in both Palestine and the Diaspora) and rural settings. Levine's description and categorization of the data is more convincing. Of course, the distinction between an external decorative focus in rural Upper Galilee versus an internal decorative focus in urban Lower Galilee was in no way absolute. After all, the Huqoq synagogue in rural Upper Galilee is home to some of the finest interior synagogue decoration known so far, particularly its mosaic carpets.

127. For example, the synagogues at Chorazin, Bar'am, Nabratein, and Meroth were clearly richly decorated but not on the scope and scale of Capernaum.

128. Schwartz, *Imperialism*, 275–289 (the reference to the "biblical people of Israel" is on p. 275).

qadishah (the holy assembly), *ha'am* (the people/nation), and *shalom 'al Yisrael* (peace upon Israel). In other words, while likely at odds with wider socioeconomic and religious realities and itself a consequence of Christianization (two very important qualifications that I address in chapter 6), Jews imagined themselves on local levels as autonomous and egalitarian communities of "religious obligation and meaning."[129] Although the inscriptions from the Capernaum synagogue do not directly mimic the language Schwartz highlights, his observations dovetail nicely with my own about the synagogue's architectural language being marked, metaphorically, by the communal flare of the first-person plural; it declares "*We* are the people of Israel." However, I suggest that what makes the Capernaum synagogue different from many other expressions of this communal ideology is that it turns this ideology *outward*, aiming it squarely at the octagonal church. From this perspective, the limestone synagogue constituted a spatial act of resistance, more specifically, to the colonial ideology of Christian supersessionism. In Collingwood's terms, the synagogue was an answer to the question of Jewish identity in the context of an expanding Christian empire.[130] If the octagon proclaimed the eternal triumph of Christianity by way of appropriating Jewish space, the synagogue, especially with its artistic and architectural focus on the motif of the Torah shrine, expressed the reclamation not only of Jewish cultural and political agency but also of Jewish *covenantal* agency: "*We*, not *you*, are the people of Israel."[131]

---

129. Schwartz, *Imperialism*, 289.

130. On Collingwood's logic of "question and answer," see note 15 in this chapter.

131. This observation provides historical context for Strange's assertion, which I find quite intriguing, that the entire limestone edifice functioned as a "solid metaphor" for the declamation of Torah. See Strange, "The Archaeology of Religion at Capernaum," 51. His idea makes sense of the art and architecture of the synagogue, which clearly draws on the Torah shrine motif in at least three separate ways (two *bema* platforms; the Torah niche with a pediment in the window above the central arch [as reconstructed by Kohl and Watzinger]; and the portable Torah shrine relief). My point is to highlight, as Ulla Tervahauta does, that the Torah shrine played important architectural and conceptual role in Jewish responses to Christianization and especially to the development of Christian notions of sacred space. See U. Tervahauta, "Sacred Space and Torah Shrines in Late Antique Synagogues," in Bonnie, Hakola, Tervahauta, *The Synagogue in Ancient Palestine*, 311–336.

CHAPTER SIX

Beyond Monumental Architecture
Jewish–Christian Relations and Everyday Life in Capernaum in Late Antiquity

1. Introduction

BY THE LATE fifth and early sixth century, Capernaum had become a Christian "holy hot spot," with pilgrims all over the Byzantine Empire trickling in to pay homage to the Cult of St. Peter, where, according to tradition, a church had been built over the supposed site of the apostle's original house. At the same time, Capernaum had become the home of one of the grandest synagogues in all of Palestine in late antiquity, erected a mere twenty-five meters to the north of the church.[1] In the sixth century, the village had reached its peak in urban development and economic prosperity, but the balance of its demographics had shifted, with Byzantine Christianity in its newly invented "Holy Land" reaching the height of its imperial power.[2] Capernaum's Jewish community—now a colonized minority attempting to carve its cultural and political agency into the landscape of Byzantine power through the architecture of its monumental synagogue[3]—shared the village as social space with politically empowered Christians emigrating from throughout the Byzantine world. And, while traces of them are ever so faint, we should allow for the possibility of a third social group: squeezed between Capernaum's Jews and

---

1. For several aerial photos of the site that helpfully contextualize both monumental buildings, see the documentary photographs in Loffreda, *Cafarnao V*, esp. DFs 1–34a.

2. On the economic environment of Capernaum in the Byzantine period, see Mattila, "Capernaum, Village of Naḥum," 217–254. On the Byzantine colonization and creation of the "Holy Land" beginning in the fourth century, see S. Fine, "Non-Jews in the Synagogues," 204; and A. Jacobs, *Remains of the Jews: The Holy Land and Christian Empire in Late Antiquity* (Stanford: Stanford University Press, 2004).

3. On which, see chapter 5.

Byzantine Christians may have been the village's historic community of Jewish Christ-followers.[4]

With these imposing structures dominating both the rhetorical and built landscapes of Capernaum, it is no wonder that most contemporary scholarly discussions about Jewish–Christian relations in the village have revolved mainly around these two buildings. Their architectures, chronologies, and proximity to one another have led to proposals of various interactional paradigms, such as conflict, coexistence, competition, or rivalry.[5] However, in view of our discussion in the previous chapter, we must be cautious, even critical, about mapping our interpretation of the monumental architecture onto the everyday experiences of Jews and Christians "on the ground."[6] To date, no study has considered the question of Jewish–Christian relations in Capernaum from the perspective of the archaeology of the village's surrounding *domestic* environment. This has led to the current status in research, in which the identity-shaping rhetoric of the octagonal church and limestone synagogue

---

4. See Runesson, "Architecture," 251. The evidence for the presence of three social groups in Capernaum during this time is as follows: (1) Byzantine Christians: (a) the octagonal church, a clear architectural expression of Byzantine religious culture (cf. also the Church of the Nativity [fourth century, Bethlehem], the Kathisma Church [fifth century, between Hebron and Jerusalem], and the Church of the Theotokos [sixth century, Mt. Gerizim]); and (b) over one-hundred pieces of imported Late Roman Fine Ware stamped with stylized crosses, the density of which is striking (for the specific find-spots, see Loffreda, *Cafarnao VI*, 400. (2) Galilean Jews: (a) a mere twenty-five meters to the north of the church was built one of the largest and most ornate synagogues of Palestine in late antiquity, outfitted with various Jewish symbols (e.g., menorah, portable Torah shrine); (b) two donor inscriptions on columns of the synagogue mention Jewish names, for example, Mo[ki]mo, Yohanan, Zebida (see T. Ilan, *Lexicon of Jewish Names in Late Antiquity*. Part II: *Palestine 200–650 CE*, TSAJ 148 [Tübingen: Mohr Siebeck, 2012], 107, 364; "Jose bar Zebida" is the name of a famous Palestinian Amoraic sage mentioned in the Bavli; the name Mo[ki]mo is Palmyran); and (c) a sixth-century donor inscription on the mosaic pavement of the synagogue at Ḥamat Gader mentions a Jewish man by the name of Yosse bar Dosti of Capernaum (*CIIP* V 2: no. 7372; Naveh, *On Stone and Mosaic*, no. 33; G. Foerster, "Dating Synagogues," 87–94 [90–91]). (3) Jewish Christ-followers: the Palestinian midrash *Qohelet Rabbah* 1:8 (redacted sixth to eighth century) mentions certain *minim* ("heretics") living in Capernaum, who are probably to be identified as Jewish followers of Jesus. While this text likely reflects, in part, some memory of a second-century rabbinic encounter with Jesus-oriented Jews, it is probably also reflective of a sixth-century polemical setting between rabbinic Jews and Jewish Christ-followers. See chapter 4.

5. For example, Runesson, "Architecture," 231–257; and Arubas and Talgam, "Jews, Christians, and *Minim*," 237–274.

6. This point is made also in Hakola, "Galilean Jews and Christians in Context," 161–164.

are often interpreted in a social and material vacuum. In this chapter, therefore, I wish to move the question of Jewish–Christian relations in Capernaum beyond the monumental architecture of the church and the synagogue and bring the village's two social-architectural spheres together analytically—the domestic and the monumental—to address the question afresh.

To do this, I suggest we adapt some of the insights offered in the work of two French social theorists, Michel de Certeau and Pierre Mayol, on the concepts of everyday life and the neighborhood, as well as Cynthia Baker's work on the architecture of gender in Galilee in late antiquity. Certain concepts from the work of these theorists, I think, will open doors for us to explore how Capernaum's neighborhood architecture—its sociomaterial network of houses, shops, and streets—can and should contribute to the way in which we imagine the functional aspects of Jews and Christians having lived together as neighbors. Once we consider the domestic remains from this perspective, we can then look back with a critical lens at the question of the supposed religious boundary projected by the architecture of Capernaum's church and synagogue. Since, as expected, there are limitations in Capernaum's archaeological record, we will need to draw upon several contemporaneous and geographically proximate literary sources that, I argue, provide further hermeneutical insight into the entangled relationship between Capernaum's monumental and domestic landscapes and generate a more robust historical imagination of Jewish–Christian interaction in the town.

2. Thinking Theoretically about "Neighborhood" and "Neighbor"

In his *The Practice of Everyday Life*, Michel de Certeau draws the now well-known distinction between strategies and tactics, two cultural categories (and metaphors taken from military parlance) that oppose one another in their calculation of power relationships within a given society.[7] Every strategic rationalization stems from the purview of power, a setting of control, in which the subjects, the producers of strategy, distinguish their own place as an in-group in the social hierarchy from an out-group, from other objects. Governments (national or local), managers of institutions (large or small),

---

7. See his discussion in M. de Certeau, *The Practice of Everyday Life*, trans. S. Randall (Berkley, CA: University of California Press, 1984), 35–38.

and city planning commissions are good examples of subjects with strategic power. Self-segregated from the invisible objects they lead, producers of strategy determine the rules of the proper; they create from a pantoptic vantage point the official environment, the public space, in which external social agents act. Tactics, on the other hand, are the everyday calculated actions of the non-powerful users of this environment. Tactics lack their own place, because they are always executed on someone else's turf, in the space of the other. Tactics are, as de Certeau puts it metaphorically, manoeuvres "within enemy territory."[8] While tactics are influenced by the rules that already exist in culture through strategic power, they operate as isolated actions, unpredictable and creative, and never wholly determined by those rules. Strategies utilize totalizing discourse to transform and control objects they wish to include within their all-encompassing scope of vision; tactical movements are opportunistic, spontaneous, and work at the ground level.

De Certeau illustrates this relationship between strategy and tactics by contrasting the concept of the city with the ordinary walker in the city.[9] The city is projected by governments and institutions as public space, as a unified whole, through maps, street grids, and urban planning. The ordinary walker—who, for example, needs to arrive at work on time—tactically adapts, manipulates, and even resists this environment by taking shortcuts, generating bypasses, hopping fences, and infracting pedestrian laws by jaywalking. The environmental "rules of the game" that strategic power produces and imposes from its surveillance tower are not necessarily rejected, but they are, indeed, poached on and transgressed in the process of everyday life, as ordinary dwellers in the city attempt what de Certeau terms "to make do."

Working within de Certeau's theoretical framework, Pierre Mayol has described how the notion of neighborhood is an important bridge concept that links the spheres of strategic power and everyday tactical action.[10] The neighborhood, for Mayol, is not a static place. Rather, it is a dynamic cultural practice involving a "progressive apprenticeship" that grows out of the repetition of a dweller's bodily engagement in the unknown totality of public space until they

---

8. de Certeau, *Everyday Life*, 37.

9. de Certeau, *Everyday Life*, 91–110.

10. P. Mayol, "The Neighborhood," in M. de Certeau, L. Giard, and P. Mayol, *The Practice of Everyday Life*, vol 2, *Living and Cooking*, trans. T. J. Tomasik (Minneapolis: University of Minnesota Press, 1998), 7–13.

achieve a kind of appropriation of this space, that is, until they have adapted it to particularized and advantageous use.[11] The neighborhood is a living and fluid extension of one's abode, which, little by little, insinuates itself into the public space of strategic power through the everyday tactical use of this space. The concept of neighborhood, therefore, both depends on and complicates the limitation between private and public space; it is always shifting as one, through repetition, becomes a master of their spatial environment. As Mayol says, "The public and the private are not both disregarded as two exogenous, though coexisting, elements: they are much more constantly interdependent, because, in the neighborhood, one has no meaning without the other."[12]

If the *repetition* of everyday cultural habits is the key to understanding the neighborhood as an environment in which a dweller appropriates (tactics) public space (strategy), then *recognition* is the key to understanding the neighborhood as a network of social relations within that appropriated environment.[13] The neighborhood is a social space known to a dweller, but it is also a social space in which a dweller knows her or himself to be recognized, to a greater or lesser degree, by others. The neighborhood is always, as Mayol asserts, "the space of a relationship to the other as a social being."[14] As soon as one steps out of their house and on to a street, they have taken up an identifiable place in a preexisting network of social signs, a place that makes them recognizable— they have a face—and, at the same time, distinguishes them from the Other. This Other is "neither intimate nor anonymous" but rather a *neighbor*.[15] The recognition of a neighbor—their being "known"—results from the repetitive and proximate performance of their commitment to the "rules of propriety," that is, the implicit social contract that makes everyday life possible rather than a living hell. Of course, this contract can experience violent

---

11. Cf. D. Martin, "Enacting Neighborhood," *Urban Geography* 24, no. 5 (2003): 365, where she articulates: "[Neighborhoods are] a particular type of place: locations where human activity is centered upon social reproduction; or daily household activities, social interaction, and engagement with political and economic structures. Neighborhoods derive their meaning or salience from individual and group values and attachments, which develop through daily life habits and interactions. Neighborhoods, like places, are 'where everyday life is situated.'"

12. Mayol, "Neighborhood," 11–12.

13. Mayol, "Neighborhood," 8–9.

14. Mayol, "Neighborhood," 12.

15. Mayol, "Neighborhood," 12.

rupture—neighborhood life can indeed become an anarchic, "monstrous" hell—and thus "making do" in the neighborhood can become impossible. Making do in everyday life, therefore, is predicated on both one's resistive adaptation of strategic power *and* the commitment of members within the social network to "pay the price" of renouncing individual impulses with the goal of gaining the symbolic benefits of being recognized.[16]

In sum, in de Certeau's and Mayol's theory, *repetition* of tactical action in concrete proximity and *recognition* of the "neither intimate nor anonymous" neighbor are the sociospatial building blocks of everyday life, of making do in the neighborhood. Together they represent adaptive responses to and within strategic power, which is, by contrast, singular and faceless. This framework goes a long way to highlight the functional interconnectivity of and, simultaneously, the discrepancy between strategic and tactical elements of society. While the society that de Certeau and Mayol have in mind here is modern— and particularly French—their theory opens up new ways of configuring social relations between Jews and Christians in an ancient context like Capernaum, where the dynamics of strategic power and tactical action can be theorized through its built environment.

3. Jews and Christians in the "Neighborhood" of Capernaum in Late Antiquity

Capernaum's grand synagogue and octagonal church are clear, if competing, expressions of ethnoreligious institutional strategy. Each functions to claim an autonomous place, to construct an official environment in which to control its objects. Together they construct sociospatial boundaries, self-segregating distinctions (concrete or conceptual) between subjects and objects, a set of rules by which those "out there" are compelled to play.

How well did the town's Jews and Byzantine Christians play by these rules? How well *could* they have played by them in light of the architecture of Capernaum's domestic landscape? In what ways and to what extent did Jews and Christians here adapt, resist, and particularize their official environment in relationship to each other as "Others"? It is impossible to answer these questions with certainty and specificity; tactical actions do not always leave

---

16. Mayol, "Neighborhood," 8.

discernible traces in the archaeological record. We can, however, get at some answers by using the de Certeau–inspired concept of neighborhood to open up Capernaum's nonmonumental landscape in relation to the landscape of the church and synagogue. I suggest we do this by considering three microzones that represent the appropriation of public space for particularized everyday use, that is, the intersection, or perhaps better, the mapping, of "private" onto "public" space. These microzones are specific areas in Capernaum's nonmonumental landscape that lend themselves the most to theorizing "life in the neighborhood, the processes of repetition and recognition, of making do, and of knowing and being known by the Other; they are houses, marketplace, and streets. I will argue that the practice of neighborhood in Capernaum draws Jewish–Christian relations into processes of liminality, fluidity, and intense sociality, while the strategy of the church and synagogue is to demarcate *place* as the primary marker of Jewish and Christian identity, that is, to distinguish between static subjects, and that we are to read a strong functional element of *resistance* to strategic power within Capernaum's domestic landscape.[17]

Capernaum's Houses and the Domestic Landscape

As in many societies today, the house in ancient Palestinian society lay at the center of the practice of neighborhood. However, in contemporary (especially European and North American) societies, as well as in de Certeau's and Mayol's social theory, the concepts of house and neighborhood are predicated upon a strong distinction between the more basic concepts of private and public space: the house is understood to exist within the realm of the private, while the neighborhood is seen as a middle concept between it and public space. As demonstrated by Cynthia Baker in her study of gender and space in Jewish society of late antiquity, houses throughout the Roman and Byzantine East entertain no such distinction.[18] That is, the house was, itself, the middle concept, the starting point for the adaptation of public space and the social processes of repetition and recognition, and, thus, for the practice of neighborhood.

---

17. Recall that "resistance" here does not imply violence, revolt, or intentional rejection of institutional strategy, but rather the principle that everyday life frequently runs against the grain of it in the attempt of individuals and groups to make do.

18. See Baker, *Rebuilding the House of Israel*, 34–76.

Ancient Mediterranean houses, especially those excavated in the region of the Galilee, were usually built in multiresidential blocks (or "*insulae*").[19] Within these blocks, lines demarcating where each dwelling unit starts and stops are often difficult or even impossible to discern. This could be due, as Baker notes, to the impartial state of preservation of many sets of remains,[20] but, in places where remains are quite well preserved, the sprawling and architecturally complex nature of such housing blocks could just as well be evidence of the intensely social and relational character of ancient dwelling units and, by implication, the dwelling practices that accompanied them.

To describe Galilean houses, therefore, as private spaces obfuscates the data.[21] Housing compounds could be relatively large and could include multi-residential complexes *set within* an even larger complex, with individual rooms and multiple courtyards communicating architecturally very closely with each other by way of, for example, shared walls or a single roof.[22] As Baker argues, it is too much to assume that such compounds were inhabited by single or extended families *or even solely by Jews*; neither archaeological remains nor textual sources support this assumption. Some rabbinic texts, for their part, envision a social environment in which it was expected that Jews would be engaged in commercial activity with non-Jews on a daily basis (as detailed, e.g., in *m. Avodah Zerah* and its expansions in the Talmudic literature) and even share or co-own living spaces with non-Jews in housing enclosures or courtyards.[23]

---

19. Hirschfeld, *The Palestinian Dwelling*, 272; Baker, *Rebuilding*, 36.

20. Baker, *Rebuilding*, 36.

21. The excavators of Capernaum routinely use the language of private versus public space to describe the town's houses in contrast to the church and synagogue. See, for example, Loffreda, *Recovering Capharnaum*, 18–26. However, housing complexes in the Galilee in late antiquity were anything but private, at least in the same way we tend to use that term today the Euro-American West.

22. See Baker, *Rebuilding*, 36, where she mentions the so-called "Triple-Courtyard House" at Capernaum (see Image 6.1—the shaded space in the plan marked #3).

23. Baker, *Rebuilding*, 37. For example, *m. Eruv.* 6:1 begins with the scenario of a Jew who "dwells in the same courtyard with a Gentile [הנכרי]" (trans. Neusner). Joint ownership of dwelling complexes or parts of dwelling complexes (e.g., courtyards, rooms) is mentioned frequently by the rabbis as well (e.g., *m. Eruv.* 6:5: "A householder who was a joint-holder [in a commercial relation] with neighbors. . ."), and was common in the ancient Mediterranean more broadly. See discussion of this (as it relates to Dura-Europos) in J. Baird, *The Inner Lives of Ancient Houses: An Archaeology Dura-Europos* (Oxford: Oxford University Press, 2014),

Beyond Monumental Architecture

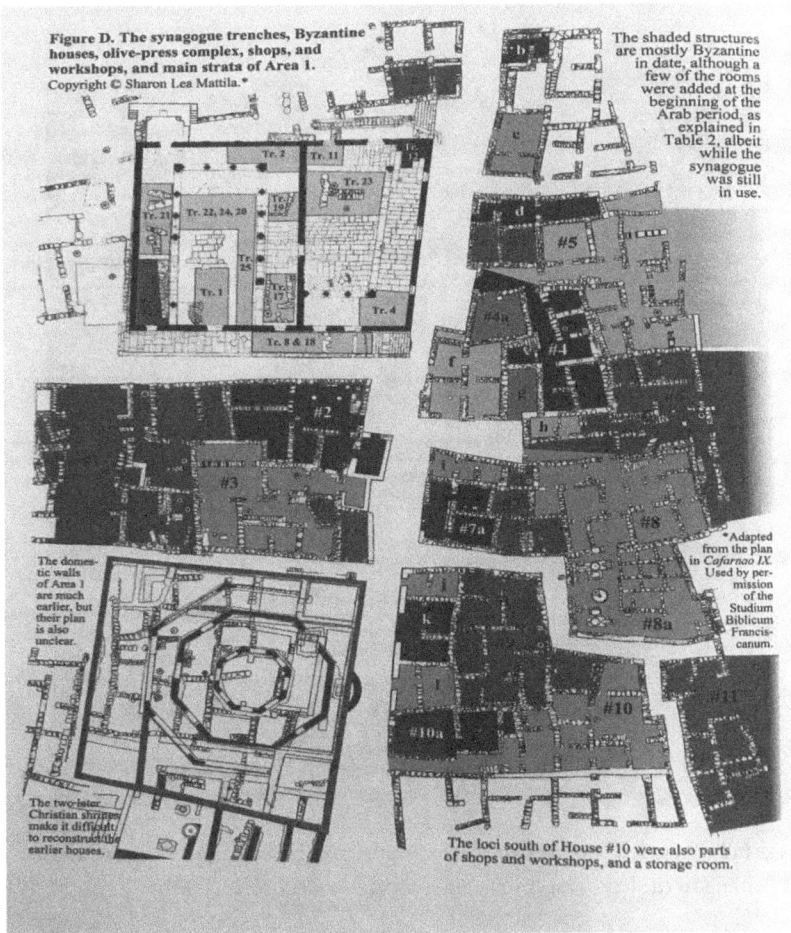

Image 6.1. Segmentation of Capernaum's Byzantine houses and shops with commentary by Sharon Mattila as published in "Capernaum, Village of Naḥum," 224.

Reproduced here with Mattila's permission. In this plan, north is at the top of the page.

While movement in and out of housing complexes was not entirely uncontrolled, the multifunctional character of houses, with their utility rooms, shops, workshops, and courtyards, meant they could experience large volumes of daily foot traffic from both residents and non-residents of the domicile. Domestic

---

50–57, especially her discussion of *P. Dura* 19, a documentary papyrus outlining the legalities of ownership of Durene houses and parts of houses.

Image 6.2. Photo looking north of Areas 3 and 4, comprised of houses and workshops, and flanked to the left (west) by the main north–south street (L39).

From Loffreda, *Cafarnao V*, 241 (DF 463). Used with permission.

workshops, often set within shared courtyards, were the most common site of production and commerce in towns and villages like Capernaum. According to *m. Baba Batra* 2:3, the coming and going of people in a shared courtyard could be dense and quite noisy, even disturbing the sleep of neighbors.[24] Everyday activities such as food preparation and doing laundry were also performed in the social space of the courtyard, using installations and manufacturing tools that were often shared among various groups. As Baker asserts, people occupying such dwellings, while in their domestic environment, were, therefore,

---

24. See Baker, *Rebuilding*, 39.

Image 6.3. Photo looking southeast of the houses in Area 2.

From Loffreda, *Cafarnao V*, 111 (DF 150). Used with permission.

in a fundamentally *social and interactive environment*.²⁵ The loud and chaotic movement of bodies and the deeply relational nature of the built environment complicate the notion of identity-bound space within the domestic landscape. The house in the Galilee of late antiquity was marked by fluidity in the spatial distribution of *ethnicity* as well as gender; it was apparently no more a strictly Jewish or Byzantine Christian space than it was a women's or men's space.²⁶

---

25. A good example of this fundamentally social environment is *m. Eruv.* 6:3, where the "men of the courtyard" are owners of dwelling units that surround said courtyard and that are mutually accessible (or not, depending on one's observance of eruv) for "bringing things in and taking things out." In other words, the halakhic status of an individual's house has a direct impact on other house owners.

26. "Byzantine Christian" should probably be understood as a broader cultural identity rather than ethnic identity. Coins and imported pottery might suggest that specific ethnic

It takes one look at a plan of ancient Capernaum to recognize in this town the kind of relationality and fluidity among its housing units that Baker has identified as characteristic of Galilean houses generally.[27]

While a main north–south street and two smaller east–west alleyways cut Capernaum into several residential blocks, these blocks do not follow an orthogonal plan.[28] Like other Galilean towns its size, such as Meiron, but unlike larger cities throughout the eastern Mediterranean, such as the lower city of Sepphoris (Galilee) and Dura-Europos (Syria), Capernaum's domestic landscape is discernibly asymmetrical in layout.[29] Houses within the residential blocks are set cheek by jowl, and it is very difficult to discern their limits.[30] Most of these complexes show remains of staircases, suggesting

---

expressions of Byzantine Christianity such as Syrian (particularly Antiochene), North African, and Asian were present in Capernaum. See footnote 55.

27. See especially the many helpful figures, including plans and reconstructions of Capernaum houses, given in Mattila, "Capernaum, Village of Naḥum." The figures on pp. 224 (plan of entire Franciscan site; reproduced with permission below), 233 (reconstruction of Houses 6 and 8), and 235 (reconstruction of Olive-Press Complex 8a and Houses 9 and 10) are particularly illustrative. For clarification, I follow the same house numbering as used by Mattila. For the plans produced by excavators V. Corbo and S. Loffreda, see any of the nine volumes produced in the series of reports, *Cafarnao I–IX* (Jerusalem: Franciscan, 1972–2008).

28. The residential block including Houses 1, 2, and 3 (block in between the synagogue and church) is the only block delimited orthogonally, with the main north–south street running along its eastern side and the two east–west streets circumscribing its northern and southern ends. It is not clear whether there are any other continuous streets in the town. One street, zig-zagging through Houses 7–10, seems to end abruptly at a wall near House 11.

29. E. M. Meyers and C. L. Meyers, "Meiron in Upper Galilee," in *Galilee in the Late Second Temple and Mishnaic Periods*, vol. 2, *The Archaeological Record from Cities, Towns, and Villages*, ed. D. A. Fiensy and J. R. Strange (Minneapolis: Fortress Press, 2015), 379–388; E. M. Meyers, C. L. Meyers, and B. Gordon, "Sepphoris: Residential Area of the Western Summit," in *Galilee*, ed. Fiensy and Strange, 2:44.

30. Mattila recognizes this difficulty in her "Capernaum, Village of Naḥum," 224. Figure D on this page clearly differentiates between houses, shops, and workshops, but it obviously includes a level of arbitrary division between, for example, Houses 4 and 5 (at what the excavators label Locus 98), and Houses 6 and 8 (at what the excavators label Locus 200). Ownership of these entryways was probably not neatly divided but rather shared between the owners of the houses (which themselves may have been jointly owned). This is not to deny that the figure is certainly helpful for clarifying some units, as it uses the general principle that independent units are defined (at least at ground level) by access to a street and lack of internal access to other units (Mattila, "Capernaum, Village of Naḥum," 229).

Beyond Monumental Architecture

Image 6.4. The photo on the left is of an area looking north of Area 3. This is Mattila's House 8 and 8a, which included an olive press complex attached to the house, labeled in the photo L270. The photo on the right is of the same area looking east.

From Loffreda, *Cafarnao V*, 216 (DF 388) and 238 (DF 455). Used with permission.

they had second-level living and working quarters,[31] which may or may not have been inhabited and used by the same group living and working on the ground level.

Let us turn to a few examples of Capernaum's housing complexes. The so-called Triple Courtyard House, which comprised the southeast third of Area 2 and designated House 3 and 3a ("a" referring specifically to the house's shop) by Mattila (see Image 6.1),[32] was almost certainly shared by multiple residents.[33] In the Byzantine period, it had an inner surface area of 135.1 m², approximately seven ancillary rooms in addition to its three courtyards, and an attached house shop that was added later (House 3a).[34] This house butted

---

31. On staircases and second levels, see Mattila, "Capernaum," 231–234

32. The specific area is designated Loci 45, 46, 51 in the official village plan produced by the excavators Corbo and Loffreda.

33. Noted by Baker, *Rebuilding*, 36.

34. Evidence that the area encompassed by House 3a (designated Loci 52, 56 by the excavators) is the remains of a house shop is (1) its lack of ovens, (2) its lack of accesses to the inner areas of the house, and (3) a direct, wide, and double-columned access to the east–west street immediately to the south (Street 41). See Mattila, "Capernaum, Village of Naḥum," 235–236, where she also draws on comparison with the house shops found in Pompeii.

up against two other houses within the block, House 1 to the west[35] and House 2 to the northeast. House 3 shared walls with both of these other houses and likely had a roof that, architecturally, communicated closely with both as well. The nature of the goods produced or sold in the house shop of the Triple Courtyard House is uncertain, but House 1's high concentration of ovens (two large ones in its southeastern-most room; see the white circular notations given in Image 21), its basalt crushing mortars, and the industrial size flour mill that was found in its courtyard have led Mattila to suggest (in agreement with Stefano De Luca) that House 1 doubled as a commercial bakery.[36] The group of houses consisting of those designated by Mattila as Houses 4 to 8 also evinces intensely social and multifunctional characteristics. Houses 6 and 8 (in Area 3) shared an entrance, with both houses having access to one another. Similarly, Houses 4 and 5 shared an entrance, which allowed even more free-flowing, mutual access between them. Mattila identifies about nine shops or workshops in this housing block, eight of which ran along the western strip of the area made up of Houses 4 to 8 and were accessible from the main north–south street (L39). A ninth shop, House 8a, was an olive press complex attached to House 8 (the use of similar roof tiles link the two structures), which was accessible from the zig-zagging east–west street and used for the production and storage of olive oil.[37]

All shops and workshops in Capernaum were attached to a domestic complex, whether or not owned and operated by the owner of the adjacent house, as was evidently the case with Houses 3/3a, 4/4a, 7a, 8/8a, and 10/10a. In other words, not only were Capernaum's housing complexes intimately connected architecturally, but they were also bound together through everyday commercial activity. Indeed, unlike in some of the larger cities of the Galilee and around the Byzantine East, there is no evidence of standalone shops or

---

35. As Mattila, "Capernaum, Village of Naḥum," 221, (in her Figure C) mentions (but presents in her Figure D on p. 224), while House 1 had a large courtyard in the early Roman period, this courtyard was divided up into smaller dwellings in the Byzantine period. As can be seen on the excavators' plan of the town, this only makes our picture of the residential block of Houses 1 to 3 more convoluted.

36. Mattila, "Capernaum," 234. For documentary photographs of these remains, see Loffreda, *Cafarnao V*, DFs 136, 152, 153, 162c (where the conical bottom of the industrial flour mill is seen *in situ* in Locus 67).

37. See the reconstructions of Stefano De Luca, presented in Mattila, "Capernaum," 233, 235.

agora- or *forum*-like spaces in Capernaum; commerce and production in the town are thoroughly embedded within its domestic landscape.

However, as in other smaller towns and villages in the region, many of Capernaum's house shops are situated along its heavily trafficked public street. Such a main street lined with house shops and workshops—called the *shuk* in rabbinic literature (lit. "street market")—created a busy thoroughfare that encompassed, as Baker observes, "the chief locale for commerce in goods, services, and information of all sorts. It is ... that place where all manner of people of local, distant, and foreign origin had access to one another, as well as to goods that were similarly of local, distant, and foreign origins."[38] Street markets, such as the one in Capernaum, made social distancing an impossibility and coexistence among Others a necessity for the survival and stability of the town; you have to play nicely with Others in your neighborhood, even if only to make a living and not to make living a living hell. Street markets, therefore, did not merely blur the boundary between domestic and public space, as they obscured the spatial limits of the neighborhood;[39] they obscured the limits of group identity, as they created a context of social flux and fluidity open, by necessity, to exchange and interaction between people of different genders, classes, and ethnoreligions.

This physical and social layout is a good example of "neighborhood-building," defined as the appropriation and particularization of public space, which I described above within Mayol's and de Certeau's social theory. The spatial semiotics of Capernaum's houses can be understood as an encroachment on and resistance to the strategy of the town's urban planning and monumental landscape. These houses were sites of everyday tactical actions that did not play by the same rules of the proper as the totalizing institutions of the church and synagogue. These dwelling complexes were predicated on processes of social fluidity and liminality, where repetitive yet unpredictable behaviors manifest as mastery of the social environment over time, for example, through buying and selling, producing and consuming, and entering and exiting spaces. In contrast to the social system of the church and synagogue, which depends on hierarchical self-segregation from the invisible objects "out there" that they attempt to control, the social system

---

38. Baker, *Rebuilding*, 105.
39. Baker, *Rebuilding*, 77–79.

of Capernaum's housing complexes, as neighborhood, was built through visibility and recognition, as dwellers increasingly inscribed their place into the sociospatial system through sharing objects, sharing courtyards, sharing greetings, and sharing the sights, sounds, and smells of the neighborhood with those in proximity to them, especially those within the same housing block. We can imagine that such repetitive, spontaneous behavior and visual recognition shaped the neither intimate nor anonymous figure of both the Jewish and Christian neighbor in Capernaum.

Imagining the Everyday Life of Jewish–Christian Relations

Reading Capernaum's neighborhood landscape as a realm of tactical action in contradistinction to its monumental landscape as the realm of strategic power can in some ways complicate and in other ways clarify our picture of Jewish–Christian relations in the town. While the church and synagogue project borders and distinction of place between Jewish and Christian identities,[40] the town's domestic environment projects a social situation that precludes such defined parameters. There is no evidence among Capernaum's housing complexes of separate Jewish and Christian spaces;[41] the intense sociality and architectural communication between dwellings seems to indicate precisely the opposite.

The image the archaeological data impresses on us is one of densely populated housing blocks, brimming with social activity from Jewish and Christian neighbors living, working, and thus, by necessity, closely interacting with each

---

40. As mentioned in note 4 in this chapter, this point is not intended to exclude the possibility (a strong one in my opinion) that Jewish Christ-followers lived in Capernaum in this period, who themselves would have blurred this boundary by way of their social identity.

41. The many fragments of imported Late Roman Fine Wares stamped with crosses, which were found scattered throughout the entire town, are evidence of neither the precise dwelling location of Byzantine Christians nor the theory that *only* Byzantine Christians inhabited Capernaum in the fifth and sixth centuries (as argued by Zvi Uri Ma'oz, "The Synagogue at Capernaum," 137–148). These fragments were found in housing complexes—especially areas of production—but also in apparently random areas such as in streets and alleyways. There is no discernible pattern in their distribution. What they demonstrate, rather, is the Byzantine strategy of colonizing through culture, in this case a particularly *visual material* culture. For documentation of the precise find-locations of the stamped pottery, see the plan presented in B. Callegher, *Cafarnao IX*, 16–17.

other in everyday life. While this image contributes little to our understanding of the psychology of Jewish–Christian relations—close interaction says nothing about whether neighbors actually like each other—it does encourage us to move away from imagining in Capernaum the presence of static and sturdy identities of Jewish versus Christian and, rather, toward envisioning these as dynamic, relational, and functional identities socially constructed through the mechanisms of repetition and recognition, which may have been manifested, for example, in commercial and real estate partnerships, labor and production cooperation, and everyday social exchanges in public areas such as the street market. Capernaum's domestic landscape signifies the implicit social contract that existed both among and between Jews and Christians, which made everyday life possible. This social contract, of course, did not involve parties of politically equal status; recall that Capernaum's Jewish community, regardless of how well resourced it might have been,[42] lived under the colonial rule of a Christian empire. The social contract undergirding everyday life in Capernaum had little to do, therefore, with establishing political or social equality but rather with, simply, making do.

The picture of everyday life of Jewish–Christian relations I have inferred from the town's domestic environment suggests that it *contrasted* and *resisted* the boundary projected by its church and synagogue. How, then, are we to imagine the on-the-ground everyday relationship between this projected religious boundary, on the one hand, and the intense social fluidity among Jews and Christians within the town's housing complexes on the other? Was the Capernaum of late antiquity a tale of two towns, characterized by close daily interaction between Jews and Christians in the sphere of the neighborhood but clear separation, rivalry, or even conflict in the sphere of "religion"?[43]

---

42. Some scholars have understood the grandeur of the limestone synagogue as evidence of a level of local wealth among Capernaum's Jewish community (e.g., Hakola, "Galilean Jews and Christians in Context," 161–164). The synagogue inscription from Hamat Gader mentioning the donation of a Jewish man from Capernaum (see note 12 above) might also be evidence of local wealth.

43. I note here my awareness of the problems involved in using the terms "religious" and "religion" as applied to antiquity. "Religion" is now widely agreed to be a defunct category as it pertains to the premodern era. On the issue, see especially B. Nongbri, *Before Religion: A History of a Modern Concept* (New Haven: Yale University Press, 2013). I use the term above in scare quotes simply as a heuristic device, without claiming that the modern concept of religion existed as a real phenomenon in late antiquity.

Capernaum's archaeological record cannot, on its own, answer this question.[44] As mentioned earlier, there is, indeed, plenty of evidence that, throughout the empire, Christians seized, vandalized, and destroyed synagogues, especially by burning.[45] But no such material evidence exists in Capernaum, and no source, literary or archaeological, indicates that the limestone synagogue had been adjudged to the Christian community there.[46] On the other hand, I suggest that some contemporaneous and geographically proximate literary sources not only provide a window to the sociosymbolic relationship between Capernaum's church and synagogue but also, and at the same time, account for the spatial semiotics of the town's domestic landscape. Of special significance is a number of ecclesiastical legal texts of Syrian origin (a region to which Capernaum clearly had a cultural and commercial attachment),[47] which indicate that in the Byzantine East the boundary between church and synagogue, or Christian space and Jewish space was, like the concept of neighborhood in Capernaum, neither always clear nor always

---

44. For such archaeological evidence from other places throughout the Mediterranean, see Eric C. Smith, *Jewish Glass and Christian Stone: A Materialist Mapping of the "Parting of the Ways"* (London: Routledge, 2018).

45. For archaeological evidence of this, see Fine, "Non-Jews in the Synagogues," 207–208. See also J. Gager, "Who Did What to Whom? Physical Violence between Jews and Christians in Late Antiquity," in *A Most Reliable Witness: Essays in Honor of Ross Shepard Kraemer*, BJS 358, ed. S. A. Harvey et al. (Providence, RI: Brown University Press, 2015), 35–48. The Theodosian Code (redacted mid-fifth century) contains numerous laws making it illegal for Christians to burn synagogues (e.g., *CTh* 16.8.21, 25, 26), suggesting that Christians throughout the empire were, indeed, engaged in such activity on a regular enough basis to spawn such legislation.

46. The major law, often repeated in both Theodosian and Justinian legislation and some ecclesiastical law collections from the Byzantine period, mandating the adjudgment of a synagogue to a Christian community was the law against the building of new synagogues. For ecclesiastical law, see the primary sources conveniently collected in A. Linder, *The Jews in the Legal Sources of the Early Middle Ages* (Detroit: Wayne State University Press, 1997), nos. 15, 23, 33, 34, 44, 99, *et passim* (hereafter: Linder).

47. See Loffreda, *Capharnaum*, 18–19, where he points to the numismatic record, imported vessels, and the town's proximity to an imperial highway that ran directly to Damascus as evidence. We can also note the discovery of Syriac graffiti in the late fourth to mid-fifth century remains under the octagonal church as a significant religiocultural connection as well. Mattila, "Capernaum, Village of Naḥum," 251, also lists Antioch, specifically, as one of the major eastern centres to which Capernaum villagers seemed to have had close economic ties.

policed, frequently transgressed and manipulated.⁴⁸ For example, *The Apostolic Canons* (ca. sixth century, Syria), in all of its recensions as well as in the commentaries of later medieval jurists who interpreted it, conveys unfeigned anxiety about the participation of Christian clerics and laypeople in synagogue life.⁴⁹ Various canons prohibit activity ranging from Christians entering a synagogue to pray with Jews, to Christians cocelebrating the Sabbath and Jewish holidays (especially Unleavened Bread)⁵⁰ and providing oil to synagogues for lamp-lighting rituals.⁵¹ *Apostolic Canons* 65, 70, and 71 are clear examples:

> If a cleric or a layman should enter a synagogue of the Jews or of heretics for prayer, he shall be deposed and excommunicated (Canon 65).⁵²

---

48. For sources and discussion going beyond what is presented below, see Levine, *The Ancient Synagogue*, 293–297. Most of Levine's discussion centers around John Chrysostom's (late fourth century) vitriolic attitudes toward Jews and Judaism presented in his homilies and his treatise *Adversus Ioudaeos*.

49. The *Apostolic Canons* is a collection of eighty-five canons forming the last part of the *Apostolic Constitutions* (8:47). The collection has a complex textual history, with multiple recensions and various receptions in the Christian East and West. The standard work on the history of the *Canons* is still F. X. Funk, *Didascalia et Constitutiones apostolorum* (Paderborn: Schöningh, 1905).

50. For example, see Linder, *Jews in the Legal Sources,* nos. 3, 121, and 124. This anxiety about the Christian cocelebration of Jewish holidays (including the Sabbath) in synagogues in the sixth century goes back several centuries. Indeed, in the second and third centuries, Origen, for example, tells his gentile Christian audience not to discuss in church questions they had heard raised in synagogue the day before, that is, on the Sabbath (*Hom. Lev.* 5.8; *Sel. Exod.* 12.46). This implies, of course, that members of his congregation were observing the seventh day by attending synagogue. In late fourth-century Antioch, John Chrysostom—whose anti-Jewish homilies and treatise *Adversus Ioudaeos* clearly influenced the development of canon law in the Christian East (perhaps even specifically the *Apostolic Canons* and its interpretation in the medieval period [see, e.g., Linder no. 353, where "Johannes of the Golden Tongue" is mentioned explicitly by a medieval jurist in his commentary on Canon 65])—decried the fact that there were many Christians in his Antiochene congregation that "fast on the same day as the Jews, and keep the Sabbaths in the same manner" (*Hom. Gal.* 1:7). On Chrysostom's portrait of Christian attraction to synagogues on Jewish holidays, see Levine, *Ancient Synagogue*, 295–296; and Wilken, *John Chrysostom and the Jews*, 140.

51. See, e.g., Linder nos. 2, 4, 103, 105, 110, 116, 120, 122, 138, 177, 354, 355, 948, 950.

52. The Greek text (from Linder no. 2) reads: Εἴ τις κληρικὸς ἢ λαϊκὸς εἰσέλθοι εἰς συναγωγὴν Ἰουδαίων ἢ αἱρετικῶν προσεύξασθαι, καθαιρείσθω καὶ ἀφοριζέσθω.

If a bishop or another cleric should fast with the Jews or celebrate holidays with them or accept their festive gifts, such as unleavened bread and anything similar to this, he shall be deposed; if a layman, excommunicated (Canon 70).[53]

If a Christian should contribute oil to a temple of the gentiles or to synagogue, or light lamps on their holidays, he shall be excommunicated (Canon 71).[54]

The *Apostolic Canons*, like earlier and ideologically similar literature from Syria (especially literature influenced by the tradition of John Chrysostom), shows that Christian attraction to synagogues (and to Jews and Judaism more broadly) was relatively widespread in the Byzantine East. Conversely, some rabbinic literature shows that Jewish attraction to churches (and to Christians and Christianity more broadly) existed as well. For example, *b. Avoda Zarah* 17a, which preserves a form of the famous Palestinian tradition about the arrest of Rabbi Eliezer on charges of entertaining "heresy" (מינות) from a disciple of "Jesus the Nazarene," presents an interpretation of the phrase "Do not come near the entrance of her [i.e., an adulterous woman's] house" from Prov. 5:8 as a warning not to enter the "house" of the politically empowered Christians (הרשות), that is, churches. In the story, the heresy of Christ adherence is likened to the lure of a "prostitute" (זונה), from whom a good rabbinic Jew must remain socially distant, four cubits (approximately two meters) to be exact. A similar interpretation of Proverbs 5:8 is given in the Rabbi Eliezer arrest tradition preserved in the sixth-century polemical midrash *Qohelet Rabbah* 1:8.[55] We discussed this text in detail in chapter 4, but what is interesting to note here is that, almost immediately following the story of Rabbi Eliezer's arrest and his interpretation of "do not come

---

53. Εἴ τις ἐπίσκοπος ἢ ἄλλος κληρικὸς νηστεύει μετὰ Ἰουδαίων ἢ ἑορτάζει μετ᾽ αὐτῶν ἢ δέχεται αὐτῶν τὰ τῆς ἑορτῆς ξένια, οἷον ἄζυμα ἤ τι τοιοῦτον, καθαιρείσθω, εἰ δὲ λαϊκός, ἀφοριζέσθω.

54. The Greek text (from Linder no. 4) reads: εἴ τις Χριστιανὸς ἔλαιον ἀπενέγκοι εἰς ἱερὸν ἐθνῶν ἢ εἰς συναγωγὴν Ἰοθδαίων, ἢ ἐν ταῖς ἑορταῖς αὐτῶν λύχνους ἅψη, ἀφοριζέσθω.

55. For a thorough study and redaction-critical comparison of the parallel tradition of Rabbi Eliezer's arrest found in the Tosefta, Bavli, and *Qohelet Rabbah*, see Schwartz and Tomson, "When Rabbi Eliezer Was Arrested," 145–181. On the sixth-century date (and other critical issues), see M. Hirshman, *Midrash Kohelet Rabbah 1–6, 79*, 122–123, 123 n. 358 (Hebrew).

near the entrance of her door" (Prov. 5:8), comes a story about a rabbinic encounter with certain "heretics" (מנים) *in Capernaum* (כפר נחם) who, like Rabbi Eliezer and his discussant Ya'akov of Kefar Sekhanya, ascribe to a Jewish identity and are portrayed as attracted to Christ adherence. It is quite possible, therefore, that this midrash is a reflection of a sixth-century polemic against non-rabbinic Jews who, in the eyes of the rabbis, had, quite literally, gotten too close to the doorstep of the church of their colonizers in Capernaum; they had not maintained their four cubits of social distance.[56] In other words, just as *The Apostolic Canons* reflects the on-the-ground social reality of

---

56. In this way, my understanding of *Qoh. Rab.* 1:8 and Jewish attraction to Christianity in Capernaum is close to the reconstruction of Arubas and Talgam (in their article "Jews, Christians, and *Minim*"). However, I disagree with their conclusion that imperial Christians necessarily *funded* the building of the town's great limestone synagogue, for which there is not one shred of evidence. It is one thing to suggest close relations between Jews and Christians but quite another to suggest that the empire was directly behind the synagogue's construction. There are a number of historical and chronological problems with Arubas's and Talgam's theory, which we addressed in chapter 5. But three points are worth making here. First, the Christianizing of Palestine through architecture, from the time of Constantine (and his mother Helena) onward, prioritized the building of churches, not synagogues. When Byzantines wished to commemorate a site believed to be significant from the time of Jesus, they did not build synagogues; they built what J. Ryan has recently called "Life-of-Jesus" churches (see his *From the Passion to the Holy Sepulcher*, ch. 6). Second, while we can, as I have done, read against the grain of imperial legislation (e.g., Theodosian Code) and canon law (e.g., *Apostolic Canons*) to ascertain what the situation between Jews and Christians might have been on the ground, this legal literature does project the will of the imperial panopticon. While it protected synagogues from being destroyed and allowed for the repair of older buildings, the overall attitude expressed is clearly negative toward synagogues: no new buildings were permitted to be erected, and several different scenarios are established that allow for their seizure and appropriation by Christians. Thus, however close and boundary-crossing the on-the-ground relations between Jews and Christians were, the idea that the Capernaum synagogue was funded by the upper echelon of Byzantine government is unconvincing. Third, Hakola ("Galilean Jews and Christians in Context," 160–161) is right to criticize Arubas's and Talgam's view for its assumption that the Jewish community in (and around) Capernaum did not have the financial resources to build such a grand synagogue on its own. Even if the building materials (esp. the limestone) came from elsewhere (e.g., Tiberias, as suggested by Runesson, "Architecture," 252–253, and supported by the recently published Kursi Synagogue Inscription; see Misgav, Artzy, and Cohen, "The Synagogue Inscription from Kursi," 67–69), other large and ornately decorated Galilean synagogues such as at Huqoq and Hurvat Kur suggest that local Jewish communities could possess the level of wealth needed to erect these kinds of buildings. Imperial funds—and even funds from more economically powerful Jews in Tiberias—were not a *requirement* for the building of the Capernaum synagogue.

Christian attraction to synagogues, so the Bavli text and the midrash reflect Jewish attraction to churches.

What we can infer from this, I think, is that the boundary between identities projected by Capernaum's church and synagogue was just as fluid, unbound, and able to be manipulated and transgressed by tactical action as the boundary between Jewish and Christian identities within the town's neighborhood landscape. We can imagine, therefore, Jewish–Christian neighborly relations as having been marked by both dynamic functional engagement and religious liminality, a compulsion to make do with, while simultaneously articulating attraction to, the Other.

4. Conclusion

There is no way to know with certainty the specific kinds of everyday boundary-crossing tactics in which Capernaum's Jews and Christians might have been engaged, whether praying in each other's buildings, contributing oil for lamp-lighting rituals,[57] or sharing festive meals.[58] But when we coordinate

---

57. The rooms labeled simply "a" in Mattila's plan (see Image 21), situated just off the northeast corner of the synagogue, has been identified as an oil lamp/pottery shop (for a description of this "bottega," see Corbo, *Cafarnao I*, 207).

58. Christian participation in Jewish healing practices might be added to this list of potential tactics. One point that Levine makes in commenting on John Chrysostom's *Adversus Ioudaeos* is that Christian attraction to synagogues seems to have been, in part, due to the powers believed to be linked to Jewish healing procedures, procedures which themselves were closely connected in the ancient world to magical practices such as incantation and amulet texts (Levine, *Ancient Synagogue*, 295). There are many sources now known that demonstrate that Jews in late antiquity were involved in this realm, and several canons of the Church indicate that Christians routinely went to the Jewish community for healing and medical attention (e.g., Canon 11 of the Council in Trullo [692 CE]: "No one of those enlisted in the sacerdotal order, nor a layman, should eat the unleavened bread of the Jews, or associate with them, or call on them in sickness and receive from them medicines, nor bathe with them in baths. If anyone should attempt to do this, if a cleric, he shall be deposed; if a layman, excommunicated" [Linder no. 124]). Among the excavations in Capernaum's Area 5, in the oil lamp shop adjacent to the northeast corner of the synagogue (L 118–119; Mattila's "a"), a Greek magical pendent was found with the words αγιος / αγιος / αγιος / Ιαω / υγι‹ει›α inscribed on the obverse and πινω / Υ / υγι‹ει›α inscribed on the reverse ("holy / holy / holy / Iao [i.e., YHWH] / health" and "I drink health"; for images, see S. Loffreda, *Cafarnao VIII: Documentazione fotografica degli oggetti [1968–2003]* [Jerusalem: Edizione Terra Santa, 2008], 120 [DF 863-31-t190]; see also Mattila, "Capernaum," 237). It is impossible to know the specific social context of its use. But it is possible—and this is my conjecture—that this

the dynamic relationality of Capernaum's domestic landscape with literary sources, we are, indeed, compelled to distinguish in the monumental landscape between the projection of strategic power and the tactics of everyday life. On the level of strategy, Capernaum's church and synagogue reflect, as Uzi Leibner says, "a struggle of monuments,"[59] a struggle between static and segregated Jewish and Christian identities built into the social environment with eight-sided shapes and white limestones. On this level, their function was simultaneously to exude and oversee the cultural-political agency of the town's colonially empowered Christians and Jewish subaltern.

However, on the level of everyday life, we can imagine Capernaum's church and synagogue as discursive spaces that mirrored the same sociality and interactivity between Jews and Christians that is reflected in the domestic landscape. Just as the town's neighborhoods were created out of the tactical fabric of social recognition, repetition, and spatial proximity, so this fabric, no matter what specific tactical actions were actually enacted, provided the building blocks of resistance to strategic power by manipulating the very *places* upon which this power hinged. The octagonal church and limestone synagogue were, therefore, not only symbols of identity seeking to control the movement of their subjects; they also, and at the same time, participated contiguously with Capernaum's dwellings in the spontaneous, opportunistic, and transgressive performance of Jewish and Christian neighbors who were, in the words of de Certeau, simply "making do."

---

amulet was produced by Capernaum Jews in the oil lamp/pottery shop near the synagogue but consumed by Capernaum Christians who, like Antiochene Christians, "ran to the Jews to be healed by 'charms, incantations and amulets' (*Jud.* 8.5; 935; 8.7; 937–38)" (Wilken, *John Chrysostom and the Jews*, 83–88, here p. 83 and quoting John Chrysostom's *Adversus Ioudeos*).

59. Leibner, *Settlment and History in Hellenistic, Roman, and Byzantine Galilee*, 403.

CHAPTER SEVEN

Capernaum and the Byzantine–Islamic Transition

1. Introduction

THE FIFTH AND sixth centuries in Capernaum were a time in which Jews and Christians ideologically shaped their competing identities yet interactively made do as neighbors, all within the larger context of a consolidating Byzantine Empire. The first half of the seventh century, however, gave rise to a very different geopolitical landscape. From the earliest days of Rome's rule over the eastern Mediterranean in the first century BCE, relations between it and the great empires of Persia had been marked by conflict as well as various types of economic, cultural, and social exchange. But, by the early seventh century, the Byzantine grip on Palestine and other provinces within its eastern dioceses was beginning to loosen, having been exhausted after two-and-a-half decades of war with the Sasanians (602–628 CE). While, for nearly seven hundred years, international affairs in this region had orbited around matters of Roman–Persian relations, neither the Byzantines nor the Sasanians, in the end, were able to hold on to their power; both eventually crumbled at the hands of the world's first Islamic empire: the Rashidun Caliphate (ca. 632–661).[1]

The early seventh century was, in a very real sense, a drama of empires, and Palestine was, in many ways, its grand theatre. Laying at or near the center of several major scene changes, Palestine passed through the hands of the Byzantines to the Sasanians (ca. 614–628), back to the Byzantines again (ca. 628–638), and then, finally, to the Rashidun and its successor Islamic empires

---

1. On the emergence of Islam in the broader context of late antiquity, see Aziz Al-Azmeh, *The Emergence of Islam in Late Antiquity: Allāh and his People* (Cambridge: Cambridge University Press, 2014).

(ca. 638–1917).² The Galilee, specifically, had a front-row seat. Several early medieval Jewish and Christian sources indicate that Jews from the Galilee, particularly from Tiberias, played an important supportive role in the Sasanian advance on Jerusalem in 614.³ And, in 636, the decisive battle of Jābiya-Yarmūk, fought between what would become Caliph Umar's victorious Rashidun and Emperor Heraclius's squashed Byzantine army, took place only about 50 km (as the crow flies) southwest of the lake of Galilee.⁴

In this chapter, then, I want to explore the experiences of Jews and Christians in Capernaum within the context of the shifting sands of the seventh-century Near East. My focus is especially on the question of the impact of the Byzantine–Islamic transition: What did the transition to early Islamic rule in Palestine *change* for Jews and Christians in Capernaum, and, perhaps more importantly, what did it *not* change? As we have become accustomed to seeing throughout this book, the sources for the Byzantine–Islamic transition in Capernaum specifically, and in Palestine generally, are tricky for the historian to handle. Literary sources will need to be considered in relation to the archaeological data, and gaps in the evidence will need to be bridged through inference and imagination.

2. The Seventh Century and the End of (Byzantine) Days in Christian and Jewish Apocalypticism

The seventh century was a time of existential crisis for the Byzantine Empire, not only because of the concrete territorial threats it faced from encroaching powers from beyond its eastern boarders, but also because of

---

2. For a general historical survey of Palestine in late antiquity up to the late seventh century, see Sivan, *Palestine in Late Antiquity*, 16–50 (47–50 discuss the seventh century specifically).

3. For example, *Armenian History Attributed to Sebeos*, 34 (seventh century); Theophanes the Confessor, *Chronicle s.v.* 627/28 CE (eighth or ninth century); Eutychius of Alexandria, *Annals* 30 (PG 111.1089B–1091B) (tenth century); *Sefer Zerubabbel* (Jewish apocalyptic work that is, at least partially, from the seventh century); and several *piyyutim*, liturgical Jewish poems, attributed to Eleazar ha-Qallir (seventh century). For discussion of these and various other sources, see H. Sivan, "From Byzantine to Persian Jerusalem: Jewish Perspectives and Jewish/Christian Polemics," *GRBS* 41 (2000): 277–306; and G. Stemberger, *Judaica Minor II: Geschichte und Literatur des rabbinischen Judentums*, TSAJ 138 (Tübingen: Mohr Siebeck, 2010), 160–171.

4. W. E. Kaegi, *Byzantium and the Early Islamic Conquests* (Cambridge: Cambridge University Press, 1992), 112–146.

the anxiety those threats induced about the fate of Christianity and its earthly kingdom. As wars raged, and as Christian armies were increasingly on the losing side of those wars, they triggered a wave of apocalyptic writings, which explained the decline of Christian political authority in the East in eschatological terms.[5] Perhaps the best known of these writings, then as well as today, is the *Apocalypse* of Pseudo-Methodius. The *Apocalypse* looks back upon the time of the invasion of the "Ishmaelites"— the phrase it, like other contemporary works, consistently uses to refer to Arab Muslims—as part of the divine ordering of world history and as punishment for Christian immorality and apostacy (*Apoc. Ps. Method.* 10.6–12.8).[6] The work paints a picture of widespread Christian suffering under Arab rule (13.1–9). Not only are great death and calamity upon the lands once held by the Byzantines, including the "Promised Land" (11.13), but also churches fall out of service and Christians are forced to carry heavy financial burdens.[7] But the *Apocalypse* then tells of a coming time, still

---

5. See, e.g., P. J. Alexander, *The Byzantine Apocalyptic Tradition* (Berkley: University of California Press, 1985); Stemberger, *Judaica Minor II: Geschichte und Literatur des rabbinischen Judentums,* TSAJ 138. (Tübingen: Mohr Siebeck, 2010), 160.

6. The *Apocalypse* of Pseudo-Methodius, wrongly attributed to the fourth-century Christian bishop Methodius of Olympus, was originally composed by an unknown author in Syriac ca. 685–692 CE, but it was quickly translated into Greek and Latin, and later Old Church Slavonic, Armenian, and Coptic. It eventually became widely read and highly influential in the eschatological thinking of medieval Europe. See B. Garstad, *Apocalypse of Pseudo-Methodius: An Alexandrian World Chronicle*, DOML 14 (Cambridge, MA: Harvard University Press, 2012), vii–xi. For an edition of the Syriac text and German translation, see G. J. Reinink, ed., *Die syrische Apokalypse des Pseudo-Methodius*, 2 vols., Corpus Scriptorum Christianorum Orientalium 540–541 (Leuven: Peeters, 1993). For an English translation of the Syriac text from Cod. Vat. Syr. 58, see Alexander, *The Byzantine Apocalyptic Tradition*, 36–51. For an edition of the Greek and Latin versions, see W. J. Alberts and G. A. A. Kortekaas, eds., *Die Apokalypse des Pseudo-Methodius: Die ältesten griechischen und lateinischen Übersetzungen*, Corpus Scriptorum Christianorum Orientalium 569 (Leuven: Peeters, 1998). For an introduction edition of the Greek and Latin texts, and English translation, see Garstad, *Apocalypse*. The references to *Apoc. Ps. Method.* given above come from Garstad's volume.

7. Garstad notes that the text's mention of these apocalyptic financial burdens probably corresponds to the tax reforms enacted by the Umayyad Caliphate from 685 to 692, which significantly increased the tax burden on Christians and, as a consequence, might have encouraged Christians to convert to Islam, something the *Apocalypse* sees as a "falling away" (*Apoc. Ps. Method.* 12) This is one reason some scholars have dated the *Apocalypse* between 685–692 (Garstad, *Apocalypse*, vii). Another is the *Apocalypse's* focus on the redemption of Jerusalem by the Roman emperor, which Reinink has interpreted as a Christian response to the building

future to the time of its composition, when the Last Roman Emperor will, in fact, rise to defeat the Ishmaelites, redeem Jerusalem for the Christians, and restore the devastated lands (13.11–18).[8]

Yet this is not the end of the *Apocalypse's* eschatological tale. The author predicts that the final demise of the Ishmaelites will only then lead to the final revelation of the "son of perdition" (13.21–14.12). He is an antichrist figure in the *Apocalypse*, whose signs and wonders will deceive the faithful, and whom even the Last Roman Emperor will not challenge. Rather, God will send his "familiar and trusted servants, Enoch and Elijah" to refute him and expose his deceit to the world (14.11). Once he stands convicted and despised, the nations who were under his thumb will abandon him and flee, but he will, nevertheless, rise in terrible wrath and slay them all. After this, finally, will come the "Son of Man," who will vanquish the son of perdition and deliver those "who worship the living God" (14:13–14).

Matthew Grey has noted that the eschatological thought of the *Apocalypse* of Pseudo-Methodius sits comfortably within the broader context of Jewish–Christian polemics in late antiquity that revolve around the messiah and the antichrist, the messiah's principal enemy.[9] In his study, Grey makes the interesting connection between the *Apocalypse's* belief that the antichrist would be a superhuman warrior descended from the tribe of Dan—a fairly common motif in ancient Christian eschatological tradition[10]—and Jewish messianism involving the expectation of a Danite Samson figure who would initiate the redemption of Israel at the end of days. Grey persuasively argues that, for Christians like Pseudo-Methodius, the antichrist was thought to be a "reverse negative of Jewish expectations. In other words, Christians believed that the messiah expected by Jews would be the coming antichrist."[11] But, perhaps even

---

of the Dome of the Rock in 692. See G. Reinink, "Der edessenische 'Pseudo-Methodius,'" *Byzantinische Zeitschrift* 83 (1990): 33–34.

8. On the theme of the Last Roman Emperor in Byzantine apocalyptic, see Alexander, *The Byzantine Apocalyptic Tradition*, 151–184; and A. Kraft, "The Last Roman Emperor 'Topos' in the Byzantine Apocalyptic Tradition," *Byzantion* 82 (2012): 213–257.

9. M. J. Grey, "'The Redeemer to Arise from the House of Dan': Samson, Apocalypticism, and Messianic Hopes in Late Antique Galilee," *JSJ* 44 (2013): 586.

10. Although earlier in date (ca. third century), Hippolytus's eschatological interpretation of Deut 33:22 explicitly ties the antichrist's coming from the tribe of Dan to the identity of Samson, at least partially (*Antichr.* 14–15).

11. Grey, "Messianic Hopes in Late Antique Galilee," 584.

more interestingly, Grey suggests that this polemic-in-the-negative between Jews and Christians was particularly strong *in the Galilee*.

Jewish texts of late antiquity that contain messianic ideas about Samson as a deliverer of Israel, such as we find in some Palestinian *piyyutim* (liturgical poems) and *targummim* (biblical "translations") used in synagogue liturgy, were likely produced in a Galilean milieu and, more specifically, around Tiberias and Mount Arbel.[12] And now, as the result of excavations during the past decade or so, these literary ideas can be connected, as Grey does, to the artistic depiction of Samson on the mosaic floors of two monumental Galilean synagogues: at Huqoq (ca. fifth century), in which two Samson scenes have been found, and at Wadi Hammam (ca. fourth century).[13] Together, literary sources and visual-archaeological remains between the fourth and seventh centuries portray the idea of a messianic Samson who was expected to bring divine restoration to Israel, starting with the Galilee. For Pseudo-Methodius, however, the Galilee is, literally, the breeding ground of the antichrist. Taking its cue from Jesus's curse in Matt 11:20–24, the *Apocalypse* claims that the antichrist is not only "born in Chorizin and raised in Bethsaida" but also "rules from Capernaum" (14:1).

How did the political context of the seventh-century map onto such Jewish–Christian polemics over hopes and expectations about the end of days? Grey's idea about Jewish–Christian "polemics-in-the-negative" provides one answer to this question. Both the Sasanian invasion of 614 and the victory of the Rashidun in 638 were, in the Byzantine apocalyptic imagination, traumatic events that were eschatologized into their thinking about the antichrist and the end of the world as they knew it. But, for at least some Jews, such as the liturgical poets of Palestine, the events were eschatologized into divinely orchestrated wars, wishfully projected to result in the deliverance of the Jewish people from imperial Christian rule.[14] Thus, it is possible that, in

---

12. Grey, "Messianic Hopes in Late Antique Galilee," 567–581.

13. See J. Magness et al., "Huqoq (Lower Galilee) and Its Synagogue Mosaics: Preliminary Report on the Excavations of 2011–13," *JRA* 27 (2014): 327–355 (esp. 340–341 and images on pp. 343, 345); Magness et al., "The Huqoq Excavation Project," 61–131; Leibner and Miller, "A Figural Mosaic in the Synagogue," 256–257. There has been some debate over the date of the Wadi Hamam synagogue. See Magness, "The Pottery from the Village of Capernaum," 112–114.

14. On the Palestinian *piyyutim* as historical documents reflecting Jewish polemical attitudes toward the Byzantine empire in its conflicts with the Sasanian Persian and Arab

some synagogues, the fires of anti-Byzantine fervor were kindled and stoked through the medium of "apocalyptic liturgy," and that such fervor may have even translated into direct action. According to some literary sources (both Jewish and Christian), some Jews from the Galilee, led by a quasimessianic figure named Nehemiah Ben Hushiel, joined the Persian army, aiding it to victory over the Byzantines.[15]

The period of Sasanian control over Palestine—and over Jerusalem specifically—must have been disappointing for Jews who had once been optimistic about life freed from Byzantine rule.[16] As Averil Cameron has noted, sources of varying date and reliability might suggest that Jews were initially allowed to access the Temple Mount and were possibly even allowed to re-establish worship there by the Persians; however, the Persians seem to have quickly reversed this policy.[17] Moreover, they seem to have been far more lenient toward Christians, at least in Jerusalem, perhaps in their attempt to win the hearts of the newly conquered.[18] In any case, Sasanian authority

---

Islamic empires, see especially Sivan, "From Byzantine to Persian Jerusalem," 286–305. Sivan is particularly interested in *piyyutim* as witness to the Byzantine–Sasanian wars and the Jewish messianic hopes that were stirred by them. But she also notes that the term these poems originally used to refer to Sasanian Persia—the biblical term "Assyria"—was quickly replaced with the term "Ishmaelites," the common word for Arab Muslims used in both Jewish and Christian literature of the seventh century (see p. 303).

15. Nehemiah Ben Hushiel is mentioned explicitly in the *Sefer Zerubbabel* and, perhaps, in some *piyyutim* by Eleazar ha-Kalir, a sixth to seventh century Jewish poet, which probably presuppose the material of *Sefer Zerubbabel*. For an excellent introduction and translation of *Sefer Zerubbabel*, see J. C. Reeves, *Trajectories in Near Eastern Apocalyptic: A Postrabbinic Jewish Apocalypse Reader* (Atlanta: SBL, 2005), 40–66. Early medieval Christian sources mention more generally Jews from the Galilee who had welcomed and joined the Persians in their fight against the Christians (e.g., *Armenian History Attributed to Sebeos* 34:115). There is no doubt that, as Averil Cameron has noted, the Christian literary accounts of Jewish partnership with the Persians against Christians are "deeply biased and distorted," but the general notion that some Jews saw the Persian invasion as a favorable development in world (i.e., eschatological) history and sought to aid its coming seems plausible, especially since it is reflected in *both* Jewish and Christian sources. For longer discussion, see A. Cameron, "The Jews in Seventh-Century Palestine," *Scripta Classica Israelica* 13 (1994): 79.

16. Sivan notes that a passage in the seventh-century Palestinian midrash *Pesikta Rabbati* 34–37 seems to reflect Jewish disillusionment with the Sasanians (= "wicked Persia"). See Sivan, "From Byzantine to Persian Jerusalem," 303 n. 60.

17. Cameron, "The Jews in Seventh-Century Palestine," 80.

18. For example, according to the *Armenian History Attributed to Sebeos*, while the Sasanians demolished a small synagogue that had been built on the esplanade of the Temple

in Palestine was simply short lived, lasting only sixteen years until Heraclius retook Jerusalem for the Byzantines, an event that many interpreted as Christianity's final eschatological victory over Zoroastrian Persia.[19] For Jews, however, the result was that they became the collective target of Heraclius's law, the first of its kind, demanding that all Jews in the Empire be baptized and forced to convert to Christianity.[20]

Less than a decade later, Umar's Rashidun army would do precisely what the Sasanians could not. The Rashidun, under the field leadership of Khalid ibn al-Walid, definitively ended Byzantine rule in Palestine, Syria, North Africa, and parts of eastern Anatolia. For Christians like the seventh-century Armenian bishop and historian Sebeos—whose account of the Arab expansion in the Near East is among our most important witnesses, despite its imaginative elements[21]—the coming of Islamic armies was like the coming of a great eschatological storm from the south, which "occupied all the land, trampled and smote it" as foretold by scripture.[22] Some Jews, on the other hand, saw it as another opportunity to shed the shackles of Christian power. Jewish poets expressed this renewed apocalyptic optimism in poetic code by applying language to the "sons of Ishmael" that they had used earlier of the Sasanians.[23] Other Jews seem to have, once again, lent a hand. Sebeos, for example, recounts that a large group of Jews who had assembled in Edessa and had been exiled by Heraclius to Tachkastan (Arabia) eventually joined forces with the early Arab armies, which had themselves been newly unified

---

Mount, they allowed Christians to rebuild their sacred shrines in the city, which had been destroyed in the previous fighting. See the historical analysis presented in R. W. Thompson, trans., and J. Howard-Johnson, *The Armenian History Attributed to Sebeos*, vol. 1, *Translation and Notes*, Translated Texts for Historians 31 (Liverpool: Liverpool University Press, 1999), 209.

19. Thompson and Howard-Johnson, *Sebeos*, 226–227.

20. For primary sources, see, again, *Armenian History Attributed to Sebeos*, 34; Theophanes the Confessor, *Chronicle s.v.* 627or 628 CE (eighth or ninth century); Eutychius of Alexandria, *Annals* 30 (PG 111.1089B–1091B) (tenth century). For discussion, see Thompson and Howard-Johnson, *Sebeos*, 227; and Cameron, "The Jews in Seventh-Century Palestine," 80–81, where she mentions that Heraclius's law was probably more symbolic than realistic.

21. See Thompson and Howard-Johnson, *Sebeos*, xxviii.

22. Thompson and Howard-Johnson, *Sebeos*, 47. Translation is from Thompson and Howard-Johnson, *Sebeos*, 133.

23. Sivan, "From Byzantine to Persian Jerusalem," 303.

under the leadership of Muhammed in the early 630s.²⁴ As Sebeos tells it, the main selling point of their partnership, for both these Jews and Muhammed, was the scriptural kinship that Jews and Arabs shared as "sons of Abraham," a kinship that Byzantine Christians could not claim.²⁵ In a joint statement delivered to Heraclius, the Jewish–Arab contingent declared: "God gave that land [Palestine] to our father Abraham as a hereditary possession and to his seed after him. We are the sons of Abraham. You [Byzantines] have occupied our land long enough. Abandon it peacefully and we shall not come into your territory. Otherwise, we shall demand that possession from you with interest" (42:136).²⁶

There is no doubt that the first half of the seventh century was a time of great political uncertainty and military conflict in Palestine, and that some Jews and Christians responded ideologically very differently—some with great angst and some with great anticipation. However, an increasing number of scholars since at least the 1990s have realized that, when it comes to the question of change—what did the emergence of Islamic rule in Palestine actually *change* for Jews and Christians on the ground?—the apocalyptic portrayals in the literary sources of death, decay, and decline of all kinds collide with a very different picture rendered by the archaeological record of Jewish and Christian settlements in the early Islamic period. And it is here—the archaeological record—that Capernaum has played an important role in the scholarly rethinking of Jewish and Christian experiences in the wake of Islamic rule in Palestine.

3. Beyond Apocalypticism
Capernaum and the Archaeology of the Byzantine–Islamic Transition

In 1992, nine years after its original publication in Hebrew, renowned Israeli historian Moshe Gil wrote the following about the "Muslim conquest" of Palestine:

---

24. On, more broadly, Jewish assistance to early Islamic expansionist armies, see M. Lecker, "The Jewish Reactions to Islamic Conquests," 184–186.
25. See Thompson and Howard-Johnson, *Sebeos*, 134–136.
26. Translation is from Thompson and Howard-Johnson, *Sebeos*, 97.

One can assume that the local population suffered immensely during the course of the war and it is very likely that many villages were destroyed and uprooted in the frontier regions, and that the lot of these local populations was very bad indeed. It appears that the period of the conquest was also that of the destruction of synagogues and churches of the Byzantine era.[27]

Gil's assumption of a brutal, indeed apocalyptic, coming of Islamic rule to Palestine, based mainly on his reading of medieval Jewish and Christian literary sources, is reflective of much of the previous generation of historiography produced about the period.[28] Indeed, a similar assumption undergirded Virgilio Corbo's interpretation of the archaeology of Capernaum at the time of the Arab conquest, a time he described, perhaps with a level of Christian bias, as "gli ultimi giorni di Cafarnao" ("the last days of Capernaum").[29] In Corbo's view, Capernaum was entirely abandoned by its Jewish and Christian populations in 636, shortly after the Rashidun victory over the Byzantines at Jābiya-Yarmūk. As he puts it, so sudden and complete was the evacuation that "life ceased in the city, like the fire that goes out in the hearth!"[30] According

---

27. M. Gil, *A History of Palestine, 634–1099* (Cambridge: Cambridge University Press, 1992 [orig. Hebrew 1983]), 61.

28. Indeed, to a large extent, Jodi Magness's book *The Archaeology of the Early Islamic Settlement in Palestine* (Winona Lake, IN: Eisenbrauns, 2003) is a direct response, based on the archaeological record, to this previous generation of historiography, as is the more recent book by Gideon Avni, *The Byzantine–Islamic Transition in Palestine: An Archaeological Approach* (Oxford: Oxford University Press, 2014). See these works for further discussions of the view represented by Gil.

29. V. Corbo, "Gli ultimi giorni di Cafarnao: Rapporto preliminare dopo la XV campagna di scavo 6 giugno—16 luglio 1983," *Liber Annuus* 33 (1983): 373–390. Corbo's use of the language of "the last days of Capernaum" (English trans. mine) clearly betrays his Christian bias concerning the history of the village. Capernaum's "days" did not end when Islam came to the region. It simply meant Christians were no longer in charge. Unfortunately, this article by Corbo is the only treatment, as far as I am aware, of Capernaum and the Byzantine–Islamic transition that the Franciscan excavation team ever produced. Although excavations continued until 2003, all of their historical studies have focused on Capernaum before the Islamic conquest. The single volume resulting from excavations carried out by Vassilios Tzaferis on the Greek Orthodox side of the site contains more discussion of early Islamic Capernaum, on which see below.

30. Corbo, "Gli ultimi giorni," 390. The English translation above is mine. The original Italian quotation is: "Cessò la vita nella città, come il fuoco che si spegne nel focolare!"

Image 7.1. The photo on the left is of an area looking southwest from Street L514, where two decorated stones are in reuse, into room L512. The photo on the right is of a detail of a stone with light scratching of a menorah.

From Loffreda, *Cafarnao V*, 155 (DFs 235 and 236). Used with permission.

to Corbo, the village laid lifeless until it was reoccupied by Umayyad settlers, presumably in the early eighth century, because of its favorable location close to the lake and the Islamic palace of Khirbat al-Minya.[31] For Corbo, the emergence of Islamic rule meant the destruction of Capernaum's synagogue and church and thus spelled the definitive end of Judaism and Christianity in the village.

The problem with Corbo's historical construction is that it rests on very little evidence, and the evidence he does marshal is now subject to criticism considering more recent research. Corbo's interpretation focuses on a single area of the Franciscan side of the Capernaum site, Area 8 (Loci 501–527).

Loffreda shares Corbo's view: "In the early seventh century many houses were abandoned and left to ruin, suggesting that the old population of Capharnaum, i.e. Jews and Christians alike, left the site. The fact that in the Early Arab period both the synagogue and the octagonal church were abandoned seems to suggest that the newcomers were predominately Moslems" (*Recovering Capharnaum*, 31).

31. Corbo, "Gli ultimi giorni," 390. Corbo is neither explicit nor does he provide any archaeological data about the date of this supposed Umayyad reoccupation of Capernaum. But since he connects the reoccupation to the Islamic palace at Khirbat al-Minya (est. ca. 705–715 CE), then one must assume he dates it to the early eighth century. On Khirbat al-Minya, see Avni, *Byzantine–Islamic Transition*, 90–92.

Specifically, he discusses several houses in the area, which, he claims, belonged to the "Umayyad period" (a term he seems to use synonymously with the "Arab invasion")[32] and which had been built over houses belonging to the Byzantine period.[33] His main evidence comes from L512, a room measuring internally 5.30 meters by 3.70 meters, in which two interesting stones were found. The first was a basalt stone that had apparently been reused as part of the door jamb (30 × 53 × 34 cm). This stone, which was found out of place but near the room's main entry door accessing Street L514, contains lightly carved images of a menorah, shofar, and palmette.[34] The second discovery was a piece of decorated limestone, which is almost certainly a fragment of a frieze from the synagogue.[35] This stone, measuring sixty centimeters by forty-five centimeters by twenty-six centimeters, was also found in secondary use, having been placed in front of the streetside threshold as a sort of stepping stone. Thus, for Corbo, the sequence of occupation of Area 8 and the decorated stones found in secondary use not only supported the theory of Capernaum's abandonment by the time of the "Arab invasion" but were also a clear indication that the town's synagogue was in ruins by this time as well.[36]

Corbo offers no archaeological evidence to support his theory that the synagogue and the structures in Area 8 were destroyed or dramatically abandoned in 636 or in the years immediately following.[37] In fact, there is evidence to the contrary. A small hoard of gold Byzantine coins, the latest of which date to the reign of Constans II in 668, was found deposited beneath the eastern benches of the synagogue's main hall.[38] Further, it is possible that some early Islamic pottery (so-called "Mefjer" ware) from the Abbasid period was found

---

32. Corbo, "Gli ultimi giorni," 383 and 387, where Capernaum's abandonment by the time of the "Umayyad period" is equated with its abandonment by the time of the "Arab invasion."

33. Corbo, "Gli ultimi giorni," 382–386.

34. Loffreda, *Cafarnao V*, DF 236 (p. 155).

35. Loffreda, *Cafarnao V*, DF 235 (p. 155).

36. Corbo, "Gli ultimi giorni," 383, where he says, "infatti é una testimonianza chiarissima che la sinagoga era già abbandonata ed in rovina al periodo omayyade." Although, as far as I know, the "last days" of the octagonal church are not discussed, Corbo and Loffreda seem to share the same general assumption that it fell out of use just before the "Arab conquest."

37. The same can be said of Loffreda in his brief statements in *Recovering Capharnaum*, 31.

38. B. Callegher, "Un ripostiglio di monete d'oro Bizantine dalla sinagoga di Cafarnao," *LA* 47 (1997): 329–338.

in the fill of Trench 11 and the foundations of a staircase near the northeast corner of the synagogue's courtyard. This might suggest, as Jodi Magness does, that the synagogue underwent repairs in the second half of the eighth century or even later.[39] Indeed, Magness points out that a bronze Tulunid coin was found between the paving stones of the synagogue's balcony, which might suggest that the synagogue remained in use even in the second half of the ninth century.[40] Magness and, more recently Rick Bonnie, have, in my view, rightly interpreted all of this evidence to mean that the synagogue was still in use well after the Islamic transition in Palestine, even if the date that the building actually fell out of use still remains difficult to pin down.[41]

There is also very little, if any, evidence that Area 8—or any other sector of the Franciscan and Greek Orthodox sides of Capernaum—was resettled by Arabs in the Umayyad period (661–750 CE).[42] The great majority of the early Islamic pottery found in Area 8 dates, according to Loffreda, not to the Umayyad but to the Abbasid period, that is, to the second half of the eighth

---

39. Magness, "The Question of the Synagogue," 36. This idea is particularly plausible in view of the likelihood that the synagogue would, indeed, have needed repair after the major earthquake of 749 CE. On the other hand, Noah Yuval-Hacham suggests that the synagogue was destroyed and fell out of use in 749 ("Mishnah Avodah Zarah 4:5—The Faces of Effacement: Between Textual and Artistic Evidence," in *Talmuda de-Eretz Israel: Archaeology and the Rabbis in Late Antique Palestine*, ed. S. Fine and A. Koller [Berlin: Walter de Gruyter, 2014], 29–52 [38 n. 28]). This position is also plausible, but it would have a more difficult time explaining the presence of Mefjer ware *beneath* parts of the synagogue.

40. This Tulunid coin is reported in A. Spijkerman, *Cafarnao III: Le monete della città* (Jerusalem: Franciscan Press, 1975), 43 (no. 346).

41. Magness, "The Question of the Synagogue," 36; R. Bonnie, "A Sustained Presence: Synagogues Buildings in Galilee during the Early Islamic Period and Later," *Journal of Eastern Mediterranean Archaeology and Heritage Studies* 9, no. 3 (2021): 282–283. In its continued use into the early Islamic period, the Capernaum synagogue would not have been a unique case. See Magness, "The Question of the Synagogue," 35–36, where she identifies the synagogues at Gush Halav, Meroth, and Nabratein among those that continued in use after the Islamic transition. We could add to this the synagogue at Hammath Tiberias, which was, in its third stage, still in use by the time of the tenth to eleventh century, although it is not clear whether it was still being used as a synagogue (see M. J. S. Chiat, *Handbook of Synagogue Architecture*, Brown Judaic Studies 29 [Chico, CA: Scholars Press, 1982], 105). Further south, the synagogue at Susia was in use until the beginning of the ninth century and the one in Na'aran until the eighth century (Yuval-Hacham, "The Faces of Effacement," 38 n. 28).

42. For overall plans of both the Franciscan and Greek Orthodox sites, see introduction chapter.

century or later.⁴³ This point coincides with Magness's re-evaluation of the early Islamic pottery from Area A of the Greek Orthodox side of the site. In a study from 1997, she argued convincingly that the pottery there, too, should be dated to the Abbasid period, nearly a century later than the date assigned by excavator Vassilios Tzaferis and his team.⁴⁴ The early Islamic numismatic data coheres with this chronology as well. In his catalogue, Bruno Callegher lists a total of sixteen Umayyad coins found on the Franciscan side of Capernaum, none of which was found in Area 8, but all of which date, at the earliest, to the eighth century, with most of them dating to its second half.⁴⁵ The mid-eighth century date of these coins also match the chronology of the Umayyad coins found in the Greek Orthodox side of Capernaum, including the fabulous hoard of 282 gold dinars of the Umayyad "post-reform" type, which was discovered in Area A.⁴⁶ While these gold coins are dated between 696–697

---

43. On the pottery from Area 8, see Loffreda, *Cafarnao VI*, 350–354, with cross-references to his *Cafarnao VII*. This would suggest, then, that the reuse of the two stones with Jewish or synagogue decoration should be associated with the second half of the eighth century, rather than, as Corbo says, with the "Umayyad period" or "Arab invasion." However, it is important to state here that the reuse of these stones—no matter the date—are not necessarily indications of the synagogue's dismantlement or abandonment. The use of two stones in secondary contexts cannot tell us this much about an entire building. Indeed, it is possible, as just an example, that these stones were among the damaged elements of the synagogue that were the result of the earthquake of 749. There are any number of other possible explanations.

44. J. Magness, "The Chronology of Capernaum in the Early Islamic Period," *JAOS* 117.3 (1997): 481–486.

45. On the numismatic data for Area 8 (Loci 501–527), see Callegher, *Cafarnao IX*, at p. 171. Most of the eight coins from Area 8 published in Callegher's catalogue date from the third to fifth century, with the one exception being a coin from the Mamluk period of Al Ashraf Sha'ban II (1363–1399 CE). For a list, with dates of the Umayyad coins, see Callegher, *Cafarnao IX*, 137–138

46. See J. F. Wilson, "The Gold Hoard," in *Capernaum I, 1978–1982*, ed. V. Tzaferis (Winona Lake, IN: Eisenbrauns, 1989), 145–179 and Plate 3 for the color image; and Callegher, *Cafarnao IX*, 142–146. "Post-reform" Umayyad coinage refers to the introduction of imageless, inscription-only coins, which was initiated during the rule of Umayyad Caliph Abd al-Malik ibn Marwan (rule 685–705 CE). The reform itself seems to have started at the very end of the seventh century and evolved over time. For a thorough discussion of the history of Umayyad coin reforms, see L. Treadwell, "Abd al-Malik's Coinage Reforms: The Role of the Damascus Mint," *Revue numismatique* 165 (2009): 357–381. The gold dinars of the Capernaum hoard are all aniconic and bear identical inscriptions. The following legend is presented in Wilson's study on p. 146 (I give only the English translation here). Obverse, in field: "There is no god except Allah alone; He has no partner." Obverse, around: "Muhammed

and 743–744, the hoard itself, as Magness notes, "could not have been buried before 744, when the latest coins it contained were minted" and "could have been deposited any time after that date."⁴⁷ Thus, a distinctly "Islamic" settlement in Capernaum—defined materially and culturally—did not emerge in the seventh century but rather in the eighth century, and most likely in the second half of it.⁴⁸

When these nodes of archaeological evidence are tallied up, the resulting portrait of the Byzantine–Islamic transition in seventh-century Capernaum is very different than the one presented by Corbo and Loffreda. It is a portrait marked not by swift abandonment and apocalyptic decline but rather by continuity in both its Christian and Jewish populations, and even growth well into the Abbasid period.⁴⁹ In other words, the change eventually brought about by the Islamic transition happened quite slowly and over a span of more than a century. Indeed, according to Gideon Avni, Capernaum's Christian population not only remained but thrived and expanded:

> The common view is that both structures [the octagonal church and limestone synagogue] declined by the end of the Byzantine period and were deserted even before the Arab conquest. However, excavations in the domestic areas of the village show that Capernaum was not destroyed and abandoned during the Arab conquest, and

---

is the Apostle of Allah whom He sent with guidance and the religion of truth that he may make it victorious over every other religion" (Sura 9:33). Reverse, in field: "All is One, Allah is the Eternal. He begets not, neither is He begotten" (Sura 112:1–3). Reverse, around: "In the name of Allah this dinar was struck in the year —." Within the multireligious context of Capernaum, it is tempting to interpret the inscriptions from the Quran on these Umayyad coins as polemical in nature. On a very general level, they, no doubt, are supersessionist and polemical in outlook, similar to the Quranic inscriptions found on the Dome of the Rock. But, first, these inscriptions are very common on Umayyad coinage as a whole and, second, the content of the inscriptions would obviously have been hidden from Jews and Christians in the village since they were part of a buried coin hoard. Thus, we should not read too much into how the ideological content of these inscriptions would have been perceived and received by non-Muslims in Capernaum specifically.

47. Magness, "Chronology of Capernaum," 482.

48. This date is supported also by Avni, *Byzantine–Islamic Transition*, 89.

49. Magness, "Chronology of Capernaum," 482, notes that the evidence from Capernaum points to its "flourishing Abbasid occupation." This seems to have been true for much of what Avni calls "the hinterland of Tiberias." See Avni, *Byzantine–Islamic Transition*, 88–93.

that the Christian settlement expanded further in the Early Islamic period. This is particularly evident from the excavations in the Greek Orthodox church area, in the northeastern section of the site. The remains of a large village (about 2.5–4 ha), consisting of a number of large residential units were discovered here. This village continued to be inhabited throughout the Early Islamic period, and was abandoned only during the eleventh century.[50]

The continued use of the synagogue suggests that Capernaum's Jewish community, too, remained visible and vibrant after the emergence of Islamic rule, at least well into the eighth century.[51] One way we are able to see this vibrancy is in the iconoclastic activity that occurred in the synagogue. As Noa Yuval-Hacham has recently noted, the systematic effacement of a significant amount of stone reliefs from the Capernaum synagogue, which once had figurative, mainly zoomorphic, depictions (especially eagles and lions), has been given hardly any scholarly attention.[52] But, when placed within the larger context of the "waves of iconoclastic eruptions" that characterized the first half of the eighth century—and impacted Jews, Christians, and Muslims—this activity has the potential to shed historical light on the dynamic and evolving character of Capernaum's Jews, particularly in relation to their Christian and early Islamic environments.[53]

---

50. Avni, *Byzantine–Islamic Transition*, 89. On p. 91, Avni comments that even the establishment of the large, fortified estate of Khirbet Minya in the early eighth century, which was clearly inhabited by Muslims and was only 4.5 km southwest of Capernaum, "did not affect the further development of the nearby Christian village of Capernaum."

51. Magness, "The Question of the Synagogue," 36, mentions as an analogous situation the continued Jewish presence at Nabratein into the eighth and ninth centuries, evidenced by a type of early Islamic bowl with the depiction of a Torah shrine on it.

52. N. Yuval-Hacham, "'You Shall Not Make for Yourself Any Given Image...': On Jewish Iconoclasm in Late Antiquity," *Ars Judaica* 6 (2010): 13–16. On p.14, she mentions that "effacement at the Capernaum synagogue extends to over twenty carved architectural designs, found both in the external parts of the structure and in the interior spaces." See also Yuval-Hacham's treatment of this topic in "The Faces of Effacement."

53. Yuval-Hacham, "Jewish Iconoclasm," 21. For a larger discussion of Near Eastern iconoclasm in its various manifestations, from late antiquity to early Islam (hence his use of "iconoclasms"), see G. W. Bowersock, *Mosaics as History: The Near East from Late Antiquity to Islam*, Revealing Antiquity 16 (Cambridge, MA: Belknap/Harvard University Press, 2006), 91–111, although he is concerned primarily with the impact of iconoclasm on the medium of mosaics.

Image 7.2. The lintel above the main entrance, southern façade, of the Capernaum synagogue, with effaced relief.

Photo by Ricardo Tulio Gandelman from Wikimedia Commons. Used under Creative Commons License 2.0.

As explained by Yuval-Hacham, the current consensus among historians is that the eighth century provides the best context for understanding the iconoclastic activity carried out in synagogues from Early Islamic Palestine, and that it was, in fact, carried out by Jews themselves rather than hostile aniconic Christians or Muslims.[54] Like the iconoclasm found in other synagogues—such as, perhaps most famously, the synagogue at Na'aran—the carved images in the Capernaum synagogue were clearly not mutilated in a fit of reckless visual violence, as one might expect to see if interreligious hostilities were in play. Rather, the images were erased precisely and with great care.[55] The

---

54. For critical discussion of this consensus and its justification, see Yuval-Hacham, "Jewish Iconoclasm," 17–19 and the extensive scholarly literature cited there.

55. The same seems to be true in the case of Christian churches in Palestine, i.e., Christians were responsible for iconoclasm in their own churches. See Bowersock, *Mosaics as History*, 98–99, who bases his views largely on the earlier work of Robert Schick, *The Christian Communities of Palestine from Byzantine to Islamic Rule: A Historical and Archaeological Study* (Princeton, NJ: Darwin Press, 1995).

meticulous execution of effacement in the Capernaum synagogue was likely carried out to *allow its continued use* by Jews living in the eighth-century village, suggesting that, at the time of effacement, certain ideological shifts internal to the local Jewish community were transpiring related to the use of figural art in the synagogue.[56] However, by the eighth century, Jews had already had a long history of expressing variegated opinions about the use of figurative images in their gathering spaces.[57] While some Jews were opposed to images, many were clearly not—not even all the rabbis were categorically against them.[58] Neither were Byzantine Christians. This raises the question, then, of why at least some Jews in Capernaum apparently took a sudden eighth-century iconoclastic turn.[59]

In 723, Umayyad Caliph Yazid II (rule 720–724 CE) issued an edict banning the use of images specifically in Christian churches within his jurisdiction.[60] The lifespan of the edict was very short, and thus not fully observed,

---

56. Yuval-Hacham, "Jewish Iconoclasm," 22; Bonnie, "A Sustained Presence," 282.

57. For larger historical discussions, see S. Schwartz, "On the Program and Reception of the Synagogue Mosaics," in *From Dura to Sepphoris: Studies in Jewish Art and Society in Late Antiquity*, ed. L.I. Levine and Z. Weiss, JRASup. 40 (Portsmouth, RI: Journal of Roman Archaeology, 2000), 165–182; S. Fine, "Iconoclasm and the Art of the Late-Ancient Palestinian Synagogues," in *From Dura to Sepphoris*, ed. Levine and Weiss, 183–194; and R. Talgam, *Mosaics of Faith: Floors of Pagans, Jews, Samaritans, Christians, and Muslims in the Holy Land* (Jerusalem/University Park, PA: Yad Ben-Zvi Press/Penn State University Press, 2014), 405–409.

58. Fine has even argued that there is evidence in the Talmud of some rabbis defending the use of images. See Fine, "Iconoclasm," 183–194.

59. For broader discussion, see Talgam, *Mosaics of Faith*, 405–409, 425–430. This question of why, seemingly all of a sudden, iconoclastic activity appears in the eighth century equally relates to the destruction of figurative art in Christian churches in Palestine. See Bowersock, *Mosaics as History*, 100–103, where he discusses five securely dated church mosaics from Palestine and the Transjordan that demonstrate that Christians apparently had no problem with laying mosaic carpets containing figurative art all the way up to the year 722.

60. The traditional date of the iconoclastic edict of Yazid II is 721, but Bowersock demonstrates that almost all of the primary sources actually put it in 723, shortly before Yazid's death in 724. This means, according to Bowersock's interpretation, the enforcement of the edict lasted only a matter of months, being overturned by Yazid's successor Hisham ibn Abd al-Malik (rule 724–743) (see Bowersock, *Mosaics as History*, 105–106, 109–110). Scholars have debated whether the edict of Yazid somehow influenced the prohibition of holy icons issued by Byzantine Emperor Leo III in 726. This idea is suggested in some medieval Greek Christian sources, which, unsurprisingly, paint a malicious portrait of Yazid and the "Jewish magician" who had supposedly influenced Yazid's own edict (Cameron, "The Jewish in

but it seems to have been strong enough that a significant number of Christian communities in Palestine attempted to implement it.⁶¹ The reason behind Yazīd's edict remains somewhat of a mystery, but Bowersock has proposed an interesting hypothesis. Bowersock suggests that Yazīd's edict flowed from his desire to conform churches "to the strict injunctions that were applied to mosques and found expression in the Hadīth."⁶² But from whence this desire to conform? A number of sources, both archaeological and literary, suggest that it was not uncommon for early Muslims to engage directly and intensively with Christianity and to use churches for a variety of purposes, not least of which was prayer.⁶³ In my view, one of the best pieces of evidence for this, which Bowersock does not mention, is the *mihrab* (Islamic prayer niche) that was added to the Kathisma Church (on Hebron Road between Jerusalem and Bethlehem) in the southern part of its ambulatory in the first half of the eighth century.⁶⁴ Among the remains of this building, in one of the

---

Seventh-Century Palestine," 87; Bowersock, *Mosaics as History*, 92). While the Christian literary tradition might reflect, on a very abstract level, the perception that Jewish, Christian, and Muslim discourses on the use of images show some level of entanglement, Bowersock notes that the two edicts were fundamentally different and emerged from entirely different social and geopolitical contexts. Leo's ban was on, specifically, the use of holy icons and emerged from an intra-Christian theological conflict raging in Byzantium for decades prior. Yazīd's edict, on the other hand, banned representations of every living thing in Christian churches and, thus, seems to have been "an aberrant and overzealous extension" of an early Islamic doctrine that was only meant to apply to mosques (*Mosaics as History*, 97). After all, in addition to the fact that Yazīd's edict was immediately repealed by Hisham, there is plenty of evidence—for example, Hisham's own palace at Khirbet al-Mafjar—that Muslims themselves were not opposed to representing living things in nonmosque contexts. See M. Louhivuori, "The Palace of Hisham and 8th Century C.E. Iconoclasm," in *Encounters of the Children of Abraham from Ancient to Modern Times*, ed. A. Laato and P. Lindqvist, Studies on the Children of Abraham 1 (Leiden: Brill, 2010), 199–213.

61. For evidence of this, see especially Schick's list of churches with iconoclastic damage from around the period of Yazīd's edict. The effacement activity, as Bowersock has discussed, is like synagogue iconoclasm—precise, careful, and systematic—indicating Christian responsibility, and it does not follow the stipulations of Leo III's ban on only holy icons but rather the ban of Yazīd on any living thing (see *Mosaics as History*, 99–100).

62. Bowersock, *Mosaics as History*, 110.

63. Bowersock, *Mosaics as History*, 109.

64. The niche's date firmly in the first half of the eighth century and its southern orientation toward Mecca lead Rina Aver to interpret it as a *mihrab*. See R. Avner, "The Dome of

annexes, was also found a ninth-century Christian inscription, decorated with a cross, which strongly suggests that Christians continued to use the building as a church even while it was also used for Muslim prayer.[65] Therefore, to my mind, Bowersock's claim, that at least one of the driving causes of Christian iconoclasm in early Islamic Palestine could have been Yazid's desire to accommodate churches for use by Muslims, is quite compelling.

What is particularly interesting for us now is that the case of Jewish iconoclasm in many ways ran parallel with the Christian case.[66] While Yazid's edict did not have synagogues specifically in view, the sudden rise of iconoclastic activity in synagogues in the eighth century can also be explained by Jewish attempts to implement it. In doing so, as Steven Fine asserts, "Jews simply adopted and adapted the aesthetics of the new colonial power."[67] This ability to adopt and adapt the visual program of their synagogue would have had internal and external effects for a Jewish community like the one in Capernaum—a community, we might recall, that had already had centuries of experience making-do with life under colonial rule. Internally, as Yuval-Hacham has suggested, Jews in the village with an aniconic bent could have seen Yazid's edict—and early Islamic attitudes towards images in religious spaces in general—as a welcome shift that gelled with their sense of Jewish identity.[68] Externally, as Bowersock has argued regarding the Christian case noted above, adapting the artwork in the synagogue toward aniconic sensibilities would have accommodated the building for use by Muslims.

---

the Rock in Light of the Development of Concentric Martyria in Jerusalem," *Muqarnas* 27 (2010): 31–49 (41–42).

65. Avner, "Dome of the Rock," 41–42. Avner mentions that there are two possible interpretations of these remains: they indicate either that Christians and Muslims prayed "side by side in the same building or that these were Christian converts to Islam who were apparently reluctant to abandon pervious beliefs and attachments" (42). In light of the evidence that Bowersock also marshals, the first interpretation mentioned by Avner seems likely. Additionally, Talgam mentions that the mosaics of the Kathisma reflect not only the well-known patterns of the Byzantine tradition but also exhibit "acceptance of influences from contemporary Muslim art and the Sassanian art that nourished it" (Bowersock, *Mosaics of Faith*, 399).

66. Bowersock, *Mosaics as History*, 108.

67. S. Fine, *Art and Judaism in the Greco-Roman World: Toward a New Jewish Archaeology* (Cambridge: Cambridge University Press, 2005), 123.

68. Yuval-Hacham, "The Faces of Effacement," 51; see also Fine, *Art and Judaism*, 123.

We do not, as far as I am aware, have direct evidence from early Islamic Palestine of Muslim participation in synagogues, as we do for Muslims in churches.[69] But Bowersock is correct that the possibility is worth considering, and, in my view, it is worth considering specifically with reference to Capernaum, a village which, in the early eighth century, seems to have had Jewish, Christian, and Muslim populations.[70] By the early Islamic period, synagogues in general had already had a long history of non-Jewish participation, and, as I argued in the previous chapter, it is quite possible that the Capernaum synagogue had itself attracted participation from non-Jewish Christians in the fifth and sixth centuries. Synagogues, as buildings and sociocultural institutions, had always possessed a high level of social and cultural flexibility and fluidity in relation to the Greco-Roman world, even as they variously housed and interpreted Jewish ancestral tradition. For us to assume that synagogues were any different in relation to early Islam—an ethnoreligious movement that Jews in Palestine, on the whole, greeted positively—would stem from prejudicial bias. According to Fine, Islam was typically not viewed with the same level of scorn that Jews sometimes felt toward Byzantine Christianity, and, in the end, Judaism came to be impacted more significantly by "the artistic and religious mores of Islamic Palestine" than any other non-Jewish influence.[71] After all, while early Islam certainly did contain ideological threads of polemical supersessionism, they, for whatever reason, never crystalized into the same sort of discourses produced by Christians to systematically subjugate Jews. Indeed, an argument could be made that early Islamic supersessionism was general in nature, and when it did sink its teeth into specifics, it more often targeted distinctly Christian teachings—such

---

69. However, there is an interesting tradition in the Hadīth collected in the Sunan ibn Mājah that imagines the possibility of Muhammad's close companion, 'Ubadah bin Samit, and Mu'awiya, the first Umayyad caliph, having a meeting "either in a church or in a synagogue" to discuss business (Hadīth 2254 [ca. 250 AH; ninth century CE]; Darussalam edition).

70. Bowersock, *Mosaics as History*, 110–111. While Capernaum's octagonal church seems to have continued in use after the emergence of Islamic rule, I see no evidence that it was adapted for Muslim use, at least not in the same way that, for example, the Kathisma was adapted. The central image of the peacock was never effaced and no later installations, such as a *mihrab*, appears to have been added. This, of course, does not mean Muslims could not have used the building anyway. Bowersock notes evidence of early Muslim use of a variety of churches in Palestine, which apparently were not all physically altered, whether through iconoclasm or additional installations.

71. Fine, *Art and Judaism*, 123.

as the divinity of Jesus and the trinity—than Jewish ones.[72] In any case, if early Muslims could nevertheless acknowledge the holiness of churches as a part of the culturally conglomerate world that they inherited, Bowersock sees no reason to doubt that they acknowledged the holiness of synagogues as well.[73] And I see no reason to doubt that Muslims in Capernaum would have acknowledged this about the limestone synagogue. To my mind, it is hard *not* to imagine that Muslims in Capernaum used the limestone synagogue in some way, even if specifics are impossible to come by.

There are also more pragmatic and contextual reasons to think that early Muslims in Capernaum engaged positively with the village's synagogue and church. Even if, as Avni notes, Capernaum was an expanding settlement in the eighth century (at most 4 hectares = .04 km^2), it was still not very large—about the area of 7.5 football fields—and it lacked a mosque.[74] New building projects, while desirable, can be costly and slow. Thus, it is easier in times of political transition to make use of preexisting infrastructures, both social and material. For example, when it came to satisfying the monetization needs of their expanding economies, the Rashidun and early Umayyad caliphates imported and imitated the preexisting system of Byzantine coinage, in particular the Byzantine follis, including its explicitly Christian iconography.[75] The Arab-Islamic identity of these so-called "Arab-Byzantine" coins is often only distinguishable by their dating, which follows the year of the *hijra*. As Clive Foss has noted, rather than simply "barbarous imitations," this coinage should be described as "transitional"

---

72. This general early Islamic supersessionism, which at times sharpens to target Christianity, is seen most famously in the Kufic inscriptions on the Dome of the Rock. It is also seen in the hoard of "post-reform" Umayyad gold dinars found in Capernaum (mentioned above), which include passages from the Quran about, on the one hand, the religion of Muhammad being generally "victorious over every other religion" (Sura 9:33), and, on the other hand, the fact that Allah "begets not, neither is He begotten" (Sura 112:1–3), which is clearly directed at Christianity's theology of Christ as the begotten son of God.

73. Bowersock, *Mosaics as History*, 110–111.

74. Avni, *Byzantine–Islamic Transition*, 89–91. The closest mosque would have been 4.5 km away at the fortified estate of Khirbet al-Minya, not built until the early eighth century. However, I am uncertain whether this mosque served only those Muslims inhabiting the estate or served also a broader Muslim public.

75. See C. Foss, *Arab-Byzantine Coins: An Introduction, with Catalogue of the Dumbarton Oaks Collection* (Cambridge: Dumbarton Oaks Research Library and Collection, 2008), 23–33. For images of the "Arab-Byzantine" coins from Capernaum, see Tavola XVII in Callegher, *Cafarnao IX*.

in nature, embodying the social, economic, and material processes involved in the slow movement from Byzantine to Islamic rule.[76] According to Callegher, twelve such coins were found in Capernaum, several of them dated as early as H 17 (639 CE), which suggests that the new empire's need to work within already existing economic structures—until it could establish its own[77]—was felt there as well. For Christians in Capernaum, the early circulation of "Byzantine–Muslim transitional coinage" could have functioned socially as a sign of continuity amidst the change, or at least a sign that change was happening slowly. For Jews, however, the transitional coinage likely represented a mixed bag of emotions: hope of a better future for some, fear of a worse future for others, and apathy for everyone else who simply wanted to make-do.

Regardless, we should remember that the Capernaum synagogue and church remained the largest and most conspicuous built spaces in the village, and they continued to operate in proximity to the busy commercial area of town that still ran along its main north–south street. It is possible, then, that, even if Muslims in the village were not attracted to these spaces for religious reasons, they might have been pulled into their orbit for purposes of business and trade. After all, in one ninth-century Hadīth, ʿUbadah bin Samit, a close colleague of Muhammad himself, and Muʿawiya, the first Umayyad caliph, are said to have had a meeting "either in a church or in a synagogue" to discuss business.[78] Interestingly, on the Franciscan side of Capernaum, only sixteen post-transitional, eighth-century Umayyad coins were found, but they were all found in loci lining the main north–south street, where shops and industrial activities had taken place during the Byzantine period.[79] Of course, we do not know who actually handled these coins, but we do know that they did not have to travel very far, being minted in the provincial capital of Tiberias (Ṭabariyya). It is not too difficult to imagine that they ended up in Capernaum as a result of Muslims participating—along with Jews and Christians—in the buying and selling that transpired in the town's marketplace, right next to the church and the synagogue that had recently been visually altered to accommodate early Islamic artistic sensibilities.

---

76. Foss, *Arab-Byzantine Coins*, viii–ix.

77. On this process, see Treadwell, "Coinage Reforms."

78. See note 69 above.

79. See the list in Callegher, *Cafarnao IX,* 137–138. On the shops and industrial areas of Byzantine Capernaum, see chapter 6.

4. Conclusion

While the seventh century brought cataclysmic clashes between armies on the battlefield and in the minds of literary apocalypticists, it brought little-to-no change to Jews and Christians making do on the village streets of Capernaum. Although signs of the transition were visible in that century—such in the circulation of "Arab-Byzantine" coinage—a distinct "early Islamic" Capernaum did not emerge until the eighth century and perhaps more so in its second half. But even when an Islamic presence did take shape in the village, there are reasons to believe that not only did Jews and Christians continue to interact in ways they had done before, but also that early Muslims may have, indeed, joined in on this interaction. Umayyad coins found lining Capernaum's main artery (i.e., its *cardo*) might mean that early Muslims were involved in the heartbeat of its commercial life. The lack of a mosque in the village and, to use Bonnie's language, the "sustained presence" of Capernaum's monumental synagogue and, I would add, its octagonal church, might suggest that early Muslims there were compelled to engage in their own type of "making do" concerning their need for assembly space.

To be clear, this historical construction does not mean that Jews, Christians, and Muslims necessarily always peacefully coexisted in Capernaum. On the other hand, it does seem to suggest that, as Bonnie notes, "strict rulings in the Abbasid period regarding the *dhimmī* (non-Muslims) population were, at least at times, not enforced in practice."[80] In other words, the demands of everyday life may have proved, once again, to be a stronger driving force in relations between Jews, Christians, and their new colonial overlords. Such a practical scenario should remind us, as discussed in the previous chapter, that the possibility of coexistence between different ethnoreligious groups in Capernaum does not mean that the village was a bastion of our modern-day value of religious pluralism. We would be naïve to neglect in our histories the imbalance in social relationships that colonial power generates. Coexistence among Others is often a necessity for the survival and stability of a group, of a town; you have to play nicely with Others in your neighborhood, even if only to make a living and not to make living a living hell. This type of everyday pragmatism must certainly factor into our characterization of interreligious relations in Capernaum in the late seventh and eighth centuries.

---

80. Bonnie, "A Sustained Presence," 283.

Epilogue
In Lieu of a Conclusion

IN THE LATE 1980s, work began on a major building project that would establish in Capernaum a new memorial to St. Peter. According to the Custodia Terrae Sanctae's own account, the need for this memorial grew out of a desire—it was evidently Virgilio Corbo's "grand wish"—to engender a "revival of worship" at the House of Peter "as it had been carried out in the first century CE."[1] The memorial, designed by the Italian architect Ildo Avetta, "sought to emphasize the importance of the location by creating a structure that would invoke the profound importance of the archaeological site, its history and, above all, the events of Jesus' and Peter's lives." The memorial was erected over top of the remains of the octagonal church, but visitors were given visual access to Room 1 by means of a quadrangular oculus inside the memorial. Its form was envisaged as "a ship whose hull would appear to hover above the Apostles house, an image alluding to the call of the Apostle Peter, who from simple fisherman became a fisher of men and head of the Church of Christ."[2] The memorial was officially consecrated on June 29, 1990. Fra Corbo had received his wish, but he died the following year and was buried next to the memorial, which is today marked by a small cross.

However important it is to religious believers today, the modern memorial project in Capernaum is interesting to reflect upon from some of the historical perspectives that were investigated in this book. For example, the memorial project is an explicit attempt to construct a modern institutional context (the Roman Catholic Church) and a socioreligious network (Christian pilgrims) for the formation of contemporary religious identity and the production of cultural memory. Throughout this book, I have highlighted the importance of institutions in Capernaum—associations, synagogues, churches—and what they provided the village in terms of social networks, connectivity, and

---

1. See the presentation on the Custodia's website: https://www.custodia.org/en/sanctuaries/capernaum

2. https://www.custodia.org/en/sanctuaries/capernaum

Image E.1. Aerial view of Capernaum's modern memorial erected over the remains of the octagonal church. Picture taken in 1999.

From Loffreda, *Cafarnao V*, 51 (DF 34). Used with permission.

belonging. Indeed, institutions were part and parcel to the very development of Judaism and Christianity, and perhaps also Islam, in Capernaum, and, as we saw in some of the book's chapters, even their physical manifestations played an important role in the mediation of cultural knowledge and memory. There is no doubt that the modern memorial, just like the ancient ones below it and beside it, also plays a role in the mediation of memory. But this also brings the memorial into the orbit of questions about architecture and power. Of course, it is not surprising that, in its presentation to the public, the Custodia says nothing about this. So, I will. However, I do so because I think there are issues at stake here that are connected to several central ideas discussed earlier in the book.

All memorials, in some way or another, are an attempt to connect the present to the past. While some memorials and their makers, out of a critical awareness, eschew notions of preserving the memory of people and places "as they really were back then," others, like the memorial in Capernaum, make this their stated aim. The memorial, it is said, "preserves the memory of the

Apostle's home and of the places where Christ preached and was active."³ But it is unclear to me how a structure, described in the Custodia's own words as an "audacious and ultramodern project," accomplishes this aim. Indeed, at least one prominent scholar has quipped that the memorial appears, visually, less like an ancient fishing boat and more like a "flying saucer."⁴ To be clear, my goal here is not to pronounce judgment on the aesthetics of the building or to lessen its religious significance for pilgrims today. Far be it from me. My aim, rather, is to encourage more critical reflection on what it is that this building is doing in its social-spatial setting. The modern church, as built space, fundamentally conditions and controls the processing of knowledge and the production of memory at the site. It mediates not only *what* is remembered but also *how* it is remembered. It is naïve to think that the memorial somehow distills and preserves an ancient memory that exists as a static object to be gazed upon "down there" amidst the hallowed remains of Room 1. And, to be quite honest, the visibility is not very good. Access to the center of the oculus is restricted by a square railing and, sometimes (often? always?), there is a potted plant sitting right in the middle of the glass. Visitors get only a marginal glimpse of "ancient things" down below, but, without a trusted guide, most will find it difficult to interpret what they see, as is, understandably, often the case with the popular consumption of archaeology. The view from the street is not much better. Thus, it is difficult to know what role the actual ancient remains play in a modern pilgrim's act of remembering. Their experience is almost entirely conditioned by interacting with the space of a modern church. As such, the memorial clearly does more than simply "preserve" an ancient memory; it *constructs* it.

The memorial also does something to the broader landscape of the Capernaum archaeological site. Before it was erected, the remains of the *insula sacra*, including those of the octagonal church, basically rested at street level. The tallest, most visible, and most accessible set of remains at the site was the limestone synagogue. The modern church, however, extends the most explicitly Christian part of the site upward to a height that now rivals, and perhaps even exceeds, the height of the synagogue. In other words, the "struggle of monuments" that we observed especially in chapter 5 evidently did not end in the fifth and sixth

---

3. https://www.custodia.org/en/sanctuaries/capernaum

4. P. Richardson, *Building Jewish in the Roman East*, 105, where he calls the memorial a "flying-saucer church hovering above an octagonal fifth-century church."

centuries when the octagonal church and limestone synagogue were built, or in the eighth century when the synagogue probably underwent repairs. The struggle endured into the late twentieth century, when the modern memorial gave Roman Christianity a final boost (literally) and the struggle's last word.

Seen from this perspective, the memorial competes with and diminishes the village's Jewish past.[5] It is a material reassertion and reproduction of Christianity's power to possess at Judaism's expense. Thus, the memorial works ideologically quite closely with other claims at the site of Christianity's superiority, such as the imagery of the Crusader-inspired fivefold cross and the description of Capernaum as "the Town of Jesus." Even the synagogue, which to many is the quintessential mark of Jewishness, is tagged for Christianity with a little white and blue sign that points out the alleged "Synagogue of Jesus." Similar to Egeria's Christianizing testimony about her travels in the "Holy Land," ancient Jews and Judaism have no life of their own, even though they certainly did during most of the history of the ancient village.[6] To my mind, then, the modern memorial stands quite squarely—even if unintentionally—in the tradition of Christian supersessionism. And this is to say nothing of the presentation of Islam at the site, whether on the Franciscan side or the Greek Orthodox side. Excavations on both sides have turned up rich Islamic material culture—such as the 282 Umayyad gold dinars found on the Greek Orthodox side, which bear inscriptions from the Quran—but none of it is represented to the public. One has to read about it in less-than-accessible archaeological reports. Capernaum's significant Islamic past, nebulously referred to on a guidepost as the "Arabic period (seventh to twelfth century)," is essentially invisible.

* * *

There is one last angle on the modern memorial in Capernaum that I would like to shed a tiny bit of light on, and perhaps strike a slightly different but no less relevant tone. In the Custodia's account of the execution of the project, it names no less than five actors involved: the main architect, Ildo Avett; Cesare Pocci, an engineer; the Technion (the Israel Institute of Technology); Solel

---

5. Indeed, this seems to be Richardson's concern and the larger context of his quip quoted in the note above. The larger context of the quote is: "Capernaum's excavations feature a fifth- (sixth?) century limestone synagogue, now rivaled in impact by a flying-saucer church hovering above an octagonal fifth-century church." Richardson, *Building Jewish*, 105.

6. Jacobs, "Visible Ghosts and Invisible Demons," 359–376.

Epilogue

Boneh (which means "Paving, Building"), one of the largest and oldest construction and civil engineering companies in Israel; and Anis Srouji, an engineer from Nazareth. What is striking about this conglomeration of people and institutions has to do with the makeup of the last three members of the list. The Technion and Solel Boneh are two historic Israeli institutions, which, while their origins predate the creation of the State of Israel in 1948, have been deeply tied to Israel's nation-building projects from the beginning. Golda Meir, Israel's fourth prime minister from 1969–1974, even considered Solel Boneh "a national tool of the highest degree."[7] Anis Srouji, on the other hand, was a Palestinian man who, along with his brother Elias and the rest of their family, lived through the 1948 Palestine War. While the Israeli army apparently allowed Anis and his family to stay in Nazareth—the family has roots in the town going back to 1772[8]—he and Elias had the tragic experience of witnessing the expulsion of many Palestinians from their Galilean homes.[9]

It is difficult to grasp how two groups of people not only from different ethnic backgrounds but, more crucially, from two radically different, that is, asymmetrical experiences of power could sit in the same room and work together on a project that has religion as its central subject. To be sure, I have no knowledge of what Anis Srouji and the agents of the Technion and Solel Boneh actually thought about each other or how they interacted, whether in friendship or hostility. Similarly, I do not know how early Christ-followers who were members of fishing associations in and around Capernaum actually interacted with their non-Christ-following Jewish compatriots, or whether Jews and Byzantine Christians in the asymmetrical setting of the village in late antiquity liked or hated each other. But I am convinced of two things

---

7. H. Yacobi, *Israel and Africa: A Genealogy of Moral Geography* (London: Routledge, 2016), 38–39.

8. This information is according to the Srouji family tree published by the family at www.sroujifamily.com.

9. Elias Srouji was a medical doctor in Nazareth until 1967, but he ended up emigrating to the United States and going on to become a renowned professor of medicine at the University of Oklahoma. In 2003, he self-published his memoirs as *Cyclamens from Galilee: Memoirs of a Physician from Nazareth*, in which he recounts these experiences. Several long excerpts from the book, however, were published in the *Journal of Palestine Studies*. One in which he mentions his brother, Anis, and their experiences during the 1948 war is titled "The Fall of a Galilean Village during the 1948 Palestine War: An Eyewitness Account," *Journal of Palestine Studies* 33 (2004): 71–80.

that, I think, are generally applicable to both the ancient and the modern situations just mentioned. One is that, on the level of "making do," employment and a paycheck can go a long way to motivate people to get along just enough to be productive, accomplish a task, and not make life a living hell. This was one of my arguments about Jewish–Christian relations in chapter 6, as I reinterpreted the limestone synagogue and octagonal church within the productive contexts of Capernaum's domestic remains. The second thing I am convinced of is something that Elias Srouji mentions in his memoirs, that "even in the bitterest of conflicts, individuals can still be decent and remember with gratitude past kindnesses."[10] And perhaps this, simple individual human decency and kindness, is precisely what allowed Anis Srouji to work effectively on the Capernaum memorial church with two Israeli institutions and vice versa. And perhaps this, individual human decency and kindness, is precisely what allowed Jews and Christians of various types to endure side by side in Capernaum for nearly seven hundred years, making the village much more than just "the Town of Jesus."

---

10. Srouji, "Fall of a Galilean Village," 80.

BIBLIOGRAPHY

Abel, F.-M. "Le nom de Capharnaum." *Journal of the Palestine Oriental Society* 8 (1928): 24–34.
Adams, E. *The Earliest Christian Meeting Places: Almost Exclusively Houses?* Revised edition. London: T&T Clark, 2016.
Adler, Y. *The Origins of Judaism: An Archaeological-Historical Reappraisal.* New Haven: Yale University Press, 2022.
Al-Azmeh, A. *The Emergence of Islam in Late Antiquity: Allāh and his People.* Cambridge: Cambridge University Press, 2014.
Alberts, W. J. and G. A. A. Kortekaas, editors. *Die Apokalypse des Pseudo-Methodius: Die ältesten griechischen und lateinischen Übersetzungen,* Corpus Scriptorum Christianorum Orientalium 569. Leuven: Peeters, 1998.
Alexander, P. J. *The Byzantine Apocalyptic Tradition.* Berkley: University of California Press, 1985.
Arubas, B. Y., and R. Talgam. "Jews, Christians, and 'Minim': Who Really Built and Used the Synagogue at Capernaum—A Stirring Appraisal." In *Knowledge and Wisdom: Archaeological and Historical Essays in Honour of Leah Di Segni,* edited by G. C. Bottini, L. D. Chrupcala, and J. Patrich, 237–274. SBFCM 54. Milano: Edizioni Terra Santa, 2014.
Ascough, R. "Paul, Synagogues, and Associations: Reframing the Question of Models for Pauline Christ Groups." *Journal of the Jesus Movement in its Jewish Setting* 2 (2015): 27–52.
———. "Translocal Relationships among Voluntary Associations and Early Christianity." *JECS* 5, no. 2 (1997): 223–241.
Avi-Yonah, M. "Editor's Note." *Israel Exploration Journal* 23, no. 1 (1973): 43.
Aviam, M. "Capernaum I." In *Encyclopaedia of the Bible and Its Reception.* Vol. 4, edited by H.-J. Klauck et al, 944–948. Berlin: De Gruyter, 2012.
———. "Christian Galilee in the Byzantine Period." In *Galilee through the Centuries: Confluence of Cultures.* 281–300. Winona Lake, IN: Eisenbrauns, 1999.
———. "People, Land, Economy, and Belief in First-Century Galilee and Its Origins: A Comprehensive Archaeological Synthesis." In *The Galilean Economy*, edited by Fiensy and Hawkins, 5–48.
Avner, R. "The Dome of the Rock in Light of the Development of Concentric Martyria in Jerusalem." *Muqarnas* 27 (2010): 31–49.

Avni, G. *The Byzantine–Islamic Transition in Palestine: An Archaeological Approach.* Oxford: Oxford University Press, 2014.
Avshalom-Gorni, D., and A. Najar. "Migdal: Preliminary Report." *Hadashot* 125 (2013). Accessed April 5, 2021. www.hadashot-esi.org.il/report_detail_eng.aspx?id=2304&mag_id=120.
Bagatti, B. *Ancient Christian Villages of Galilee.* Jerusalem: Franciscan, [Reprint 2001].
———. *The Church from the Circumcision: History and Archaeology of the Judaeo-Christians.* Translated by E. Hoade. Jerusalem: Franciscan, 1971. [Reprint 1984].
Baird, J. *The Inner Lives of Ancient Houses: An Archaeology Dura-Europos.* Oxford: Oxford University Press, 2014.
Baird, J. A. "The Graffiti of Dura-Europos: A Contextual Approach." In *Ancient Graffiti in Context*, edited by J. A. Baird and C. Taylor, 49–68. London: Routledge, 2011.
Baird, J. A., and C. Taylor. "Ancient Graffiti in Context." In *Ancient Graffiti in Context*, edited by J. A. Baird and C. Taylor, 1–17. London: Routledge, 2011.
Baird, J. A., and C. Taylor. "Ancient Graffiti." In *The Routledge Handbook of Graffiti and Street Art*, edited by J. I. Ross, 17–26. London: Routledge, 2016.
Baker, C. *Rebuilding the House of Israel: Architectures of Gender in Jewish Antiquity.* Stanford: Stanford University Press, 2002.
Bar-Asher Siegal, M. *Jewish–Christian Dialogues on Scripture in Late Antiquity.* Cambridge: Cambridge University Press, 2019.
———. "Judaism and Syriac Christianity." In *The Syriac World*, edited by D. King, 146–157. London: Routledge, 2018.
Bar, D. "The Christianisation of Rural Palestine during Late Antiquity." *JEH* 54, no. 3 (2003): 401–421.
Barton, C. E. "Duality and Invisibility: Race and Memory in the Urbanism of the American South." In *Sites of Memory: Perspectives on Architecture and Race*, edited by C. E. Barton, 1–12. New York: Princeton Architectural Press, 2001.
Bauckham, R. "James and the Jerusalem Community." In *Jewish Believers in Jesus: The Early Centuries*, edited by O. Skarsaune and R. Hvalvik, 55–95. Peabody, MA: Hendrickson, 2007.
———. *Jude and the Relatives of Jesus in the Early Church.* Edinburgh: T&T Clark, 1990.
———. "Magdala and the Fishing Industry." In *Magdala of Galilee: A Jewish City in the Hellenistic and Roman Period*, edited by Bauckham, 185–268. Waco, TX: Baylor University Press.
———, editor. *Magdala of Galilee: A Jewish City in the Hellenistic and Roman Period.* Waco, TX: Baylor University Press, 2018.

———. "The Origin of the Ebionites." In *The Image of the Judaeo-Christians in Ancient Jewish and Christian Literature*, edited by P. J. Tomson and D. Lambers-Petry, 162–181. WUNT 158. Tübingen: Mohr Siebeck, 2003.

Becker, A. H., and A. Y. Reed, editors. *The Ways That Never Parted: Jews and Christians in Late Antiquity and the Early Middle Ages*. Minneapolis: Fortress Press, 2007.

Becker, E.-M. "Jesus and Capernaum in the Apostolic Age: Balancing Sources and Their Evidence." In *The Mission of Jesus: Second Nordic Symposium on the Historical Jesus, Lund, 7–10 October 2012*, edited by S. Byrskog and T. Hägerland, 118. Tübingen: Mohr Siebeck, 2015.

Berlin, A. "Household Judaism." In *Galilee in the Late Second Temple and Mishnaic Period*. 2 vols, edited by D. A. Fiensy and J. R. Strange, 208–215. Minneapolis: Fortress Press, 2014.

Bernier, J. *Apsynagōgos and the Historical Jesus in John: Rethinking the Historicity of the Johannine Expulsion Passages*. BibInt 122. Leiden: Brill, 2013.

———. *The Quest for the Historical Jesus after the Demise of Authenticity: Toward a Critical Realist Philosophy of History in Jesus Studies*. LNTS 540. London: T&T Clark, 2016.

Binder, D. *Into the Temple Courts: The Place of the Synagogues in the Second Temple Period*. Atlanta: SBL, 1999.

Bishop, E. "Jesus and Capernaum." *CBQ* 14 (1953): 427–437.

Bloedhorn, H. *Die Kapitelle der Synagoge von Kapernaum: Ihre zeitliche und stilistische Einordnung im Rahmen der Kapitellentwicklung in der Dekapolis und in Palaestina*. ADVP 11. Wiesbaden: Harrassowitz, 1988.

———. "The Capitals of the Synagogue of Capernaum—Their Chronological and Stylistic Classification with regard to the Development of Capitals in the Decapolis and in Palestine." In *Ancient Synagogues in Israel: Third–Seventh Century*, edited by R. Hachlili, 49–54. BAR International Series 499. Oxford: Oxford University Press, 1989.

Bockmuehl, M. "Syrian Memories of Peter: Ignatius, Justin, and Serapion." In *The Image of the Judaeo-Christians in Ancient Jewish and Christian Literature*, edited by P. J. Tomson and D. Lambers-Petry, 124–146. WUNT 158. Tübingen: Mohr Siebeck, 2003.

Bonnie, R. "A Sustained Presence: Synagogue Buildings in Galilee during the Early Islamic Period and Later." *Journal of Eastern Mediterranean Archaeology and Heritage Studies* 9, no. 3 (2021): 278–298.

———. *Being Jewish in Galilee, 100–200 CE: An Archaeological Study*. SEMA 11. Turnhout: Brepols, 2019.

Borgen, P. *Bread from Heaven: An Exegetical Study of the Concept of Manna in the Gospel of John and the Writings of Philo*. NovTSupp 10. Leiden: Brill, 1965.

Bowersock, G. W. *Mosaics as History: The Near East from Late Antiquity to Islam*, Revealing Antiquity 16. Cambridge, MA: Belknap/Harvard University Press, 2006.

Bowman, S. "Jews in Byzantium." In *The Cambridge History of Judaism*. Vol. 4, *The Late Roman–Rabbinic Period*, edited by S. T. Katz, 1035–1052. Cambridge: Cambridge University Press, 2006.

Boyarin, D. *Borderlines: The Partition of Judaeo-Christianity*. Philadelphia: University of Pennsylvania Press, 2004.

———. "Rethinking Jewish Christianity: An Argument for Dismantling a Dubious Category (to which is Appended a Correction of my Border Lines." *JQR* 99, no. 1 (2009): 7–36.

Breytenbach, C. "Mark and Galilee: Text World and Historical World." In *Galilee through the Centuries: Confluence of Cultures*, edited by E. Meyers, 75–85. Winona Lake, IN: Eisenbrauns, 1999.

Buchli, V. *An Anthropology of Architecture*. London: Bloomsbury, 2013.

Burke, P. *History and Social Theory*. Ithaca, NY: Cornell University Press, 1992.

Burns, J. E. *The Christian Schism in Jewish History and Jewish Memory*. New York: Cambridge University Press, 2016.

Butz, E.-M., and A. Zettler. "Pilgrim's Devotion? Christian Graffiti from Antiquity to the Middle Ages." In *Travel, Pilgrimage, and Social Interaction from Antiquity to the Middle Ages*, edited by J. Kuuliala and J. Rantala, 141–164. London: Routledge, 2020.

Callegher, B. *Cafarnao IX: Monete dall'area urbana di Cafarnao (1968–2003)*. Jerusalem: Franciscan, 2007.

———. "Un ripostiglio di monete d'oro Bizantine dalla sinagoga di Cafarnao." *LA* 47 (1997): 329–338.

Cameron, A. "The Jews in Seventh-Century Palestine." *Scripta Classica Israelica* 13 (1994): 75–93.

Casson, L. *The Periplus Maris Erythraei: Text with Introduction, Translation, and Commentary*. Princeton, NJ: Princeton University Press, 1989.

Catto, S. K. *Reconstructing the First-Century Synagogue: A Critical Analysis of Current Research*. LNTS 363. London: T&T Clark, 2007.

Chancey, M. A. *Greco-Roman Culture and the Galilee of Jesus*, SNTSMS 134. Cambridge: Cambridge University Press, 2005.

———. *The Myth of a Gentile Galilee*. SNTSMS 134. Cambridge: Cambridge University Press, 2002.

Chen, D. "On the Chronology of the Ancient Synagogue at Capernaum." *Zeitschrift des Deutschen Palästina-Vereins* 102 (1986): 134–143.

Chiat, M. J. S. *Handbook of Synagogue Architecture,* Brown Judaic Studies 29. Chico, CA: Scholars Press, 1982.

Cirafesi, W. V. "The Socio-Economic Context of Capernaum's Limestone Synagogue and Jewish–Christian Relations in the Late Ancient Town." *Scandinavian Jewish Studies* 32, no. 1 (2021): 46–65.

Claußen, C. "Jesus und die Versammlungen Galiläas: Zur Frage nach der Bedeutung ἡ συναγωγή." In *Jesus und die Archäologie Galiläas,* edited by C. Claußen and J. Frey, 227–244. BThSt 87. Neukirchen-Vluyn: Neukirchener Verlag, 2008.

———. *Versammlung, Gemeinde, Synagog: Das hellenistisch–jüdische Umfeld der frühchristlichen Gemeinden.* StUNT 27. Göttingen: Vandenhoeck & Ruprecht, 2002.

Claußen, C., and J. Frey, eds. *Jesus und die Archäologie Galiläas.* BThSt 87. Neukirchen-Vluyn: Neukirchener Verlag, 2008.

Collar, A. *Religious Networks in the Roman Empire: The Spread of New Ideas.* Cambridge: Cambridge University Press, 2013.

Collingwood, R. G. "Hadrian's Wall: 1921–1930." *Journal of Roman Studies* 21 (1931): 36–64.

———. "Lectures on the Philosophy of History." 75 pp. (lecture given January 1926).

———. "Outlines of a Philosophy of History." 69 pp. (lecture given in April 1928).

———. "Lectures on Philosophy of History." 38 pp. (lecture given Trinity Term 1929).

———. *Speculum Mentis, or The Map of Knowledge.* Oxford: Clarendon, (1924) 1963.

———. *The Archaeology of Roman Britain.* London: Methuen, 1930.

———. *The Idea of History,* revised edition, edited by J. van der Dussen. Oxford: Oxford University Press, 1994 [originally published in 1946].

Concannon, C. *Assembling Early Christianity: Trade Networks, and the Letters of Dionysios of Corinth.* Cambridge: Cambridge University Press, 2017.

Corbo, V. *Cafarnao I: Gli edifici della città.* Jerusalem: Franciscan, 1975.

———. "Edifici antichi sotto la sinagoga di Cafarnao." In *Studia Hierosolymitana I: Studi Archeologici,* edited by E. Testa, B. Bagatti, and G. C. Bottini, 159–176. Jerusalem: Franciscan, 1976.

———. "Gli ultimi giorni di Cafarnao: Rapporto preliminare dopo la XV campagna di scavo 6 giugno—16 luglio 1983." *Liber Annuus* 33 (1983): 373–390.

———. "La città romana di Magdala." In *Studia Hierosolymitana I,* 355–378. Jerusalem: Franciscan Printing Press, 1976.

———. *La sinagoga di Cafarnao dopo gli scavi del 1969.* Jerusalem: Franciscan, 1970.

———. "Resti della sinagoga del primo secolo a cafarnao." In *Studia Hierosolymitana III,* edited by G. C. Bottini, 313–357. Jerusalem: Franciscan Printing Press, 1982.

———. "The Late Chronology of the Synagogue of Capernaum." In *Ancient Synagogues Revealed,* edited by L. Levine, Jerusalem: Israel Exploration Society, 1982.

———. *The House of Saint Peter at Capharnaum.* Jerusalem: Franciscan, 1969.

Czachesz, I. "Speaking Asses in the Acts of Thomas: An Intertextual and Cognitive Perspective." In *The Prestige of Balaam in Judaism, Early Christianity, and Islam,* edited by G. H. van Kooten and J. van Ruiten, 275–286. Leiden: Brill, 2008.

Dal Santo, Gitte Lønstrup. "Concordia Apostolorum—Concordia Augustorum. Building a Corporate Image for the Theodosian Dynasty." In *East and West in the Roman Empire of the Fourth Century: An End to Unity?* Edited by R. Dijkstra, S. van Poppel, and D. Slootjes, 99–120. Leiden: Brill, 2015.

Daniélou, J. *Théologie du judéo-christianisme.* Paris: Cerf, 1958. [English translation, 1964].

Davis, R., translator. *The Book of Pontiffs (Liber Pontificalis)*, 2nd ed., Translated Texts for Historians 6. Liverpool: Liverpool University Press, 2000.

de Certeau, M. *The Practice of Everyday Life,* translated by S. Randall. Berkley, CA: University of California Press, 1984.

de Lange, N. "Jews in the Age of Justinian." In *Cambridge Companion to the Age of Justinian,* edited by M. Maas, 401–426. Cambridge: Cambridge University Press, 2005.

De Luca, S. "Capernaum." In *The Oxford Encyclopaedia of the Bible and Archaeology,* edited by D. M. Master, 168–180. Oxford: Oxford University Press, 2013.

De Luca, S., and A. Lena. "The Harbor of the City of Magdala/Tarichaea on the Shores of the Sea of Galilee, from the Hellenistic to the Byzantine Times: New Discoveries and Preliminary Results." In *Harbors and Harbor Cities in the Eastern Mediterranean from Antiquity to the Byzantine Period: Recent Discoveries and Current Approaches,* edited by S. Ladstätter, F. Pirson, and T. Schmidts, 113–163. BYZAS 19. Istanbul: Yayinlari, 2014.

de Quiroga, P. "Patronage and Slavery in the Roman World: The Circle of Power." In *The Oxford Handbook of Greek and Roman Slaveries,* edited by S. Hodkinson, M. Kleijwegt, and K. Vlassopoulos. Oxford: Oxford University Press, 2020. Published online: https://doi.org/10.1093/oxfordhb/9780199575251.013.31.

de Vaux, R. "On the Right and Wrong Uses of Archaeology." In *Near Eastern Archaeology in the Twentieth Century,* edited by J. A. Sanders, 64–80. Garden City, NY: Doubleday, 1970.

Deines, R. "Galiläa und Jesus: Anfragen zur Funktion der Herkunftsbezeichnung 'Galiläa' in der neueren Jesusforschung." In *Jesus und die Archäologie Galiläas.* Edited by C. Claußen and J. Frey. BThSt 87. Neukirchen-Vluyn: Neukirchener Verlag, 2008.

Dray, Y., I. Gonen, and C. Ben David. "The Synagogue of Umm el-Qanatir: Preliminary Report." *Israel Exploration Journal* 67, no. 2 (2017): 209–231.

Dyson, S. L. *Rome: A Living Portrait of an Ancient City.* Baltimore: Johns Hopkins University Press, 2010.

Edwards, D. R. "Identity and Social Location in Roman Galilean Villages." In *Religion, Ethnicity, and Identity in Ancient Galilee: A Region in Transition,* edited by J. Zangenberg, H.W. Attridge, and D. Martin. WUNT 210. Tübingen: Mohr Siebeck, 2007.

Evola, G., L. Marlettaa, S. Natarajanb, and E. MariaPatanè. "Thermal Inertia of Heavyweight Traditional Buildings: Experimental Measurements and Simulated Scenarios," *Energy Procedia* 133 (2017): 42–52.

Fear, C. "Collingwood's Logic of Question and Answer: Against the Relativization of Reason." In *Other Logics: Alternatives to Formal Logic in the History of Thought and Contemporary Philosophy,* edited by A. Skodo, 81–100. Leiden: Brill, 2014.

——. "The Question-and-Answer Logic of Historical Context." *History of the Human Sciences* 26, no. 3 (2013): 68–81.

Fiensy, D. A. "Introduction." In *The Galilean Economy in the Time of Jesus*, edited by D. A. Fiensy and R. K. Hawkins, 1–4. ECL 11. Atlanta: SBL, 2013.

Fiensy, D. A., and J. R. Strange, eds. *Galilee in the Late Second Temple and Mishnaic Periods*. 2 vols. Minneapolis: Fortress Press, 2014, 2015.

Filipczak, P. *An Introduction to the Byzantine Administration in Syro-Palestine on the Eve of the Arab Conquest*, translated by A. Mękarski. Byzantina Lodziensia 26. Lodz: Wydawnictwo Uniwersytetu Łódzkiego, 2015.

Findley, L. *Building Change: Architecture, Politics, and Culture Agency*. London: Routledge, 2005.

Fine, S. *Art and Judaism in the Greco-Roman World: Toward a New Jewish Archaeology*. Cambridge: Cambridge University Press, 2005.

———. "Iconoclasm and the Art of the Late-Ancient Palestinian Synagogues." In *From Dura to Sepphoris*, edited by Levine and Weiss, 183–194.

———. "Non-Jews in the Synagogues of Late-Antique Palestine: Rabbinic and Archaeological Evidence." In *Jews, Christians, and Polytheists in the Ancient Synagogue: Cultural Interaction During the Greco-Roman Period*, edited by S. Fine, 204–207. London: Routledge, 1999.

Fischer, M. L. "Marble Imports and Local Counterparts: Luxury Business in Roman Palestine." *Topoi: Orient—Occident* 8 (2007): 249–269.

Foerster, G. "Dating Synagogues with a 'Basilical' Plan and an Apse." In *Ancient Synagogues: Historical Analysis and Archaeological Discovery*. 2 vols, edited by D. Urman and P. V. M Flesher, 87–94. Leiden: Brill, 1995.

Foerster, G. "Recent Excavations at Capernaum." *IEJ* 21 (1971): 207–211.

Foss, C. *Arab-Byzantine Coins: An Introduction, with Catalogue of the Dumbarton Oaks Collection*. Cambridge: Dumbarton Oaks Research Library and Collection, 2008.

Foucault, Michel. *Power/Knowledge: Selected Interviews and Other Writings 1972–1977*, edited by Colin Gordon. New York: Pantheon Books, 1980.

Fowler, R. "'The Insanity of Heretics Must Be Restrained': Heresiology in the Theodosian Code." In *Theodosius II: Rethinking the Roman Empire in Late Antiquity*, 172–194. Cambridge: Cambridge University Press, 2013.

Francis, E. D. "Mithraic Graffiti from Dura-Europos." In *Mithraic Studies*, edited by J. R. Hinnells, 424–445. Manchester: Manchester University Press, 1971.

Frankfurter, D. "Beyond 'Jewish Christianity': Continuing Religious Sub-Cultures of the Second and Third Centuries and Their Documents." In *The Ways That Never Parted: Jews and Christians in Late Antiquity and the Early Middle Ages*, edited by A. H. Becker and A. Y. Reed, 131–143. Minneapolis: Fortress Press, 2007.

Fredriksen, P. *Augustine and the Jews: A Christian Defense of Jews and Judaism*. New York: Doubleday, 2008.

———. "Divinity, Ethnicity, Identity: 'Religion' as a Political Category in Christian Antiquity." In *An End to Antisemitism!* Vol. 3, *Comprehending Antisemitism through the Ages: A Historical Perspective*, edited by A. Lange et al., 101–120. Berlin: Walter de Gruyter, 2021.

———. "'If It Looks like a Duck, and It Quacks like a Duck...': On *Not* Giving Up the Godfearers." In *A Most Reliable Witness: Essays in Honor of Ross Shepard Kraemer*, edited by S. A. Harvey et al. Brown Judaic Studies 358. Providence, RI: Brown University Press, 2015.

———. *When Christians Were Jews: The First Generation*. New Haven: Yale University Press, 2018.

Freyne, S. *Galilee from Alexander the Great to Hadrian: A Study of Second Temple Judaism*. Wilmington, Del.: Glazier, 1980.

———. "Galilean Studies: Old Issues and New Questions." In *Religion, Ethnicity, and Identity in Ancient Galilee: A Region in Transition*. Edited by J. Zangenberg et al. WUNT 210. Tübingen: Mohr Siebeck, 2007.

Frøyshov, S. S. R. "The Early Development of the Liturgical Eight-Mode System in Jerusalem." *St. Vladimir's Theological Quarterly* 51, no. 2–3 (2007): 139–178.

Funk, F. X. *Didascalia et Constitutiones apostolorum*. Paderborn: Schöningh, 1905.

Gager, J. "Who Did What to Whom? Physical Violence between Jews and Christians in Late Antiquity." In *A Most Reliable Witness: Essays in Honor of Ross Shepard Kraemer*, BJS 358, edited by S. A. Harvey et al., 35–48. Providence, RI: Brown University Press, 2015.

Garstad, B. *Apocalypse of Pseudo-Methodius: An Alexandrian World Chronicle*, DOML 14. Cambridge, MA: Harvard University Press, 2012.

Gil, M. *A History of Palestine, 634–1099*. Cambridge: Cambridge University Press, 1992 (orig. Hebrew 1983).

Goodblatt, D. "The Political and Social History of the Jewish Community in the Land of Israel, c. 235–638." In *The Cambridge History of Judaism*. Vol. 4, *The Late Roman–Rabbinic Period*, edited by S. T. Katz, 404–431. Cambridge: Cambridge University Press, 2006.

Goranson, S. C. "The Joseph of Tiberias Episode in Epiphanius: Studies in Jewish and Christian Relations." PhD diss., Duke University, 1990.

Graf, F. "Laying Down the Law in Ferragosto: The Roman Visit of Theodosius in Summer 389." *JECS* 22, no. 2 (2014): 219–242.

Grenfell, B. P., A. S. Hunt, and D. G. Hogarth. *Fayûm Towns and Their Papyri*. London: Offices of the Egypt Exploration Fund, 1900.

Grey, M. J. "Jewish Priests and the Social History of Post-70 Palestine." PhD diss., University of North Carolina, 2011.

———. "Simon Peter in Capernaum: An Archaeological Survey of the First-Century Village." In *The Ministry of Peter, the Chief Apostle*, edited by F. Judd Jr., E. D. Huntsman, and S. D. Hopkin. Provo, 27–66. UT: Religious Studies Center; Salt Lake City: Deseret Book, 2014.

———. "'The Redeemer to Arise from the House of Dan': Samson, Apocalypticism, and Messianic Hopes in Late Antique Galilee." *JSJ* 44 (2013): 553–589.

Guttman, S. "The Synagogue at Gamla." In *Ancient Synagogues Revealed*, edited by L. Levine, 30–34. Jerusalem: Israel Exploration Society, 1982.

Hachlili, R. *Ancient Synagogues—Archaeology and Art: New Discoveries and Current Research*. Leiden: Brill, 2013.

———. "The Niche and the Ark in Ancient Synagogues." *BASOR* 223 (1976): 43–53.

———. "Torah Shrine and Ark in Ancient Synagogues: A Re-evaluation." *ZDP* 116, no. 2 (2000): 146–183.

Hakola, R. "Galilean Jews and Christians in Context: Spaces Shared and Contested in the Eastern Galilee in Late Antiquity." In *Spaces in Late Antiquity: Cultural, Theological, and Archaeological Perspectives*, edited by Juliette Day et al., 141–165. London: Routledge, 2016.

———. "Galilean Synagogues as Local Responses to Cultural Globalization in Late Antiquity." In *The Synagogue in Ancient Palestine: Current Issues and Emerging Trends*, edited by R. Bonnie, R. Hakola, and U. Tervahauta, 271–288. Göttingen: Vandenhoeck & Ruprecht, 2021.

———. "The Production and Trade of Fish as a Source of Economic Growth in First Century CE Galilee." *Novum Testamentum* 59, no. 2 (2017): 111–130.

Hall, J. M. *Ethnic Identity in Greek Antiquity*. Cambridge: Cambridge University Press, 1997.

Harland, P. *Associations, Synagogues, and Congregations: Claiming a Place in Ancient Mediterranean Society*, 2nd rev. ed. Kitchener, ON: Philip Harland, 2013.

———. *Greco-Roman Associations: Texts, Translations, and Commentary*. Vol. 2, *North Coast of the Black Sea, Asia Minor*. BZNW 204. Berlin: Walter de Gruyter, 2014.

Harvey, S. A., et al., editors. *A Most Reliable Witness: Essays in Honor of Ross Shepard Kraemer*. BJS 358. Providence, RI: Brown University Press, 2015.

Hawkins, R. K., and D. A. Fiensy, editors. *The Galilean Economy in the Time of Jesus*. ECL 11. Atlanta: SBL, 2013.

Herford, R. *Christianity in the Talmud and Midrash*. 1903. Reprint, New York: Ktav, 2007.

Hezser, C. *The Social Structure of the Rabbinic Movement in Roman Palestine*. TSAJ 66. Tübingen: Mohr Siebeck, 1997.

Hirschfeld, Y. *Roman, Byzantine, and Early Muslim Tiberias: A Handbook of Primary Sources*. Bloomington, IN: Indiana University Press, 2005.

———. *The Palestinian Dwelling in the Roman Byzantine Period*. Jerusalem: Franciscan Printing Press, 1995.

Hirshman, M. *Midrash Kohelet Rabbah 1–6: Critical Edition based on Manuscripts and Genizah Fragments, with an Introduction, References, Variant Readings and Commentary*. Jerusalem: Schechter Institute of Jewish Studies, 2016. (Hebrew)

Horsley, R. A. "Synagogues in Galilee and the Gospels." In *Evolution of the Synagogue: Problems and Prospects*, edited by H. C. Kee and L. H. Cohick, 46–69. Harrisburg: Trinity Press International, 1999.

Ilan, T. *Lexicon of Jewish Names in Late Antiquity. Part II: Palestine 200–650 CE,* TSAJ 148. Tübingen: Mohr Siebeck, 2012.
Irshai, O. "Confronting a Christian Empire: Jewish Culture in the World of Byzantium." In *Cultures of the Jews: A New History,* edited by D. Biale, 181–222. New York: Schocken Books, 2002.
Jackson-McCabe, M. *Jewish Christianity: The Making of the Christianity-Judaism Divide.* New Haven: Yale University Press, 2020.
———. "What's in a Name? The Problem of 'Jewish Christianity.'" In *Jewish Christianity Reconsidered: Rethinking Ancient Groups and Texts,* edited by M. Jackson-McCabe, 7–38. Minneapolis: Fortress Press, 2007.
Jacobs, A. *Remains of the Jews: The Holy Land and Christian Empire in Late Antiquity.* Stanford: Stanford University Press, 2004.
———. "Visible Ghosts and Invisible Demons: The Place of Jews in Early Christian Terra Sancta." In *Galilee Through the Centuries: Confluence of Cultures,* edited by E. M. Meyers, 359–376. Winona Lake, IN: Eisenbrauns, 1999.
Jensen, R. M. *Understanding Early Christian Art.* London: Routledge, 2000, 159.
Jones, F. S. *An Ancient Jewish Christian Source on the History of Christianity: Pseudo-Clementine Recognitions 1.27–71.* Atlanta: Scholars Press, 1995.
Kaegi, W. E. *Byzantium and the Early Islamic Conquests.* Cambridge: Cambridge University Press, 1992.
Kampen, J. *Matthew within Sectarian Judaism.* New Haven: Yale University Press, 2016.
Keddie, A. *Class and Power in Roman Palestine: The Socioeconomic Setting of Judaism and Christian Origins.* Cambridge: Cambridge University Press, 2019.
Kee, H. C. "Defining the First-Century CE Synagogue: Problems and Progress." *New Testament Studies* 41 (1995): 481–500.
———. "Early Christianity in the Galilee: Reassessing the Evidence from the Gospels." In *The Galilee in Late Antiquity,* edited by L.I. Levine, 3–22. New York: JTS Press, 1992.
———. "The Transformation of the Synagogue after 70 CE: Its Import for Early Christianity." *New Testament Studies* 36 (1990): 1–24.
Kee, H. C. and L. H. Cohick, eds. *Evolution of the Synagogue: Problems and Progress.* Harrisburg, PA: Trinity Press International, 1999.
Kelly, C. "Rethinking Theodosius." In *Theodosius II: Rethinking the Roman Empire in Late Antiquity,* 1–64. Cambridge: Cambridge University Press, 2013.
Killebrew, A. "Village and Countryside." In *The Oxford Handbook of Jewish Daily Life in Roman Palestine,* edited by C. Hezser, 189–209. Oxford: Oxford University Press, 2010.
Kimelman, R. "Rabbi Yohanan of Tiberias: Aspects of Social and Religious History of Third Century Palestine." PhD dissertation, 187, 202. Yale University, 1977.
Kloppenborg, J. S. *Greco-Roman Associations: Texts, Translations, and Commentary.* Vol. 3, *Ptolemaic and Early Roman Egypt.* Berlin: Walter de Gruyter, 2020.

———. "Jesus, Fishermen, and Tax Collectors: Papyrology and the Construction of the Ancient Economy of Roman Palestine." *Ephemerides Theologicae Lovanienses* 94, no. 4 (2018): 571–599.

Kloppenborg Verbin, J. S. "Dating Theodotos (CIJ II 1404)." *Journal of Jewish Studies* 51, no. 2 (2000): 243–280.

Kohl, H., and K. Watzinger. *Die antiken Synagogen in Galiläa*. Leipzig: J.C. Hinrichs'sche Buchhandlung, 1916.

Kraemer, R. S. *The Mediterranean Diaspora in Late Antiquity: What Christianity Cost the Jews*. Oxford: Oxford University Press, 2020.

———. *Unreliable Witnesses: Religion, Gender, and History in the Greco-Roman Mediterranean*. Oxford: Oxford University Press, 2011.

Kraft, A. "The Last Roman Emperor 'Topos' in the Byzantine Apocalyptic Tradition." *Byzantion* 82 (2012): 213–257.

Kuhnen, H.-P. *Kalifenzeit am See Genezareth: Der Palast von Khirbat al-Minya*. Nünnerich-Asmus Verlag & Media GmbH, 2014.

———. *Palästina in griechisch-römischer Zeit*. Handbuch der Archäologie 2.2. Munich: Beck, 1990.

Lapin, H. "Palestinian Inscriptions and Jewish Ethnicity in Late Antiquity." In *Galilee through the Centuries: Confluence of Cultures,* edited by E. Meyers, 239–267. Winona Lake, IN: Eisenbrauns, 1999.

Last, R. "The Other Synagogues." *Journal for the Study of Judaism in the Persian, Hellenistic, and Roman Period* 47 (2016): 330–363.

Laughlin, J. C. H. "Capernaum: From Jesus' Time and After." *Biblical Archeology Review* 19 (1993): 54–61.

———. "The Identification of the Site." In *Excavations at Capernaum*. Vol. 1, *1978–1982*, edited by V. Tzaferis. Winona Lake, IN: Eisenbrauns, 1989.

Lecker, M. "The Jewish Reactions to Islamic Conquests." In *Dynamics in the History of Religions between Asia and Europe: Encounters, Notions, and Comparative Perspectives,* Dynamics in the History of Religions 1, 177–190. Leiden: Brill, 2012.

Lee, A. D. *From Rome to Byzantium AD 363–565: The Transformation of Ancient Rome*. Edinburgh: Edinburgh University Press, 2013.

Leibner, U. "Identifying Gennesar on the Sea of Galilee." *JRA* 19 (2006): 229–245.

———. *Settlement and History in Hellenistic, Roman, and Byzantine Galilee: An Archaeological Survey of the Eastern Galilee*. TSAJ 127. Tübingen: Mohr Siebeck, 2009.

———. "The Dating of the 'Galilean'-Type Synagogues: Khirbet Wadi Ḥamam as a Case-Study." In *Synagogues in the Hellenistic and Roman Periods: Archaeological Finds, New Methods, New Theories,* Ioudaioi 11, edited by L. Doering and A. Krause, 43–69. Göttingen: Vandenhoeck & Ruprecht, 2020.

Leibner, U., and B. Arubas. "Invisible Synagogues from the Second Temple Period." Paper presented at Les premiers synagogues en Galilée, University of Lausanne, Switzerland, 9–11 April.

Leibner, U. and S. Miller. "A Figural Mosaic in the Synagogue at Khirbet Wadi Hamam." *JRA* 23 (2010): 238–264.
Levine, L. "Diversity in the Ancient Synagogue of Roman-Byzantine Palestine: Historical Implications." In *Diversity and Rabbinization: Jewish Texts and Societies between 400 and 1,000 CE,* edited by G. McDowell, R. Naiweld, and D. Stökl Ben Ezra, 3–32. Cambridge: Cambridge University Press, 2021.

———. *The Ancient Synagogue: The First Thousand Years,* 2nd ed. New Haven: Yale University Press, 2005.

———. "The Nature and Origin of the Palestinian Synagogue Reconsidered." *Journal of Biblical Literature* 115, no. 3 (1996): 425–448.

———. *Visual Judaism in Late Antiquity: Historical Contexts of Jewish Art.* New Haven: Yale University Press, 2012.

Lieu, J. *Neither Jew nor Greek? Constructing Early Christianity.* 2nd ed. London: T&T Clark, 2016.

———. "The Synagogue and the Separation of the Christians." In *The Ancient Synagogue: From Its Origins until 200 CE,* edited by B. Olsson and M. Zetterholm, 189–207, CBNTS 39. Stockholm: Almqvist & Wiksell International, 2003.

Linder, A. *The Jews in the Legal Sources of the Early Middle Ages.* Detroit: Wayne State University Press, 1997.

Loffreda, S. *Cafarnao II: La ceramica.* Jerusalem: Franciscan, 1974.

———. *Cafarnao V: Documentazione fotografica degli scavi (1968–2003).* Jerusalem: Franciscan, 2005.

———. *Cafarnao VI: Tipologie e contesti stratigrafici della ceramica (1968–2003).* Jerusalem: Edizioni Terra Santa, 2008.

———. *Cafarnao VII: Documentazione grafica della ceramica (1968–2003).* Jerusalem: Edizioni Terra Santa, 2008.

———. *Cafarnao VIII: Documentazione fotografica degli oggetti [1968–2003].* Jerusalem: Edizione Terra Santa, 2008.

———. "Ceramica ellenistico-romana nel sottosuolo della sinagoga di Cafarnao." In *Studia Hierosolymitana III,* edited by G. C. Bottini, 273–312. Jerusalem: Franciscan, 1982.

———. "Coins from the Synagogue of Capharnaum." *Liber Annuus* 47 (1997): 223–244.

———. "The Late Chronology of the Synagogue of Capernaum." *Israel Exploration Journal* 23, no. 1 (1973): 37–42.

———. "The Synagogue of Capharnaum: Archaeological Evidence for its Late Chronology." *Liber Annuus* 22 (1972): 5–29.

———. *Recovering Capharnaum,* Studium Biblicum Franciscanum Guides 1. Jerusalem: Franciscan, 1993.

Louhivuori, M. "The Palace of Hisham and 8th Century C.E. Iconoclasm." In *Encounters of the Children of Abraham from Ancient to Modern Times,* edited by A. Laato and P. Lindqvist, 199–213. Studies on the Children of Abraham 1. Leiden: Brill, 2010.

Luomanen, P. *Recovering Jewish-Christian Sects and Gospels*. VC 110. Leiden: Brill, 2012.

Lytle, E. "A Customs House of Our Own: Infrastructure, Duties and a Joint Association of Fishermen and Fishmongers (IK, 11.1a-Ephesos, 20)." In *Tout vendre, tout acheter: structures et équipements des marchés antiques,* edited by V. Chankowski and P. Karonis. Bordeaux: Ausonius, 2012.

Maʻoz, Z. U. "The Synagogue at Capernaum: A Radical Solution." In *The Roman and Byzantine Near East.* Vol. 2, *Some Recent Archaeological Research,* JRASup. 31, edited by J. H. Humphrey, 137–148. Ann Arbor: University of Michigan Press, 1999.

MacMullen, R. "The Historical Role of the Masses in Late Antiquity." In *Changes in the Roman Empire: Essays in the Ordinary,* 250–276. Princeton, NJ: Princeton University Press, 1990.

———. "The Preacher's Audience (AD 350–400)." *JTS* 40, no. 2 (1990): 503–511.

Magen, Y., and Y. Zionit. "Kiryat Sefer—A Jewish Village and Synagogue from the Second Temple Period." *Qadmoniot* 117 (1999): 25–32 (Hebrew).

Magness, J. "Did Galilee Decline in the Fifth Century? The Synagogue at Chorazin Reconsidered." In *Religion, Ethnicity, and Identity in Ancient Galilee: A Region in Transition,* WUNT 210, edited by J. Zangenberg, H. Attridge, and D. Martin, 259–274. Tübingen: Mohr Siebeck, 2007.

———. "The Chronology of Capernaum in the Early Islamic Period." *JAOS* 117, no. 3 (1997): 481–486.

———. "The Date of the Sardis Synagogue in Light of the Numismatic Evidence." *AJA* 109 (2005): 443–475.

———. "The Huqoq Synagogue: A Regional Variant of the Galilean Type." In *The Synagogue in Ancient Palestine: Current Issues and Emerging Trends,* FRLANT 279, edited by R. Bonnie, R. Hakola, and U. Tervahauta, 155–174. Göttingen: Vandenhoeck and Ruprecht, 2021.

———. "The Pottery from the Village of Capernaum and the Chronology of Galilean Synagogues." *Tel Aviv* 39 (2012): 110–122.

———. "The Question of the Synagogue: The Problem of Typology." In *Judaism in Antiquity. Part 3/Vol. 4: Where We Stand: Issues and Debates in Ancient Judaism: The Special Problem of the Synagogue,* edited by A. J. Avery-Peck and J. Neusner, 1–48. Leiden: Brill, 2001.

Magness, J. et al. "Huqoq (Lower Galilee) and Its Synagogue Mosaics: Preliminary Report on the Excavations of 2011–13." *JRA* 27 (2014): 327–355.

Magness, J. et al. "The Huqoq Excavation Project: 2014–2017 Interim Report." *BASOR* 380 (2018): 61–131.

Markus, T. *Buildings and Power: Freedom and Control in the Origin of Modern Buildings.* London: Routledge, 1993.

Martin, D. "Enacting Neighborhood." *Urban Geography* 24, no. 5 (2003): 361–385.
Martindale, J. R. *The Prosopography of the Later Roman Empire*. Vol. 2, *A.D. 395–527.* Cambridge: Cambridge University Press, 1980.
Matassa, Lidia. *Invention of the First-Century Synagogue*. Ancient Near Eastern Monographs 22. Atlanta: SBL, 2018.
Mattila, S. L. "Capernaum, Village of Naḥum, from Hellenistic to Byzantine Times." In *Galilee in the Late Second Temple and Mishnaic Periods*. Vol. 2, *The Archaeological Record from Cities, Towns, and Villages*, edited by D. A. Fiensy and J. R. Strange. Minneapolis: Fortress Press, 2015, 217–257.
———. "Inner Village Life in Galilee: A Diverse and Complex Phenomenon." In *Galilee in the Late Second Temple and Mishnaic Periods*. Vol. 1, *Life, Culture, and Society*, edited by D. A. Fiensy and J. R. Strange, 312–345. Minneapolis: Fortress Press, 2014.
———. "Revisiting Jesus' Capernaum: A Village of Only Subsistence-Level Fishers and Farmers?" In *The Galilean Economy in the Time of Jesus*, edited by D. A. Fiensy and R. K. Hawkins. 75–138. ECL 11. Atlanta: SBL, 2013.
Mayol, P. "The Neighborhood." In *M. de Certeau, L. Giard, and P. Mayol, The Practice of Everyday Life*. Vol. 2, *Living and Cooking*, translated by T. J. Tomasik, 7–13. Minneapolis: University of Minnesota Press, 1998.
Maza, S. *Thinking about History*. Chicago: University of Chicago Press, 2017.
Meyers, E. M., and C. L. Meyers. *Excavations at Ancient Nabratein: Synagogue and Environs*. Winona Lake, IN: Eisenbrauns, 2009.
———. "Meiron in Upper Galilee," in *Galilee in the Late Second Temple and Mishnaic Periods*. Vol. 2, *The Archaeological Record from Cities, Towns, and Villages*, edited by D. A. Fiensy and J. R. Strange (Minneapolis: Fortress Press, 2015).
Meyers, E. M., C. L. Meyers, and B. Gordon. "Sepphoris: Residential Area of the Western Summit." In *Galilee in the Late Second Temple and Mishnaic Periods*. 2 vols, edited by D. A. Fiensy and J. R. Strange. Minneapolis: Fortress Press, 2014, 2015.
Meyers, E. M., and J. F. Strange. *Archaeology, the Rabbis, and Early Christianity*. London: SCM Press, 1981.
Miller, S. *At the Intersection of Texts and Material Finds: Stepped Pools, Stone Vessels, and Ritual Purity among the Jews of Roman Galilee*. Göttingen: Vandenhoeck & Ruprecht, 2015.
———. "The Minim of Sepphoris Reconsidered." *HTR* 86, no. 4 (1993): 377–402.
Milson, D. *Art and Architecture of the Synagogue in Late Antique Palestine: In the Shadow of the Church*. AJEC 65. Leiden: Brill, 2007.
Mimouni, S. *Les fragments évangéliques judéo-chrétiens apocryphisés: Recherches et perspectives*. Paris: Gabalda, 2006.
Misgav, H., M. Artzy, and H. Cohen. "The Synagogue Inscription from Kursi." *JJMJS* 3 (2016): 167–169.
Morgenstern, M. "Christian Palestinian Aramaic." In *The Semitic Languages*, edited by S. Weninger, 628–637. Berlin: De Gruyter, 2012.

Mumford, L. *The City in History*. New York: Harcourt, Brace, and World, 1961.
Naveh, J. *On Stone and Mosaic: The Aramaic and Hebrew Inscriptions from Ancient Synagogues*. Jerusalem: Israel Exploration Society, 1978.
Nongbri, B. *Before Religion: A History of a Modern Concept*. New Haven: Yale University Press, 2013.
Nun, M. "Cast Your Net Upon the Waters." *Biblical Archaeology Review* 19, no. 6 (1993): 46–49, 51–56, 70.
———. "Ports of Galilee." *Biblical Archaeology Review* 25, no. 4 (1999): 18–23, 25–31, 64.
Oakman, D. E., and J. A. Overman. "Debate: Was the Galilean Economy Oppressive or Prosperous?" In *Galilee in the Late Second Temple and Mishnaic Period*, vol. 1, *Life, Culture, and Society*, edited by D. A. Fiensy and J. R. Strange, 346–365. Minneapolis: Fortress Press, 2014.
Oehl, B. "Die Altercatio Ecclesiae et Synagogae: Ein antijudaistischer Dialog der Spätantike." PhD dissertation, Universität Bonn, 2012.
Oliver, P. *Built to Meet Needs: Cultural Issues in Vernacular Architecture*. Oxford: Architectural Press, 2006.
Olsson, B. "'All My Teaching Was Done in Synagogues . . .' (John 18,20)." In *Theology and Christology in the Fourth Gospel: Essays by the Members of the SNTS Johannine Writings Seminar*, edited by G. van Belle, J. G. van der Watt, and P. J. Martin, 203–224. Leuven: Peeters, 2005.
Onn, A., and S. Weksler-Bdolah. "Horbat Umm el-'Umdan—A Jewish Village with a Synagogue from the Second Temple Period at Modi'in." *Qadmoniot* 130 (2005): 107–116 (Hebrew).
Orfali, G. *Capharnaüm et ses ruines. D'après les fouilles accomplies à Tell-Houm par la Custodie Franciscaine de Terre Sainte (1905–1921)*. Paris: Auguste Picard, 1922.
Ousterhout, R.G., ed. *The Blessings of Pilgrimage*. Champagne-Urbana: University of Illinois Press, 1990.
Overman, J. Andrew. *Church and Community in Crisis: The Gospel According to Matthew*. Valley Forge, PA: Trinity Press International, 1996.
Paget, J. C. "The Definition of the Terms Jewish Christian and Jewish Christianity in the History of Research." In *Jewish Believers in Jesus*, Skarsaune and Hvalvik, 22–52.
Patrich, J. "The Early Christianization of the Holy Land—The Archaeological Evidence." *Studi di Antichità Cristiana* 66 (2016): 265–293.
Rajak, T., and D. Noy. "Archisynagogoi: Office, Title and Social Status in the Greco-Jewish Synagogue." *Journal of Roman Studies* 83 (1993): 75–93.
Reed, J. *Archaeology and the Galilean Jesus: A Re-examination of the Evidence*. Harrisburg, PA: Trinity Press International, 2000.
Reeves, J. C. *Trajectories in Near Eastern Apocalyptic: A Postrabbinic Jewish Apocalypse Reader*. Atlanta: SBL, 2005.

Reinink, G. "Der edessenische 'Pseudo-Methodius.'" *Byzantinische Zeitschrift* 83 (1990): 31–45.
Reinink, G. J., editor. *Die syrische Apokalypse des Pseudo-Methodius*. 2 vols., Corpus Scriptorum Christianorum Orientalium 540–541. Leuven: Peeters, 1993.
Rhodes, P. "Demagogues and Demos in Athens." *Polis* 33, no. 2 (2016): 243–264.
Richardson, P. "An Architectural Case for Synagogues as Associations." In *The Ancient Synagogue: From Its Origins until 200 CE*, edited by B. Olsson and M. Zetterholm, 90–117. CBNTS 39. Stockholm: Almqvist & Wiksell, 2001.
———. *Building Jewish in the Roman East*. Waco, TX: Baylor University Press, 2004.
Riesner, R. "What Does Archaeology Teach Us about Early House Churches." *TTK* 78, no. 3–4 (2007): 159–185.
Richardson, P. "Early Synagogues as Collegia in the Diaspora and Palestine." In *Voluntary Associations in the Graeco-Roman World*, edited by J. S. Kloppenborg and S. G. Wilson. London: Routledge, 1996.
Robinson, E. *Biblical Researches in Palestine, Mount Sinai, and Arabia Petraea: A Journal of Travels for the Year 1838*. London: John Murray, 1841.
———. *Later Biblical Researches in Palestine and the Adjacent Regions: A Journal of Travels in the Year 1852*. London: John Murray, 1856.
Runesson, A. "Architecture, Conflict, and Identity Formation: Jews and Christians in Capernaum from the First to the Sixth Century." In *Religion, Ethnicity, and Identity in Ancient Galilee: A Region in Transition*, edited by J. Zangenberg, H. Attridge, and D. Martin, 231–257. WUNT 210. Tübingen: Mohr Siebeck, 2007.
———. "Rethinking Early Jewish–Christian Relations: Matthean Community History as Pharisaic Intragroup Conflict." *JBL* 127, no. 1 (2008): 95–132.
———. "Synagogues without Rabbis or Christians? Ancient Institutions beyond Normative Discourses." *Journal of Belief and Values* 38, no. 2 (2017): 159–172.
———. *The Origins of the Synagogue: A Socio-Historical Study*. CBNT 37. Stockholm: Almqvist & Wiksell International, 2001.
———. "The Question of Terminology: The Architecture of Contemporary Discussions on Paul." In *Paul within Judaism: Restoring the First-Century Context to the Apostle*, edited by M. D. Nanos and M. Zetterholm, 53–78. Minneapolis: Fortress Press, 201.
———. "What Does It Mean to Read New Testament Texts 'within Judaism'?" *NTS* 69 (2023): 299–312.
———. "What Never Belonged Together Cannot Part: Rethinking the So-Called Parting of the Ways Between Judaism and Christianity." In *Jews and Christians: Parting Ways in the First Two Centuries C.E.? Reflections on the Gains and Losses of a Model*, edited by J. Schröter, B. A. Edsall, and J. Verheyden. Berlin: De Gruyter, 2021.
Runesson, A., and W. V. Cirafesi. "Art and Architecture at Capernaum, Kefar 'Othnay, and Dura Europos." In *The Reception of Jesus in the First Three Centuries*. Vol. 3,

From Celsus to the Catacombs: Visual, Liturgical, and Non-Christian Receptions of Jesus in the Second and Third Centuries CE, edited by Chris L. Keith, 151–200. London: T&T Clark, 2020.

Runesson, A., D. Binder, and B. Olsson. *The Ancient Synagogue from its Origins to 200 CE*. AJEC 72. Leiden: Brill, 2008.

Runesson, A., and W. V. Cirafesi. "Reassessing the Impact of 70 CE on the Origins and Development of Palestinian Synagogues." In *The Synagogue in Ancient Palestine: Current Issues and Emerging Trends*, edited by R. Bonnie, R. Hakola, and U. Tervahauta, 37–57. Göttingen: Vandenhoeck & Ruprecht, 2021.

Runesson, R. "Centurions in the Jesus Movement? Rethinking Luke 7:1–5 in Light of the Gaianus Inscription at Kefar 'Othnay." *JBL* 142, no. 1 (2023): 129–149.

Rüpke, J. *Religious Deviance in the Roman World: Superstition or Individuality?* Translated by D.M.B. Richardson. Cambridge: Cambridge University Press, 2016.

Rutgers, L. V. "The Synagogue as Foe in Early Christian Literature." In *"Follow the Wise": Studies in Jewish History and Culture in Honor of Lee I. Levine*, edited by Z. Weiss et al., 449–468. Winona Lake, IN: Eisenbrauns, 2010.

Ryan, J. *From the Passion to the Holy Sepulcher: Memories of Jesus in Place, Pilgrimage, and Early Commemorative Churches over the First Three Centuries*. The Reception of Jesus in the First Three Centuries 7. London: T&T Clark, 2021.

———. "Jesus and Synagogue Disputes: Recovering the Institutional Context of Luke 13:10–17." *Catholic Biblical Quarterly* 79, no. 1 (2017): 41–59.

———. "Jesus at the Crossroads of Inference and Imagination: The Relevance of R. G. Collingwood's Philosophy of History for Current Methodological Discussions in Historical Jesus Research." *Journal for the Study of Historical Jesus* 13 (2015): 66–89.

———. *The Role of the Synagogue in the Aims of Jesus*. Minneapolis: Fortress Press, 2017.

Said, E. *Orientalism*. New York: Random House, 1978.

Saldarini, A. J. "The Gospel of Matthew and Jewish–Christian Conflict in the Galilee." In *The Galilee in Late Antiquity*, edited by Lee I. Levine, 23–38. Cambridge, MA: Harvard University Press, 1992.

Sanders, E.P. *Judaism: Practice and Belief 63 BCE–66 CE*. Philadelphia: SCM Press, 1992.

Sanders, J. T. *Schismatics, Sectarians, Dissidents, Deviants: The First One Hundred Years of Jewish–Christian Relations*. London: SCM Press, 1993.

Schäfer, P. *Jesus in the Talmud*. Princeton, NJ: Princeton University Press, 2007.

Scheidel, W. "Slavery." In *The Cambridge Companion to the Roman Economy*, edited by W. Scheidel, 89–113. Cambridge: Cambridge University Press, 2012.

Schick, R. *The Christian Communities of Palestine from Byzantine to Islamic Rule: A Historical and Archaeological Study*. Princeton, NJ: Darwin Press, 1995.

Schneider, A. M. "Ḥirbet El-Minje am See Genesareth." *Annales archéologiques de Syrie* 2 (1952): 23–45.

Schremer, A. *Brothers Estranged: Heresy, Christianity and Jewish Identity in Late Antiquity.* Oxford: Oxford University Press, 2010.

Schröter, J., B.A. Edsall, and J. Verheyden, eds. *Jews and Christians: Parting Ways in the First Two Centuries C.E.? Reflections on the Gains and Losses of a Model.* Berlin: De Gruyter, 2021.

Schwartz, D. "Was 70 CE a Watershed in Jewish History?" In *Was 70 CE a Watershed in Jewish History? On Jews and Judaism before and after the Destruction of the Second Temple,* edited by D. R. Schwartz and Zeev Weiss, 1–19. Leiden: Brill, 2012.

Schwartz, J., and P. J. Tomson. "When Rabbi Eliezer Was Arrested for Heresy." *JSIJ* 10 (2012): 145–181.

Schwartz, S. *Imperialism and Jewish Society, 200 BCE to 640 CE.* Princeton, NJ: Princeton University Press, 2001.

———. "On the Program and Reception of the Synagogue Mosaics." In *From Dura to Sepphoris: Studies in Jewish Art and Society in Late Antiquity,* edited by L. I. Levine and Z. Weiss, 165–182. JRASup. 40. Portsmouth, RI: Journal of Roman Archaeology, 2000.

Seland, E. H. *A Global History of the Ancient World: Asia, Europe, and Africa Before Islam.* London: Routledge, 2021.

Seymour, W. W. *The Cross in Tradition, History, and Art.* London: G. P. Putnam's Sons, 1898.

Shalev-Hurvitz, Vered. *Holy Sites Encircled: The Early Byzantine Concentric Churches of Jerusalem.* Oxford: Oxford University Press, 2015.

Shay, O. "Collectors and Collections in Palestine at the Conclusion of the Ottoman Era." *Le Muséon* 122, no. 3 (2009): 449–471.

Shepherdson, C. *Anti-Judaism and Christian Orthodoxy: Ephrem's Hymns in Fourth-Century Syria.* NAPSMS 20. Washington, DC: Catholic University of America Press, 2008.

Shepardson, C. "Between Polemic and Propaganda: Evoking the Jews of Fourth-Century Antioch." *Journal of the Jesus Movement in its Jewish Setting* 2 (2015): 151–182.

Sim, D. C. "The Gospel of Matthew and Galilee: An Evaluation of an Emerging Hypothesis." *ZNW* 107, no. 2 (2016): 141–169.

Sivan, H. "From Byzantine to Persian Jerusalem: Jewish Perspectives and Jewish/Christian Polemics." *GRBS* 41 (2000): 277–306.

———. *Palestine in Late Antiquity.* Oxford: Oxford University Press, 2008.

Skarsaune, O. "Jewish Believers in Jesus in Antiquity—Problems of Definition, Method, and Sources." In *Jewish Believers in Jesus,* edited by O. Skarsaune and R. Hvalvik, 3–21. Peabody, MA: Hendrickson, 2007.

Smith, E. C. *Jewish Glass and Christian Stone: A Materialist Mapping of the "Parting of the Ways."* London: Routledge, 2018.

Snyder, G. *Ante-Pacem: Archaeological Evidence of Church Life before Constantine*, 2nd ed. Macon: Mercer University Press, 2003.

Spigel, C. *Ancient Synagogue Seating Capacities: Methodology, Analysis, and Limits.* TSAJ 149. Tübingen: Mohr Siebeck, 2012.

———. "Reconsidering the Question of Separate Seating in Ancient Synagogues." *JJS* 63, no. 1 (2012): 62–83.

Spijkerman, A. *Cafarnao III: Le monete della città.* Jerusalem: Franciscan Press, 1975.

Srouji, E. "The Fall of a Galilean Village during the 1948 Palestine War: An Eyewitness Account." *Journal of Palestine Studies* 33 (2004): 71–80.

Stegemann, E. W., and W. Stegemann. *The Jesus Movement: A Social History of Its First Century.* Minneapolis: Fortress Press, 1999.

Stemberger, G. *Judaica Minor II: Geschichte und Literatur des rabbinischen Judentums*, TSAJ 138. Tübingen: Mohr Siebeck, 2010.

Stern, K. "Prayer as Power: Amulets, Graffiti, and Vernacular Writing in Ancient Levantine Synagogues," in *The Synagogue in Ancient Palestine: Current Issues and Emerging Trends*, edited by R. Bonnie, R. Hakola, and U. Tervahauta, 221–245. FRLANT 279. Göttingen: Vandenhoeck & Ruprecht, 2021.

Stern, K. B. *Writing on the Wall: Graffiti and the Forgotten Jews of Antiquity.* Princeton, NJ: Princeton University Press, 2018.

Strange, J. F. "Archaeological Evidence of Jewish Believers?" In *Jewish Believers in Jesus*. Edited by O. Skarsaune and R. Hvalvik, 729

———. "The Archaeology of Religion at Capernaum, Synagogue and Church." In *Religious Texts and Material Contexts*, edited by J. Neusner and J. F. Strange, 43–63. Studies in Ancient Judaism. Lanham, MD: University Press of America, 2001.

———. "The Capernaum and Herodium Publications (Part 1)." *BASOR* 226 (1977): 65–73.

———. "The Capernaum and Herodium Publications (Part 2)." *BASOR* 233 (1979): 63–69 (66–67).

Strange, J. F., and H. Shanks. "Synagogue Where Jesus Preached Found at Capernaum." *Biblical Archaeology Review* 9, no. 6 (1983): 24–32.

Strange, J. R. *Archaeology, Bible, Politics, and the Media: Proceedings of the Duke University Conference, April 23–24, 2009.* Vol. 6. Göttingen: Vandenhoeck & Ruprecht, 2012.

———. "Christianity: The Fourth Century Christian Basilica." In *Religious Texts and Material Contexts*, edited by J. Neusner and J. F. Strange, 89–138. Lanham, MD: University Press of America, 2001.

———. "Does Archaeology Generate Propositions about Religion?" In *A City Set on a Hill: Essays in Honor of James F. Strange*, 298–317. Mountain Home, AZ: BorderStone Press, 2014.

Talgam, R. *Mosaics of Faith: Floors of Pagans, Jews, Samaritans, Christians, and Muslims in the Holy Land.* Jerusalem/University Park, PA: Yad Ben-Zvi Press/Penn State University Press, 2014.

Tarkhanova, S. "The Friezes with the 'Peopled Scrolls' Motif in the Capernaum Synagogue: Dating by Stylistic Method and Some Aspects of the Reconstruction." In *The Synagogue in Ancient Palestine,* 195–218.

Taylor, J. "Capernaum and its 'Jewish–Christians': A Re-Examination of the Franciscan Excavations." *BAIAS* 9 (1989–90): 7–28.

———. *Christians and the Holy Places: The Myth of Jewish–Christian Origins.* Oxford: Oxford University Press, 1993.

Tervahauta, U. "Sacred Space and Torah Shrines in Late Antique Synagogues." In *The Synagogue in Ancient Palestine,* edited by Bonnie, Hakola, Tervahauta, 311–336.

Testa, E. *Cafarnao IV: I graffiti della casa di S. Pietro.* Jerusalem: Franciscan, 1972.

———. *Il simbolismo dei giudeo-cristiani.* Jerusalem: Franciscan, 1962.

———. *The Faith of the Mother Church: An Essay on the Theology of the Judeo-Christians.* Translated by P. Rotondi. Jerusalem: Franciscan, 1992.

Theodoropoulou, T. "Salting the East: Evidence for Salt Fish and Fish Products from the Aegean Sea in Roman Times." In *Fish & Ships: Production et commerce des salsamenta durant l'Antiquité,* edited by E. Botte and V. Leitch. Bibliothèque d'Archéologie Méditerranéenne et Africaine 17. Arles Cédex: Édition Errance, 2014.

Thompson, R. W., translator, and J. Howard-Johnson. *The Armenian History Attributed to Sebeos.* Vol. 1, *Translation and Notes.* Translated Texts for Historians 31. Liverpool: Liverpool University Press, 1999.

Treadwell, L. "Abd al-Malik's Coinage Reforms: The Role of the Damascus Mint." *Revue numismatique* 165 (2009): 357–381.

Trebilco, P. *Jewish Communities in Asia Minor.* SNTSMS 69. Cambridge: Cambridge University Press, 1991.

Tsafrir, Y. "The Byzantine Setting and Its Influence on Ancient Synagogues." In *The Synagogue in Late Antiquity,* edited by L.I. Levine. Philadelphia: ASOR Press, 1987, 147–157.

———. "The Synagogues in Capernaum and Meroth and the Dating of the Galilean Synagogue." In *The Roman and Byzantine Near East.* Vol. 2, *Some Recent Archaeological Research,* edited by John H. Humphrey, 151–161. JRASup 14. Ann Arbor: Journal of Roman Archaeology, 1995.

Tzaferis, V. "Capernaum." In *NEAEHL* 1: 291–296.

———., ed. *Excavations at Capernaum.* Vol. 1, *1978–1982.* Winona Lake, IN: Eisenbrauns, 1989.

van der Dussen, W. J. *History as a Science: The Philosophy of R.G. Collingwood.* The Hauge: Martinus Nijhoff, 1981.

Verheyden, J., ed. *Jesus in the Galilean Crisis: New Perspectives from Qumran.* BETL 163. Leuven: Peeters, 2002.

Visotzky, B. "Overturning the Lamp." *JJS* 38 (1987): 72–80.
Whitcomb, D. "From Pastoral Peasantry to Tribal Urbanites: Arab Tribes and the Foundation of the Islamic State in Syria." In *Nomads, Tribes, and the State in the Ancient Near East,* edited by J. Szuchman, 241–259. Chicago: University of Chicago Press, 2009.
White, L. M. *Building God's House in the Roman World: Architectural Adaptation among Pagans, Jews, and Christians.* Baltimore: Johns Hopkins University Press, 1990.
———. "Early Christian Architecture: The First Five Centuries." In *The Early Christian World,* edited by P. Esler, 2 vols. London: Routledge, 2017, 1: 673–746.
———. *From Jesus to Christianity: How Four Generations of Visionaries and Storytellers Created the New Testament and Christian Faith.* New York: HarperSanFrancisco, 2004.
———. *The Social Origins of Christian Architecture.* Vol. 1, *Building God's House in the Roman World: Architectural Adaptation among Pagans, Jews, and Christians.* Baltimore: Johns Hopkins University Press, 1990.
———. *The Social Origins of Christian Architecture.* Vol. 2, *Texts and Monuments for the Christian Domus Ecclesiae in its Environment.* Harvard Theological Studies 42. Valley Forge, PA: Trinity Press International, 1997.
Wilken, R. L. *John Chrysostom and the Jews: Rhetoric and Reality in the 4th Century.* Berkley, CA: University of California Press, 1983.
Wilkinson, J. *Egeria's Travels.* London: SPCK, 1971.
Williams, F., translator. *The Panarion of Epiphanius of Salamis: Book I (Sects 1–46),* 2nd rev. exp. ed. (Leiden: Brill, 2009).
Wilson, C. W. *The Recovery of Jerusalem: A Narrative of Exploration and Discovery in the City and the Holy Land.* London: Richard Bentley & Son, 1871.
Wilson, J. *The Lands of the Bible Visited and Described,* Vol. 2. Edinburgh: William Whyte, 1847.
Wilson, J. F. "The Gold Hoard." In *Capernaum I, 1978–1982,* edited by V. Tzaferis, 145–179. Winona Lake, IN: Eisenbrauns, 1989.
Xenophontos, C., C. Elliot, and J. G. Malpas. "Major and Trace-Element Geochemistry Used in Tracing the Provenance of Late Bronze Age and Roman Basalt Artefacts from Cyprus Edwards." *Levant* 20 (1988): 169–183.
Yacobi, H. *Israel and Africa: A Genealogy of Moral Geography.* London: Routledge, 2016.
Yasin, A. M. "Prayers on Site: The Materiality of Devotional Graffiti and the Production of Early Christian Sacred Space." In *Viewing Inscriptions in the Late Antique and Medieval World,* edited by A. Eastmond, 36–60. Cambridge: Cambridge University Press, 2015.
Yeivin, Z. *The Synagogue at Korazim: The 1962–1964, 1980–1987 Excavations.* IAA Reports 10. Jerusalem: IAA, 2000 (Hebrew and English).

Yuval-Hacham, N. "Mishnah Avodah Zarah 4:5—The Faces of Effacement: Between Textual and Artistic Evidence." In *Talmuda de-Eretz Israel: Archaeology and the Rabbis in Late Antique Palestine,* edited by S. Fine and A. Koller, 29–52. Berlin: Walter de Gruyter, 2014.

———. "'You Shall Not Make for Yourself Any Given Image...': On Jewish Iconoclasm in Late Antiquity." *Ars Judaica* 6 (2010): 7–22.

Zangenberg, J. "From the Galilean Jesus to the Galilean Silence: Earliest Christianity in the Galilee until the Fourth Century CE." In *The Rise and Expansion of Christianity in the First Three Centuries of the Common Era,* edited by C. K. Rothschild and J. Schröter, 75–108. Tübingen: Mohr Siebeck, 2013.

Zangenberg, J., H. Attridge, and D. Martin, eds. *Religion, Ethnicity, and Identity in Ancient Galilee: A Region in Transition.* WUNT 210. Tübingen: Mohr Siebeck, 2007.

Zangenberg, J. K. "The Menorah on the Mosaic Floor from the Late Roman/Early Byzantine Synagogue at Ḥorvat Kur." *Israel Exploration Journal* 67 (2017): 110–126.

Zeichmann, C. "Capernaum: A 'Hub' for the Historical Jesus or the Markan Evangelist?" *Journal for the Study of Historical Jesus* 15 (2017): 147–165.

———. "Loanwords or Code-Switching? Latin Transliteration and the Setting of Mark's Composition." *Journal of the Jesus Movement in its Jewish Setting* 4 (2017): 42–64.

———. *The Roman Army and the New Testament.* Lanham: Lexington/Fortress Academic, 2018.

Zetterholm, K. H. "Alternate Visions of Judaism and Their Impact on the Formation of Rabbinic Judaism." *Journal of the Jesus Movement in its Jewish Setting* 1 (2014): 127–153.

———. "Israel and the Nations in the Pseudo-Clementine Homilies and Recognitions 1.27–72: Receptions of the Gospel of Matthew." In *Matthew within Judaism,* edited by A. Runesson and D. Gurtner. ECL. Atlanta: SBL, 2020, 399–426.

———. *Jews and Gentiles in the Early Jesus Movement: An Unintended Journey.* Minneapolis: Fortress Press, 2013.

Zetterholm, K. H., A. Runesson, C. Wassén, and M. Zetterholm, editors. *Negotiating Identities: Conflict, Conversion, and Consolidation in Early Judaism and Christianity (200 BCE—600 CE).* Lanham/Minneapolis: Lexington Books/Fortress Academic, 2022.

Zetterholm, K. H., and A. Runesson, editors. *Within Judaism? Interpretive Trajectories in Judaism, Christianity, and Islam from the First to the Twenty-First Century.* Lanham/Minneapolis: Lexington Books/Fortress Academic, 2023.

Zetterholm, M. "A Struggle among Brothers: An Interpretation of the Relations between Jews and Christians in Ostia." In *The Synagogue of Ancient Ostia and the Jews of Rome,* edited by B. Olsson et al., 101–113. Stockholm: Paul Åström, 2001.

ANCIENT SOURCES INDEX

Hebrew Bible

Exodus
16   76

Numbers
11:4–9   76

Psalms
55:24   97 n.64

Proverbs
1:14   95
5:8   220

Isaiah
53:14   76

Second Temple Jewish Literature

Josephus

Antiquities of the Jews
14:213–216   55 n.35
16:42–43   56 n.42, 113 n.108
17:282–283   24 n.32

Jewish War
2:411   114 n.114
3:506–521   18 n.9

Life
276–281   57 n.43, 113 n.109
294–295   57 n.43, 113 n.109
403   18 n.8

LXX

Susana (Old Greek)
28   57 n.43, 113 n.107

New Testament

Gospel of Matthew
4:12–22   19
4:13   5
4:18–22   40 n.92
8:5–13   74 n.94
8:5   20 n.15
8:14–15   102
8:14   84 n.15
9:9   19
10:17   57 n.43, 113 n.107
11:20–24   229
11:23   19
13:47–50   40 n.92
23:24   57 n.43
23:34   113 n.107

Gospel of Mark
1:16–21   19
1:16–20   40 n.92
1:21–28   74
1:21–22   76
1:21   20
1:23   76
1:29–35   102
1:29   75, 84 n.15, 114 n.115

2:1–2	114 n.115	9:31	115
2:1	5, 19	15:21	56 n.42, 113 n.108
2:13–14	32–33		
2:14	19	Philo	
3:1–6	74, 76		
3:6	76	*Contempl.*	
		25–33	113
Gospel of Luke			
4:16–31	56–57 n.42, 113 nn.108–109	*Hypoth.*	
		7:13	76 n.102
4:20	58 n.45		
4:31	19, 76	*Prob.*	
4:33	74, 76	80–83	54–55 n.35
4:38–39	102	**Rabbinic Literature**	
4:38	75 n.98, 84 n.15		
5:1–11	19, 37, 40 n.92	Mishnah	
5:27	19	*B. Bat.*	
7:1–5	19, 24	2:3	210
7:3	24, 76		
7:5	20, 45, 48 n.13, 74, 75	*Ber.*	
		7:3	56 n.40
10:13–15	19		
		Bik.	
Gospel of John		1:4	56 n.40
2:12	5		
4:46–54	20 n.15	*'Eruv.*	
6:22–59	19	6:1	208 n.23
6:25–71	76	6:5	208 n.23
6:41	76	10:10	56 n.40, 76 n.102
6:45	76		
6:52	76	*Mak.*	
6:59	20, 74, 76	3:12	56 n.40, 57 n.43, 58 n.45
18:20	75		
21:1–14	40 n.92		
		Meg.	
Acts		3:1–3	56 n.40
2:44	95	3:1	113 n.110
6:9–10	55 n.35	3:4–4:10	56 n.40

Ancient Sources Index

Ned.
5:4–5   56 n.40
5:5   76 n.101
9:2   56 n.40

Neg.
13:12   56 n.40

Pesaḥ.
4:4   56 n.40

Rosh Hash.
3:7   56 n.40

Sanh.
10:1   96 n.64

Shebu.
4:10   56 n.40

Sotah
7:7–8   56 n.40, 58 n.45

Sukkah
3:13   56 n.40

Ter.
11:10   56 n.40

Yoma
7:1   56 n.40, 58 n.45

Tosefta

Ḥul.
2:20–24   91, 94 n.55
2:24   99

Meg.
3:21   58 n.45, 76 n.102

Sukkah
4:6   41 n.97, 76 n.102

Ter.
2:13   58 n.45

Jerusalem Talmud (Yerushalmi)

Avodah Zarah
2:2   94 n.55

Meg.
1.9.3   142

Shabb.
14:4   94 n.55

Sotah
7.2.3   142

Babylonian Talmud (Bavli)

Avodah Zarah
16b–17a   94 n.55, 99
17a   220
27b   94 n.55

Bava Kamma
82b–83a   142

Ber.
17a–b   96 n.64

Git.
55b–57a   96 n.64

Sanh.
61b   199
106a   97 n.64
106b   97 n.64
107b   97 n.64

Shabb.
72b	199
116a–b	96 n.62

Sotah
49b	110 n.100, 140 n.61, 142

Midrashim

Qohelet Rabbah
1:8	45 n.5, 83–85, 92–94, 94 n.55, 96, 98–99, 111, 115, 202 n.4, 220–221, 221 n.56
7:26	83, 84, 93–94, 128 n.33, 131

Pesikta de Rav Kahana
18:5	133

Pesikta Rabbati
34–37	230 n.16

Greek and Latin Literature

Dio Cassius

Hist. rom.
69.12.2	24 n.32

Periplus of the Erythraean Sea
No. 19	21

Plato

Laws
7:824	40 n.91

Tacitus

Ann.
13:50–51	38 n.85

Hist.
5	96 n.62

Ancient Christian Literature

Acts of Thomas
39	97 n.64
69	97 n.64

Altercatio ecclesiae et synagogae
194–95

Apostolic Canons (with entry number from Linder, *Early Middle Ages*)
11 (Linder no. 124)	219 n.50, 222 n.58
65 (Linder nos. 2, 103, 116, 120, 177, 948)	219, 219 nn.50–52
70 (Linder nos. 3, 121, 116, 177)	219, 219 n.50, 220
71 (Linder nos. 4, 105, 122, 138, 950)	219, 219 n.51, 220
72 (Linder nos. 110, 138)	219 n.51

Armenian History Attributed to Sebeos
34	226 n.3, 231 n.20
34:115	230 n.15
42:136	232

Augustine

Civ. Dei
21:4	173 n.53

Ancient Sources Index

Epiphanius of Salamis

Panarion   82
30   82 n.11
30:2:7–9   92
30:5:1   128 n.30
30:5:5   93
30:11:9–10   92, 127 n.27
30:11:10   44–45 n.5, 93 n.50
30:12   131 n.42
30:12.2–3   128 n.32
30:12:4   132
30:12:9   132
30:16:7   91 n.45

Epistle of Barnabas
15:8–9   173 n.55
15:8   175

Eusebius

Onom.
172   94

Eutychius of Alexandria

Annals
30   226 n.3, 231 n.20

Gospel of the Hebrews   81 n.6

Gospel of Peter
14:60   40 n.92

Gospel of Thomas
8   40 n.92

Hippolytus

Antichr.
14–15   229 n.10

John Chrysostom

Adversos Ioudaeos   219 nn. 48, 50

Hom. Gal.
1:7   219 n.50

Julius Africanus

Letter to Aristides (*apud* Eusebius, *Hist. eccl.* 1:7:14)   92

Justin Martyr

Dial.
10   95 n.59
41   174 n.55
137   58 n.45
138   174 n.55

Justinian I (entry number from Linder, *Early Middle Ages*)

Justinian Code (*CJust*)
1:6   175 n.62
1:9:18 (Linder no. 44)   218 n.46

Novels of Justinian (entry number from Linder, *Early Middle Ages*)
131 (Linder nos. 15, 23, 33, 34, 99)   218 n.46

Liber Pontificalis
1   177 n.65

Origen

Contra Celsum
6:27   95 n.59
6:40   95 n.59

Hom. Lev.
5.8   12 n.12, 219 n.50

Sel. Exod.
12.46   12 n.12, 219 n.50

Pilgrim Literature

Itinerarium Egeriae (*Corpus Scriptorum Ecclesiasticorum Latinorum* [*CSEL*])
39:112–113   107 n.90, 120 n.8

Piacenza Pilgrim (CSEL)
39:163   168 n.37

Pseudo-Clementines

Rec.
1:27–71   91, 91 n.45, 92 n.46

Pseudo-Methodius

Apocalypse
10:6–12:8   227
11:13   227
12   227 n.7
13:1–9   227
13:11–18   228
13:21–14:12   228
14:1   229
14:11   228
14:13–14   228

Tertullian

Apol.
16:1–2   96 n.62

Theodosian Code (CTh)
15:5:5   177, 177 n.63, 178
16   194
16:6   175 n.62
16:7:4   176 n.62
16:8   187
16:8:21   218 n.45
16:8:25   154, 218 n.45
16:8:26   218 n.45

Theophanes the Confessor

Chronicle
627–628 CE   226 n.3, 231 n.20

Early Islamic Literature

Sunan ibn Mājah

Hadīth 2254   244 n.69, 246

Quran
9:33   237–38 n.46, 245 n.72
112:1–3   238 n.46, 245 n.72

Papyri

Aegyptische Urkunden aus den Königlichen (later *Staatlichen*) *Museen zu Berlin, Griechische Urkunden (BGU)*
4.1118   33 n.67

Chrest. Wilck.
223   33 n.67

Corpus Papyrorum Judaicarum (CPJ)
1.129   58 n.45

O. Wilck.
326   37 n.83

P. Dura
19   209 n.23

P. Fayûm
67–76   33 n.68

P. Hev/Se
60 (Greek)   110 n.100, 140 n.61

Ancient Sources Index

63 (Greek)   110 n.100, 140 n.61

P. Masada
722   24

P. Sijp. (= *P. Gen.* Inv. 181)
30   37 n.83, 38, 38 n.86

P. Yadin
18   110 n.100, 140 n.61
52 (= 5/6 *Hev* 52; *SB* VIII)   110 n.100, 140 n.61

Papiri greci e latini (PSI)
4.383   33 n.67, 38 n.85

Sammelbuch griechischer Urkunden aus Ägypten (SB)
1.5729   33 n.67
10.10266   33 n.67

Urkunden der Ptolemäerzeit (UPZ)
1.112.8   33 n.67

Inscriptions

Corpus Inscriptionum Iudaeae / Palaestinae (CIIP)
I 2: no. 1119   58 n.45, 110 n.100
I 2: no. 1120   58 n.45, 110 n.100
V 1: no. 6081   156 n.12
V 1: no. 6415   140 n.61, 189
V 1: no. 6416   189
V 1: no. 6651   140 n.61

Corpus Inscriptionum Judaicarum (CIJ)
II 1400   110 n.100, 140 n.61
II 1402   110 n.100, 140 n.61
II 1404 (Theodotos Inscription)   58 n.45, 75, 76 n.102

Die Inschriften von Ephesos (IEph)
20   33 n.69, 34 n.71, 36
1503   33 n.69

Greco-Roman Associations (GRA)
II 113 (= *IJO* II 168)   23 n.30
III 156 (= *JIGRE* 24)   23 n.29

Inscriptiones Latinae Selectae (ILS)
8858   33 n.69

Inscriptiones Scythiae Minoris graecae et latinae (IGLS)
16.1475   21 n.19

Kursi Synagogue Inscription   191–93

L'année épigraphique (AE)
1966.493   21 n.19

Monumenta Asiae Minoris Antiqua (MAMA)
VI 263   23 n.30
VI 264   23 n.30

Runesson, Binder, and Olsson, *The Ancient Synagogue from Its Origins to 200 CE: A Source Book (ASSB)*
No. 103 (= *IJO* II 168; *CIJ* 2.766; *MAMA* VI 264; Julia Severa Inscription)   75 n.94
No. 151 (= *JIGRE* 27 // *CIJ* 2.1443)   23 n.29

SUBJECT INDEX

Abbasids, 235–38, 238 n.49, 247
Abd al-Malik ibn Marwan, 237 n.46
Anti-Jewish polemic, 8, 100, 126, 132, 137, 142, 154–56, 173, 179, 195 n.112, 219 n.50
Antioch, 12 n.12, 91 n.41, 101 n.77, 141 n.63, 142, 177 n.65, 212 n.26, 218 n.47, 219 n.50, 223 n.58
Apocalypticism (in Late Antiquity, Jewish and Christian), 11, 226–33, 238
Arab / Islamic expansion ("conquest"), 225, 226, 231, 232–39
Architecture (anthropology of)
    Monumental architecture, 10, 153, 157, 158–162, 167
    Ritual killing and ruination, 162, 163
    Vernacular architecture, 117–125, 137, 138, 139, 144, 148, 149, 153, 167, 168 n.38
Attraction to Christianity, 221, 222
Attraction to Judaism / "Judaizers," 10, 78, 139, 141, 142, 154, 156, 219 n.50, 220, 222
Asclepiodotus (Praetorian Prefect of the East, 423–425 CE), 187
Associations, Greco-Roman (general), 106 n.88, 113, 114
    Cult associations, 9, 54, 122, 123, 144, 145
    Philosophical associations, 54, 55 n.35
    Trade/occupational associations, 9, 17, 22, 32, 36–38, 41, 54, 55 n.35, 193

Basilica (churches and synagogues), 41 n.97, 98, 101 n.77, 122, 157, 168 n.37, 170, 170 n.42, 171 n.48, 197, 198
Basalt stone, 27, 29–31, 41, 60, 61–64, 65 n.64, 66, 67, 69–71, 73, 105 n.84, 187 n.87, 195, 197, 214, 235
Battle of Jābiya-Yarmūk, 226, 233
Bordeaux Pilgrim, 118, 135, 168 n.38

Capernaum
    As the "Town of Jesus," 1, 4–7, 252, 254
    Its identification, 5 n.4, 43 n.1, 100
    Its purchase by the Franciscans, 6–7
    Modern archaeological park, 1–7, 249–54
    Modern memorial church, 249–54
Centurions, 20–25, 45, 63, 76, 78
Coins/Numismatics (in Capernaum), 28, 60, 61, 68, 186 n.82, 211 n.26, 218 n.47, 235, 237, 238, 245–47
Commemoration and memory (in architecture), 83 n.14, 118 n.6, 124, 139, 143, 145–50, 154, 161,

163, 164, 168, 169, 170, 171 n.48,
173, 174, 187, 249, 250, 251
Concentric churches (general), 122,
169–70, 171 n.46, 171 n.48,
172–74, 175 n.59, 179
In Capernaum (octagonal church),
10, 39, 98, 101–3, 112, 121,
138, 150, 157, 158, 162,
163–76, 178, 179, 182, 184,
193, 195, 197, 198, 200, 202,
206, 218 n.47, 223, 234 n.30,
235 n.36, 238, 244 n.70, 247,
249–52, 254
Other sites
Golden Church (Antioch), 101 n.77
San Vitale (north Italy), 101 n.77
Constantine, 8, 80, 86, 89 n.36, 90, 92,
111, 116–18, 125, 127, 129, 131
n.43, 132, 138, 168, 221 n.56
Constantinople, 156, 177
Courtyards (in Capernaum), 29, 30, 39,
40, 61, 66–68, 71, 72, 103, 181,
182, 198, 208–10, 213, 214, 216,
236
Custodia Terra Sancta, 6–8, 249–52

Dome of the Rock, 228 n.7, 238 n.46,
245 n.72
Domus ecclesia / house church /
christaeum 10, 106, 117, 123,
123 n.16, 125, 127–34, 136–41,
143–45, 148–51, 153, 162, 163,
167, 168 –69 n.38, 171, 178 n.66
Dura Europos (general), 108, 146, 208
n.23, 212
Christ-oriented building, 106–7
n.89, 112, 122, 123, 144
Mithraeum, 144, 145
Synagogue, 144

Edward Robinson, 43, 44, 180
Egeria, Pilgrim, 70 n.79, 107, 120 n.8,
124, 126, 135, 139, 143, 144, 150,
169 n.38, 186 n.84, 252

Festival of Peter and Paul, 177, 178
Fishing (fisherman, industry), 16, 17,
19, 20, 22, 32–41, 78, 249, 251,
253

Galilee, other sites
Bar'am, 44, 188, 199 n.127
Chorazin (Korazim), 180 n.71, 182
n.77, 188, 199 n.127
Gush Ḥalav, 70 n.79, 180 n.71, 188,
236 n.41
Hamat Gader, 45 n.5, 189, 190, 202,
217
Huqoq, 10, 188, 189 n.91, 199
n.126, 221 n.56, 229
Hurvat Kur, 10, 221 n.56
Magdala (Migdal), 17, 33, 34 n.73,
55, 57, 59 n.47, 69, 70 n.81,
73, 75
Meiron, 30, 44, 180 n.71, 188, 212
Meroth, 199 n.127, 236 n.41
Nabratein, 70 n.79, 156 n.12, 180
n.71, 188, 199 n.127, 236
n.41, 239 n.51
Nazareth, 4, 16, 26, 41, 45, 58 n.45,
80, 91 n.44, 92, 93, 127, 130,
186, 253
Sepphoris, 31, 33, 40 n.90, 45 n.5,
91–93, 127, 127 n.28, 133,
136, 190 n.95, 212
Tiberias, 27, 32, 33, 40 n.90, 45
n.5, 70 n.79, 92, 93 n.50, 127,
128, 131, 132, 136, 140 n.61,
166–67 n.35, 187, 191–93,

Subject Index

196, 221 n.56, 226, 229, 236
  n.41, 238 n.49, 246
Wadi Hamam, 10, 70 n.79, 188, 189
  n.91, 229
Golan Heights (general), 82 n.91, 192
  n.101
  Gamla, 55, 56, 73
  Kursi, 192 n.101
  Umm el-Qanatir, 70 n.79
Graffiti
  At Capernaum, 107–11, 123, 125,
    126, 135, 139–41, 143–48,
    218 n.47
  At other sites, 96, 144–47

Harbor
  of Capernaum, 25, 32–34, 37–39, 41
  of Roman Ephesos, 36
  Other sites, 21
Heraclius, Byzantine Emperor, 226,
  231, 232
Heresiology, 10, 11, 13, 82, 83 n.14,
  100, 129, 130, 131, 133, 154 n.5,
  178, 179, 195 n.112
Hisham ibn Abd al-Malik, 241–42 n.60
Historical Jesus, 5, 15, 19 n.11, 76, 81, 90
Historiography, 48–51, 53, 74, 77, 82,
  86, 124 n.18, 129, 156, 233
Houses (in Capernaum), 29–31, 39, 39
  n.88, 63, 65, 66, 71, 72, 103, 118,
  122, 167, 203, 207–12, 214, 215,
  234 n.30, 235

Iconoclasm, 239–45

Jerusalem temple, 17, 75, 125
Jewish Patriarch, 126, 127, 131, 132,
  191 n.100
Joseph of Tiberias, 92, 93, 127–29, 131,
  136

Judea, villages with early Roman
  synagogues
  Umm el-Umdan, 55, 73
  Kiryat Sefer, 55, 73
Justinian I, 13, 100, 135, 155, 175

Kathisma Church, 170, 171, 202, 242,
  243, 244 n.70
Kefar 'Othnay, 20, 90, 106–7 n.89, 112,
  121–23
Khirbet al-Mafjar, 242 n.60
Khirbet al-Minya, 43 n.1, 234, 239
  n.50, 245 n.74
Kirk-Bizzeh, 121, 123

Limestone (material), 31, 180, 183,
  196, 197, 221 n.56, 235

Markets (including marketplaces and
  street markets), 17, 24, 25, 27,
  32–34, 36–39, 41, 135, 155, 184
  n.81, 191, 207, 215, 217, 246
Messianism (in the time of Jesus and
  in Late Antiquity), 41, 78, 178,
  228–30
Min/Minim, 45 n.5, 80, 82, 83, 85,
  86, 91, 93–99, 115, 127 n.28,
  131–33, 153 n.3, 190 n.95, 202
  n.4, 221
Mithraeum, 122, 123, 144–46
Muhammad, 232, 237 n.46

Na'aran (synagogue), 240
Networks (social, economic, religious),
  17, 18, 24, 26, 27, 28, 35, 36, 38,
  40, 41, 54, 77, 78, 113, 145, 190,
  193, 203, 205, 206, 249

Ogdoad, 173, 174
Ostia, 55 n.35

Parting of the ways, 11
Patronage (including patrons), 18, 20, 22–25, 137, 170, 186
Pharisees, 57, 76, 78, 114
Piacenza Pilgrim, 168 n.37, 186 n.84
Pilgrimage (ancient and modern), 4, 5, 12, 13, 106, 107 n.89, 108, 110 n.100, 111, 116–20 n.8, 124, 126, 129, 134–36, 141, 143–45, 168 n.37, 168 n.38, 175, 178, 179 n.66, 186 n.84, 191, 192 n.101, 201, 249, 251
Piyyutim, 156, 226 n.3, 229, 229–30 n.14, 230 n.15
Pompeii, 31, 213 n.34
Pottery/ceramics (in Capernaum, general), 18, 26–28, 60, 61, 61 n.54, 62 n.55, 64, 103 n.81, 104–5 n.84, 186 n.82, 211 n.26, 223 n.58
  Hellenistic Rhodian amphorae, 27
  Terra Sigillata (including ETSA), 27, 28
  Herodian oil lamps, 103–5, 105 n.84
  Late Roman Fine Ware (stamped with crosses), 134, 135, 165 n.34, 198, 202 n.4, 216 n.41, 222 n.57
  "Mefjer" Ware, 235, 236, 237
Ptolemaic Egypt, 23, 34, 35, 58 n.45

Rabbis, 57, 58, 82, 95, 99, 110 n.100, 115, 131–33, 137, 141, 142, 143 n.69, 190 n.95, 191 n.100, 199, 208 n.23, 221, 241
Rashidun, 225, 226, 229, 231, 233, 245
Ritual purity, 25, 25 n.39, 26, 28, 106 n.87
Roman Asia, 23 n.30, 28, 37, 156, 165, 212 n.26

Roman Egypt, 21, 30, 33, 34
Roman military, 20 n.15, 21 n.19, 22, 25 n.36, 232
Rome, 96 n.62, 122, 129 n.37, 170 n.40, 177, 177 n. 65
Room 1 / *sala venerata* / House of Peter, 9, 10, 83, 85, 86, 89, 102–14, 117–25, 127, 128, 130, 135, 136, 143, 144, 147–49, 154, 162, 163, 165, 167–70, 172, 179, 249, 251

Sardis, 198
Serapaeum, 123
Slaves, 20 n.15, 24
Streets (in Capernaum), 39, 184, 203, 207, 212 n.30, 213 n.34, 214, 215, 216 n.41, 217, 234, 235, 247
  Main east–west street (*decumanus*), 39, 184, 212, 212 n.28
  Main north–south street (*cardo*), 39, 41, 184, 184 n.81, 210, 212, 212 n.28, 214, 215, 246
Supersessionism, 12, 129, 137, 138, 141 n.65, 174, 179, 195, 200, 238 n.46, 244, 245 n.72, 252
Synagogues
  Association-type (including Jewish Christ-groups), 54, 55, 55 n. 35, 76, 78, 113–16, 118, 122, 123, 132–34, 144, 145, 149, 150, 179
  Byzantine synagogues, see *Galilee, othersites.*
  First-century synagogues, 8, 22 n.26, 46 n.9, 47–51, 53, 54, 57 n.42, 59, 63, 65, 67 n.71, 74 n.91, 75, 77, 113 n.108

Subject Index

Limestone synagogue (in Capernaum), 5, 10, 31, 39, 45, 46, 60–63, 65–72, 101, 110 n.100, 129 n.37, 137, 140, 153, 157, 158, 164, 179, 180, 182–87, 195, 196, 199, 200, 202, 217 n.42, 218, 221 n.56, 223, 238–241, 245, 251, 252, 254

Public-assembly-type, 55–59, 76–78, 114, 115, 132, 133, 134, 137

Tax booth / customs office / *telōnion*, 19, 19 n.14, 20, 32–34, 36–39

Tax collectors (tax collection), 21, 25, 32, 36, 40, 41

Theodosius I (Byzantine Emperor), 177

Theodosius II (Byzantine Emperor), 135, 154 n.5, 155, 155 n.7, 175, 176, 177 n.64, 187

Therapeutae, 55 n.35, 113, 113 n.112, 114

Umar (Rashidun Caliph), 226, 231

Umayyads, 43 n.1, 187 n.86, 227 n.7, 234, 234 n.31, 235, 235 n.32, 236, 237, 237 nn.43–46, 238 n.46, 241, 244 n.69, 245, 245 n.72, 246, 247, 252

Workshops (in Capernaum), 209, 210, 212 n.30, 214, 215

Yazid II (Umayyad Caliph), 241, 241–242 n.60, 242, 243